AA002155

3rd Workshop on Computational Linguistics and Clinical Psychology: From Linguistic Signal to Clinical Reality 2016

Held at the 2016 Conference of the North American Chapter of the Association for Computational Linguistics: Human Language Technologies (NAACL HLT 2016)

San Diego, California, USA
16 June 2016

ISBN: 978-1-5108-2527-7

Printed from e-media with permission by:

Curran Associates, Inc.
57 Morehouse Lane
Red Hook, NY 12571

Some format issues inherent in the e-media version may also appear in this print version.

Copyright© (2016) by the Association for Computational Linguistics
All rights reserved.

Printed by Curran Associates, Inc. (2016)

For permission requests, please contact the Association for Computational Linguistics
at the address below.

Association for Computational Linguistics
209 N. Eighth Street
Stroudsburg, Pennsylvania 18360

Phone: 1-570-476-8006
Fax: 1-570-476-0860

acl@aclweb.org

Additional copies of this publication are available from:

Curran Associates, Inc.
57 Morehouse Lane
Red Hook, NY 12571 USA
Phone: 845-758-0400
Fax: 845-758-2634
Email: curran@proceedings.com
Web: www.proceedings.com

NAACL HLT 2016

Computational Linguistics and Clinical Psychology:
From Linguistic Signal to Clinical Reality

Proceedings of the Third Workshop

June 16, 2016
San Diego, California, USA

Platinum Sponsor:

Introduction

In the United States, mental and neurological health problems are among the costliest challenges we face. Depression, Alzheimer's disease, bipolar disorder, and attention deficit hyperactivity disorder (ADHD) are only a handful of the many illnesses that contribute to this cost. The global cost of mental health conditions alone was estimated at $2.5 trillion in 2010, with a projected increase to over $6 trillion in 2030. Neurological illnesses and mental disorders cost the U.S. more than $760 billion a year. The World Health Organization (WHO) estimates one out of four people worldwide will suffer from a mental illness at some point in their lives, while one in five Americans experience a mental health problem in any given year. Mental, neurological, and substance use disorders are the leading cause of disability worldwide, yet most public service announcements and government education programs remain focused on physical health issues such as cancer and obesity. Despite the substantial and rising burden of such disorders, there is a significant shortage of resources available to prevent, diagnose, and treat them; thus technology must be brought to bear.

For clinical psychologists, language plays a central role in diagnosis, and many clinical instruments fundamentally rely on manual coding of patient language. Applying language technology in the domain of mental and neurological health could lead to inexpensive screening measures that may be administered by a wider array of healthcare professionals. Researchers had begun targeting such issues prior to this workshop series, using language technology to identify emotion in suicide notes, analyze the language of those with autistic spectrum disorders, and aid the diagnosis of dementia.

The series of Computational Linguistics and Clinical Psychology (CLPsych) workshops began at ACL 2014, while NAACL 2015 hosted the second such workshop with a near-doubling in attendance. The 2015 workshop additionally hosted a Shared Task for detecting depression and post-traumatic stress disorder (PTSD) based on social media posts. The CLPsych workshops diverge from the conventional "mini-conference" workshop format by inviting clinical psychologists and researchers to join us at the workshop as discussants, to provide real-world points of view on the potential applications of NLP technologies presented during the workshop. We hope to build the momentum towards releasing tools and data that can be used by clinical psychologists.

NAACL 2016 hosts the third CLPsych workshop, with another shared task. Published papers in this proceedings propose methods for aiding the diagnosis of dementia, analyzing sentiment as related to psychotherapy, assessing suicide risk, and quantifying the language of mental health. The 2016 CLPsych Shared Task centered on the classification of posts from a mental health forum to assist forum moderators in triaging and escalating posts requiring immediate attention. We accepted 11 submissions for the main workshop and 16 for the shared task. Each oral presentation will be followed by discussions led by one of our discussants, subject matter experts working in the fields of behavioral and mental health and with clinical data, including: Dr. Loring Ingraham and Dr. Bart Andrews.

We wish to thank everyone who showed interest and submitted a paper, all of the authors for their contributions, the members of the Program Committee for their thoughtful reviews, our clinical discussants for their helpful insights, and all the attendees of the workshop. We also wish to extend thanks to the Association for Computational Linguistics for making this workshop possible, and to Microsoft Research for its very generous sponsorship.

– Kristy and Lyle

Organizers:

Kristy Hollingshead, IHMC
Lyle Ungar, University of Pennsylvania

Clinical Discussants:

Loring J. Ingraham, George Washington University
Bart Andrews, Behavioral Health Response

Program Committee:

Steven Bedrick, Oregon Health & Science University
Archna Bhatia, IHMC
Wilma Bucci, Adelphi University
Wei Chen, Nationwide Children's Hospital
Leonardo Claudino, University of Maryland, College Park
Mike Conway, University of Utah
Glen Coppersmith, Qntfy
Brita Elevåg, Department of Clinical Medicine, University of Tromsø
Peter Foltz, Pearson
Dan Goldwasser, Purdue University
Ben Hachey, University of Sydney
Graeme Hirst, University of Toronto
Christopher Homan, Rochester Institute of Technology
Jena Hwang, IHMC
Zac Imel, University of Utah
Loring Ingraham, George Washington University
William Jarrold, Nuance Communications
Yangfeng Ji, School of Interactive Computing, Georgia Institute of Technology
Dimitrios Kokkinakis, University of Gothenburg
Tong Liu, Rochester Institute of Technology
Shervin Malmasi, Harvard Medical School
Bernard Maskit, Stony Brook University
Margaret Mitchell, Microsoft Research
Eric Morley, Oregon Health & Science University
Danielle Mowery, University of Utah
Sean Murphy, John Jay College of Criminal Justice; City University of New York
Cecilia Ovesdotter Alm, Rochester Institute of Technology
Ted Pedersen, University of Minnesota
Craig Pfeifer, MITRE
Glen Pink, University of Sydney
Daniel Preotiuc, University of Pennsylvania
Emily Prud'hommeaux, Rochester Institute of Technology

Matthew Purver, Queen Mary University of London
Philip Resnik, University of Maryland
Rebecca Resnik, Mindwell Psychology
Brian Roark, Google
Mark Rosenstein, Pearson
Masoud Rouhizadeh, Stony Brook University & University of Pennsylvania
J. David Schaffer, Binghamton University
Ronald Schouten, Harvard Medical School
H. Andrew Schwartz, Stony Brook University
J. Ignacio Serrano, Spanish National Research Council
Richard Sproat, Google
Hiroki Tanaka, Nara Institute of Science and Technology
Michael Tanana, University of Utah
Paul Thompson, Dartmouth College
Jan van Santen, Oregon Health & Science University
Eleanor Yelland, University College London
Dan Yoo, Cambia Health

Table of Contents

This page intentionally left blank.

Conference Program

2016/06/16

09:00–09:20   *Opening Remarks*
Kristy Hollingshead and Lyle Ungar

09:20–10:30   Oral Presentations, Session 1

Detecting late-life depression in Alzheimer's disease through analysis of speech and language
Kathleen C. Fraser, Frank Rudzicz and Graeme Hirst

Towards Early Dementia Detection: Fusing Linguistic and Non-Linguistic Clinical Data
Joseph Bullard, Cecilia Ovesdotter Alm, Xumin Liu, Qi Yu and Rubén Proaño

10:30–11:00   Break

11:00–11:45   Poster Presentations

Self-Reflective Sentiment Analysis
Benjamin Shickel, Martin Heesacker, Sherry Benton, Ashkan Ebadi, Paul Nickerson and Parisa Rashidi

Is Sentiment in Movies the Same as Sentiment in Psychotherapy? Comparisons Using a New Psychotherapy Sentiment Database
Michael Tanana, Aaron Dembe, Christina S. Soma, Zac Imel, David Atkins and Vivek Srikumar

Building a Motivational Interviewing Dataset
Verónica Pérez-Rosas, Rada Mihalcea, Kenneth Resnicow, Satinder Singh and Lawrence An

Crazy Mad Nutters: The Language of Mental Health
Jena D. Hwang and Kristy Hollingshead

The language of mental health problems in social media
George Gkotsis, Anika Oellrich, Tim Hubbard, Richard Dobson, Maria Liakata, Sumithra Velupillai and Rina Dutta

Exploring Autism Spectrum Disorders Using HLT
Julia Parish-Morris, Mark Liberman, Neville Ryant, Christopher Cieri, Leila Bateman, Emily Ferguson and Robert Schultz

11:45–1:00   **Lunch**

1:00–2:45   **Oral Presentations, Session 2**

Generating Clinically Relevant Texts: A Case Study on Life-Changing Events
Mayuresh Oak, Anil Behera, Titus Thomas, Cecilia Ovesdotter Alm, Emily Prud'hommeaux, Christopher Homan and Raymond Ptucha

Don't Let Notes Be Misunderstood: A Negation Detection Method for Assessing Risk of Suicide in Mental Health Records
George Gkotsis, Sumithra Velupillai, Anika Oellrich, Harry Dean, Maria Liakata and Rina Dutta

Exploratory Analysis of Social Media Prior to a Suicide Attempt
Glen Coppersmith, Kim Ngo, Ryan Leary and Anthony Wood

2:45–3:00   **Break**

3:00–3:15   **Shared Task Introduction**

CLPsych 2016 Shared Task: Triaging content in online peer-support forums
David N. Milne, Glen Pink, Ben Hachey and Rafael A. Calvo

3:15–3:40   **Shared Task Poster Presentations, Session 1**

Data61-CSIRO systems at the CLPsych 2016 Shared Task
Sunghwan Mac Kim, Yufei Wang, Stephen Wan and Cecile Paris

Predicting Post Severity in Mental Health Forums
Shervin Malmasi, Marcos Zampieri and Mark Dras

Classifying ReachOut posts with a radial basis function SVM
Chris Brew

Triaging Mental Health Forum Posts
Arman Cohan, Sydney Young and Nazli Goharian

Detecting late-life depression in Alzheimer's disease through analysis of speech and language

Kathleen C. Fraser[1] and **Frank Rudzicz**[2,1] and **Graeme Hirst**[1]
[1]Department of Computer Science, University of Toronto, Toronto, Canada
[2]Toronto Rehabilitation Institute-UHN, Toronto, Canada
{kfraser,frank,gh}@cs.toronto.edu

Abstract

Alzheimer's disease (AD) and depression share a number of symptoms, and commonly occur together. Being able to differentiate between these two conditions is critical, as depression is generally treatable. We use linguistic analysis and machine learning to determine whether automated screening algorithms for AD are affected by depression, and to detect when individuals diagnosed with AD are also showing signs of depression. In the first case, we find that our automated AD screening procedure does not show false positives for individuals who have depression but are otherwise healthy. In the second case, we have moderate success in detecting signs of depression in AD (accuracy = 0.658), but we are not able to draw a strong conclusion about the features that are most informative to the classification.

1 Introduction

Depression and dementia are both medical conditions that can have a strong negative impact on the quality of life of the elderly, and they are often co-morbid. However, depression is often treatable with medication and therapy, whereas dementia usually occurs as the result of an irreversible process of neurodegeneration. It is therefore critical to be able to distinguish between these two conditions.

However, distinguishing between depression and dementia can be extremely difficult because of overlapping symptoms, including apathy, crying spells, changes in weight and sleeping patterns, and problems with concentration and attention.

It is also important to detect when someone has both AD and depression, as this serious situation can lead to more rapid cognitive decline, earlier placement in a nursing home, increased risk of depression in the patient's caregivers, and increased mortality (Thorpe, 2009; Lee and Lyketsos, 2003).

Separate bodies of work have reported the utility of spontaneous speech analysis in distinguishing participants with depression from healthy controls, and in distinguishing participants with dementia from healthy controls. Here we consider whether such analyses can be applied to the problem of detecting depression in Alzheimer's disease (AD). In particular, we explore two questions: (1) In previous work on detecting AD from speech (elicited through a picture description task), are cognitively healthy people with depression being misclassified as having AD? (2) If we consider only participants with AD, can we distinguish between those with depression and those without, using the same picture description task and analysis?

2 Background

There has been considerable work on detecting depression from speech and on detecting dementia from speech, but very little which combines the two. We will first review the two tasks separately, and then discuss some of the complexity that arises when depression and AD co-occur.

2.1 Detecting depression from speech

Depression affects a number of cognitive and physical systems related to the production of speech, including working memory, the phonological loop, ar-

1

Proceedings of the 3rd Workshop on Computational Linguistics and Clinical Psychology: From Linguistic Signal to Clinical Reality, pages 1–11,
San Diego, California, June 16, 2016. ©2016 Association for Computational Linguistics

ticulatory planning, and muscle tension and control (Cummins et al., 2015). These changes can result in word-finding difficulties, articulatory errors, decreased prosody, and lower verbal productivity.

Over the past decade or so, there has been growing interest in measuring properties of the speech signal that correlate with the changes observed in depression, and using these measured variables to train machine learning classifiers to automatically detect depression from speech.

Ozdas et al. (2004) found that mean jitter and the slope of the glottal flow spectrum could distinguish between 10 non-depressed controls, 10 participants with clinical depression, and 10 high-risk suicidal participants.

Moore et al. (2008) considered prosodic features as well as vocal tract and glottal features. They performed sex-dependent classification and found that glottal features were more discriminative than vocal tract features, but that the best results were achieved using all three types of features.

Cohn et al. (2009) examined the utility of facial movements and vocal prosody in discriminating participants with moderate or severe depression from those with no depression. They achieved 79% accuracy using only two prosodic features: variation in fundamental frequency, and latency of response to interviewer questions. They used a within-subjects design, in which they predicted which participants had responded to treatment in a clinical trial.

Low et al. (2011) analyzed speech from adolescents engaged in normal conversation with their parents (68 diagnosed with depression, 71 controls). They grouped their acoustic features into 5 groups: spectral, cepstral, prosodic, glottal, and those based on the Teager energy operator (TEO, a nonlinear energy operator). They achieved higher accuracies using sex-dependent models than sex-independent models, and found that the best results were achieved using the TEO-based features (up to 87% for males and 79% for females).

Cummins et al. (2011) distinguished 23 depressed participants from 24 controls with a best accuracy of 80% in a speaker-dependent configuration and 79% in a speaker-independent configuration. Spectral features, particularly mel-frequency cepstral coefficients (MFCCs), were found to be useful.

Alghowinem et al. (2012) analyzed speech from 30 participants with depression and 30 healthy controls. The speech was elicited through interview questions about situations that had aroused significant emotions. Higher accuracy was achieved on detecting depression in women than in men. Energy, intensity, shimmer, and MFCC features were all informative, and positive emotional speech was more discriminatory than negative emotional speech.

Scherer et al. (2013) differentiated 18 depressed participants from 18 controls with 75% accuracy, using interviews captured with a simulated virtual human. They found that glottal features such as the normalized amplitude quotient (NAQ) and quasi-open quotient (QOQ) differed significantly between the groups.

Alghowinem et al. (2013) compared four classifiers and a number of different feature sets on the task of detecting depression from spontaneous speech. They found loudness and intensity features to be the most discriminatory, and suggested pitch and formant features may be more useful for longitudinal comparisons within individuals.

While most of the literature concerning the detection of depression from speech has focused solely on the speech signal, there is an associated body of work on detecting depression from writing that focuses on linguistic cues. Rude et al. (2004) found that college students with depression were significantly more likely to use the first-person pronoun *I* in personal essays than college students without depression, and also used more words with negative emotional valence. Other work has found differences in the frequency of different parts-of-speech (POS) (De Choudhury et al., 2013) and in the general topics chosen for discussion (Resnik et al., 2015). Other work has accurately identified depression (and differentiated PTSD and depression) in Twitter social media texts with high accuracies using n-gram language models (Coppersmith et al., 2015). Similarly, Nguyen et al. (2014) showed that specialized lexical norms and Linguistic Inquiry and Word Count[1] features significantly differentiate clinical and control groups in blog post texts. Howes et al. (2014) showed that lexical features (in style and dialogue) could also be used to predict the severity of depression and anxiety during Cognitive Be-

---

[1] http://liwc.wpengine.com.

havioural Therapy treatment. It is not obvious that these results generalize to the case where the topic and structure of the narrative is constrained to a picture description.

2.2 Detecting Alzheimer's disease from speech

A growing number of researchers have tackled the problem of detecting dementia from speech and language. Most of this work has focused on Alzheimer's disease (AD), which is the most common cause of dementia. Although the primary diagnostic symptom of AD is memory impairment, this and other cognitive deficits often manifest in spontaneous language through word-finding difficulties, a decrease in information content, and changes in fluency, syntactic complexity, and prosody. Other work, including that of Roark et al. (2007), focuses on mild cognitive impairment, which is also broadly applicable.

Thomas et al. (2005) classified spontaneous speech samples from 95 AD patients and an unspecified number of controls by treating the problem as an authorship attribution task, and employing a "common N-grams" approach. They were able to distinguish between patients with severe AD and controls with a best accuracy of 94.5%, and between patients with mild AD and controls with an 75.3% accuracy.

Habash and Guinn (2012) built classifiers to distinguish between AD and non-AD language samples using 80 conversations between 31 AD patients and 57 cognitively normal conversation partners. They found that features such as POS tags and measures of lexical diversity were less useful than measuring filled pauses, repetitions, and incomplete words, and achieved a best accuracy of 79.5%.

Meilán et al. (2012) distinguished between 30 AD patients and 36 healthy controls with temporal and acoustic features alone, obtaining an accuracy of 84.8%. For each participant, their speech sample consisted of two sentences read from a screen. The discriminating features were percentage of voice breaks, number of voice breaks, number of periods of voice, shimmer, and noise-to-harmonics ratio.

Jarrold et al. (2014) used acoustic features, POS features, and psychologically-motivated word lists to distinguish between semi-structured interview responses from 9 AD participants and 9 controls with an accuracy of 88%. They also confirmed their hypothesis that AD patients would use more pronouns, verbs, and adjectives and fewer nouns than controls.

Rentoumi et al. (2014) considered a slightly different problem: they used computational techniques to differentiate between picture descriptions from AD participants with and without additional vascular pathology ($n = 18$ for each group). They achieved an accuracy of 75% when they included frequency unigrams and excluded binary unigrams, syntactic complexity features, measures of vocabulary richness, and information theoretic features.

Orimaye et al. (2014) obtained F-measure scores up to 0.74 on transcripts from DementiaBank, combining participants with different etiologies rather than focusing on AD. In previous work, we also studied data from DementiaBank (Fraser et al., 2015). We computed acoustic and linguistic features from the "Cookie Theft" picture descriptions and distinguished 240 AD narratives from 233 control narratives with 81% accuracy using logistic regression.

2.3 Relationship between dementia and depression

The relationship between dementia and depression is complicated, as the two conditions are not independent of each other and in fact frequently co-occur. When someone is diagnosed with dementia, feelings of depression are common. At the same time, depression is a risk factor for developing Alzheimer's disease (Korczyn and Halperin, 2009). The diagnosis of a third medical condition (e.g., heart disease) can trigger depression and also independently increase the risk of dementia. Similarly, some risk factors for depression and dementia are the same, such as alcohol use and cigarette smoking (Thorpe, 2009). Furthermore, changes in white matter connectivity have been linked to both depression (Alexopoulos et al., 2008) and dementia (Prins et al., 2004).

The prevalence of depression in AD has been estimated to be 30–50% (Lee and Lyketsos, 2003), although these figures have been shown to vary widely depending on the diagnostic method used (Müller-Thomsen et al., 2005). In contrast, the prevalence of depression in the general population older than 75 is estimated to be 7.2% (major depression) and 17.1% (depressive disorders) (Luppa et al., 2012).

The prevalence of Alzheimer's disease is 11% for people aged 65 and older, increasing to 33% for people ages 85 and older (Alzheimer's Association, 2015).

Symptoms which are common in both depression and dementia include: poor concentration, impaired attention (Korczyn and Halperin, 2009), apathy (Lee and Lyketsos, 2003), changes to eating and sleeping patterns, and reactive mood symptoms, e.g., tearfulness (Thorpe, 2009). However, both dementia and depression are heterogeneous in presentation, which can lead to many possible combinations of symptoms when they co-occur.

Studies examining spontaneous speech tasks to discriminate between dementia and depression are rare. Murray (2010) investigated whether clinical depression could be distinguished from AD by analyzing narrative speech. She found that there were significant differences in the amount of information that was conveyed in a picture description task, with depressed participants communicating the same amount of information as healthy controls, and AD patients showing a reduction in information content. Other discourse measures relating to the quantity of speech produced and the syntactic complexity of the narrative did not differ between the groups. In contrast to the current work, the study described in Murray (2010) did not include participants with *both* dementia and depression, involved a much smaller data set (49 participants across 3 groups), and did not seek to make predictions from the data.

3 Methods

3.1 Data

We use narrative speech data from the Pitt corpus in the DementiaBank database[2]. These data were collected between 1983 and 1988 as part of the Alzheimer Research Program at the University of Pittsburgh. Detailed information about the study cohort is available from Becker et al. (1994), and demographic information is presented for each experiment below in Tables 1 and 3. Diagnoses were made on the basis of a personal history and a neuropsychological battery; a subset of these diagnoses were confirmed post-mortem. The language samples were elicited using the "Cookie Theft" picture

---

[2] https://talkbank.org/DementiaBank/

description task from the Boston Diagnostic Aphasia Examination (BDAE) (Goodglass and Kaplan, 1983), in which participants are asked to describe everything they see going on in a picture. We extract features from both the acoustic files (converted from MP3 to 16-bit mono WAV format with a sampling rate of 16 kHz) and the associated transcripts. All examiner speech is excluded from the sample.

A subset of the participants also have Hamilton Depression Rating Scale (HAM-D) scores (Hamilton, 1960). The HAM-D is still one of the gold standards for depression rating (although it has also received criticism; see Bagby et al. (2014) for an example). It consists of 17 questions, for which the patient's responses are rated from 0–4 or 0–2 by the examiner. A total score between 0–7 is considered normal, 8–16 indicates mild depression, 17–23 indicates moderate depression, and greater than 24 indicates severe depression (Zimmerman et al., 2013).

3.2 Features

We extract a large number of textual features (including part-of-speech tags, parse constituents, psycholinguistic measures, and measures of complexity, vocabulary richness, and informativeness), and acoustic features (including fluency measures, MFCCs, voice quality features, and measures of periodicity and symmetry). A complete list of features is given in the Supplementary Material, and additional details are reported by Fraser et al. (2015).

3.3 Classification

We select a subset of the extracted features using a correlation-based filter. Features are ranked by their correlation with diagnosis and only the top N features are selected, where we vary N from 5 to 400. The selected features are fed to a machine learning classifier; in this study we compare logistic regression (LR) with support vector machines (SVM) (Hall et al., 2009). We use a cross-validation framework and report the average accuracy across folds. The data is partitioned across folds such that samples from a single speaker occur in either the training set or test set, but never both. Error bars are computed using the standard deviation of the accuracy across folds. In some cases we also report *sensitivity* and *specificity*, where sensitivity indicates the proportion of people with AD (or depression) who were

	AD $n = 196$	Controls $n = 128$	Sig.
Age	71.7 (8.7)	63.7 (7.6)	**
Education	12.4 (2.9)	13.9 (2.4)	**
Sex (M/F)	66/130	49/79	

Table 1: Mean and standard deviation of demographic information for participants in Experiment I. ** indicates $p < 0.01$.

correctly identified as such, and specificity indicates the proportion of controls who were correctly identified as such.

4 Experiment I: Does depression affect classification accuracy?

Our first experiment examines whether depression is a confounding factor in our current diagnostic pipeline. To answer this question, we consider the subset of narratives for which associated HAM-D scores are available. This leaves a set of 196 AD narratives and 128 control narratives from 150 AD participants and 80 control participants. Since participants may have different scores on different visits, we consider data per narrative, rather than per speaker. Demographic information is given in Table 1. The groups are not matched for age or education, which is a limitation of the complete data set as well; the AD participants tend to be both older and less educated.

We then perform the classification procedure using the analysis pipeline described above, with 10-fold cross-validation. The results for a logistic regression and SVM classifier are shown in Figure 1. This is a necessary first step to examine if depression is a confounding factor.

Choosing the best result of 0.799 (SVM classifier, 70 features), we then perform a more detailed analysis. Accuracy, sensitivity, and specificity for the full data set are reported in the first row of Table 2. We first break down the data into two separate groups: those with a Hamilton score greater than 7 (i.e., "depressed") and those with a Hamilton score less than or equal to 7 ("non-depressed") (Zimmerman et al., 2013). The accuracy, sensitivity, and specificity for these sub-groups are also reported in Table 2. Because there are far more AD participants with depression ($n = 65$) than controls with

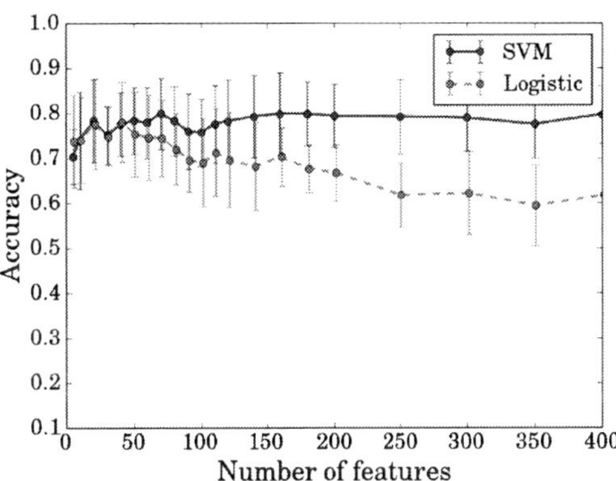

Figure 1: Classification accuracy on the task of distinguishing AD from control narratives for varying feature set sizes.

Data set	Baseline	Accuracy	Sens.	Spec.
All	0.605	0.799	0.826	0.758
Depressed	0.743	0.864	0.846	1.000
Non-depressed	0.552	0.780	0.816	0.739

Table 2: Accuracy, sensitivity, and specificity for all participants, depressed participants, and non-depressed participants.

depression ($n = 9$), we also report the accuracy of a majority class classifier as a baseline with which to compare the reported accuracies. Alternatives to this approach, including synthetically balancing the classes, e.g., with synthetic minority oversampling (Chawla et al., 2002), is to be the subject of future work.

A key result from this experiment is that although there are only a few control participants who are depressed, none of those are misclassified as AD (specificity = 1.0 in this case).

Furthermore, if we partition the participants by accuracy (those who were classified correctly versus incorrectly), we find no significant difference on HAM-D scores ($p > 0.05$). This suggests that the accuracy of the classifier is not affected by the presence or absence of depression.

5 Experiment II: Can we detect depression in Alzheimer's disease?

In our second experiment, we tackle the problem of detecting depression when it is comorbid with

	Depressed $n = 65$	Non-dep. $n = 65$	Sig.
Age	71.4 (8.6)	71.6 (8.6)	
Education	11.7 (2.6)	12.9 (3.0)	*
Sex (M/F)	21/44	19/46	
MMSE	18.1 (5.5)	17.9 (5.4)	

Table 3: Mean and standard deviation of demographic information for AD participants in Experiment II. * indicates $p < 0.05$.

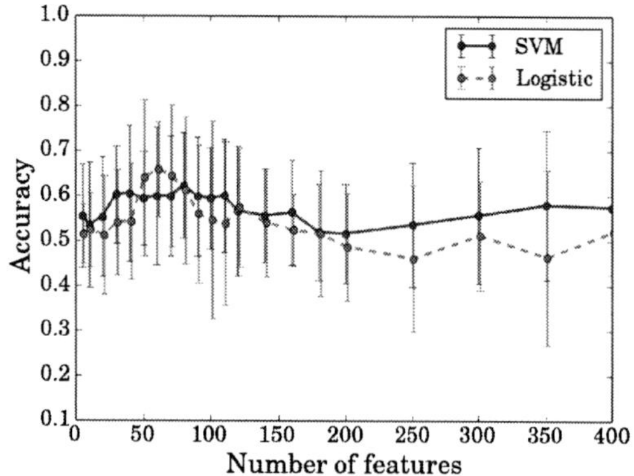

Figure 2: Classification accuracy on the task of distinguishing depressed from non-depressed AD narratives for varying feature set sizes.

Alzheimer's disease. From the previous section, we have 65 narratives from participants with both AD and depression (HAM-D > 7). We select an additional 65 narratives from participants with AD but no depression. These additional data are selected randomly but such that participants are matched for dementia severity, age, and sex. Demographic information is given in Table 3.

5.1 Standard processing pipeline

We begin by using our standard processing pipeline to assess whether it is capable of detecting depression. The classification accuracies are given in Figure 2. In this case, since the groups are the same size, the baseline accuracy is 0.5. The best accuracy of 0.658 is achieved with the LR classifier using 60 features (sensitivity: 0.707, specificity: 0.610). This represents a significant increase (paired t-test, $p < 0.05$) of 15 percentage points over the random baseline, but there is clearly room for improvement.

Rank	Feature	r	Trend
1	Skewness MFCC 1	0.270	↑
2	Info unit: *boy*	−0.265	↓
3	Mean ΔΔMFCC 8	0.229	↑
4	VP → VB NP	−0.223	↓
5	Kurtosis MFCC 4	0.223	↑
6	Kurtosis MFCC 3	0.217	↑
7	Kurtosis ΔMFCC 2	0.213	↑
8	Skewness ΔΔMFCC 2	0.211	↑
9	Kurtosis MFCC 10	0.209	↑
10	Determiners	−0.206	↓

Table 4: Highly ranked features for distinguishing people with AD and depression from people with only AD. The third column shows the correlation with diagnosis, and the fourth column shows the direction of the trend (increasing or decreasing) with depression.

Data set	Baseline	Accuracy	Sens.	Spec.
All	0.500	0.658	0.707	0.610
Females	0.511	0.588	0.519	0.653
Males	0.525	0.650	0.580	0.717

Table 5: Accuracy, sensitivity, and specificity for all participants, just females, and just males.

Table 4 shows the features which are most highly correlated with diagnosis (over all data). Even for the top-ranked features, the correlation is weak, and the difference between groups is not significant after correcting for multiple comparisons. We therefore cannot conclusively draw conclusions about the selected features, although we do note the apparent importance of the MFCC features here.

5.2 Sex-dependent classification

Given that acoustic features naturally vary across the sexes, and that previous work achieved better results using sex-dependent classifiers, we also consider a sex-dependent configuration. The drawback to this approach is the reduction in data, particularly for males. In these experiments we attempt to classify 21 males with depression+AD versus 19 males with AD only, and 44 females with depression+AD versus 46 females with AD only. The results for these experiments are shown in Figure 3, and the best accuracies are given in Table 5.

The features which are most correlated with di-

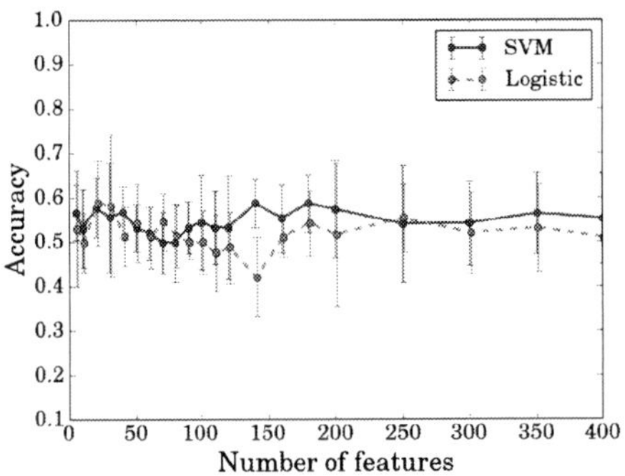

(a) Females

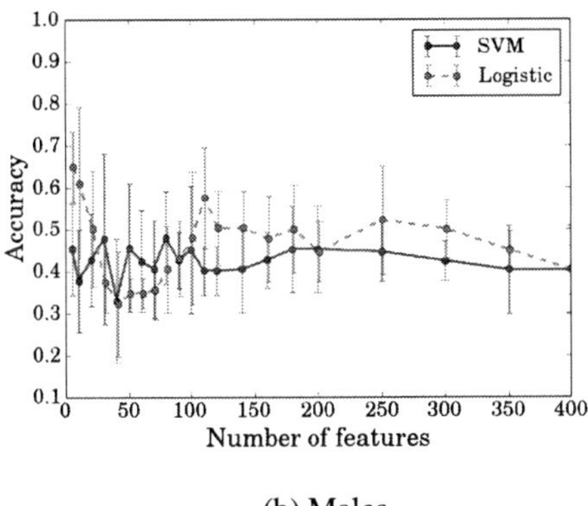

(b) Males

Figure 3: Sex-dependent classification accuracy on the task of distinguishing depressed from non-depressed AD narratives for varying feature set sizes.

Rank	Feature	r	Trend
1	Info unit: *boy*	-0.323	↓
2	Mean ΔMFCC 9	0.284	↑
3	VP → VB NP	-0.274	↓
4	Kurtosis MFCC 3	0.266	↑
5	Kurtosis Δ energy	0.261	↑
6	Skewness MFCC 1	0.260	↑
7	Kurtosis MFCC 4	0.256	↑
8	NP → PRP\$ NNS	0.251	↑
9	Skewness $\Delta\Delta$MFCC 2	0.249	↑
10	NP → NP NP .	0.243	↑

(a) Females

Rank	Feature	r	Trend
1	Mean $\Delta\Delta$MFCC 9	0.447	↑
2	Skewness $\Delta\Delta$MFCC 12	-0.406	↓
3	VP → VB S	0.405	↑
4	Mean $\Delta\Delta$MFCC 2	-0.381	↓
5	Info unit: *stool*	0.352	↑
6	VP → VBG NP	-0.351	↓
7	Key word: *chair*	0.346	↑
8	Mean ΔMFCC 11	-0.325	↓
9	Key word: *girl*	-0.318	↓
10	Mean $\Delta\Delta$MFCC 8	0.316	↑

(b) Males

Table 6: Highly ranked features for distinguishing individuals with AD and depression from individuals with only AD, in the sex-dependent case. (No differences are significant after correcting for multiple comparisons.)

agnosis for females are listed in Table 6a, and those which are most correlated with diagnosis for males are listed in Table 6b. Again, the selected features tend to be either informational, grammatical, or cepstral in nature, although none of the differences are significant after correcting for multiple comparisons.

5.3 Additional features

To help our classifiers better distinguish between people with and without depression, we implement a number of additional features which have been reported to be valuable in detecting depression. Many of the acoustic features from the literature were already present in our feature set, but we now consider a number of glottal features, including the mean and standard deviations of the maximum voiced frequency, glottal closure instants, linear prediction residuals, peak slope, glottal flow (and derivative), normalized amplitude quotient (NAQ), quasi-open quotient (QOQ), harmonic richness factor, parabolic spectral parameter, and cepstral peak prominence. These features are implemented in the COVAREP toolkit (version 1.4.1) (Degottex et al., 2014).

We also include three additional psycholinguistic variables relating to the affective qualities of words: valence, arousal, and dominance. Valence describes the degree of positive or negative emotion associated with a word, arousal describes the intensity of the emotion associated with a word, and dominance describes the degree of control associated with a word. We use the crowd-sourced norms presented by Warriner et al. (2013) for their broad coverage, and measure the mean and maximum value of each variable.

Finally, we count the frequency of occurrence of first-person words (*I*, *me*, *my*, *mine*). In general, the picture description task is completed in the third person, but first-person words do occur.

However, including these new features actually had a slightly negative effect on the sex-independent classification, reducing the maximum accuracy from 0.658 to 0.650, as well as on the males-only case, reducing maximum accuracy from 0.650 to 0.585. This suggests that some of the new features are being selected in individual training folds, but not generalizing to the test folds. In contrast, the new features did make a small, incremental improvement in the females-only case, from 0.588 to 0.609 for females. The new features that were most highly ranked for females were the standard deviation of the peak slope (rank 12, $r = -0.237$) and the standard deviation of NAQ (rank 35, $r = -0.186$), both showing a weak negative correlation with diagnosis. The most useful new feature for males was the mean QOQ (rank 16, $r = 0.273$), with a weak positive correlation with diagnosis.

6   Conclusion

In this paper, we considered two questions. The first is related to previous work in the field showing that speech analysis and machine learning can lead to good, but not perfect, differentiation between participants with AD and healthy controls. We wondered whether some control participants were being misclassified as having AD when in fact they were depressed. However, in our experiment we found that none of the 9 depressed controls were misclassified as having AD. This is a small sample, but it is consistent with the findings of Murray (2010), who found that although AD participants and controls could be distinguished through analysis of their picture descriptions, there were no differences between depressed participants and controls.

We then considered only participants with AD, and tried to distinguish between those with comorbid depression and those without. Our best accuracy for this task was 0.658, which is considerably lower than reported accuracies for detecting depression in the absence of AD, but reflects the difficulty of the task given the wide overlap of symptoms in the two conditions. In fact, previous work on detecting depression from speech has focused overwhelmingly on young and otherwise healthy participants, and much work is needed on detecting depression in other populations and with other comorbidities.

One limitation of this work is the type of speech data available; previous work suggests that emotional speech is more informative for detecting depression. Another limitation is that we are assigning our participants to the depressed and non-depressed groups on the basis of a single test score, rather than a confirmed clinical diagnosis. A related factor to consider is the relatively mild depression that is observed in this data set, which was developed for the study of AD rather than depression – only 8 participants met the criteria for "moderate" depression, and none met the criteria for severe depression. Furthermore, while the controls in Experiment 2 all had scores below the threshold for mild depression, in most cases the scores were still non-zero, and so the classification task is not as clearly binary as we have framed it here. Finally, limitations of the dataset introduced issues of confounding variables (namely age and education), and prohibited us from contrasting speech from participants with only depression versus those with only AD. We are currently undertaking our own data collection to overcome the various challenges of this dataset.

Depression and Alzheimer's disease both present in different syndromes, and so it is probably unrealistic to clearly delineate between the many potential combinations of depression, AD, and other possible medical conditions through the analysis of a single language task. On the other hand, previous work suggests that this type of analysis can be very fine-grained and sensitive to subtle cognitive impairments. Ideally, future work will focus directly on the task of distinguishing AD from depression, using clinically validated data with a stronger emotional component.

Acknowledgments

The authors would like to thank Dr. John Strauss for his comments on an early draft of this paper. This work was supported by the Natural Sciences and Engineering Research Council of Canada (NSERC), grant number RGPIN-2014-06020.

References

George S. Alexopoulos, Christopher F. Murphy, Faith M. Gunning-Dixon, Vassilios Latoussakis, Dora Kanellopoulos, Sibel Klimstra, Kelvin O. Lim, and Matthew J. Hoptman. 2008. Microstructural white matter abnormalities and remission of geriatric depression. *The American Journal of Psychiatry*, 165(2):238–244.

Sharifa Alghowinem, Roland Goecke, Michael Wagner, Julien Epps, Michael Breakspear, Gordon Parker, et al. 2012. From joyous to clinically depressed: Mood detection using spontaneous speech. In *Proceedings of the Florida Artificial Intelligence Research Society (FLAIRS) Conference*, pages 141–146.

Sharifa Alghowinem, Roland Goecke, Michael Wagner, Julien Epps, Tom Gedeon, Michael Breakspear, and Gordon Parker. 2013. A comparative study of different classifiers for detecting depression from spontaneous speech. In *Acoustics, Speech and Signal Processing (ICASSP), 2013 IEEE International Conference on*, pages 8022–8026.

Paavo Alku, Helmer Strik, and Erkki Vilkman. 1997. Parabolic spectral parameter – a new method for quantification of the glottal flow. *Speech Communication*, 22(1):67–79.

Alzheimer's Association. 2015. 2015 Alzheimer's disease facts and figures. *Alzheimer's & Dementia*, 11(3):332.

R. Michael Bagby, Andrew G. Ryder, Deborah R. Schuller, and Margarita B. Marshall. 2014. The Hamilton Depression Rating Scale: has the gold standard become a lead weight? *American Journal of Psychiatry*, 161(12):2163–2177.

James T. Becker, François Boiler, Oscar L. Lopez, Judith Saxton, and Karen L. McGonigle. 1994. The natural history of Alzheimer's disease: description of study cohort and accuracy of diagnosis. *Archives of Neurology*, 51(6):585–594.

Sarah D. Breedin, Eleanor M. Saffran, and Myrna F. Schwartz. 1998. Semantic factors in verb retrieval: An effect of complexity. *Brain and Language*, 63:1–31.

Étienne Brunet. 1978. *Le vocabulaire de Jean Giraudoux structure et évolution*. Éditions Slatkine.

Marc Brysbaert and Boris New. 2009. Moving beyond Kučera and Francis: A critical evaluation of current word frequency norms and the introduction of a new and improved word frequency measure for American English. *Behavior Research Methods*, 41(4):977–990.

Romola S. Bucks, Sameer Singh, Joanne M. Cuerden, and Gordon K. Wilcock. 2000. Analysis of spontaneous, conversational speech in dementia of Alzheimer type: Evaluation of an objective technique for analysing lexical performance. *Aphasiology*, 14(1):71–91.

Jieun Chae and Ani Nenkova. 2009. Predicting the fluency of text with shallow structural features: case studies of machine translation and human-written text. In *Proceedings of the 12th Conference of the European Chapter of the Association for Computational Linguistics*, pages 139–147.

Nitesh V. Chawla, Kevin W. Bowyer, Lawrence O. Hall, and W. Philip Kegelmeyer. 2002. SMOTE: Synthetic Minority Over-sampling Technique. *Journal of Artificial Intelligence Research*, 16:321–357.

Jeffrey F. Cohn, Tomas Simon Kruez, Iain Matthews, Ying Yang, Minh Hoai Nguyen, Margara Tejera Padilla, Feng Zhou, and Fernando De La Torre. 2009. Detecting depression from facial actions and vocal prosody. In *Affective Computing and Intelligent Interaction and Workshops, 2009. ACII 2009. 3rd International Conference on*, pages 1–7.

Glen Coppersmith, Mark Dredze, Craig Harman, Kristy Hollingshead, and Margaret Mitchell. 2015. CLPsych 2015 shared task: Depression and PTSD on Twitter. In *Proceedings of the Shared Task for the NAACL Workshop on Computational Linguistics and Clinical Psychology*.

Michael A. Covington and Joe D. McFall. 2010. Cutting the Gordian knot: The moving-average type–token ratio (MATTR). *Journal of Quantitative Linguistics*, 17(2):94–100.

Bernard Croisile, Bernadette Ska, Marie-Josee Brabant, Annick Duchene, Yves Lepage, Gilbert Aimard, and Marc Trillet. 1996. Comparative study of oral and written picture description in patients with Alzheimer's disease. *Brain and Language*, 53(1):1–19.

Nicholas Cummins, Julien Epps, Michael Breakspear, and Roland Goecke. 2011. An investigation of depressed speech detection: Features and normalization. In *Proceedings of the 12th Annual Conference of the International Speech Communication Association (INTERSPEECH 2011)*, pages 2997–3000.

Nicholas Cummins, Stefan Scherer, Jarek Krajewski, Sebastian Schnieder, Julien Epps, and Thomas F Quatieri. 2015. A review of depression and suicide risk assessment using speech analysis. *Speech Communication*, 71:10–49.

Munmun De Choudhury, Scott Counts, and Eric Horvitz. 2013. Social media as a measurement tool of depression in populations. In *Proceedings of the 5th Annual ACM Web Science Conference*, pages 47–56.

Gilles Degottex, John Kane, Thomas Drugman, Tuomo Raitio, and Stefan Scherer. 2014. COVAREP – a collaborative voice analysis repository for speech technologies. In *Acoustics, Speech and Signal Processing (ICASSP), 2014 IEEE International Conference on*, pages 960–964.

Thomas Drugman and Yannis Stylianou. 2014. Maximum voiced frequency estimation: Exploiting amplitude and phase spectra. *Signal Processing Letters, IEEE*, 21(10):1230–1234.

Thomas Drugman, Baris Bozkurt, and Thierry Dutoit. 2012. A comparative study of glottal source estimation techniques. *Computer Speech & Language*, 26(1):20–34.

Thomas Drugman. 2014. Maximum phase modeling for sparse linear prediction of speech. *Signal Processing Letters, IEEE*, 21(2):185–189.

Rubén Fraile and Juan Ignacio Godino-Llorente. 2014. Cepstral peak prominence: A comprehensive analysis. *Biomedical Signal Processing and Control*, 14:42–54.

Kathleen C. Fraser, Jed A. Meltzer, and Frank Rudzicz. 2015. Linguistic features identify Alzheimer's disease in narrative speech. *Journal of Alzheimer's Disease*, 49(2):407–422.

Ken J. Gilhooly and Robert H. Logie. 1980. Age-of-acquisition, imagery, concreteness, familiarity, and ambiguity measures for 1,944 words. *Behavior Research Methods*, 12:395–427.

Harold Goodglass and Edith Kaplan. 1983. *Boston diagnostic aphasia examination booklet*. Lea & Febiger Philadelphia, PA.

Anthony Habash and Curry Guinn. 2012. Language analysis of speakers with dementia of the Alzheimer's type. In *Association for the Advancement of Artificial Intelligence (AAAI) Fall Symposium*, pages 8–13.

Mark Hall, Eibe Frank, Geoffrey Holmes, Bernhard Pfahringer, Peter Reutemann, and Ian H. Witten. 2009. The WEKA data mining software: an update. *ACM SIGKDD Explorations Newsletter*, 11(1):10–18.

Max Hamilton. 1960. A rating scale for depression. *Journal of Neurology, Neurosurgery, and Psychiatry*, 23(1):56–62.

Antony Honoré. 1979. Some simple measures of richness of vocabulary. *Association for Literary and Linguistic Computing Bulletin*, 7(2):172–177.

Christine Howes, Matthew Purver, and Rose McCabe. 2014. Linguistic indicators of severity and progress in online text-based therapy for depression. In *In Proceedings of the ACL Workshop on Computational Linguistics and Clinical Psychology*.

William Jarrold, Bart Peintner, David Wilkins, Dimitra Vergryi, Colleen Richey, Maria Luisa Gorno-Tempini, and Jennifer Ogar. 2014. Aided diagnosis of dementia type through computer-based analysis of spontaneous speech. In *Proceedings of the ACL Workshop on Computational Linguistics and Clinical Psychology*, pages 27–36.

John Kane and Christer Gobl. 2011. Identifying regions of non-modal phonation using features of the wavelet transform. In *12th Annual Conference of the International Speech Communication Association 2011 (INTERSPEECH 2011)*, pages 177–180.

Amos D. Korczyn and Ilan Halperin. 2009. Depression and dementia. *Journal of the Neurological Sciences*, 283(1):139–142.

Hochang B. Lee and Constantine G. Lyketsos. 2003. Depression in Alzheimer's disease: heterogeneity and related issues. *Biological Psychiatry*, 54(3):353–362.

Lu-Shih Alex Low, Namunu C. Maddage, Margaret Lech, Lisa B. Sheeber, and Nicholas B. Allen. 2011. Detection of clinical depression in adolescents' speech during family interactions. *Biomedical Engineering, IEEE Transactions on*, 58(3):574–586.

Xiaofei Lu. 2010. Automatic analysis of syntactic complexity in second language writing. *International Journal of Corpus Linguistics*, 15(4):474–496.

Melanie Luppa, Claudia Sikorski, Tobias Luck, L. Ehreke, Alexander Konnopka, Birgitt Wiese, Siegfried Weyerer, H-H. König, and Steffi G. Riedel-Heller. 2012. Age-and gender-specific prevalence of depression in latest-life–systematic review and meta-analysis. *Journal of Affective Disorders*, 136(3):212–221.

Juan J.G. Meilán, Francisco Martínez-Sánchez, Juan Carro, José A. Sánchez, and Enrique Pérez. 2012. Acoustic markers associated with impairment in language processing in Alzheimer's disease. *The Spanish Journal of Psychology*, 15(02):487–494.

Elliot Moore, Mark Clements, John W. Peifer, and Lydia Weisser. 2008. Critical analysis of the impact of glottal features in the classification of clinical depression in speech. *Biomedical Engineering, IEEE Transactions on*, 55(1):96–107.

Tomas Müller-Thomsen, Sönke Arlt, Ulrike Mann, Reinhard Maß, and Stefanie Ganzer. 2005. Detecting depression in Alzheimer's disease: evaluation of four different scales. *Archives of Clinical Neuropsychology*, 20(2):271–276.

Laura L. Murray. 2010. Distinguishing clinical depression from early Alzheimer's disease in elderly people: Can narrative analysis help? *Aphasiology*, 24(6-8):928–939.

Thin Nguyen, Dinh Phung, Bo Dao, Svetha Venkatesh, and Michael Berk. 2014. Affective and content analysis of online depression communities. *IEEE Transactions on Affective Computing*, 5(3):217–226.

Sylvester Olubolu Orimaye, Jojo Sze-Meng Wong, and Karen Jennifer Golden. 2014. Learning predictive linguistic features for Alzheimer's disease and related dementias using verbal utterances. In *Proceedings of the 1st Workshop on Computational Linguistics and Clinical Psychology (CLPsych)*, pages 78–87.

Asli Ozdas, Richard G. Shiavi, Stephen E. Silverman, Marilyn K. Silverman, and D. Mitchell Wilkes. 2004. Investigation of vocal jitter and glottal flow spectrum as possible cues for depression and near-term suicidal risk. *Biomedical Engineering, IEEE Transactions on*, 51(9):1530–1540.

Niels D. Prins, Ewoud J. van Dijk, Tom den Heijer, Sarah E. Vermeer, Peter J. Koudstaal, Matthijs Oudkerk, Albert Hofman, and Monique M.B. Breteler. 2004. Cerebral white matter lesions and the risk of dementia. *Archives of Neurology*, 61(10):1531–1534.

Vassiliki Rentoumi, Ladan Raoufian, Samrah Ahmed, Celeste A. de Jager, and Peter Garrard. 2014. Features and machine learning classification of connected speech samples from patients with autopsy proven Alzheimer's disease with and without additional vascular pathology. *Journal of Alzheimer's Disease*, 42:S3–S17.

Philip Resnik, William Armstrong, Leonardo Claudino, and Thang Nguyen. 2015. The University of Maryland CLPsych 2015 shared task system. In *Proceedings of the 2nd Workshop on Computational Linguistics and Clinical Psychology: From Linguistic Signal to Clinical Reality*, pages 54–60, Denver, Colorado, June 5.

Brian Roark, John-Paul Hosom, Margaret Mitchell, and Jeffrey A. Kaye. 2007. Automatically derived spoken language markers for detecting mild cognitive impairment. In *Proceedings of the 2nd International Conference on Technology and Aging (ICTA)*, Toronto, ON, June.

Stephanie Rude, Eva-Maria Gortner, and James Pennebaker. 2004. Language use of depressed and depression-vulnerable college students. *Cognition & Emotion*, 18(8):1121–1133.

Stefan Scherer, Giota Stratou, Jonathan Gratch, and Louis-Philippe Morency. 2013. Investigating voice quality as a speaker-independent indicator of depression and PTSD. In *Proceedings of Interspeech*, pages 847–851.

Hans Stadthagen-Gonzalez and Colin J. Davis. 2006. The Bristol norms for age of acquisition, imageability, and familiarity. *Behavior Research Methods*, 38(4):598–605.

Calvin Thomas, Vlado Keselj, Nick Cercone, Kenneth Rockwood, and Elissa Asp. 2005. Automatic detection and rating of dementia of Alzheimer type through lexical analysis of spontaneous speech. In *Proceedings of the IEEE International Conference on Mechatronics and Automation*, pages 1569–1574.

Lilian Thorpe. 2009. Depression vs. dementia: How do we assess? *The Canadian Review of Alzheimer's Disease and Other Dementias*, pages 17–21.

Amy Beth Warriner, Victor Kuperman, and Marc Brysbaert. 2013. Norms of valence, arousal, and dominance for 13,915 English lemmas. *Behavior Research Methods*, 45(4):1191–1207.

Victor Yngve. 1960. A model and hypothesis for language structure. *Proceedings of the American Physical Society*, 104:444–466.

Mark Zimmerman, Jennifer H. Martinez, Diane Young, Iwona Chelminski, and Kristy Dalrymple. 2013. Severity classification on the Hamilton depression rating scale. *Journal of Affective Disorders*, 150(2):384–388.

Towards Early Dementia Detection:
Fusing Linguistic and Non-Linguistic Clinical Data

Joseph Bullard[1], Cecilia Ovesdotter Alm[2], Xumin Liu[1], Rubén A. Proaño[3], Qi Yu[1]
[1]College of Computing & Information Sciences, [2]College of Liberal Arts, [3]College of Engineering
Rochester Institute of Technology, Rochester, NY
{jtb4478,coagla,xmlics,qyuvks,rpmeie}@rit.edu

Abstract

Dementia is an increasing problem for an aging population, with a lack of available treatment options, as well as expensive patient care. Early detection is critical to eventually postpone symptoms and to prepare health care providers and families for managing a patient's needs. Identification of diagnostic markers may be possible with patients' clinical records. Text portions of clinical records are integrated into predictive models of dementia development in order to gain insights towards automated identification of patients who may benefit from providers' early assessment. Results support the potential power of linguistic records for predicting dementia status, both in the absence of, and in complement to, corresponding structured non-linguistic data.

1 Introduction

Dementia is a problem for the aging population, and it is the 6th leading cause of death in the US (Alzheimer's Association, 2014). Around 35 million people worldwide suffer from some form of dementia, and this number is expected to double by 2030 (Prince et al., 2013). The most common form of dementia is Alzheimer's Disease, which has no known cure and limited treatment options. The clinical care for dementia focuses on prolonged symptom management, resulting in high personal and financial costs for patients and their families, straining the healthcare system in the process. Early detection is critical for potential postponement of symptoms, and for allowing families to adjust and adequately plan for the future. Despite this importance, current detection methods are costly, invasive, or unreliable, with most patients not being diagnosed until their symptoms have already progressed. Dementia diagnosis is a life-changing event not only for the patient but for the caretakers that have to adjust to the ensuing life changes. Improved understanding and recognition of early warning signs of dementia would greatly benefit the management of the disease, and enable long-term planning and logistics for healthcare providers, health systems, and caregivers.

With the advent of electronic clinical records comes the potential for large-scale analysis of patients' clinical data to understand or discover warning signs of dementia progression. The ability to follow the evolution of the disease based on patients' records would be key to develop intelligent support systems to assist medical decision-making and the provision of care. Current research using records mainly focuses on structured data, i.e. numerical or categorical data, such as test results or patient demographics (Himes et al., 2009). However, unstructured data, such as text notes taken during interactions between patients and doctors, presents a potentially rich source of information that may be both more straightfowardly interpretable for humans, as well as helpful for early dementia detection. Structured data from innovative diagnostic tests are often absent due to their cost and accessibility, text notes are generated for nearly every visit of a patient. Moreover, text notes in medical records are a source of natural language, and potentially more flexibly encode the diagnostic expertise and reasoning of the clinical professionals who write them.

Proceedings of the 3rd Workshop on Computational Linguistics and Clinical Psychology: From Linguistic Signal to Clinical Reality, pages 12–22,
San Diego, California, June 16, 2016. ©2016 Association for Computational Linguistics

Processing and computationally analyzing natural language remains a formidable task, but insights gleaned from it may translate particularly well into actual clinical practice, given its interpretable and accessible nature. Therefore, the ability to predict dementia development based on both structured and unstructured data would be useful for intelligent support systems which could automatically flag individuals who will benefit for further evaluation, reducing the impact of late diagnosis.

1.1 Related Work

Structured clinical data has been useful for identifying known disease markers (Himes et al., 2009). Procedural and diagnostic codes (e.g., ICD-9) can provide high specificity for identifying a disease, but may not provide sufficient sensitivity (Birman-Deych et al., 2005; Kern et al., 2006). A patient's history, however, is typically summarized by a clinician in text form, and can provide informative expressiveness and granularity not adequately captured by ICD-9 codes (Li et al., 2008). Interestingly,

Prior work has shown that natural language data can help synthesize details and discover trends in medical records. Natural language processing and text mining have been applied to the identification of various known medical conditions. One method maps specific conditions to relevant terms from ontologies (curated knowledge bases). For example, SNOMED-CT predicted post-operative patient complications (Murff et al., 2011), and MedLEE (Friedman et al., 1995) identified colorectal cancer cases (Xu et al., 2011), suspicious mammogram findings (Jain and Friedman, 1997), and adverse events related to central venous catheters (Penz et al., 2007). Similarly, the language analysis-based resource SymText (Haug et al., 1995) has been used for detecting bacterial pneumonia cases from descriptions of chest X-ray (Fiszman et al., 2000).

While such studies with medical knowledge bases are useful for disease identification, they mostly involve conditions with well known markers and known relationships between words and clinical concepts typically available once the patient is symptomatic. However, many cognitive conditions, such as dementia, as well as other illnesses of interest, are not well understood and their onsets gradually evolve over long periods of time. Further-more, diagnosing such conditions is often primarily a function of experts' analysis, transcribed into notes. Thus, discovering lexical associations with the progression of these conditions could be tremendously beneficial, and could also help to validate and enhance the use of resources such as the Alzheimer's Disease Ontology (Malhotra et al., 2013).

Topic models have produced interesting results across domains (Chan et al., 2013; Resnik et al., 2013; McCallum et al., 2007; Paul and Dredze, 2011). Latent Semantic Indexing (LSI) has been used in medicine to discover statistical relationships between lexical items in a corpus. LSI has been used to supplement the development of a clinical vocabulary associated with post-traumatic stress disorder (Luther et al., 2011), and for forecasting ambulatory falls in elderly patients (McCart et al., 2013). However, LSI often requires around 300–500 concepts or dimensions to produce stable results (Bradford, 2008). This limitation can be overcome by using LDA, whose identified groups of related terms are also more intuitive for human interpretation than LSI results. Additionally, representing documents by their LDA topic distribution reduces the dimensionality of the feature space. Furthermore, a study with microtext data demonstrated that document length influences topic models, and that aggregating short documents by author can be beneficial (Hong and Davison, 2010). This finding is relevant for this study due to the short nature of clinical texts.

This study is concerned with the fusion of linguistic data with structured non-linguistic data, as well as the integration of distinct models suitable for each. Approaches to the former case, have been studied (Ruta and Gabrys, 2000). For the latter case, integration of classifiers typically involves multiple models of the same data, e.g. ensemble methods such as random forests, and often utilizes voting algorithms to produce the final combined output. However, here we focus on the combination of two distinct models: one based on linguistic data and one on structured non-linguistic data. This setup complicates the use of typical voting methods, and thus we explore a less frequently studied solution that leverages Bayesian probability to produce posterior distributions (Bailer-Jones and Smith, 2011).

1.2 Our Contributions

(1) We compare performance of predictive modeling with linguistic vs. non-linguistic features, studying if linguistic features used alone as predictors yield performance comparable to that of non-linguistic record data – especially when the latter exclude cognitive assessment scores from expert-administered tests. Our results show the utility of linguistic data for dementia prediction, e.g., when relevant structured data are unavailable in the records, as is often the case. (2) We explore the use of Latent Dirichlet Allocation (LDA) (Blei et al., 2003) as textually interpretable dimensionality reduction of the lexical feature space into a topic space. We examine if LDA can transform the sparse term space into a reduced topic space that meaningfully characterizes the texts, and we discuss its practical value for classification. (3) We study the challenge of fusing linguistic and non-linguistic data from records in additional classification experiments. If fusion improves performance, this would strengthen the utility of records-based linguistic features for disease prediction. We explore two integration methods: combining feature vectors computed independently from structured and text data, or leveraging probabilistic outputs of their respective trained classifiers.

This paper is organized as follows. Section 2 describes the data for the dementia detection problem. Section 3 presents our framework and integration. Section 4 outlines experiments and results. We conclude with future directions in Section 5.

2 Dementia Detection Problem: Data

This study makes a secondary use of a data set from the Alzheimer's Disease Neuroimaging Initiative (ADNI) (`adni.loni.usc.edu`). The ADNI study contains mostly structured data, such as measurements from brain imaging scans, blood, and cerebrospinal fluid biomarkers. The dataset also contains optional text fields in which examiners include notes or descriptions at their discretion.

Each ADNI subject[1] is labeled upon entering the study. ADNI's original labeling scheme was modified in later phases of the study, resulting in some subjects having updated labels, while others remain unchanged. Therefore, only subjects who joined the

---

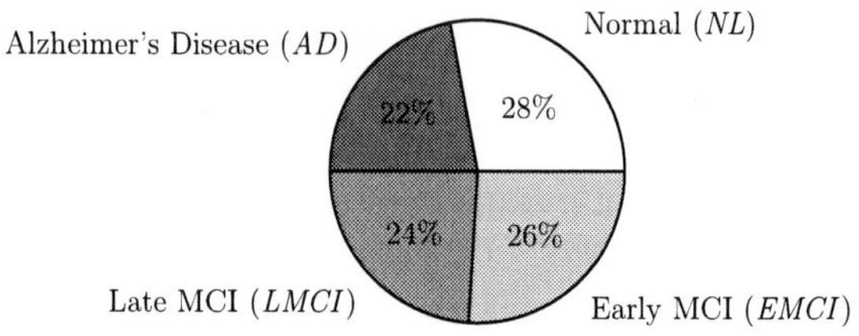

Figure 1: Distribution of subject diagnostic labels ($n =$ 679). MCI = Mild Cognitive Impairment.

study under the most recent phase, *ADNI-2*, are included in this work. Subjects with a label of *SMC* (Significant Memory Complaint; reflecting a self-reported memory issue) are excluded as it is not a real diagnostic category outside of ADNI. A subject's record must have both unstructured text and structured data to be included, resulting in 679 usable subjects; from here on we refer to their data.

The *ADNI-2* phase of the ADNI collection uses several labels to indicate the progression to Alzheimer's Disease: *NL* (Normal), *EMCI* (Early Mild Cognitive Impairment), *LMCI* (Late MCI), and *AD* (Alzheimer's Disease). The label (class) distribution of the remaining 679 subjects is relatively balanced (see Figure 1). Moderately-sized data sets are common in clinical NLP contexts, where data is understandably more challenging to collate and access. For the text data, we considered text source files with considerable quantities of information.[2] All 679 subjects possess text notes in at least one of these four files. Entries from these files are aggregated by subject and concatenated to yield one text document per subject.

There are 22 structured data fields in this ADNI subset. The problem of missing values in the structured data was handled through multiple imputation (using the Amelia II package in R). This process uses log-likelihoods to generate probable complete datasets. Most structured data comes from either cerebrospinal fluid samples or brain imaging scans, while three fields correspond to scores on cognitive exam evaluations: the Clinical Dementia Rating (CDR), the Mini Mental State Examination (MMSE), and the Alzheimer's Disease Assessment Scale (ADAS13). Importantly, a meaningful distinction can be made between structured data from cognitive assessments versus those from biophys-

---

[1] The ADNI study refers to its participants as *subjects*.

[2] See Table in the supplementary documentation.

ical tests/markers. A cognitive assessment is administered by a clinical professional, and thus is a reflection of that person's opinion and expertise. Essentially, cognitive assessment scores are outputs of professional interpretation, whereas other structured data are inputs for future interpretation. Cognitive assessments are also usually administered when providers already suspect dementia, and thus can be regarded as post-symptomatic. Patients, providers, and families will benefit from early detection, and such automated detection can also help prioritize the scheduling of expert-based cognitive assessments in resource-strained healthcare environments.

3 Modeling of Linguistic Data

There are three main feature representations for the linguistic data: *bag-of-words* (BOW), *term-frequency inverse-document-frequency* (*tf-idf*) on top of BOW, and *topics* from LDA.

Preprocessing and text normalization were performed in Python and NLTK, involving lowercasing, punctuation removal, stop-listing, and number removal (with exception of age mentions). Besides regular stop-listing, words or phrases revealing a subject's diagnostic state (for example *MCI*) were removed. Words in a document were lemmatized to merge inflections (removing distinctions between for instance *cataracts* and *cataract*). Abbreviation expansion used lexical lists. The 200 most frequent lexical content bigrams and trigrams were extracted and concatenated (*breast cancer → breast_cancer*). Lastly, while dates were removed, age expressions were kept after conversion and binning (*AGE_>=70_<80*), as they may be important for this problem. Ages below 40 were represented as *AGE_<40* and ages at or above 90 as *AGE_>=90*.

BOW and tf-idf were implemented using `gensim` (Řehůřek and Sojka, 2010). The standard BOW representation is very sparse, since any document only contains a small subset of the vocabulary. An extension weights the terms based on their distribution in the corpus using *tf-idf*. Thus higher weights are assigned to terms which appear more times in fewer documents, and lower weights to terms which appear fewer times and/or in more documents. The feature space of tf-idf corresponds to standard BOW, but the values are the weights.

LDA is a generative model for identifying latent topics of related terms in a text corpus, D, which consists of M documents and is assumed to contain K topics. Each topic k is essentially follows a multinomial distribution over the corpus vocabulary, parameterized by ϕ_k, which is drawn from a Dirichlet distribution, i.e., $\phi_k \sim \mathrm{Dir}(\beta)$. Similarly, each *document* follows a multinomial distribution over the set of topics in the corpus, also assumed to have a Dirichlet probability, denoted $\theta_i \sim \mathrm{Dir}(\alpha)$. Working backwards, the probability of each term in a document is determined by the term distribution of its topic, which is in turn determined by the topic distribution of the document (Blei et al., 2003).

Under LDA, a document is modeled as a probabilistic distribution over topics, learned from the occurrence of terms through Collapsed Variational Bayesian (CVB) inference methods using the Stanford Topic Modeling Toolbox (Teh et al., 2007).[3] Since topics are determined based on statistical relationships of terms, the effectiveness of the model can be hampered by extremely frequent or infrequent terms. For these reasons, we filter out the vocabulary (Boyd-Graber et al., 2014, p. 9) for terms appearing less than 3 times and the 30 most common terms.[4]

3.1 Integration with Structured Data Models

Integration is performed on the results of each unstructured modeling experiment (BOW, tf-idf, and LDA) and those of each structured ones–with vs. without cognitive assessment features. For LDA, only the parameters with the highest performance are used in integration. The most intuitive form of integration is concatenation of the feature vectors for structured and unstructured data. Hence, *concatenation* refers to joining two vectors of length n and m into a single new vector of length $n + m$. This concatenated feature vector is used in classification.

The second approach of integration leverages posterior probabilities from the individual (linguistic vs. non-linguistic) classification models. For each input, a classifier produces a posterior probability of each class label and selects the most probable as its output. One classifier is trained on structured data

---

[3]Compared to Gibbs sampling (also explored initially), CVB converged on more sensible topics and performed better in model development.

[4]Other cutoff values were explored initially.

features X_s, and another on unstructured data features X_u, resulting in two posterior distributions. The probability of a class C_k is then denoted as $p(C_k \mid X_s, X_u)$. If these distributions are assumed to be conditionally independent with respect to their class labels, then by Bayes' theorem:

$$p(C_k \mid X_s, X_u) \propto \frac{p(C_k \mid X_s)\, p(C_k \mid X_u)}{p(C_k)} \quad (1)$$

From here, the class label with the highest probability is selected as the output; for details see Bailer-Jones and Smith (Bailer-Jones and Smith, 2011).

For integration purposes, we use logistic regression for all classification experiments, implemented in `scikit-learn` (Pedregosa et al., 2011) to compute the posterior probabilities of all classes. We adopt a regularized logistic regression model to further improve the predictive accuracy. By incorporating a regularization term into the basic logistic regression model, regularized logistic regression is able to reach a good bias-variance trade-off and hence achieve a better generalization capability. The regularization term is comprised of two parameters, which are C, the inverse of regularization strength,[5] and the penalty function (either the L^1 or L^2 vector norm). A smaller C corresponds to harsher penalties for large coefficients. The values of these parameters are selected through a grid search of possible values, evaluated by accuracy in cross validation. The process is repeated for each labeling scheme.

4   Experimental Study

Each subject is annotated with a dementia status class label. Each subject's linguistic and structured non-linguistic data are used separately or integrated, as instances for classification. Two different classification problems are reported on. One involves all four classes (*NL, EMCI, LMCI, AD*). This 4-class problem is henceforth referred to as *Standard*. As discussed, early detection of dementia is critical. Accordingly, *EMCI* subjects are of particular interest, as they represent the beginning of the disease's progression. In the second experiment, we use 367 subjects having one of these two class labels (187

NL, 180 *EMCI*). While this does not perfectly match the reality of diagnosis, as it excludes the later dementia stages, it could be argued that those later stages are in less need of automatic analysis since they are more readily observable. The resulting binary problem is referred to here as *Early Risk*.

The results and discussions presented later in this paper include a comparison to a majority class baseline, however, this is included merely as a standard comparison, while the actual comparison of interest is between integration of non-linguistic (with vs. without cognitive assessment scores) and linguistic features compared to those groups in isolation.

Held-out Data   The data set is randomly split into 80% ($n = 544$ subjects) for model development (*dev* set), and 20% ($n = 135$ subjects) for final evaluation (*held-out* set). Models are only exposed to the *held-out* set after satisfactory performance is achieved using the *dev* set. Class distributions are preserved in the *dev* and *held-out* sets.

LOO Cross-Validation   Although the *dev* and *held-out* sets have similar class distributions, overfitting is still a potential issue. For this reason, after the held-out evaluation is complete, a leave-one-out cross-validation (LOO or LOOCV) procedure is run on the entire merged dataset to serve as an additional evaluation, to either confirm or call into question the trends from held-out testing, which may be evident through differences in performance of the same features and models. LOOCV is a case of k-fold cross-validation where k is equal to the number of training instances, resulting in one fold for every data point in which all other data points are used for training.

4.1   Topic Exploration and Evaluation

Tuning of the topic number parameter is essential to finding an appropriate LDA model. This process is performed by iteratively measuring classification accuracy at values of K ranging from 5 to 100, in multiples of 5, using the training data from the held-out evaluation split. LDA is being used here with two goals in mind: to improve classification performance as a form of dimensionality reduction, as well as to provide human-interpretable topics. The former is more convenient and appropriate in the context of this work, but does not necessarily imply good results for the latter. A clinical expert view-

---

[5]It is common in other sources to use λ for the regularization strength, but the employed `scikit-learn` library instead uses $C = 1/\lambda$, i.e. the *inverse* of regularization strength.

ing the output of such a model would likely prefer fewer topics, each with higher interpretability. Accordingly, LDA models in classification are examined with various per-topic metrics known to correlate well with human evaluation. Thus, the best-performing reduced topic-feature space is selected for classification results and then additionally analyzed using the *topic coherence* metric (Mimno et al., 2011), which measures how often the most probable words of a topic appear together in documents, and has been shown to match well with human evaluation of topic quality (Boyd-Graber et al., 2014).

4.2 Classification of *Standard* Labels

The upper part of Table 1 shows the results of structured vs. linguistic features in isolation for the *Standard* problem, while the rest of the table shows results of integration techniques. Overall, performance improved in LOOCV, with a few exceptions (e.g. *tf-idf*), which is likely due to the greater number of available training instances in this evaluation.

The performance of structured data alone is substantially higher than the majority class baseline, and more so when cognitive assessment features were included (+*cognitive*), as expected. Importantly, the BOW representation for text data achieved similar performance compared to the structured data without cognitive assessment scores, showing that simple text modeling can be useful in the common event that structured data are missing.

The benefit of tf-idf appears inconsistent between held-out and LOOCV evaluations, possibly attributable to differences in document frequency of important terms in the different training data (*dev* vs. *dev+held-out*, respectively).

For LDA, performance was dependent on the number of topics, as seen in Figure 2, with two performance peaks (at $K = 60$ and $K = 85$) surpassing BOW. This supports that dimensionality reduction by LDA can improve performance, but data size may influence results. This is a limitation of using an unsupervised algorithm for a supervised task. Performance differences between held-out and LOOCV indicate overfitting to the *dev* set in particular.

Table 2a shows 5 of the top 10 topics from the 60 topic model, based on topic coherence. This metric appears to aid in identifying interpretable topics. For example, Topic 2 is about cognitive assessment,

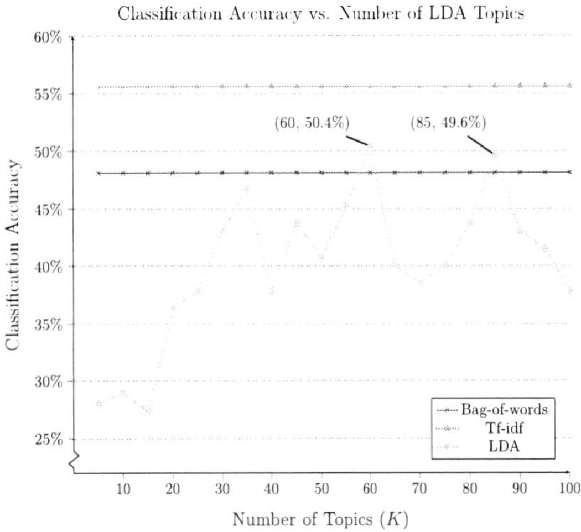

Figure 2: Classification accuracy of LDA features on the *held-out* set, with increasing number of topics K (increments of 5).

referencing people in their 60's. Topic 45 pertains to regular medical visits (*PCP* is *primary care physician*), with some common concerns of elderly patients (*back*, *heart*). Topic 25 captures heart disease (*cardiac*, *stent*, *chest_pain*) and related visits (*hospitalization*, *admitted*, *discharged*).

Linguistic and non-linguistic models are integrated to improve classification performance. Table 1 shows results for 16 integrated models (2 non-linguistic models × 4 linguistic models × 2 integration methods). Similar trends were observed for BOW and tf-idf in most cases. Interestingly, integrating with BOW is better than including cognitive assessment scores for held-out. The LDA-reduced features are again less consistent than other text features, but still comparatively improved performance in many cases. LDA integration experiments appear more robust between held-out and LOOCV than when LDA features were used alone, likely due to structured features taking the brunt of the decision.

It was predicted that the posterior probability composition method would yield better results than vector concatenation. Interestingly, this is not apparent, with many cases revealing the opposite. Yet overall, the best performing cases include results where integration is done by this method. One potential limitation of the posterior probability composition is that a stronger decision is made when each of the underlying classifiers produces an asymmetric posterior class distribution. A limitation of

| Features | | Held-out Evaluation | | | | | Leave-one-out Cross-validation | | | | |
| | | | NL | EMCI | LMCI | AD | | NL | EMCI | LMCI | AD |
	Acc.	P / R	P / R	P / R	P / R	Acc.	P / R	P / R	P / R	P / R
Baseline (majority class)	32.6%	33 / 100	− / 0	− / 0	− / 0	27.5%	28 / 100	− / 0	− / 0	− / 0
Structured (−cognitive)	51.9%	68 / 73	27 / 28	47 / 23	55 / 88	53.9%	57 / 77	43 / 34	40 / 26	66 / 81
Structured (+cognitive)	55.6%	80 / 84	35 / 38	33 / 20	56 / 79	62.7%	70 / 86	52 / 48	50 / 33	71 / 85
Bag-of-words	48.1%	67 / 55	32 / 38	52 / 46	43 / 54	50.2%	59 / 67	40 / 39	43 / 42	60 / 51
Tf-idf	55.6%	61 / 61	37 / 63	78 / 40	74 / 58	48.9%	49 / 75	39 / 43	49 / 32	73 / 42
LDA($K = 85$)	49.6%	57 / 48	39 / 72	65 / 37	53 / 42	39.3%	39 / 62	34 / 32	39 / 29	52 / 32
LDA($K = 60$)	50.4%	64 / 61	37 / 66	53 / 23	57 / 50	37.4%	39 / 54	32 / 33	35 / 28	48 / 33
S_{-cog} ∪ Bag-of-words	61.5%	77 / 68	41 / 50	70 / 46	62 / 88	59.8%	69 / 79	48 / 44	45 / 41	73 / 76
S_{-cog} ⊕ Bag-of-words	57.0%	90 / 59	41 / 53	47 / 40	59 / 83	58.3%	69 / 73	46 / 46	45 / 44	75 / 71
S_{+cog} ∪ Bag-of-words	58.5%	78 / 71	35 / 41	59 / 46	61 / 79	61.3%	72 / 79	48 / 43	47 / 44	74 / 80
S_{+cog} ⊕ Bag-of-words	59.3%	88 / 64	39 / 53	56 / 43	63 / 83	61.9%	74 / 80	48 / 48	48 / 45	77 / 75
S_{-cog} ∪ Tf-idf	53.3%	74 / 71	31 / 34	45 / 26	55 / 88	58.0%	62 / 83	49 / 38	45 / 31	68 / 81
S_{-cog} ⊕ Tf-idf	51.1%	83 / 55	37 / 59	39 / 14	51 / 88	59.6%	63 / 83	52 / 43	46 / 30	70 / 82
S_{+cog} ∪ Tf-idf	59.3%	79 / 86	41 / 44	45 / 26	58 / 79	64.7%	73 / 88	53 / 53	52 / 34	72 / 84
S_{+cog} ⊕ Tf-idf	61.5%	95 / 80	45 / 72	42 / 14	57 / 83	65.4%	73 / 89	55 / 53	54 / 35	73 / 85
S_{-cog} ∪ LDA($K = 85$)	54.8%	73 / 73	31 / 34	56 / 29	55 / 88	56.4%	60 / 82	46 / 33	42 / 31	70 / 80
S_{-cog} ⊕ LDA($K = 85$)	44.4%	80 / 46	28 / 50	27 / 09	50 / 88	56.3%	60 / 79	45 / 36	42 / 30	71 / 81
S_{+cog} ∪ LDA($K = 85$)	58.5%	84 / 86	39 / 44	38 / 23	58 / 79	62.0%	70 / 86	49 / 45	46 / 34	74 / 84
S_{+cog} ⊕ LDA($K = 85$)	58.5%	90 / 77	44 / 69	36 / 11	53 / 79	63.6%	71 / 87	52 / 48	49 / 35	75 / 85
S_{-cog} ∪ LDA($K = 60$)	51.1%	69 / 61	30 / 34	48 / 29	55 / 88	55.7%	59 / 78	47 / 37	40 / 28	69 / 82
S_{-cog} ⊕ LDA($K = 60$)	45.9%	78 / 48	30 / 53	33 / 09	49 / 88	56.4%	60 / 78	47 / 37	40 / 30	71 / 82
S_{+cog} ∪ LDA($K = 60$)	60.0%	88 / 86	44 / 53	37 / 20	56 / 79	62.4%	72 / 86	50 / 47	45 / 33	74 / 85
S_{+cog} ⊕ LDA($K = 60$)	59.3%	92 / 77	45 / 72	33 / 11	54 / 79	62.9%	74 / 86	51 / 48	44 / 34	75 / 84

Table 1: Results on *Standard* problem (4-classes). Integration by *vector concatenation* is indicated by ∪, and *posterior probability composition* by ⊕. Structured (−cognitive) = S_{-cog} , Structured (+cognitive) = S_{+cog}.

ID	Top 10 Words
3	*corroborated, subjective, continues_meet, score, factor, other, SP, AGE_>=60_<70, controlled_medication, unremarkable*
2	*impression, CDR, MMSE, ADLS, AGE_>=60_<70, cog, amnestic, global, function, score*
17	*medical, consistent, status, function, continues, health, occasional, active, daily, functional*
45	*blood, pressure, month, visit, PCP, diagnosed, dizziness, back, doctor, heart*
25	*hospital, admitted, discharged, stent, cardiac, went, chest_pain, AE, anxiety, total*

Table 2a: Five high-ranked topics from the *Standard* problem with $K = 60$ (ranked by *topic coherence*).

ID	Top 10 Words
38	*completed, visit, reported, mg, performed, protocol, testing, study_partner, blood, year*
25	*criterion, subjective, corroborated, factor, other, AGE_>=60_<70, continues_meet, score, memory_problems, confounding*
55	*hip, left, right, removed, normal, arthritis, cataract, eye, allergy, hand*
36	*year, smoked, ago, pack, o, quit, per_day, c, urinary_frequency, memory_problems*
56	*work, up, valve, cardiac, aortic, ER, heart, x, cardiologist, visit*

Table 2b: Five high-ranked topics from the *Early Risk* problem with $K = 100$ (ranked by *topic coherence*).

this method is its dependence on strong or accurate decisions from the underlying models. Vector concatenation is not subject to this limitation, but has the drawback of potentially overwhelming a smaller feature set with a larger sparse one. As for class-specific differences, the *NL* (normal) and *AD* (Alzheimer's disease) subjects were classified with higher precision and recall scores than were the MCI classes in nearly all integration experiments, pointing to the challenge of subtler disease stages.

4.3 Classification of *Early Risk*

In addition to the experiments above, the more specific problem of distinguishing normal (*NL*) subjects from those with early mild cognitive impairment (*EMCI*) was also explored. Only LOOCV is performed because the subsampling of *NL* and *EMCI* subjects slightly distorts the class distributions in the original held-out set. Results are given in Table 3.

As in the *Standard* problem, all non-linguistic and linguistic feature types perform well above the majority class baseline. One major difference here is that all linguistic data types outperform the structured features when cognitive assessments are excluded. This may suggest a potential linguistic difference in clinical notes at the onset of MCI.

The number of LDA topics is selected as before (but using the whole *Early Risk* subsample, as opposed to the *Standard dev* set). Two peaks found at $K = 65$ and $K = 100$ achieve the same classification accuracy, but do not outperform BOW and tf-idf. The difficulties LDA faced in the *Standard* problem are also faced here, and thus similar performance shortcomings are observed. The ability to approximately match tf-idf performance is still noteworthy since the LDA features are a smaller and denser representation than tf-idf, which may be more easily interpretable by clinical professionals.

Table 2b shows 5 of the top 10 topics from the 100 topic model trained on the *Early Risk* subset, based on the topic coherence metric. A consequence of a smaller sample of subjects is a smaller vocabulary and thus weaker statistical judgments, Topics 38, 25, 36, and 56 appear to be about routine visits/tests, cognitive evaluations, smoking habits, and cardiac issues, respectively. Topic 55 is an example of a *chained* topic (Boyd-Graber et al., 2014, p. 17), where unrelated words are linked together through

| Features | LOOCV | | |
| | | NL | EMCI |
	Acc.	P / R	P / R
Baseline	51.0%	51 / 100	− / 0
Structured (−cognitive)	67.6%	67 / 73	69 / 62
Structured (+cognitive)	79.8%	78 / 84	82 / 76
Bag-of-words	70.8%	71 / 73	71 / 69
Tf-idf	69.2%	68 / 75	71 / 63
LDA($K = 65$)	68.9%	67 / 76	71 / 62
LDA($K = 100$)	68.9%	68 / 74	70 / 63
$S_{-cog} \cup$ Bag-of-words	76.8%	76 / 79	78 / 74
$S_{-cog} \oplus$ Bag-of-words	76.0%	77 / 77	76 / 76
$S_{+cog} \cup$ Bag-of-words	77.1%	76 / 80	78 / 74
$S_{+cog} \oplus$ Bag-of-words	80.7%	80 / 82	81 / 79
$S_{-cog} \cup$ Tf-idf	72.2%	71 / 78	74 / 66
$S_{-cog} \oplus$ Tf-idf	72.8%	71 / 79	75 / 66
$S_{+cog} \cup$ Tf-idf	80.7%	79 / 85	83 / 77
$S_{+cog} \oplus$ Tf-idf	83.1%	82 / 86	84 / 81
$S_{-cog} \cup$ LDA($K = 65$)	72.2%	71 / 78	74 / 67
$S_{-cog} \oplus$ LDA($K = 65$)	72.5%	71 / 78	74 / 67
$S_{+cog} \cup$ LDA($K = 65$)	79.0%	78 / 82	81 / 76
$S_{+cog} \oplus$ LDA($K = 65$)	79.3%	78 / 83	81 / 76
$S_{-cog} \cup$ LDA($K = 100$)	71.4%	70 / 77	73 / 66
$S_{-cog} \oplus$ LDA($K = 100$)	71.9%	70 / 76	74 / 66
$S_{+cog} \cup$ LDA($K = 100$)	80.4%	80 / 82	81 / 78
$S_{+cog} \oplus$ LDA($K = 100$)	80.9%	80 / 83	82 / 79

Table 3: Classification performance on *Early Risk* (2 classes). *Vector concatenation* is indicated by $\cup$, and *posterior probability composition* by $\oplus$. Structured with (S_{+cog}) and without (S_{-cog}) cognitive.

shared co-occurring words, in this case with *left* and *right* seeming to link *eye* and *hand*, along with their associated terms *cataract* and *arthritis*.

The performance trends for the integrated models are slightly more consistent for the *Early Risk* problem than they were for the *Standard* problem. When excluding cognitive assessment scores, all integration experiments result in a modest improvement, although there is little to no difference between the two integration methods employed. This may suggest that results can be achieved without extra sophistication provided by posterior probability composition, or that further sophistication is needed beyond either of these techniques. In general, our results further justify the integration of linguistic and non-linguistic features and/or models.

5 Conclusion and Future Work

We explored classification of dementia progression status of subjects from a study on Alzheimer's disease, and the integration of text data models with those of structured data, with vs. without cognitive assessment scores. Experiments support texts' viability as a useful source for dementia classification, as an important complement to structured data, or alone when structured data are missing. LDA was also studied as interpretable dimensionality reduction. With a larger sample size, the LDA model may converge to a more stable set of topics, but other appropriate public datasets (with both linguistic and non-linguistic data) are presently not available. An alternative is to apply supervised versions of LDA (Blei and McAuliffe, 2007; Ramage et al., 2009). Furthermore, with access to a pool of clinical specialists, it would be useful to integrate experts in evaluating the latent topics. Chang et al. (2009) proposed various such human evaluation techniques, such as the *word intrusion* task, in which human evaluators are presented with a list of n high probability terms of a randomly chosen topic, and one additional low probability term from that topic, and asked to identify the former. A drawback is that it would require access to a large enough pool of dementia specialists.

Other avenues of future work would include the incorporation of lexical similarity measures from sources like WordNet.

Acknowledgement

This study was supported by a Kodak Endowed Chair award form the Golisano College of Computing and Information Sciences at the Rochester Institute of Technology.

We are thankful for being able to use the ADNI projects dataset in this work. As per the data-use agreement, information about the ADNI data are included verbatim. Data collection and sharing for this project was funded by the Alzheimers Disease Neuroimaging Initiative (ADNI) (National Institutes of Health Grant U01 AG024904) and DOD ADNI (Department of Defense award number W81XWH-12-2-0012). ADNI is funded by the National Institute on Aging, the National Institute of Biomedical Imaging and Bioengineering, and through generous contributions from the following: Alzheimers Association; Alzheimers Drug Discovery Foundation; BioClinica, Inc.; Biogen Idec Inc.; Bristol-Myers Squibb Company; Eisai Inc.; Elan Pharmaceuticals, Inc.; Eli Lilly and Company; F. Hoffmann-La Roche Ltd and its affiliated company Genentech, Inc.; GE Healthcare; Innogenetics, N.V.; IXICO Ltd.; Janssen Alzheimer Immunotherapy Research & Development, LLC.; Johnson & Johnson Pharmaceutical Research & Development LLC.; Medpace, Inc.; Merck & Co., Inc.; Meso Scale Diagnostics, LLC.; NeuroRx Research; Novartis Pharmaceuticals Corporation; Pfizer Inc.; Piramal Imaging; Servier; Synarc Inc.; and Takeda Pharmaceutical Company. The Canadian Institutes of Health Research is providing funds to support ADNI clinical sites in Canada. Private sector contributions are facilitated by the Foundation for the National Institutes of Health (www.fnih.org). The grantee organization is the Northern California Institute for Research and Education, and the study is coordinated by the Alzheimers Disease Cooperative Study at the University of California, San Diego. ADNI data are disseminated by the Laboratory for Neuro Imaging at the University of Southern California.

References

Alzheimer's Association. 2014. 2014 Alzheimer's Disease Facts and Figures. *Alzheimer's & Dementia*, 10.

C.A.L. Bailer-Jones and K. Smith. 2011. Combining probabilities. GAIA-C8-TN-MPIA-CBJ-053, July.

Elena Birman-Deych, Amy D. Waterman, Yan Yan, David S. Nilasema, Martha J. Radford, and Brian F. Gage. 2005. Accuracy of ICD-9-CM codes for identifying cardiovascular and stroke risk factors. *Medical Care*, 43:480–485.

David M. Blei and Jon D. McAuliffe. 2007. Supervised topic models. In *Advances in Neural Information Processing Systems 20, Proceedings of the Twenty-First Annual Conference on Neural Information Processing Systems*, pages 121–128, Vancouver, B.C., Canada.

David M. Blei, Andrew Y. Ng, and Michael I. Jordan. 2003. Latent Dirichlet Allocation. *Journal of Machine Learning Research*, 3:993–1022.

Jordan Boyd-Graber, David Mimno, and David Newman, 2014. *Care and Feeding of Topic Models: Problems, Diagnostics, and Improvements*. CRC Handbooks of Modern Statistical Methods. CRC Press, Boca Raton, Florida.

Roger B Bradford. 2008. An empirical study of required dimensionality for large-scale latent semantic indexing applications. In *Proceedings of the 17th ACM Conference on Information and Knowledge Management*, CIKM '08, pages 153–162.

Katherine Redfield Chan, Xinghua Lou, Theofanis Karaletsos, Christopher Crosbie, Stuart Gardos, David Artz, and Gunnar Rätsch. 2013. An empirical analysis of topic modeling for mining cancer clinical notes. In *13th IEEE International Conference on Data Mining Workshops*, pages 56–63, Dallas, Texas, December 7–10.

Jonathan Chang, Jordan Boyd-Graber, Chong Wang, Sean Gerrish, and David M. Blei. 2009. Reading tea leaves: How humans interpret topic models. In *Neural Information Processing Systems*, Vancouver, British Columbia.

Marcelo Fiszman, Wendy Webber Chapman, Dominik Aronsky, R. Scott Evans, and Peter J. Haug. 2000. Automatic detection of acute bacterial pneumonia from chest x-ray reports. *Journal of the American Medical Informatics Association*, 7(6):593–604.

Carol Friedman, Stephen B. Johnson, Bruce Forman, and Justin Starren. 1995. Architectural requirements for a multipurpose natural language processor in the clinical environment. In *Proceedings of the Annual Symposium on Computer Application in Medical Care*, pages 347–351.

Peter J. Haug, Spence Koehler, Lee Min Lau, Ping Wang, Roberto Rocha, and Stanley M. Huff. 1995. Experience with a mixed semantic/syntactic parser. In *Proceedings of the Annual Symposium on Computational Application in Medical Care*, pages 284–288.

Blanca E. Himes, Yi Dai, Isaac S. Kohane, Scott T. Weiss, and Marco F. Ramoni. 2009. Prediction of chronic obstructive pulmonary disease (COPD) in asthma patients using electronic medical records. *Journal of the American Medical Informatics Association*, 16:371–379.

Liangjie Hong and Brian D. Davison. 2010. Empirical study of topic modeling in Twitter. In *Proceedings of the First Workshop on Social Media Analytics*, SOMA '10, pages 80–88, Washington DC, USA.

Nilesh L. Jain and Carol Friedman. 1997. Identification of findings suspicious for breast cancer based on natural language processing of mammogram reports. In *Proceedings of the American Medical Informatics Association Annual Fall Symposium: American Medical Informatics Association*, pages 829–833.

Elizabeth F. O. Kern, Miriam Maney, Donald R. Miller, Chin-Lin Tseng, Anjali Tiwari, Mangala Rajan, David Aron, and Leonard Pogach. 2006. Failure of ICD-9-CM codes to identify patients with comorbid chronic kidney disease in diabetes. *Health Services Research*, 41(2):564–580.

Li Li, Herbert S. Chase, Chintan O. Patel, Carol Friedman, and Chunhua Weng. 2008. Comparing ICD9-encoded diagnoses and NLP-processed discharge summaries for clinical trials pre-screening: A case study. In *American Medical Informatics Association Annual Symposium Proceedings 2008*, pages 404–408.

Stephen Luther, Donald Berndt, Dezon Finch, Michael Richardson, Edward Hickling, and David Hickam. 2011. Using statistical text mining to supplement the development of an ontology. *Journal of Biomedical Informatics*, 44:S86–S93.

Ashutosh Malhotra, Erfan Younesi, Michaela Gündel, Müller, Michael T. Heneka, and Martin Hofmann-Apitius. 2013. ADO: A disease ontology representing the domain knowledge specific to Alzheimer's disease. *Alzheimer's and Dementia*, 10:238–246.

Andrew McCallum, Xuerui Wang, and Andrés Corrada-Emmanuel. 2007. Topic and role discovery in social networks with experiments on Enron and academic email. *Journal of Artificial Intelligence Research*, 30(1):249–272, Oct.

James A. McCart, Donald J. Berndt, Jay Jarman, Dezon K. Finch, and Stephen Luther. 2013. Finding falls in ambulatory care clinical documents using statistical text mining. *The Journal of American Medical Informatics Association*, 20(5):906–914.

David Mimno, Hanna M. Wallach, Edmund Talley, Miriam Leenders, and Andrew McCallum. 2011. Optimizing semantic coherence in topic models. In *Proceedings of the Conference on Empirical Methods in Natural Language Processing*, EMNLP '11, pages 262–272, Edinburgh, United Kingdom.

Harvey J. Murff, Fern FitzHenry, Michael E. Matheny, Nancy Gentry, Kristen L. Kotter, Kimberly Crimin, S. Dittus, Robert, Amy K. Rosen, Peter L. Elkin, Steven H. Brown, and Theodore Speroff. 2011. Automated identification of postoperative complications within an electronic medical record using natural language processing. *The American Journal of Medicine*, 306(8):848–855, August.

Michael J. Paul and Mark Dredze. 2011. You are what you tweet: Analyzing Twitter for public health. In *Proceedings of the Fifth International Conference on Weblogs and Social Media*, pages 265–272, Barcelona, Catalonia, Spain, July 17–21.

Fabian Pedregosa, Gael Varoquaux, Alexandre Gramfort, Vincent Michel, Bertrand Thirion, Olivier Grisel, Mathieu Blondel, Peter Prettenhofer, Ron Weiss, Vincent Dubourg, Jake Vanderplas, Alexandre Passos, David Cournapeau, Matthieu Brucher, Matthieu Perrot, and Edouard Duchesnay. 2011. Scikit-learn: Machine learning in Python. *Journal of Machine Learning Research*, 12:2825–2830.

Janet F. E. Penz, Adam B. Wilcox, and John F. Hurdle. 2007. Automated identification of adverse events related to central venous catheters. *Journal of Biomedical Informatics*, 40(2):174–182, April.

Martin Prince, Matthew Prina, and Maëlenn Guerchet. 2013. *World Alzheimer Report 2013*. Alzheimer's Disease International (ADI), London, September.

Daniel Ramage, David Hall, Ramesh Nallapati, and Christopher D. Manning. 2009. Labeled LDA: A supervised topic model for credit attribution in multi-labeled corpora. In *Proceedings of the 2009 Conference on Empirical Methods in Natural Language Processing: Volume 1 - Volume 1*, EMNLP '09, pages 248–256, Stroudsburg, PA, USA. Association for Computational Linguistics.

Philip Resnik, Anderson Garron, and Rebecca Resnik. 2013. Using topic modeling to improve prediction of neuroticism and depression in college students. In *Proceedings of the 2013 Conference on Empirical Methods in Natural Language Processing, EMNLP 2013*, pages 1348–1353, Seattle, Washington, USA, 18–21 October.

Dymitr Ruta and Bogdan Gabrys. 2000. An overview of classifier fusion methods. *Computing and Information Systems*, 7:1–10.

Yee Whye Teh, David Newman, and Max Welling. 2007. A collapsed variational Bayesian inference algorithm for latent Dirichlet allocation. In *Advances in Neural Information Processing Systems*, volume 19.

Radim Řehůřek and Petr Sojka. 2010. Software framework for topic modelling with large corpora. In *Proceedings of the LREC 2010 Workshop on New Challenges for NLP Frameworks*, pages 45–50, Valletta, Malta, May. ELRA.

Hua Xu, Zhenming Fu, Anushi Shah, Yukun Chen, Neeraja B. Peterson, Qingxia Chen, Subramani Mani, Mia A. Levy, Qi Dai, and Josh C. Denny. 2011. Extracting and integrating data from entire electronic health records for detecting colorectal cancer cases. In *American Medical Informatics Association Annual Symposium Proceedings 2011*, pages 1564–1572, Washington, DC, USA.

Self-Reflective Sentiment Analysis

Benjamin Shickel
University of Florida
Gainesville, FL 32611
shickelb@ufl.edu

Martin Heesacker
University of Florida
Gainesville, FL 32611
heesack@ufl.edu

Sherry Benton
TAO Connect, Inc.
Gainesville, FL 32601
sherry.benton@taoconnect.org

Ashkan Ebadi
University of Florida
Gainesville, FL 32611
ashkan.ebadi@ufl.edu

Paul Nickerson
University of Florida
Gainesville, FL 32611
pvnick@ufl.edu

Parisa Rashidi
University of Florida
Gainesville, FL 32611
parisa.rashidi@ufl.edu

Abstract

As self-directed online anxiety treatment and e-mental health programs become more prevalent and begin to rapidly scale to a large number of users, the need to develop automated techniques for monitoring patient progress and detecting early warning signs is at an all-time high. While current online therapy systems work based on explicit quantitative feedback from various survey measures, little attention has been paid thus far to the large amount of unstructured free text present in the monitoring logs and journals submitted by patients as part of the treatment process. In this paper, we automatically categorize patients' internal sentiment and emotions using machine learning classifiers based on n-grams, syntactic patterns, sentiment lexicon features, and distributed word embeddings. We report classification metrics on a novel mental health dataset.

1 Introduction

As mental health awareness becomes more widespread, especially among at-risk populations such as young adults and college-aged students, many institutions and universities are beginning to offer online anxiety and depression treatment programs to supplement traditional therapy services. A key component of these largely self-directed programs is the regular completion of journals, in which patients describe how they are feeling. These journals contain a wide variety of information, including a patient's specific fears, worries, triggers, reactions, or simply status updates on their emotional state. At current time, these journals are either reviewed by therapists (who are vastly outnumbered by the users) or left unused, with the assumption that simply talking about negative emotions is therapy in and of itself. We see a large and novel opportunity for applying natural language techniques to these unstructured mental health records. In this paper, we focus on analyzing the sentiment of patient text.

The largest motivator of existing sentiment analysis research has arguably been the detection of user sentiment towards entities, such as products, companies, or people. We define this type of problem as *external* sentiment analysis. In contrast, when working in the mental health domain (particularly with self-reflective textual journals), we are trying to gauge a patient's *internal* sentiment towards their own thoughts, feelings, and emotions. The differences in goals, types of sentiment, and distribution of polarity presents unique challenges for applying sentiment analysis to this new domain.

One key aspect that sets our task apart from traditional sentiment analysis is our treatment of polarity classes. Traditionally, sentiment is categorized as either *positive*, *negative*, or *neutral*. In contrast, we subdivide the *neutral* polarity class into two distinct classes: *both positive and negative* and *neither positive nor negative*. We justify this decision based on several studies showing the independent dimensions of positive and negative affect in human emotion (Warr et al., 1983; Watson et al., 1988; Diener et al., 1985; Bradburn, 1969), and feel that is a more appropriate framework for our domain. This choice represents a novel characterization of sentiment analysis in mental health, and is one we hope

Proceedings of the 3rd Workshop on Computational Linguistics and Clinical Psychology: From Linguistic Signal to Clinical Reality, pages 23–32,
San Diego, California, June 16, 2016. ©2016 Association for Computational Linguistics

to see made in future studies in this domain.

Our primary focus in this paper is on the automatic and reliable categorization of patient responses as *positive, negative, both positive and negative*, or *neither positive nor negative*. Such a system has far-reaching implications for the online therapy setting, in which automatic language analysis can be incorporated into existing patient evaluation and progress monitoring, or serve as an early warning indicator for patients with severe cases of depression and/or risk of suicide. Additionally, tools based on this type of internal sentiment analysis can provide immediate feedback on mental health and thought processes, which can become distorted and unclear in patients stuck in anxiety or depression. In the future, sentiment-based mental health models can be incorporated into the characterization and treatment of patients with autism, dementia, or other broadly-defined language disorders.

In short, our main contributions are summarized by the following:

- We present a novel sentiment analysis dataset, annotated by psychology experts, specifically targeted towards the mental health domain.

- We introduce the notion of subdividing the traditional *neutral* polarity class into both a dual polarity sentiment (*both positive and negative*) and a *neither positive nor negative* sentiment.

- We identify the unique challenges faced when applying existing sentiment analysis techniques to mental health.

- We present an automatic model for classifying the polarity of patient text, and compare our work to models trained on existing sentiment corpora.

2   Related Work

From a technical point of view, our methods fall squarely in the realm of sentiment analysis, a field of computer science and computational linguistics primarily concerned with analyzing people's opinions, sentiments, attitudes, and emotions from written language (Liu, 2010). In our paper, we apply sentiment analysis and polarity detection techniques to the largely untapped mental health domain.

In the past decade, sentiment analysis techniques have been applied to a wide variety of areas. Although the majority of work has dealt in areas outside of mental health, we must discuss the bulk of previous sentiment analysis research, from which our techniques are derived.

Given the explosive rise in popularity of social media platforms, a large number of studies have focused on user sentiment in microblogs such as Twitter (Barbosa and Feng, 2010; Pak and Paroubek, 2010; Agarwal et al., 2011; Kouloumpis et al., 2011; Nielsen, 2011; Wang et al., 2011; Zhang et al., 2011; Montejo-Ráez et al., 2012; Spencer and Uchyigit, 2012; Montejo-Ráez et al., 2014; Tang et al., 2014). Other studies have explored user sentiment in web forum opinions (Abbasi et al., 2008), movie reviews (Agrawal and Siddiqui, 2009), blogs (Melville et al., 2009), and Yahoo! Answers (Kucuktunc et al., 2012). As we will show, the models proposed in all of these works cannot be directly transferred to polarity detection in mental health (as sentiment analysis remains a largely domain-specific task), but our initial techniques are largely based on these previous works.

Although the majority of sentiment analysis has focused on user opinions towards entities, there are studies in domains more directly related to our area. One such study analyzed the sentiment of suicide notes (Pestian et al., 2012). Another mined user sentiment in MOOC discussion forums (Wen et al., 2014).

Sentiment analysis and polarity detection techniques are widely varied (Mejova and Srinivasan, 2011; Feldman, 2013), and as this research area is still garnering a great deal of interest, many studies have proposed novel methods. These include topic-level sentiment analysis (Nasukawa and Yi, 2003; Kim and Hovy, 2004), phrase-level sentiment analysis (Wilson et al., 2009), linguistic approaches (Wiegand et al., 2010; Benamara et al., 2007; Tan et al., 2011), semantic word vectorization (Maas et al., 2011; Tang et al., 2014), various lexicon-based approaches (Taboada et al., 2011; Baccianella et al., 2010), information-theoretic techniques (Lin et al., 2012), and graph-based methods (Montejo-Ráez et al., 2014; Pang and Lee, 2004; Wang et al., 2011). In recent years, approaches based on deep learning architectures have also shown promising results (Glorot et al., 2011; Socher et al., 2013). As a starting point for our new *internal* sentiment analysis framework, in this paper we apply more straightforward approaches based on linear classifiers.

3   Dataset

In this section, we detail the construction of our mental health sentiment dataset. While not yet publicly available, we plan to release our data in the near future.

In order to build a dataset of real patient responses, we partnered with TAO Connect, Inc.[1], an online therapy program designed to treat anxiety, depression, and stress. This program is being implemented in several universities around the country, and as such, the primary demographic is college-aged students.

As part of the TAO program, patients complete several self-contained content modules designed to teach awareness and coping strategies for anxiety, depression, and stress. Additionally, patients regularly submit several types of journals and logs pertaining to monitoring, anxiety, depression, worries, and relaxation. The free text contained in these logs is the source of our dataset. In total, we collected 4021 textual responses from 342 unique patients, with submission dates ranging from April 2014 to November 2015. Patients were de-identified and the collection process was part of an IRB-approved study. Responses typically range from single sentences to a single paragraph, with an average of 39 words per response. We show a complete word count distribution in Figure 1.

To help transform our collection of free text responses into a classification dataset suitable for polarity prediction, we solicited the expertise of three psychology undergraduates (all female) under the supervision of one psychology professor (male) to provide polarity labels for our response documents. The annotators were tasked with reading each individual response, and assigning it a label of *positive*, *negative*, *both positive and negative*, or *neither positive nor negative*. The inter-rater agreement reliability (Cohen's kappa) between annotators 1 and 2 was 0.5, between annotators 2 and 3 was 0.67, and between annotators 1 and 3 was 0.48. The overall

---

[1]http://www.taoconnect.org/

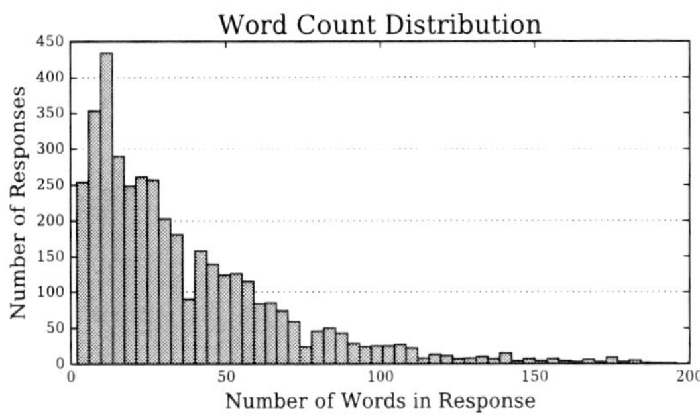

Figure 1: Distribution of word counts per response for our collected dataset. On average, each response contains 39 words, with a minimum of two words and a maximum of 762 words. 30 responses had more than 200 words, which we do not show.

Annotator	POS	NEG	BOTH	NEITHER
Annotator 1	494	2569	556	402
Annotator 2	321	2509	552	638
Annotator 3	531	2152	383	954
Final	414	2545	510	548

Table 1: Label counts per annotator, as well as the the final dataset label counts obtained via a majority-voting scheme. For brevity, we denote the *positive* label as POS, *negative* as NEG, *both positive and negative* as BOTH, and *neither positive nor negative* as NEITHER.

agreement reliability between all annotators (Fleiss' kappa) was 0.55. We used a majority-vote scheme to assign a single label to each piece of text, where 62% of the documents had full annotator agreement, 35% had a clear label majority, and only 3% had no majority, in which case we picked the label from the annotator with the best aggregate reliability. Table 1 shows label counts for each annotator, as well as the final count after applying the majority-vote process.

To provide a clearer picture of the types of responses in our dataset, we present one short concrete example of each polarity class below.

- **Positive** - *I tried to say good things for them since I know there was a lot of arguments happening.*

- **Negative** - *I don't do well at parties, I'm not interesting.*

- **Both Positive and Negative** - *I shouldn't have taken things so seriously.*

- **Neither Positive nor Negative** - *I wrote in my*

In the above examples, the challenges of applying sentiment analysis and traditional text classification techniques to self-reflective text becomes more apparent. For instance, the *positive* example mentions arguments, typically associated with negative sentiment, while the *negative* example mentions parties, a word usually associated with a positive connotation. Additionally, the *both positive and negative* example exhibits subtle cues that differentiate it from the other three polarity classes.

4 Method

To predict polarity from patient text, we employ several established machine learning and text classification techniques. We begin by preprocessing the annotated patient responses, which we refer to interchangeably as *documents*. We then extract several types of attributes from each response, referred to as *features*. The extracted features and polarity annotations are used to build a logistic regression *classifier*, which is a linear machine learning model we use to predict the final polarity label. In this section, we describe each step in detail.

4.1 Preprocessing

Starting with the raw documents obtained from our data collection process, we apply several traditional preprocessing steps to the text. First, based on experimental feedback, we convert all the text to lowercase and strip all documents of punctuation following a standard tokenization phase. While these are relatively standard steps, it should be explicitly noted that we did *not* remove stop words from our corpus, which is a common preprocessing technique in other domains, due to lowered classification performance. This can be partially explained by the nature of our domain; for example, the phrase "what if" tended to be associated with worrying about the future - traditionally, both of these words are considered stop words and filtered out, losing valuable information for our task.

4.2 Feature Extraction

Next, we extract several types of features from the preprocessed documents. In our experiments, we evaluate classification performance with various feature subsets.

4.2.1 N-Gram Features and POS Tags

As a starting point for our experiments with this new domain, the most numerous of our extracted features are derived from a traditional "bag of n-grams" approach, in which we create document vectors comprised of word unigrams, bigrams, and/or trigram counts. As previous works have shown, this allows the capture of important syntactical information like negation, which would otherwise be missed in a standard "bag of words" (i.e., unigrams only) model.

In order to constrain the scope of later feature subset experiments, we first obtain the n-gram combination resulting in the best performance for our newly created dataset. We denote this optimal n-gram setting as the "n-grams only" model in later experiments. In this experiment, we perform a 10-fold cross-validated randomized parameter search using six possible word n-gram combinations: unigrams, bigrams, trigrams, unigrams + bigrams, bigrams + trigrams, and unigrams + bigrams + trigrams. We split cross-validation folds on responses, as we expect patient responses to be independent over time. All extracted n-gram counts are normalized by tf-idf (term frequency-inverse document frequency), a common technique used for describing how important particular n-grams are to their respective documents. The results of this n-gram comparison experiment are shown in Figure 2, where it is clear that using a combination of unigrams and bigrams resulted in the best performance.

In an effort to capture more subtle patterns of grammatical structure, we also experiment with augmenting each document with each word's Penn-Treebank part-of-speech (POS) tag. In these experiments, we augment our documents by appending these tags, in order, to the end of every sentence, allowing for our n-gram extraction methods to capture syntactic language patterns. During the tokenization process, we ignore any n-grams consisting of both words and part-of-speech tags.

4.2.2 Sentiment Lexicon Word Counts

One of the more rudimentary sentiment analysis techniques stems from the use of a sentiment dictio-

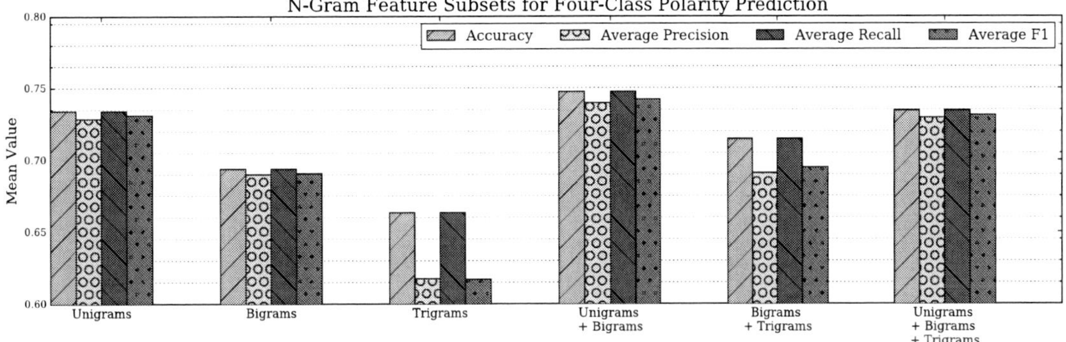

Figure 2: Classification results using only word n-gram features for our 4-class polarity dataset. Results were obtained following a 10-fold cross-validated randomized hyperparameter search. A combination of unigrams and bigrams resulted in the best metrics. As seen by the final cluster, adding trigrams to this subset resulted in a performance decrease. Thus, when we use n-gram features in later experiments, we only consider the combination of unigrams and bigrams.

nary, or lexicon, which is a pre-existing collection of subjective words that are labeled as either *positive* or *negative*. Using the sentiment lexicon from (Liu, 2012)[2], we count the number of positive and negative words occurring in each document and incorporate the counts as two additional features.

4.2.3 Document Word Count

In our initial analysis, we discovered that oftentimes the most negative text responses were associated with a larger word count. Although the correlation is relatively weak across the entire corpus, we nonetheless include a word count of each document as a feature.

4.2.4 Word Embeddings

Based on the recent successes of distributed word representations like Word2Vec (Mikolov et al., 2013) and GloVe (Pennington et al., 2014), we sought to harness these learned language models for predicting sentiment polarity. Although primarily used in deep learning architectures, we show that these representations can also be useful with linear models. Unlike our other features, the individual features contained in word embeddings are indecipherable; however, as we show in the results section, they contribute to the overall success of our classification.

In our experiments, we utilize a publicly available Word2Vec model pre-trained on Google News[3], containing 100 billion words. Each unique word in the model is associated with a 300-dimensional vector. For each of our documents, we include the mean word vector derived from each individual word's embedding as 300 additional features.

5 Four-Class Polarity Prediction

Because our new dataset introduces a clear distinction between text labeled as *both positive and negative* and *neither positive nor negative* (traditionally, both of these classes are grouped together as *neutral*), there are no baselines for which to compare our experiments. We offer our results for this scenario as a launching point for future studies on polarity detection in mental health. For this scenario, we show the results of each feature extraction method individually, as well as the results for the combination of all features. All results are evaluated via 10-fold cross-validation, with folds split on responses. Results are shown in Figure 3, where it is clear that optimal performance is achieved using the model trained on all features. Our methods gave rise to an overall classification accuracy of 78%.

From Figure 3, it is apparent that of all individual features, n-grams perform the best. The relatively strong performance of n-gram features tends to align with our expectations, given the widespread use of n-gram features across all types of text classifica-

---

[2]https://www.cs.uic.edu/ liub/FBS/sentiment-analysis.html

[3]https://code.google.com/p/word2vec/

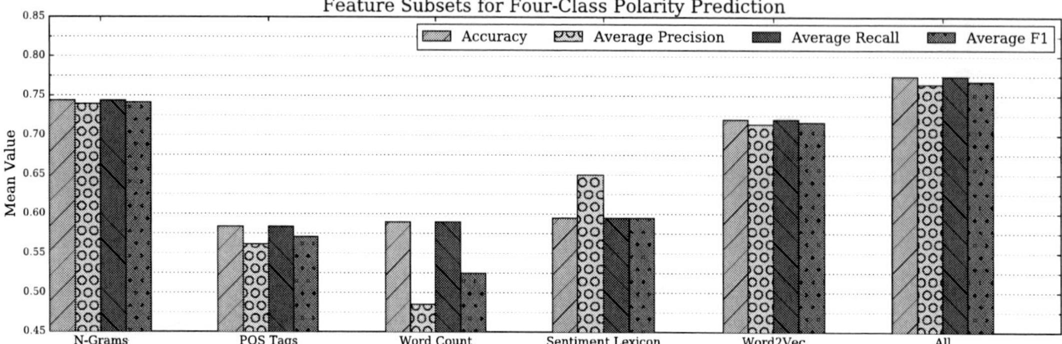

Figure 3: Classification performance for the 4-class polarity prediction task. We show results for each feature set individually, as well as the combination of all features. Using all extracted features results in the highest accuracy, F1, precision, and recall.

tion problems. However, what is more surprising is the relatively weak results for the sentiment lexicon features, given their popularity in modern sentiment analysis. Additionally, the word embedding features also gave rise to better performance than expected, especially considering that we used the Word2Vec embeddings with linear models as opposed to the more traditional deep learning architectures. Finally, we see optimal performance across all metrics when using the combination of all features.

Using the optimal model from Figure 3, we show the individual class metrics for precision, recall, F1, and overall accuracy in Table 2. It is apparent that the *both positive and negative* class proves especially difficult to classify. This is explained in part by the previously mentioned class imbalance issue - when the majority of the corpus is negative, it becomes difficult for the classifier to differentiate between sentiment comprising of *mostly* positive polarity, and sentiment comprising of *some* positive polarity. The low recall of the *both positive and negative* class clearly points towards the need for more research in this area.

6   Binary Polarity Prediction

In this section, we experiment with using existing sentiment analysis corpora to perform traditional two-class polarity prediction on our dataset, and compare the results to a cross-validation approach, split on responses, trained on our dataset alone. The primary purpose is to gauge the effectiveness of classifiers trained on existing sentiment corpora as applied to the mental health domain. State of

Class	Precision	Recall	F1
Positive	0.63	0.32	0.42
Negative	0.74	0.96	0.84
Both	0.58	0.16	0.26
Neither	0.77	0.47	0.59
Overall Accuracy	**0.78**		

Table 2: Polarity prediction results for the full 4-class version of our dataset. For brevity, the polarity class *both positive and negative* is denoted as *Both*, and the class *neither positive nor negative* is denoted as *Neither*.

the art sentence-level binary polarity detection accuracy is reported as 85.4% (Socher et al., 2013) using deep learning models and a specialized movie review dataset, and while our models are computationally more simple and use different features, we incorporate such existing corpora in our experiments. Since our full dataset consists of four polarity labels, whereas traditional sentiment analysis only uses two, for these experiments we only consider the responses from our dataset belonging to the *positive* and *negative* classes.

We begin by training our model on existing sentiment datasets only. The first is a large-scale Twitter sentiment analysis dataset[4] which automatically assigns polarity labels based on emoticons present in user tweets (we denote this dataset as "Twitter"). The next is a collection of IMDB movie reviews published by (Maas et al., 2011) at Stanford University[5] (we denote this dataset as "Stanford"). We also use two movie reviews datasets from (Pang et al.,

---

[4]http://help.sentiment140.com/for-students/
[5]http://ai.stanford.edu/ amaas/data/sentiment/

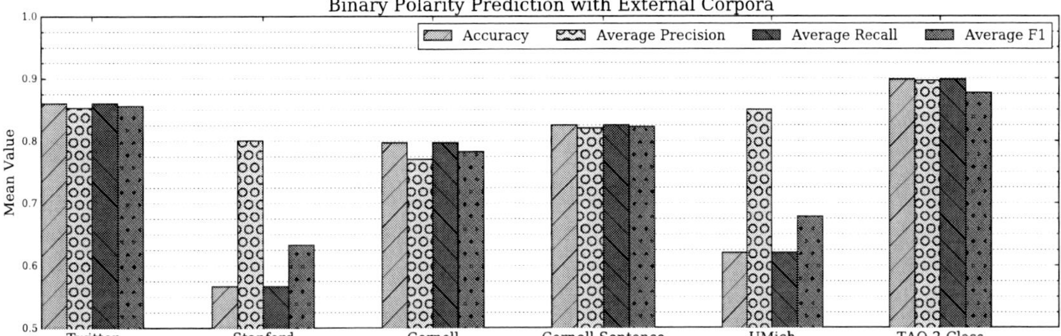

Figure 4: Classification results for the *positive* vs. *negative* prediction setting using 5 external sentiment corpora and cross-validated results on our own binary dataset (TAO 2-Class). The precision, recall, and F1 scores are reported using a weighted average incorporating the support of each class label. For all metrics, training on our dataset (TAO 2-Class) yields better results than using models trained on existing sentiment corpora.

Dataset	# Positive	# Negative
Twitter	797792	798076
Stanford	25000	25000
Cornell	1000	1000
Cornell Sentence	5221	5212
UMich	3995	3091

Table 3: Existing sentiment corpora summary.

2002) at Cornell University[6], where one is geared towards document-level sentiment classification (denoted as "Cornell"), and the other towards sentence-level classification (denoted as "Cornell Sentence"). Our final dataset is a collection of web forum opinions collected by the University of Michigan as part of a Kaggle competition[7] (which we denote as "UMich"). The number of documents of each sentiment class, per dataset, is given in Table 3.

Using all features from the previously outlined extraction process, we train a separate model on each of the five existing sentiment analysis corpora. Optimal hyperparameters for each experiment were selected via a randomized parameter search in conjunction with three-fold cross validation. In each case, the trained models were tested against the binary version of our dataset. Additionally, we perform the same extraction and fine-tuning process to construct a model trained on our new dataset alone. For this experiment, we report the results after a 10-fold cross-validation process split on responses. A summary of accuracy, precision, recall, and F1 score for the binary prediction setting is shown in Figure 4, where it is apparent that the best performance occurs when using our dataset, pointing towards the need for collecting custom mental health datasets for this new type of internal sentiment analysis. Our binary polarity model resulted in 90% classification accuracy.

7 Important Features

In this section, we wish to understand which features are most discriminative in predicting whether a piece of text is *positive, negative, both positive and negative,* or *neither positive nor negative*. These features (all of which are naturally-interpretable aside from the word embeddings) can serve as useful indicators for therapists and future mental health polarity studies.

To evaluate our features, we examine the weight matrix of a randomized logistic regression classifier trained on our full four-class polarity dataset. The feature weights corresponding to each of the four classes give an idea of the relative importance of each feature, and how discriminative they are as compared to the remaining three classes. We summarize the 10 most important features per class in Table 4.

Much can be gleaned from an informal inspection of these top features. For example, while the words found in the *positive* and *negative* polarity

---

[6]https://www.cs.cornell.edu/people/pabo/movie-review-data/

[7]https://inclass.kaggle.com/c/si650winter11/data

Positive	Negative	Both Positive and Negative	Neither Positive nor Negative
was able	worried	but	work
no anxiety	$RB $VBG	okay	nothing
calm	<W2V-81>	nt worry	$IN $NNP
nothing terrible	$VBN $IN	$NNS $PRP	to the
great	worried about	$VB $RB	slowly
better	worried that	eventually	can
did well	nt do	not as	<W2V-129>
no worries	<W2V-96>	instead	<W2V-230>
not anxious	stressed	although	study
hopeful	<W2V-168>	actually	not sure

Table 4: Top 10 features per class from a randomized logistic regression model, trained on our mental health dataset. Features with a $ symbol are part-of-speech tags (using our POS n-gram method). All individual word embedding features, obtained via a pre-trained Word2Vec embedding, are denoted as <W2V-X>, where X is the dimension index of the embedding vector. The POS tags shown are are as follows: $RB = adverb, $VBG = present participle verb, $VBN = past participle verb, $IN = preposition, $JJ = adjective, $NNS = plural noun, $PRP = personal pronoun, $VB = base form verb, $NNP = singular proper noun.

classes are clearly characteristic of their respective labels (with *negative* words pertaining mostly to worry and stress), the words found in the *both positive and negative* class are more indecisive in nature ('but', 'eventually', 'although', 'actually'). Words from the *neither positive nor negative* class carry less surface-level emotional significance. The part-of-speech patterns are more difficult to interpret, but these results point towards the need for future exploration.

8 Conclusion

In this paper, we introduced the notion of applying sentiment analysis to the mental health domain, and show that existing techniques and corpora cannot be simply transferred to this new setting. We developed baseline classification techniques grounded in the results from previous works, and show the benefit of spending resources on creating new mental health datasets explicitly focused on patient sentiment. We introduced the notion of splitting the polarity class traditionally defined as *neutral* into two sub-classes, and demonstrated the new challenges that decision brings as it pertains to the automatic classification of patient sentiment in mental health text.

References

Ahmed Abbasi, Hsinchun Chen, and Arab Salem. 2008. Sentiment analysis in multiple languages: Feature selection for opinion classification in web forums. *ACM Transactions on Information Systems*, 26(3):1–34.

Apoorv Agarwal, Boyi Xie, Ilia Vovsha, Owen Rambow, and Rebecca Passonneau. 2011. Sentiment analysis of Twitter data. In *Proceedings of the Workshop on Languages in Social Media*, pages 30–38.

Shaishav Agrawal and Tanveer J Siddiqui. 2009. Using syntactic and contextual information for sentiment polarity analysis. In *Proceedings of the 2nd International Conference on Interaction Sciences: Information Technology, Culture and Human*, pages 620–623.

Stefano Baccianella, Andrea Esuli, and Fabrizio Sebastiani. 2010. SentiWordNet 3.0: An enhanced lexical resource for sentiment analysis and opinion mining. In *Proceedings of the Seventh International Conference on Language Resources and Evaluation (LREC'10)*, pages 2200–2204.

Luciano Barbosa and Junlan Feng. 2010. Robust sentiment detection on Twitter from biased and noisy data. In *Proceedings of the 23rd International Conference on Computational Linguistics: Posters*, pages 36–44.

Farah Benamara, Carmine Cesarano, Antonio Picariello, Diego Reforgiato, and V.S. Subrahmanian. 2007. Sentiment analysis: adjectives and adverbs are better than adjectives alone. In *Proceedings of the International Conference on Weblogs and Social Media (ICWSM)*, pages 203–206.

Norman M. Bradburn. 1969. The structure of psychological well-being.

E Diener, R J Larsen, S Levine, and R a Emmons. 1985. Intensity and frequency: dimensions underlying positive and negative affect. *Journal of personality and social psychology*, 48(5):1253–1265.

Ronen Feldman. 2013. Techniques and applications for sentiment analysis. *Communications of the ACM*, 56(4):82–89.

X Glorot, A Bordes, and Y Bengio. 2011. Domain adaptation for large-scale sentiment classification: A deep learning approach. *Proceedings of the*.

Soo-Min Kim and Eduard Hovy. 2004. Determining the sentiment of opinions. In *Proceedings of the 20th International Conference on Computational Linguistics*, pages 1367–1373, Morristown, NJ, USA.

Efthymios Kouloumpis, Theresa Wilson, and Johanna Moore. 2011. Twitter sentiment analysis: The good the bad and the omg! In *Proceedings of the Fifth International AAAI Conference on Weblogs and Social Media (ICWSM 11)*, pages 538–541.

Onur Kucuktunc, Ingmar Weber, B. Barla Cambazoglu, and Hakan Ferhatosmanoglu. 2012. A large-scale sentiment analysis for Yahoo! Answers. In *Proceedings of the 5th ACM International Conference on Web Search and Data Mining*, pages 633–642.

Yuming Lin, Jingwei Zhang, Xiaoling Wang, and Aoying Zhou. 2012. An information theoretic approach to sentiment polarity classification. In *Proceedings of the 2nd Joint WICOW/AIRWeb Workshop on Web Quality*, pages 35–40.

Bing Liu. 2010. *Sentiment Analysis and Subjectivity*. 2 edition.

Bing Liu. 2012. Sentiment analysis and opinion mining. *Synthesis Lectures on Human Language Technologies*, 5(1):1–167.

Andrew L Maas, Raymond E. Daly, Peter T. Pham, Dan Huang, Andrew Y. Ng, and Christopher Potts. 2011. Learning word vectors for sentiment analysis. In *Proceedings of the 49th Annual Meeting of the Association for Computational Linguistics: Human Language Technologies*, pages 142–150. Association for Computational Linguistics.

Yelena Mejova and Padmini Srinivasan. 2011. Exploring feature definition and selection for sentiment classifiers. In *Proceedings of the Fifth International AAAI Conference on Weblogs and Social Media*, pages 546–549.

Prem Melville, Wojciech Gryc, and Richard D. Lawrence. 2009. Sentiment analysis of blogs by combining lexical knowledge with text classification. In *Proceedings of ACM SIGKDD International Conference on Knowledge Discovery and Data Mining*, pages 1275–1284, New York, New York, USA. ACM Press.

Tomas Mikolov, Kai Chen, Greg Corrado, and Jeffrey Dean. 2013. Efficient estimation of word representations in vector space. In *Proceedings of International Conference on Learning Representations (ICLR)*, pages 1–12.

Arturo Montejo-Ráez, Eugenio Martínez-Cámara, M. Teresa Martín-Valdivia, and L. Alfonso Ureña-López. 2012. Random walk weighting over SentiWordNet for sentiment polarity detection on Twitter. In *Proceedings of the 3rd Workshop in Computational Approaches to Subjectivity and Sentiment Analysis*, pages 3–10. Association for Computational Linguistics.

Arturo Montejo-Ráez, Eugenio Martínez-Cámara, M. Teresa Martín-Valdivia, and L. Alfonso Ureña-López. 2014. Ranked WordNet graph for sentiment polarity classification in Twitter. *Computer Speech & Language*, 28(1):93–107.

Tetsuya Nasukawa and Jeonghee Yi. 2003. Sentiment analysis: Capturing favorability using natural language processing. In *Proceedings of the 2nd International Conference on Knowledge Capture*, pages 70–77, New York, New York, USA.

Finn Årup Nielsen. 2011. A new ANEW: Evaluation of a word list for sentiment analysis in microblogs. In *ESWC2011 Workshop on Making Sense of Microposts*, pages 93–98.

Alexander Pak and Patrick Paroubek. 2010. Twitter as a corpus for sentiment analysis and opinion mining. In *Proceedings of the Seventh Conference on International Language Resources and Evaluation (LREC'10)*, pages 19–21.

Bo Pang and Lillian Lee. 2004. A sentimental education: Sentiment analysis using subjectivity summarization based on minimum cuts. In *Proceedings of the 42nd Annual Meeting on Association for Computational Linguistics*, pages 271–278.

Bo Pang, Lilian Lee, and Shivakumar Vaithyanathan. 2002. Thumbs up? Sentiment classification using machine learning techniques. In *Proceedings of the Conference on Empirical Methods in Natural Language Processing*, pages 79–86.

Jeffrey Pennington, Richard Socher, and Christopher D Manning. 2014. GloVe: Global vectors for word representation. In *Proceedings of the Empiricial Methods in Natural Language Processing*, pages 1532–1543.

John Pestian, John Pestian, Pawel Matykiewicz, Brett South, Ozlem Uzuner, and John Hurdle. 2012. Sentiment analysis of suicide notes: A shared task. *Biomedical Informatics Insights*, 5(1):3–16.

Richard Socher, Alex Perelygin, Jean Y Wu, Jason Chuang, Christopher D Manning, Andrew Y Ng, and Christopher Potts. 2013. Recursive deep models for semantic compositionality over a sentiment treebank. In *Proceedings of the Conference on Empirical Methods in Natural Language Processing*, pages 1631–1642.

James Spencer and Gulden Uchyigit. 2012. Sentimentor: Sentiment analysis of Twitter data. In *Proceedings of European Conference on Machine Learning and Principles and Practice of Knowledge Discovery in Databases*, pages 56–66.

Maite Taboada, Julian Brooke, Milan Tofiloski, Kimberly Voll, and Manfred Stede. 2011. Lexicon-based methods for sentiment analysis. *Computational Linguistics*, 37(2):267–307.

Luke Kien Weng Tan, Jin Cheon Na, Yin Leng Theng, and Kuiyu Chang. 2011. Sentence-level sentiment polarity classification using a linguistic approach. In *Proceedings of 13th International Conference on Asia-Pacific Digital Libraries*, pages 77–87.

Duyu Tang, Furu Wei, Nan Yang, Ming Zhou, Ting Liu, and Bing Qin. 2014. Learning sentiment-specific word embedding for Twitter sentiment classification. In *Proceedings of the 52nd Annual Meeting of the Association for Computational Linguistics*, pages 1555–1565.

Xiaolong Wang, Furu Wei, Xiaohua Liu, Ming Zhou, and Ming Zhang. 2011. Topic sentiment analysis in Twitter: A graph-based hashtag sentiment classification approach. In *Proceedings of the 20th ACM International Conference on Information and Knowledge Management*, pages 1031–1040, New York, New York, USA. ACM Press.

Peter Warr, Joanna Barter, and Garry Brownbridge. 1983. On the Independence of Positive and Negative Affect. *Journal of Personality and Social Psychology*, 44(3):644–651.

D Watson, L A Clark, and A Tellegen. 1988. Development and Validation of Brief Measures of Positive and Negative Affect - the Panas Scales. *Journal of Personality and Social Psychology*, 54(6):1063–1070.

Miaomiao Wen, Diyi Yang, and Cp Rosé. 2014. Sentiment analysis in MOOC discussion forums: What does it tell us? In *Proceedings of Educational Data Mining*, pages 1–8.

Michael Wiegand, Alexandra Balahur, Benjamin Roth, Dietrich Klakow, and Andrés Montoyo. 2010. A survey on the role of negation in sentiment analysis. In *Proceedings of the Workshop on Negation and Speculation in Natural Language Processing*, pages 60–68.

Theresa A. Wilson, Janyce Wiebe, and Paul Hoffmann. 2009. Recognizing contextual polarity: An exploration of features for phrase-level sentiment analysis. *Computational Linguistics*, 35(3):399–433.

Lei Zhang, Riddhiman Ghosh, Mohamed Dekhil, Meichun Hsu, and Bing Liu. 2011. Combining lexicon-based and learning-based methods for Twitter sentiment analysis. Technical report.

Is Sentiment in Movies the Same as Sentiment in Psychotherapy? Comparisons Using a New Psychotherapy Sentiment Database

Michael Tanana[1], Aaron Dembe[1], Christina S. Soma[1], David Atkins[2], Zac Imel[1] and Vivek Srikumar[3]

[1] Department of Educational Psychology, University of Utah, Salt Lake City, UT

[2] Department of Psychiatry and Behavioral Sciences, University of Washington, Seattle, WA

[3] School of Computing, University of Utah, Salt Lake City, UT

michael.tanana@utah.edu aaron.dembe@utah.edu CSoma@sa.utah.edu
zac.imel@utah.edu datkins@u.washington.edu svivek@cs.utah.edu

Abstract

The sharing of emotional material is central to the process of psychotherapy and emotional problems are a primary reason for seeking treatment. Surprisingly, very little systematic research has been done on patterns of emotional exchange during psychotherapy. It is likely that a major reason for this void in the research is the enormous cost of annotating sessions for affective content. In the field of NLP, there have been major strides in the creation of algorithms for sentiment analysis, but most of this work has focused on written reviews of movies and twitter feeds with little work on spoken dialogue. We have created a new database of 97,497 utterances from psychotherapy transcripts labeled by humans for sentiment. We describe this dataset and present initial results for models identifying sentiment. We also show that one of the best models from the literature, trained on movie reviews, performed below many of our baseline models that trained on the psychotherapy corpus.

1 Introduction

People often seek psychotherapy because they feel emotionally distressed (e.g. anxious, unable to sleep). For well over a century, researchers and practitioners have consistently acknowledged the central role emotions play in psychotherapy (Freud and Breuer, 1895; Lane et al., 2015). Emotion, or affect, is directly involved in key concepts of psychotherapeutic process and outcome, including the formation of the therapeutic alliance (Safran and Muran, 2000), an individual's process of decision making (Bar-On et al., 2004; Isen, 2008) , behavior change (Lang and Bradley, 2010), personality style (Mischel, 2013), and happiness (Gross and Levenson, 1997). Affect is implicated in human memory (Schacter, 1999), and is an essential building block of empathy (Elliott et al., 2011; Imel et al., 2014a). The particular role of affect in different psychotherapy theories varies from encouraging patients to access and release suppressed emotions (as in psychoanalysis; e.g. (Kohut, 2013)) to identifing the impact of cognition on emotion (as in rational-emotive behavior therapy; (Ellis, 1962)). Carl Rogers, a progenitor of humanistic / person-centered therapy, theorized that empathy involved a therapist experiencing a client's affect as if it were his or her own, and that empathy constituted a necessary ingredient for human growth and change (Rogers, 1975). Empathy and emotion continues to be a primary area of research in psychological science (Decety and Ickes, 2009).

In psychotherapy, there are many ways that clients and therapists communicate how they are feeling (e.g., facial expression (Haggard and Isaacs, 1966), body positioning (Beier and Young, 1998), vocal tone (Imel et al., 2014a), but clearly one is the words they use. For example, there is evidence that greater use of affect words predicts positive treatment outcome (Anderson et al., 1999; Stalikas, 1995). Similarly, Mergenthaler (1996) developed a theory on how the pattern of emotional expression should proceed between a client and therapist. However, this research has been limited to dictionary based methods (see also Mergenthaler (2008)). Until very re-

Proceedings of the 3rd Workshop on Computational Linguistics and Clinical Psychology: From Linguistic Signal to Clinical Reality, pages 33–41,
San Diego, California, June 16, 2016. ©2016 Association for Computational Linguistics

cently, the exploration of emotion in psychotherapy has been limited by the lack of methodology for looking at sentiment in a more nuanced way.

2 Sentiment Analysis

There is a long tradition in the field of Natural Language Processing (NLP) for trying to correctly identify the sentiment of passages of text and as a result there are a large number of techniques that have been tested (for a review on the subject, see Pang and Lee (2008)). Some common methods involve using n-grams combined with classifier models (SVM, CRF, Naive Bayes) to identify the sentiment of sentences or passages (Pak and Paroubek, 2015). Another method involves using pre-compiled dictionaries of common terms with their polarity (positive or negative) (Baccianella et al., 2010). As with many NLP methods, researchers have attempted to go beyond the mere presentation of words and use sentence structure and contextual information to improve accuracy. Along these lines, more recently researchers have used deep learning techniques to improve accuracy on sentiment datasets, with some success (Maas et al., 2011; Socher et al., 2013).

2.1 Domain Adaptation: Why Create A New Sentiment Dataset

The purpose of this project is to create and evaluate a dataset for training machine learning sentiment analysis models that could then be applied to the domain of psychotherapy and mental health. Pang and Lee (2008) have pointed out that sentiment analysis is domain specific. Thus, creating a sentiment dataset specific to psychotherapy addresses the possibility that the words and ratings used to train models in other contexts may have very different connotations than those in spoken psychotherapy. For example, if one were reviewing a movie and wrote that 'the movie was very effective emotionally, deeply sad', this might be rated as a very positive statement. But in a therapy session, the word 'sad' would be more likely to be used in the context 'I am feeling very sad'. Moreover, there are many words that might be extremely rare in other datasets, but are very common in psychotherapy. For example, the word 'Zoloft' (an anti-depression medication) may never occur in a movie review dataset, but it occurs

381 times in our collection of therapy transcripts. Moreover, psychotherapy text typically comes from transcribed dialogue - not written communication. Modeling strategies that work well on written text may perform poorly on spoken language. For example, methods that require parse trees (recursive neural nets) may have difficulty on the disfluencies, fillers and fragments that come from dialogue.

Databases used for sentiment analysis have come from a variety of written prose ranging from classic literature (Yussupova et al., 2012; Qiu et al., 2011; Liu and Zhang, 2012), news articles (see Pang and Lee (2008) for a list of databases), to social media text (for examples see Bohlouli et al. (2015), Gokulakrishnan et al. (2012) and Pak and Paroubek (2015)). Databases have been created from archived text via the Internet. Additionally, researchers have used a variety of techniques to harvest a live feed of tweets and posts from social media outlets as Twitter and Facebook, respectively, so as to access fresh data (Bohlouli et al., 2015). Virtually all of the databases for sentiment analysis are written and none (that we are aware of) come from a mental health domain.

3 Data Collection

Data were obtained from a large corpus of psychotherapy transcripts that are published by Alexander Street Press (http://alexanderstreet.com/). These transcripts come from a variety of different theoretical perspectives (Psychodynamic, Experiential/Humanistic, Cognitive Behavioral and Drug Therapy/Medication Management) (Imel et al., 2014b). Importantly, these transcripts are available through library subscription and can be downloaded from the web. As a result they can be shared more easily than a typical psychotherapy datasets. At the time of writing, there were 2,354 sessions, with 514,118 talk turns.

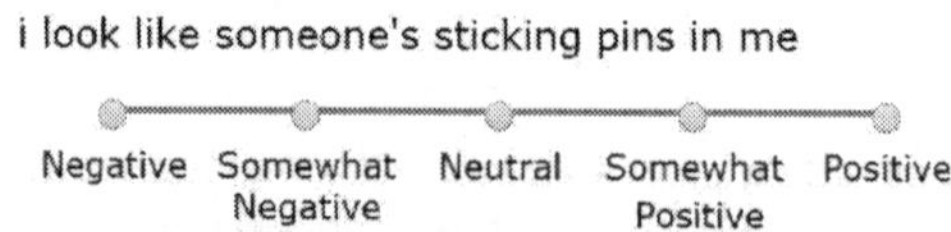

Figure 1: Example Mechanical Turk Rating

Before sampling from the dataset, we segmented

talk turns on sentence boundaries (based on periods, exclamation and question marks). We refer to these discrete units as 'utterances'. We also excluded any talk turns that were shorter than 15 characters (a large part of the dataset consists of short filler text like 'mm-hmm', 'yeah', 'ok' that are neutral in nature). We left in non-verbal indicators that were transcribed like '(laugh)' or '(sigh)'. We randomly sampled from the entire dataset of utterances that met the criteria for length, without any stratification by session.

We used Amazon Mechanical Turk (MTurk) to code the dataset for sentiment. We limited the workers to individuals in the United States to reduce the variability in the ratings to only US English speakers. In addition, we required that workers were all 'master' certified by the system (which means that they had a track record of successfully performing other tasks). We packaged each utterance with a set of 7 others that were all completed at the same time (though all were selected randomly and were not in order). Workers were told that the utterances came from transcripts of spoken dialogue, and as a result are sometimes messy, but to try their best to rate each one. For each rating, workers were given the following five options: Negative, Somewhat Negative, Neutral, Somewhat Positive, Positive (see figure 1 to see the exact presentation). Each utterance in the main dataset was rated by one person.

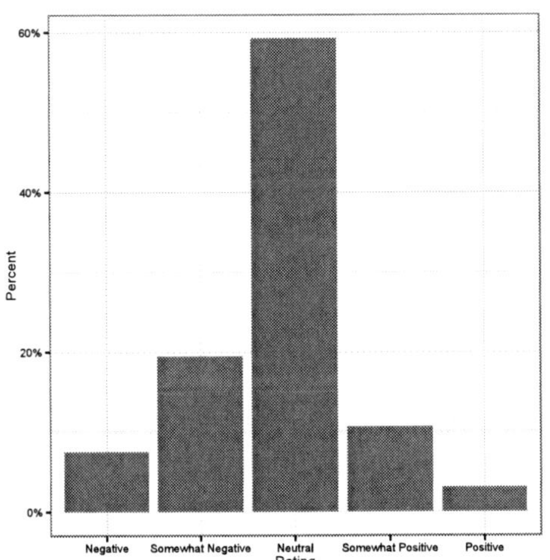

Figure 2: Distribution of Sentiment Ratings

3.1 Interrater Dataset

In addition to the main dataset, where one worker rated each utterance, we created another dataset where a random selection of 100 utterances were rated by 75 workers each. The purpose of this dataset was 1) to estimate the numeric interrater reliability of human coding of sentiment and 2) to be able to see the distribution of sentiment ratings for different utterances.

4 Data Description

4.1 Sentiment Dataset Description

The sentiment ratings were completed by 221 different workers on MTurk. The workers completed 97,497 ratings. The mean length of the utterances was 13.6 (SD = 11.1) and the median length was 10 words. The most frequent rating was neutral (59.2%) and the ratings generally skewed more negative than positive (see figure 2).

There was a similar trend to the one observed by Socher et al. (2013) that shorter sentences tended to be more neutral than longer ones. Though in contrast, even in longer phrases, our dataset skewed more negative and had a larger neutral percentage. This makes sense, given that the dataset comes from a collection of psychotherapy transcripts where participants are likely to be discussing the problems that brought the client to psychotherapy.

4.2 Data Splits

From the overall collection of 97,497 ratings we randomly split the data into a training, development and test set. We allocated 60% to the training set (58,496), 20% to the development (19,503) and 20% to the test set (19,498).

4.3 Interrater Dataset Description

The interrater dataset was used to determine the level of interrater agreement when rating sentiment in this dataset. We used the Intraclass Correlation Coefficient (ICC) to assess this agreement (Shrout and Fleiss, 1979). Using a two way random effects model for absolute agreement, treating the data as ordinal, the ICC was .54[1]. (95% CI [.47, .62])[2].

---

[1]This rated "fair" by the criterion of Cicchetti (1994)
[2]CI=Confidence Interval

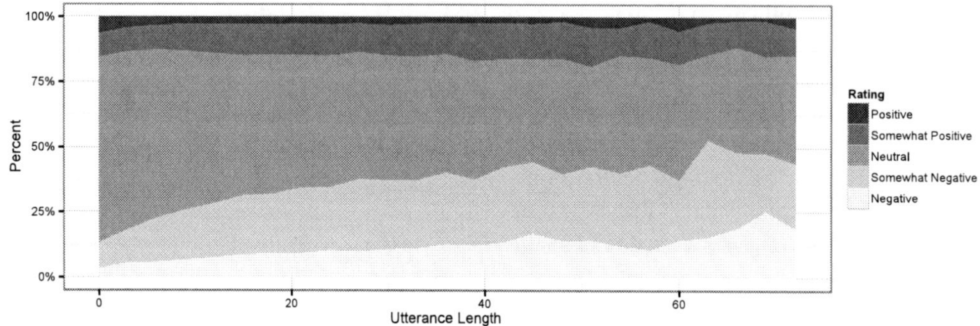

Figure 3: Distribution of Sentiment Ratings by Length of Utterance

The interrater set provides an illustration of how different types of utterances produce different responses in people. We present several examples in figure 4 that were chosen to illustrate different patterns in ratings. As can be seen in the examples, there are certain ratings where the vast majority of raters agree on the sentiment. For example 'and then left the house' was rated neutral by most of the raters. Another example, 'no, I don't even like him' was agreed to be some degree of negative by most raters. Another utterance that was generally rated positive was '(chuckling) but I know I didn't feel as good as I do now'. But even in examples where the vast majority of raters agreed on the direction of the rating (positive or negative) there was almost never complete agreement on the degree of sentiment. This finding lends support to the method of training models that predict the polarity of the sentiment, but not the degree (Socher et al., 2013). In many utterances a large proportion of raters agreed a phrase was not neutral, but there was low agreement on what direction of the sentiment was. The example 'see I don't need any therapy' illustrates this point. The modal rating was neutral, but the example had a wide distribution of ratings. Different raters had very different views on the sentiment of the sentence. It is possible that these different assesments could map onto ways in which therapists might view such a statement - some taking it at face value and an indicator a client was doing well, while others might view it as a failure to acknowledge problems that brought them to psychotherapy.

5 Models

We tested several common NLP models to predict the labels on the dataset from the text. The purpose of the modeling was to build baseline measures that could serve as comparisons for future studies.

5.1 Features

We tested the models with several n-gram combinations. Grams were created by parsing on word boundaries without separating out contractions. For example, the word "don't" would be left as a single gram. Each model was tested with 1) unigram features 2) unigram + bigram features 3) unigram, bigram and trigram features.

5.2 Evaluation

All of the models were evaluated on how well they predicted the course sentiment labels, which were 'positive', 'negative' and 'neutral'. We used several metrics: 1) Overall accuracy predicting labels 2) F1-Score for each of the labels and 3) Cohen's Kappa (weighted). Because the base rate for neutral was high in our dataset, the Kappa metric probably gives the best overall measure of the performance of these models, correcting for chance agreement on neutral ratings. Although accuracy is reported in the table, we feel that Kappa is a better metric because in our dataset, an accuracy of .59 could be achieved by guessing the majority class.

All models were tuned against the development set. Once the final hyperparameters were selected for each model, they were trained on both the training and development set and run once against the test set.

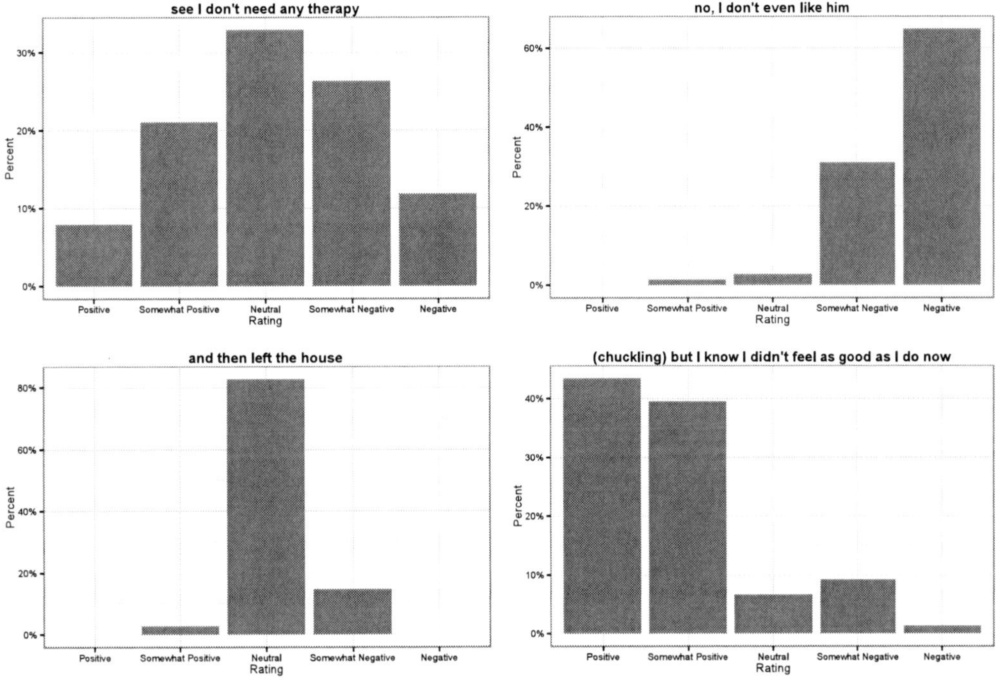

Figure 4: Examples Rating Distributions from Interrater Set

6 Classifier Model

We tested each of the feature sets with a Maximum Entropy Model. The L1 regularization on each of the models was tuned against the development set. The model functioned as local classifier (that is, they could only see each utterance in isolation, without any surrounding information from the session from which it was drawn).

In addition, we tested a pre-trained version of the Stanford sentiment model based on a Recursive Neural Network as a comparison for how a model that was trained on movie reviews would perform on psychotherapy dialogue (Socher et al., 2013). Because of the way that this model is set up to learn, it was not possible to train it on our data[1]. The RNN

---

[1]As a side note: this is not a limitation of Recursive Neural Networks (RNN) in general, but rather the way that Socher's implementation was designed to learn. The movie dataset that their group created labeled all of the sections of a parse tree and gave these labeled tree structures to the RNN. One could have designed an RNN to learn from just the top label of a tree, but then one would have to use a different implementation of an RNN. It may also surprise readers to learn that Socher's model in this paper relied on the Stanford parser to pre-parse the sentence trees, instead of letting the RNN parse the sentence.

model from the previously mentioned paper requires parse trees of the training set, labeled at each node. Our training dataset only has the top level of the sentence labeled. In our tables, the specific model is identified as a Recursive Neural Tensor Network (RNTN).

7 Results

In general, we found that the n-gram models trained on this dataset had similar accuracy on the categorization of the course sentiment rating, but varied to a large degree in their F1 scores and Kappa statistics (see table 1). The maxent trigram model had the best overall accuracy, but by a relatively small margin.

The best F1 for positive statements was from the maxent unigram and bigram models and the best F1 for negative statements was from the maxent model as well. The maxent model had the highest Kappa score. Surprisingly, there was not a wide divergence in scores by the length of the grams in the models. The Kappa score for the maxent model did not change by more than .01 between a unigram and a tri-gram model.

The RNTN from Socher, et al. (2013) that was

Model	Accuracy	F1-Neutral	F1-Positive	F1-Negative	Kappa
Unigram Features					
Maxent	.601	.706	**.339**	**.451**	**.308**
Bigram Features					
Maxent	.603	.709	**.339**	.446	.306
Trigram Features					
Maxent	**.606**	**.714**	.337	.434	.300
RNN					
RNTN Trained on Movie Reviews	.484	.559	.319	.450	.227

Table 1: Results Test Set. Best scores for each category are bolded.

only pretrained on the movie review data had much lower accuracy than the other models (.484) and a lower Kappa score than the maxent models. The F1 scores for positive and negative statements were comparable to the best models, but the F1 score for negative was lower than any of the other models tested (.559).

In table 2 we present the best predictors of the positive and negative classes from the unigram maxent model. It is interesting to note that these words give some insight into why it is important to have a sentiment dataset that is specific to psychotherapy. We can see that 'scary' is one of the top ten negative words in the dataset. We should note that in a movie review, the word 'scary' might be a positive indicator. Additionally, psychologically relevant words are frequent on the list of good predictors like 'depressed' and 'relaxed'.

The confusion matrix for the maxent unigram model (see figure 5) shows that the basic model is generally accurate in the polarity of the statement (that is, there are very few errors of positive sentences coded as negative, or negative sentences coded as positive). The errors are generally classifying a positive utterance as neutral or a neutral utterance as positive.

8 Discussion

Psychotherapy is an often emotional process, and most theories of psychotherapy involve hypotheses about emotional expression, but very few researchers have systematically explored how affect works empirically in these situations. There are several databases of sentiment ratings in text but few of them involve dialogue and none are from a mental health setting. This dataset represents an initial step towards the study of sentiment in psychotherapy.

Most Positive Words
nice
thank, amazing
glad, good
proud, great
relaxed, helpful
fine, interesting
forward, helped
special, helps
cool, better
enjoyed, excited

Most Negative Words
sad, crap
hated, screwed
afraid, terrible
fear, can't
bothers, rejection
worst, death
hard, scary
horrible, worse
stupid, ugly
pissed, depressed

Table 2: Most Positive and Negative Words from Maxent Unigram Model

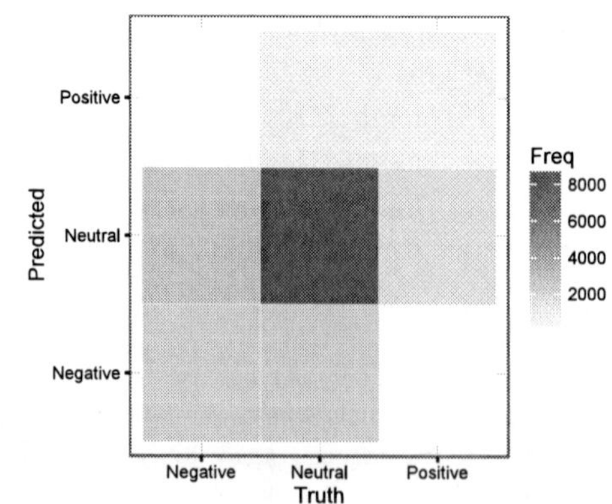

Figure 5: Confusion Matrix for Maxent Unigram Model (Test Set)

38

One of the novel contributions of this dataset to the area of sentiment analysis in general is the interrater reliability subset. In our literature search we were unable to find examples where researchers had estimated what human agreement was on different datasets used for sentiment analysis. This will allow us to compare our models to human-human agreement and also provide a qualitative sense for what kinds of utterances humans agree on and on which ones they disagree.

We hope that the creation of this dataset will improve researchers' ability to predict sentiment from dialogue and in psychotherapy settings. It is clear from the interrater reliability dataset that we should not expect models to perfectly rate sentiment because even humans do not completely agree on many types of utterances. However, it may be reasonable for machine rated reliability to approach the human range of reliability.

The models suggested by this paper are not intended to be a comprehensive list of models that may work well on the dataset, but are intended to be a baseline for other work to compare to. There is a long list of possible models that should be tried in the future, including LIWC counts, LDA models, word vectors and more comprehensive tests with Recursive Neural Networks. Testing all of these models and their variations is beyond the scope of this paper, but we hope that this dataset will give a baseline for different groups to test what works well in this type of data.

One of the interesting findings of this paper was the comparison of the RNTN model from Socher et al. (2013) that was only trained on the original movie review data. This dataset, it should be noted, is much larger than our own, but it is from a very different context. This is consistent with the conclusions of Pang and Lee (2008) that context is extremely important in identifying sentiment. Our work provides a test of the viability of domain adaption of models trained on very different datasets. It would appear accuracy will suffer if we use models that were trained on datasets like movie reviews and apply them directly to mental health contexts.

Finally, there were not substantial differences in accuracy between unigram models and the bigram, trigram models, suggesting that the more complex word patterns to not necessarily improve accuracy.

This may be a side effect of the characteristics of dialogue, which are not always as gramatically clear as written text.

8.1 Psychotherapy Compared to Other Sentiment Domains

It may be surprising that the accuracy of some of our initial models are lower than other similar models used on other sentiment datasets. Part of this is may be a result of our decision to not use extremely short phrases (our dataset has a large number of neutral listening utterances like 'mm-hmm' and 'yeah' that we wanted to exclude). It should be noted that even in Socher et al. (2013) all of the models tested had an accuracy below .6 on anything that had 5 words or more (see figure 6 in their paper).

However, there may be a larger issue in the psychotherapy domain that makes labeling these utterances more difficult in general. For example, when rating movies, the typical subject of the sentence is going to be the movie and whether or not the reviewer enjoyed it. While you may have sentences that express both positive and negative attitudes, but there is some sense that the purpose is always going to be to evaluate the movie. In psychotherapy, an utterance like "(chuckling) but I know I didn't feel as good as now" has a complicated temporal aspect to it. The rater may be confused about whether this should be positive because the person feels good now, or negative because they were not feeling good prior to now. An utterance like "see I don't need any therapy" is complicated because some raters may see this as a person in recovery and others may see a person in denial.

Consequently, our models may not necessarily be evaluating how a person is *feeling* about another person or themselves in a given moment. Instead raters evaluated the emotional valence of a statement which could target the speaker, another person, or something unspecified. The psychotherapy domain clearly presents a more complicated task than answering the question "is this movie review a positive one or a negative one?" which is a better defined tasks. Future work may attempt more challenging classification tasks like asking a rater to guess how a client or therapist may be feeling from text - similar to how a human interacting with a client or therapist might attempt to understand their partners internal state. However, even if models could be trained to accurately capture this particular aspect of sentiment, we could not be sure that models were capturing an actual internal state. Instead they would be learning human perception of this state, which in and of itself can be error prone.

8.2 Future Directions

Beyond the practical question of whether we can accurately rate sentiment in psychotherapy, we hope that models trained on this dataset will eventually be able to code entire psychotherapy sessions so that we can ask larger questions about how sentiment expressed by clients and therapists influences outcomes. For example, would we expect to see the largest improvement in symptoms from positive client expression or negative client expression? Or should there be a pattern from negative expressed sentiment to positive? Another important question is whether we would see the most improvement from therapists who focus on positive aspects of a client's experience or more negative ones. To answer these questions, we need to be able to label more data than is practical to do with just human raters.

Acknowledgments

We would like to thank Padhraic Smyth for his helpful thoughts on early versions of this manuscript. Funding for this project was provided by NIH/NIDA R34 DA034860.

References

Timothy Anderson, Edward Bein, Brian Pinnell, and Hans Strupp. 1999. Linguistic analysis of affective speech in psychotherapy: A case grammar approach. *Psychotherapy research*, 9(1):88–99.

Stefano Baccianella, Andrea Esuli, and Fabrizio Sebastiani. 2010. Sentiwordnet 3.0: An enhanced lexical resource for sentiment analysis and opinion mining. In *LREC*, volume 10, pages 2200–2204.

Reuven Bar-On, Daniel Tranel, Natalie L Denburg, and Antoine Bechara. 2004. Emotional and social intelligence. *Social neuroscience: key readings*, 223.

Ernst G Beier and David M Young. 1998. *The silent language of psychotherapy*. Aldine.

M. Bohlouli, J. Dalter, M. Dronhofer, J. Zenkert, and M. Fathi. 2015. Knowledge discovery from social media using big data-provided sentiment analysis (somabit). *Journal of Information Science*, 41(6):779–798.

Domenic V. Cicchetti. 1994. Guidelines, criteria, and rules of thumb for evaluating normed and standardized assessment instruments in psychology. *Psychol. Assess.*, 6(4):284–290.

J. Decety and W. Ickes. 2009. *The social neuroscience of empathy*. MIT Press, Cambridge, MA.

R. Elliott, A. C. Bohart, J. C. Watson, and L. S. Greenberg. 2011. Empathy. *Psychotherapy*, 48(1):43.

Albert Ellis. 1962. *Reason and emotion in psychotherapy*. Lyle Stuart.

Sigmund Freud and Josef Breuer. 1895. Studies on hysteria. se, 2. *London: Hogarth*.

B. Gokulakrishnan, P. Priyanthan, T. Ragavan, N. Prasath, and A. Perera. 2012. Opinion mining and sentiment analysis on a twitter data stream. in advances in ict for emerging regions (icter), 2012 international conference. *IEEE*, pages 182–188.

James J Gross and Robert W Levenson. 1997. Hiding feelings: the acute effects of inhibiting negative and positive emotion. *Journal of abnormal psychology*, 106(1):95.

Ernest A Haggard and Kenneth S Isaacs. 1966. Micromomentary facial expressions as indicators of ego mechanisms in psychotherapy. In *Methods of research in psychotherapy*, pages 154–165. Springer.

Z. E. Imel, J. S. Barco, H. J. Brown, B. R. Baucom, J. S. Baer, J. C. Kircher, and D. C. Atkins. 2014a. The association of therapist empathy and synchrony in vocally encoded arousal. *Journal of counseling psychology*, 61(1):146.

Zac E Imel, Mark Steyvers, and David C Atkins. 2014b. Psychotherapy Computational Psychotherapy Research : Scaling up the Evaluation of Patient Provider Interactions Computational. *Psychotherapy*.

Alice M Isen. 2008. Some ways in which positive affect influences decision making and problem solving. *Handbook of emotions*, 3:548–573.

H. Kohut. 2013. *The analysis of the self: A systematic approach to the psychoanalytic treatment of narcissistic personality disorders*. University of Chicago Press.

Richard D Lane, Lee Ryan, Lynn Nadel, and Leslie Greenberg. 2015. Memory reconsolidation, emotional arousal, and the process of change in psychotherapy: New insights from brain science. *Behavioral and Brain Sciences*, 38:e1.

Peter J Lang and Margaret M Bradley. 2010. Emotion and the motivational brain. *Biological psychology*, 84(3):437–450.

B. Liu and L. Zhang. 2012. A survey of opinion mining and sentiment analysis. *Mining Text Data*, pages 415–463.

Andrew L Maas, Raymond E Daly, Peter T Pham, Dan Huang, Andrew Y Ng, and Christopher Potts. 2011. Learning word vectors for sentiment analysis. In *Proceedings of the 49th Annual Meeting of the Association for Computational Linguistics: Human Language Technologies-Volume 1*, pages 142–150. Association for Computational Linguistics.

Erhard Mergenthaler. 1996. Emotion–abstraction patterns in verbatim protocols: A new way of describing psychotherapeutic processes. *Journal of consulting and clinical psychology*, 64(6):1306.

Erhard Mergenthaler. 2008. Resonating minds: A school-independent theoretical conception and its empirical application to psychotherapeutic processes. *Psychotherapy Research*, 18(2):109–126.

Walter Mischel. 2013. *Personality and assessment*. Psychology Press.

A. Pak and P. Paroubek. 2015. Twitter as a corpus for sentiment analysis and opinion mining. *In LREc*, 10:1320–1326.

Bo Pang and Lillian Lee. 2008. Opinion Mining and Sentiment Analysis. *Found. Trends Inf. Retreival*, 1(2):91–231.

G. Qiu, B. Liu, J. Bu, and C. Chen. 2011. Opinion word expansion and target extraction through double propagation. *Computational Linguistics*, 37(1):9–27.

C. R. Rogers. 1975. Empathic: An unappreciated way of being. *Couns. Psychol.*, 5(2):2–10.

Jeremy D Safran and J Christopher Muran. 2000. *Negotiating the therapeutic alliance: A relational treatment guide*. Guilford Press.

Daniel L Schacter. 1999. The seven sins of memory: Insights from psychology and cognitive neuroscience. *American psychologist*, 54(3):182.

Patrick E. Shrout and Joseph L. Fleiss. 1979. Intraclass correlations: Uses in assessing rater reliability. *Psychol. Bull.*, 86(2):420–428.

Richard Socher, Alex Perelygin, Jean Y Wu, Jason Chuang, Christopher D. Manning, Andrew Y. Ng, and C. Potts. 2013. Recursive deep models for semantic compositionality over a sentiment treebank. *Proc. Conf. Empir. Methods.*

Anastassios Stalikas. 1995. Client good moments: An intensive analysis of a single session anastassios stalikas marilyn fitzpatrick mcgill university. *Canadian Journal of Counselling*, 29:2.

N Yussupova, Diana Bogdanova, and M Boyko. 2012. Applying of sentiment analysis for texts in russian based on machine learning approach. In *Proceedings of Second International Conference on Advances in Information Mining and Management*, pages 8–14.

Building a Motivational Interviewing Dataset

Verónica Pérez-Rosas[1]**, Rada Mihalcea**[1]**, Kenneth Resnicow**[2]
Satinder Singh[1]**, Lawrence An**[3]
[1]Computer Science and Engineering, University of Michigan
[2]School of Public Health, University of Michigan
[3]Center for Health Communications Research, University of Michigan
{vrncapr,mihalcea,kresnic,baveja,lcan}@umich.edu

Abstract

This paper contributes a novel psychological dataset consisting of counselors' behaviors during Motivational Interviewing encounters. Annotations were conducted using the Motivational Interviewing Integrity Treatment (MITI). We describe relevant aspects associated with the construction of a dataset that relies on behavioral coding such as data acquisition, transcription, expert data annotations, and reliability assessments. The dataset contains a total of 22,719 counselor utterances extracted from 277 motivational interviewing sessions that are annotated with 10 counselor behavioral codes. The reliability analysis showed that annotators achieved excellent agreement at session level, with Intraclass Correlation Coefficient (ICC) scores in the range of 0.75 to 1, and fair to good agreement at utterance level, with Cohen's Kappa scores ranging from 0.31 to 0.64.

Behavioral interventions are a promising approach to address public health issues such as smoking cessation, increasing physical activity, and reducing substance abuse, among others (Resnicow et al., 2002). In particular, Motivational Interviewing (MI), a client centered psychotherapy style, has been receiving increasing attention from the clinical psychology community due to its established efficacy for treating addiction and other behaviors (Moyers et al., 2009; Apodaca et al., 2014; Barnett et al., 2014; Catley et al., 2012).

Despite its potential benefits in combating addiction and in providing broader disease prevention and management, implementing MI counseling at larger scale or in other domains is limited by the need for human-based evaluations. Currently, this requires a human either watching or listening to video-tapes and then providing evaluative feedback.

Recently, computational approaches have been proposed to aid the MI evaluation process (Atkins et al., 2014; Xiao et al., 2014; Klonek et al., 2015). However, learning resources for this task are not readily available. Having such resources will enable the application of data-driven strategies for the automatic coding of counseling behaviors, thus providing researchers with automatic means for the evaluation of MI. Moreover, this can also be useful to explore how MI works by relating MI behaviors to health outcomes, and to provide counselors with evaluative feedback that helps them improve their MI skills.

In this paper, we present the construction and validation of a dataset annotated with counselor verbal behaviours using the Motivational Interviewing Treatment Integrity 4.0 (MITI), which is the current gold standard for MI-based psychology interventions. The dataset is derived from 277 MI sessions containing a total of 22,719 coded utterances.

1 Motivational Interviewing

Miller and Rollnick define MI as a collaborative, goal-oriented style of psychotherapy with particular attention to the language of change (Miller and Rollnick, 2013). MI has been widely used as a treatment method in clinical trials on psychotherapy research to address addictive behaviors such as alcohol, tobacco and drug use; promote healthier habits such as nutrition and fitness; and help clients with

Proceedings of the 3rd Workshop on Computational Linguistics and Clinical Psychology: From Linguistic Signal to Clinical Reality, pages 42–51,
San Diego, California, June 16, 2016. ©2016 Association for Computational Linguistics

psychological problems such as depression and anxiety disorders (Rollnick et al., 2008; Lundahl et al., 2010). In addition, MI has been successfully applied in different practice settings including social work in behavioral health centers, education, and criminal justice (Wahab, 2005; McMurran, 2009).

The competence of the counselor in MI delivery is measured using systematic observational methods to assess verbal behavior in MI by either focusing on therapist behaviors, client behaviors, or both (Jelsma et al., 2015). Current coding instruments for MI include the Behavior Change Counselor Index (BECCI) (Lane et al., 2005), the Client Evaluation of Motivational Interview (CEMI) (Madson et al., 2009), the Independent Tape Rating Scale (ITRS) (Martino et al., 2009), the MI Skills Code (MISC) (Moyers et al., 2003), the Stimulated Client Interview Rating Scale (SCIRS) (Arthur, 1999), the One Pass (McMaster and Resnicow, 2015), and the Motivational Interviewing Treatment Integrity (MITI) (Moyers et al., 2005).

1.1 Motivational Interviewing Treatment Integrity

The MITI coding system is currently the most frequently used instrument for assessing MI fidelity (Moyers et al., 2003). The MITI is derived from the MISC coding system and focuses exclusively on the verbal behavior of the counselor. It measures how well or poorly the clinician is using MI. The coding system evaluates MI processes related to change talk such as engagement, focus, evocation, and planning. MITI has two components: global scores and behavior counts. The global scores aim to characterize the overall quality of the interaction and include four dimensions, namely Cultivating Change Talk, Softening Sustain Talk, Partnership, and Empathy. Behavior counts are evaluated by tallying instances of particular interviewing behaviors, which can be grouped into five broad categories: questions, reflections, MI adherent behavior (MIA), MI non-adherent behavior (MINA), and neutral behaviors.

Reflections capture reflective listening statements made by the clinician in response to client statements and can be categorized as simple or complex. MIA behaviors summarize counselor adherence to core aspects of the MI strategy such as seeking collaboration, affirming, and emphasizing autonomy.

MINA includes aspects that indicate counselor deficiencies while delivering MI, such as confronting and persuading without permission. The neutral behaviors include counselor actions such as providing information and persuading with permission.

MITI evaluation is conducted by trained coders who assess the overall session scores and the occurrence of behaviors by using pen and paper. During the coding process, coders rely on audio recordings and their corresponding transcriptions. The evaluation is usually performed as a two-step process by first evaluating overall scores and next focusing on behavior counts.

MITI coding is a very time consuming and expensive process, as it requires accurate transcriptions and human expertise. The quality of the transcriptions is affected by the recoding quality and their preparation is time consuming as it might take about three times the duration of the recording (Klonek et al., 2015). Thus, estimates for a 30 min session might add up to 2.5 hours of transcriber time and about one hour of coder time.

1.2 MI reliability assessment

Reliability assessment for MI helps to validate treatment fidelity in clinical studies as it provides evidence that the MI intervention has been effective and allows comparisons across studies (Jelsma et al., 2015). MI literature suggests assessing reliability by double coding a fraction of the study sessions. The most common method to quantify the inter-annotator agreement on MI coding is computing the Intraclass Correlation Coefficient (ICC). This statistic describes how much of the total variation in MITI scores is due to differences among annotators (Dunn et al., 2015). ICC scores range in the 0 to 1 interval; relatively high ICC scores indicate that annotators scored MITI in a similar way while scores closer to 0 suggest that there is a considerable amount of variation in the way annotator's evaluated counselor MI skill. Low scores further suggest that either the measure is defective or the annotators should be retrained. Another method to measure inter-annotator reliability in MI is the Cohen's Kappa score (Lord et al., 2015a), which calculates the pair-wise agreement among annotations considering the probability of annotators agreeing by chance.

2   Related work

Current approaches for MI coding and evaluation entail extensive human involvement. Recently, there have been a number of efforts on building computational tools that assist researchers during the coding process. (Can et al., 2012) proposed a linguistic based approach to automatically detect and code counselor reflections that is based on analyzing n-grams patterns, similarity features between counselor and client speech, and contextual meta-features, which aim to represent the dialog sequence between the client and counselor. A method based on topic models is presented in (Atkins et al., 2012; Atkins et al., 2014), where authors focus on automatically identifying topics related to MI behaviors such as reflections, questions, support, and empathy, among others. Text and speech based methods have also been proposed to evaluate overall MI quality. (Lord et al., 2015b) analyzed the language style synchrony between therapist and client during MI encounters. In this work, authors relied in the psycholinguistic categories from the Linguistic Inquiry and Word Count lexicon to measure the degree in which counselor matches the client language. (Xiao et al., 2014) presents a study on the automatic evaluation of counselor empathy by analyzing correlations between prosody patterns and empathy showed by the therapist during the counseling interaction.

Although most of the work on coding of MI within session language has focused on modeling the counselor language, there is also work that addresses the client language. (Tanana et al., 2015) used recursive neural networks (RNN) to identify client change and sustain talk in MI transcripts, i.e., language that indicates commitment towards and away behavioral change. In this work, authors combined both therapist and client utterances in a single sequence model using Maximum Entropy Markov Models, NRR, and n-grams features. (Gupta et al., 2014) analyzed the valence of client's attitude towards the target behavior by using n-grams and conditional maximum entropy models. In this paper authors also present an exploration of the role laughter of both counselor and client's during the MI encounter and attempts to incorporate its occurrence as an additional source of information in the prediction model.

Research findings have shown that natural language processing approaches can be successfully applied to behavioral data for the automatic annotation of therapists' and clients' behaviors. This motivates our interest in building resources for this task as an initial step for the construction of improved coding tools. There has been work on creating annotated resources that facilitate advances in natural language processing of clinical text, including semantic and syntactic annotation of pathology reports, oncology reports, and biomedical journals (Roberts et al., 2007; Albright et al., 2013; Verspoor et al., 2012). However, to our knowledge, there are just a few psychotherapy corpora available. One of them is the "Alexander Street Press", [1] which is a large collection of transcripts and video recordings of therapy sessions on different subjects such as anxiety, depression, family conflicts, and others. There are also some other psychology datasets available under limited access from the National Institute of Mental Health (NIMH).[2] These datasets provide recorded interactions among clinicians and patients on a number of psychology styles. However, they are not annotated and validated to be used in the computational psychology domain.

In this paper, we present the development of a clinical narratives dataset that can be used to implement data-driven methods for the automatic evaluation of MI sessions.

3   Motivational Interviewing Dataset

3.1   Data collection

The dataset is derived from a collection of 284 video recordings of counseling encounters using MI. The recordings were collected from various sources, including two clinical trials, students' counseling sessions from a graduate level MI course, wellness coaching phone calls, and demonstrations of MI strategies in brief medical encounters.

The clinical trials sessions consist of interventions for smoking cessation and antiretroviral therapy adherence with electronic drug monitoring. Psychology students' sessions are conducted on standardized patients and aim at weight loss and smoke

---

[1] http://alexanderstreet.com/products/counseling-and-psychotherapy-transcripts-series

[2] http://psychiatry.yale.edu/pdc/resources/datasets.aspx

Source	No. sessions	Avg.length
Clinical trial	121	27 min
Standardized patients	138	15 min
Brief MI encounters	18	4 min
Coaching phone calls	7	15 min
Total	284	

Table 1: Data sources for the MI sessions

cessation. Wellness coaching phone calls inquired about patient health and medication adherence after surgery. The demonstration sessions are collected from online sources, i.e., YouTube and Vimeo, and present brief MI encounters on several scenarios such as dental practice, emergency room counseling, and student counseling. Table 1 presents a summary of the data sources used in the dataset collection.

All the sessions are manually anonymized to remove identifiable information such as counselor and patient names and references to counseling sites' location. Each recording is assigned a new identifier that does not include any information related to the original recording. The resulting recordings are then processed to remove the visual data stream to further prevent counselor/patient identification. After this process, we obtained a set of 277 sessions due to the exclusion of some sessions with recording errors. The final dataset comprises a total of 97.8 hours of audio with average session duration of 20.8 minutes and a standard deviation of 11.4 minutes.

3.2 Transcriptions

The sessions from clinical trials include full transcripts. However, this was not the case for the remaining set of sessions, and for these we obtained manual transcriptions via crowdsourcing using Amazon Mechanical Turk. This resource has proved to be a fast and reliable method to obtain speech transcriptions (Marge et al., 2010).

Mechanical Turk workers were provided with transcription guidelines that include clearly identifying the speaker (client or counselor), and transcribing speech disfluencies such as false starts, repetitions of whole words or parts of words, prolongations of sounds, fillers, and long pauses. Resulting transcriptions were manually verified to avoid spam and to ensure their quality. The transcriptions consist of approximately 22,719 utterances, with an average of 83 utterances per session.

3.3 MITI Annotations

Three counselors, with previous MI experience, were trained on the use of the MITI 4.1 by expert trainers from the Motivational Interviewing Network of Trainers[3] (MINT) to conduct the annotation task. Prior to the annotation phase, annotators participated in a coding calibration phase where they had discussions regarding the criteria for sentence parsing, the correct assignment of behavior codes, and conducted team coding of sample sessions.

Annotators used both audio recordings and verbatim transcriptions to conduct the annotations.

Annotators were instructed to parse the interviewer speech following the guidelines defined by MITI 4.1. The annotation was conducted at utterance level, by selecting and labeling utterances in each counselor turn that contain a specific MI behavior.

Following this strategy allowed us to obtain more accurate examples of each behavior code for cases where a turn contains multiple utterances and thus more than one behavior code. In addition, given possible inaccuracies and interruptions in the turn by turn segmentation, annotators were allowed to select the text that they considered belonging to a coded utterance, even if it spanned more than one counselor-client turn, to avoid utterance breaking.

In order to facilitate this process, annotators used a software based coding system instead of the traditional paper and pen system. Annotators were trained to code using the Nvivo software,[4] a quantitative analysis suite that allows to select and assign text segments to a given codebook. The codebook contains the following behavior codes:

Question (QUEST) All questioning statements spoken by clinicians.

Simple reflection (SR) Clinician statements that convey understanding or facilitate client-clinician exchanges.

Complex reflection (CR) Reflective statements that add substantial meaning or emphasis to what the client has said.

---

[3] http://www.motivationalinterviewing.org/
[4] http://www.qsrinternational.com/what-is-nvivo

Code	Count	Verbal example
QUEST	5262	Could you talk a little bit more about those behaviors you say that automatically makes you smoke?
SR	2690	It sounds like something that you know and feel like you can improve on in the next week.
CR	2876	So you want something that's gonna to allow you to eat the foods that you enjoy but that maybe more moderation.
SEEK	614	And, then, when we meet again, you can bring some of that information. Maybe we can discuss which of those feels right for you, and start to put together a plan for what could be your next steps.
AUTO	141	This is something that it's up to you whether you want to use it or not.
AF	499	Okay, great. So, I'm excited about this because you're obviously very motivated. And the barriers that you've presented are definitely overcomable
CON	141	Okay, well that's a good start, but cutting back isn't gonna do it. If you actually quit the smoking, you can reverse all the damage you've done in your mouth, and you can stop yourself from ... from being at risk for these other diseases. But, but as long as you're continuing to use these cigars, you're really putting yourself in a lot of danger.
PWOP	598	Okay so with all of the risks of smoking and the benefits of quitting, what is keeping you from making a plan?
N-GI	1017	There are two other over the counter options. There's a patch and that would deal with the taste you don't like. With the patch you just put it on and it slowly releases nicotine throughout the day so you don't even have to think about it. There are also lozenges, which are kind of like throat lozenges, or a hard candy and you just suck on it. And as it dissolves it releases nicotine.
N-PWP	2100	Well, if it's alright with you, umm, you know, I could toss out some ideas of things that have worked for other people and umm things that umm, could be helpful as far as reducing stress and, and really filling in other activities so you're not umm, as tempted to ... smoke

Table 2: Frequency counts and verbal examples of MI behaviors in the dataset

Seeking collaboration (SEEK) The clinician attempts to share power or acknowledge the expertise of the client.

Emphasizing autonomy (AUTO) The clinician focus the responsibility on the client for the decision and actions pertaining to change.

Affirm (AF) Clinician utterances that accentuates something positive about the client.

Persuading without permission (PWOP) The clinician attempts to change the client's opinions, attitudes, or behaviors, using tools such as logic, compelling arguments, self-disclosure or facts.

Confront (CON) Statements where the clinician confronts the client by directly disagreeing, arguing, correcting, shaming, criticizing, moralizing or questioning client's honesty.

Persuading with permission (N-PWP) Clinician statements that make emphasis on collaboration or autonomy support while persuading.

Giving information (N-GI) The clinician give information, educates, or expresses a professional opinion without persuading, advising, or warning.

The 277 sessions were randomly distributed among the three annotators. The team annotated approximately 20 sessions per week. The entire annotation process took about three months.

Annotator 1		Annotator 2		Method
So you're getting back to your old self.	SR	So you're getting back to your old self.	SR	Exact match
So it sounds like you kinda struggle with that a little bit in that sometimes	SR	So it sounds like you kinda struggle with that a little bit in that sometimes it's hard I imagine, it is sometimes hard to be financially independent I mean I, But it something it sounds like you respect in yourself that you are able to do it.	SR	Split utterances
it's hard I imagine, it is sometimes hard to be financially independent I mean I,	NL			
But it something it sounds like you respect in yourself that you are able to do it.	SR			
OK. But even though it's something that you really don't like, it's something that's not terribly bothersome.	SR	So you mentioned that one side effect of the Sustiva was that it makes you dizzy. OK. But even though it is something that you really don't like, it something that,it's not terribly bothersome.	SR	Partial match

Table 3: Sample utterance alignment for coding comparisons

After the annotation phase, transcripts were processed to extract the verbal content of each MITI annotation; non-coded utterances were also extracted and labeled as neutral. Sample annotations are presented in Table 2. The final set contains 15,886 annotations distributed among the ten codes and 6,833 neutral utterances. Table 2 shows the frequency distribution for each behavior count and neutral utterances.

4 Dataset Validation

In order to validate the annotator reliability, a sample of 10 sessions was randomly selected to be double coded by two members of the coding team.

The total amount of recoding material for this sample is about 4.5 hours. Each session has an average duration of 26 minutes, with an average of 115 counselor-client conversation turns per session, comprising a total of 1,160 utterances.

4.1 Inter-rater Reliability Analysis

Because we conducted the MITI annotation at utterance level without any pre-parsing, annotations across coders showed noticeable parsing variations. These variations consisted of differences in utter-

Code	ICC	Kappa
QUEST	0.97	0.64
CR	0.97	0.49
SR	0.89	0.34
SEEK	0.03	0.42
N-GI	0	0.28
AF	0	0.47
AUTO	0	0.31
N-PWP	0	NA
CON	NA	NA
PWOP	NA	NA

Table 4: ICC at session level and Kappa scores at utterance level for 10 double coded sessions. NA indicates that the MI behavior was not present in any session

ance boundaries such as overlaps and split utterances. In order to allow for coding comparisons, we opted for aligning annotations by utterance matching using similar methods to (Lord et al., 2015a). We considered three cases: exact match, partial match and split utterances. In the first case, we simply compare two coded utterances and define a match if both utterances contained the same words. The partial match addresses cases where two coders disagree in utterance boundaries, thus resulting in annotations from one annotator partially matching the others, i.e., some degree of overlap. The third case also deals with differences due to utterance boundaries but focuses on split utterances, i.e., an annotated utterance from one coder was split into two different annotations by the other, and cases where utterances with different annotations show some degree of overlapping. Table 3 presents sample utterances.

Using the transcript from each session, we first identified those utterances who were assigned a behavior code by either of the two annotators. Then, we compared their verbal content by applying the utterance matching methods described above. We assigned a match when both annotators agreed on their evaluations. We considered both split utterances and partial matches as a single match. Those utterances for which we were unable to find a matching pair or differed on the assigned codes were regarded as disagreements.

Table 4 presents the Intra Class Coefficient (ICC) measured at session level. Reported scores were obtained using a two-way mixed model with absolute agreement (Jelsma et al., 2015). Overall, we observe excellent ICC scores for Complex Reflections CR (CR), Simple Reflections (SR), and Questions, based on ICC reference values, where values ranging from 0.75 to 1 are considered as excellent agreement (Jelsma et al., 2015).

ICC scores suggest that annotators did not show significant variations on most of the coded behaviours, except for Seeking collaboration (SEEK), which showed considerable disagreement. We believe that this is caused by the higher variability on the frequency counts for this code across the 10 sessions.

Wanting to evaluate how well did the annotators agree while coding the same annotation, we calculated the pairwise agreement among coders using Cohen's Kappa. Results are also reported in Table 4. The Kappa values suggest fair to good levels of agreement among the different behavior codes.

In addition, we evaluate the ability of coders to distinguish the occurrence of a particular behavior code versus any other code. This allow us to answer question such as, how well did the annotators agree on what is considered a reflection as compared to what is not a reflection? This analysis provides further insights about the validity of the coding. In these comparisons, utterances coded with a different behavior than the target behavior were considered as the negative case. For instance, if the target behavior was Simple Reflection (SR), then we evaluated the identification of Simple Reflection vs non-Simple Reflection. In order to more accurately represent the human coding process, we also included non coded utterances (NL) as negatives cases. Figure 1 shows the annotation agreement between the two annotators for 10 sessions coded at utterance level in heatmap representation, where the color intensity represents the agreement distribution. In the shown matrix, the x axis indicates the MI code assigned by the first annotator and the y axis the MI code assigned by the second annotator. Each cell indicates the observed frequency of a coding pair.

From this table, we observe that questions attained the highest agreement levels among all behaviors, followed by simple reflections (SR), complex reflections (CR), seeking collaboration (SEEK), giving information (GI), and emphasizing autonomy (AUTO). From the observed disagreements, a small fraction of questions annotated by one coder were regarded as Simple Reflections or were left uncoded by the second coder. This might be related to ambiguous cases, where the counselor formulate a simple reflection but added a question tone at end of the sentence thus making the reflection sound like a question. In addition, annotators showed noticeable disagreement while distinguishing between complex and simple reflections. This was somehow expected, as the MI literature has reported similar findings given the highly subjective criteria applied while evaluating these codes (Lundahl et al., 2010). Annotators found no agreement for confronting (CON) and persuading without permission (PWOP) codes. This has to do with zero or low frequency counts e.g the first annotator found only one confrontation utterance while the second annotator found zero. Finally, annotators showed high agreement on utterances that did not contain MI behaviors, thus suggesting that 1) annotators have good agreement regarding what should be coded; and 2) differences in parsing did not affect the annotations process.

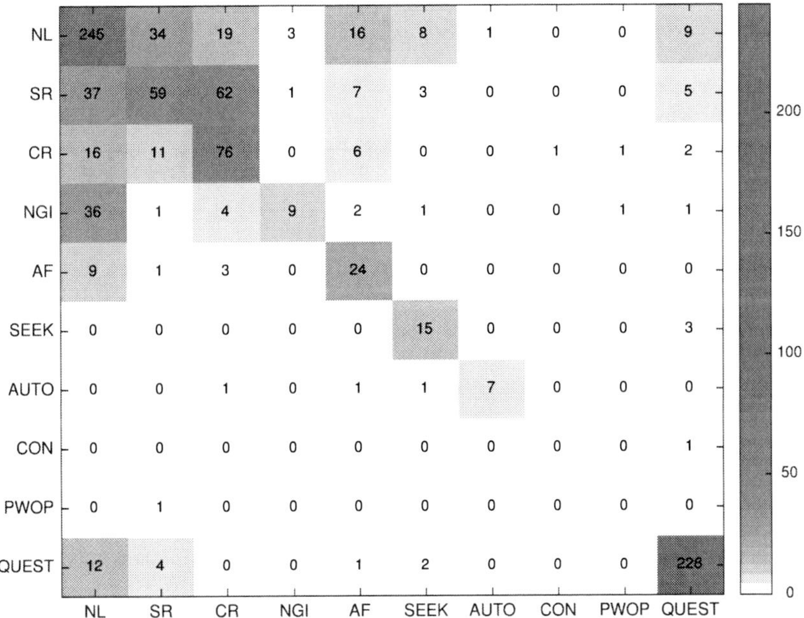

Figure 1: Annotator agreement on non-coded utterances (NL) and MI behaviors. The *x* axis indicates the MI code assigned by the first annotator and the *y* axis the MI code assigned by the second annotator.

5   Conclusion

In this paper, we introduced a new clinical narratives dataset derived from MI interventions. The dataset consists of annotations for ten verbal behaviors displayed by the counselor while conducting MI counseling. We presented a detailed description of the dataset collection and annotation process. We conducted a reliability analysis where we showed that annotators achieved excellent agreement at session level, with ICC scores in the range of 0.75 to 1, and fair to good agreement at utterance level, with Cohen's Kappa scores ranging from 0.31 to 0.64. The paper reports our initial efforts towards building accurate tools for the automatic coding of MI encounters. Our future work includes developing data-driven methods for the prediction of MI behaviors.

Acknowledgments

This material is based in part upon work supported by the University of Michigan under the MCubed program, by the National Science Foundation award #1344257, and by grant #48503 from the John Templeton Foundation. Any opinions, findings, and conclusions or recommendations expressed in this material are those of the authors and do not necessarily reflect the views of the University of Michigan, the National Science Foundation, or the John Templeton Foundation.

References

Daniel Albright, Arrick Lanfranchi, Anwen Fredriksen, William F Styler, Colin Warner, Jena D Hwang, Jinho D Choi, Dmitriy Dligach, Rodney D Nielsen, James Martin, et al. 2013. Towards comprehensive syntactic and semantic annotations of the clinical narrative.

Timothy R Apodaca, Brian Borsari, Kristina M Jackson, Molly Magill, Richard Longabaugh, Nadine R Mastroleo, and Nancy P Barnett. 2014. Sustain talk predicts poorer outcomes among mandated college student drinkers receiving a brief motivational intervention. *Psychology of Addictive Behaviors*, 28(3):631.

David Arthur. 1999. Assessing nursing students' basic communication and interviewing skills: the development and testing of a rating scale. *Journal of Advanced Nursing*, 29(3):658–665.

David C Atkins, Timothy N Rubin, Mark Steyvers, Michelle A Doeden, Brian R Baucom, and Andrew Christensen. 2012. Topic models: A novel method for modeling couple and family text data. *Journal of family psychology*, 26(5):816.

David C Atkins, Mark Steyvers, Zac E Imel, and Padhraic Smyth. 2014. Scaling up the evaluation of psychotherapy: evaluating motivational interviewing fidelity via statistical text classification. *Implementation Science*, 9(1):49.

Elizabeth Barnett, Theresa B Moyers, Steve Sussman, Caitlin Smith, Louise A Rohrbach, Ping Sun, and Donna Spruijt-Metz. 2014. From counselor skill to decreased marijuana use: Does change talk matter? *Journal of substance abuse treatment*, 46(4):498–505.

Dogan Can, Panayiotis G. Georgiou, David C. Atkins, and Shrikanth S. Narayanan. 2012. A case study: Detecting counselor reflections in psychotherapy for addictions using linguistic features. In *INTERSPEECH*, pages 2254–2257. ISCA.

Delwyn Catley, Kari J Harris, Kathy Goggin, Kimber Richter, Karen Williams, Christi Patten, Ken Resnicow, Edward Ellerbeck, Andrea Bradley-Ewing, Domonique Malomo, et al. 2012. Motivational interviewing for encouraging quit attempts among unmotivated smokers: study protocol of a randomized, controlled, efficacy trial. *BMC public health*, 12(1):456.

Chris Dunn, Doyanne Darnell, Sheng Kung Michael Yi, Mark Steyvers, Kristin Bumgardner, Sarah Peregrine Lord, Zac Imel, and David C Atkins. 2015. Should we trust our judgments about the proficiency of motivational interviewing counselors? a glimpse at the impact of low inter-rater reliability. *Motivational Interviewing: Training, Research, Implementation, Practice*, 1(3):38–41.

R Gupta, P G Georgiou, D C Atkins, and S Narayanan. 2014. Predicting client's inclination towards target behavior change in motivational interviewing and investigating the role of laughter. *Proceedings of the Annual Conference of the International Speech Communication Association, INTERSPEECH*, (September):208–212.

Judith GM Jelsma, Vera-Christina Mertens, Lisa Forsberg, and Lars Forsberg. 2015. How to measure motivational interviewing fidelity in randomized controlled trials: Practical recommendations. *Contemporary clinical trials*, 43:93–99.

Florian E Klonek, Vicenç Quera, and Simone Kauffeld. 2015. Coding interactions in motivational interviewing with computer-software: What are the advantages for process researchers? *Computers in Human Behavior*, 44:284–292.

Claire Lane, Michelle Huws-Thomas, Kerenza Hood, Stephen Rollnick, Karen Edwards, and Michael Robling. 2005. Measuring adaptations of motivational interviewing: the development and validation of the behavior change counseling index (becci). *Patient education and counseling*, 56(2):166–173.

Sarah Peregrine Lord, Doğan Can, Michael Yi, Rebeca Marin, Christopher W Dunn, Zac E Imel, Panayiotis Georgiou, Shrikanth Narayanan, Mark Steyvers, and David C Atkins. 2015a. Advancing methods for reliably assessing motivational interviewing fidelity using the motivational interviewing skills code. *Journal of substance abuse treatment*, 49:50–57.

Sarah Peregrine Lord, Elisa Sheng, Zac E Imel, John Baer, and David C Atkins. 2015b. More than reflections: empathy in motivational interviewing includes language style synchrony between therapist and client. *Behavior therapy*, 46(3):296–303.

Brad W Lundahl, Chelsea Kunz, Cynthia Brownell, Derrik Tollefson, and Brian L Burke. 2010. A meta-analysis of motivational interviewing: Twenty-five years of empirical studies. *Research on Social Work Practice*.

Michael B Madson, E Bullock, A Speed, and S Hodges. 2009. Development of the client evaluation of motivational interviewing. *Motivational Interviewing Network of Trainers Bulletin*, 15:6–8.

Matthew Marge, Satanjeev Banerjee, Alexander Rudnicky, et al. 2010. Using the amazon mechanical turk for transcription of spoken language. In *Acoustics Speech and Signal Processing (ICASSP), 2010 IEEE International Conference on*, pages 5270–5273. IEEE.

Steve Martino, Samuel A Ball, Charla Nich, Tami L Frankforter, and Kathleen M Carroll. 2009. Informal discussions in substance abuse treatment sessions. *Journal of substance abuse treatment*, 36(4):366–375.

Fiona McMaster and Ken Resnicow. 2015. Validation of the one pass measure for motivational interviewing competence. *Patient education and counseling*, 98(4):499–505.

Mary McMurran. 2009. Motivational interviewing with offenders: A systematic review. *Legal and Criminological Psychology*, 14(1):83–100.

William R Miller and Stephen Rollnick. 2013. *Motivational interviewing: Helping people change, Third edition*. The Guilford Press.

Theresa Moyers, Tim Martin, Delwyn Catley, Kari Jo Harris, and Jasjit S Ahluwalia. 2003. Assessing the integrity of motivational interviewing interventions: Reliability of the motivational interviewing skills code. *Behavioural and Cognitive Psychotherapy*, 31(02):177–184.

Theresa B Moyers, Tim Martin, Jennifer K Manuel, Stacey ML Hendrickson, and William R Miller. 2005.

Assessing competence in the use of motivational interviewing. *Journal of substance abuse treatment*, 28(1):19–26.

Theresa B Moyers, Tim Martin, Jon M Houck, Paulette J Christopher, and J Scott Tonigan. 2009. From in-session behaviors to drinking outcomes: a causal chain for motivational interviewing. *Journal of consulting and clinical psychology*, 77(6):1113.

Ken Resnicow, Colleen DiIorio, Johana E Soet, Belinda Borrelli, Denise Ernst, Jacki Hecht, and Angelica Thevos. 2002. Motivational interviewing in medical and public health settings. *Motivational interviewing: Preparing people for change*, 2:251–269.

Angus Roberts, Robert Gaizauskas, Mark Hepple, Neil Davis, George Demetriou, Yikun Guo, Jay Kola, Ian Roberts, Andrea Setzer, Archana Tapuria, and Bill Wheeldin. 2007. The CLEF corpus: semantic annotation of clinical text. *AMIA ... Annual Symposium proceedings / AMIA Symposium. AMIA Symposium*, pages 625–629.

Stephen Rollnick, William R Miller, Christopher C Butler, and Mark S Aloia. 2008. Motivational interviewing in health care: helping patients change behavior. *COPD: Journal of Chronic Obstructive Pulmonary Disease*, 5(3):203–203.

Michael Tanana, Kevin Hallgren, Zac Imel, David Atkins, Padhraic Smyth, and Vivek Srikumar. 2015. Recursive Neural Networks for Coding Therapist and Patient Behavior in Motivational Interviewing. *2nd Workshop on Computational Linguistics and Clinical Psychology: From Linguistic Signal to Clinical Reality*, pages 71–79.

Karin Verspoor, Kevin Bretonnel Cohen, Arrick Lanfranchi, Colin Warner, Helen L Johnson, Christophe Roeder, Jinho D Choi, Christopher Funk, Yuriy Malenkiy, Miriam Eckert, et al. 2012. A corpus of full-text journal articles is a robust evaluation tool for revealing differences in performance of biomedical natural language processing tools. *BMC bioinformatics*, 13(1):1.

StÉphanie Wahab. 2005. Motivational interviewing and social work practice. *Journal of Social Work*, 5(1):45–60.

Bo Xiao, Daniel Bone, Maarten Van Segbroeck, Zac E Imel, David C Atkins, Panayiotis G Georgiou, and Shrikanth S Narayanan. 2014. Modeling therapist empathy through prosody in drug addiction counseling. In *Fifteenth Annual Conference of the International Speech Communication Association*.

Crazy Mad Nutters: The Language of Mental Health

Jena D. Hwang and **Kristy Hollingshead**
Institute for Human and Machine Cognition (IHMC)
Ocala, FL 34470, USA
`{jhwang,kseitz}@ihmc.us`

Abstract

Many people with mental illnesses face challenges posed by stigma perpetuated by fear and misconception in society at large. This societal stigma against mental health conditions is present in everyday language. In this study we take a set of 14 words with the potential to stigmatize mental health and sample Twitter as an approximation of contemporary discourse. Annotation reveals that these words are used with different senses, from expressive to stigmatizing to clinical. We use these word-sense annotations to extract a set of mental health–aware Twitter users, and compare their language use to that of an age- and gender-matched comparison set of users, discovering a difference in frequency of stigmatizing senses as well as a change in the target of pejorative senses. Such analysis may provide a first step towards a tool with the potential to help everyday people to increase awareness of their own stigmatizing language, and to measure the effectiveness of anti-stigma campaigns to change our discourse.

1 Introduction

The World Health Organization (WHO) estimates that one in four people worldwide will suffer from a mental illness at some point in their lives (World Health Organization, 2011). One in five Americans experience a mental health problem in any given year (Kessler et al., 2007; Substance Abuse and Mental Health Services Administration, 2014). Many people with a mental illness experience social and economic hardship as a direct result of their illness. They must cope with their symptoms, but also

with the stigma and discrimination that result from misconceptions about such illnesses (McNair et al., 2002; Corrigan et al., 2003). In fact, the stigma and discrimination related to mental illnesses have been described as having worse consequences than the conditions of the mental illnesses themselves, contributing to people's hesitation to seek treatment for a mental health condition (Corrigan et al., 2014).

Many studies in Linguistics and Cognitive Science have shown that word choice and language use have direct influences on the speaker's thought and actions (c.f., linguistic relativism (Boroditsky, 2011; Berlin and Kay, 1991; Lakoff, 1990)). Word choice and the context to which the words are attributed serve to foster stigma and prejudice toward people with mental health conditions, trivializing serious mental health conditions and their accompanying experiences. Anti-stigma campaigns, designed to raise public awareness of mental stigma, have in recent years focused on bringing public attention to the negative impact of the choice of their words. For example, reporters are advised that, as with any disparaging words related to race and ethnicity, some words should never be used in reporting, including 'crazy', 'nuts', 'lunatic', 'deranged', 'psycho', and 'wacko'. The premise behind anti-stigma campaigns is that increased awareness of the detrimental effects of stigmatizing language associated with mental health will help the public become more judicious in their word choice and, consequently, change their attitudes and behaviors toward mental illnesses and those suffering from them.

One might ask, then, whether these anti-stigma campaigns are effective; are they changing the dis-

Proceedings of the 3rd Workshop on Computational Linguistics and Clinical Psychology: From Linguistic Signal to Clinical Reality, pages 52–62,
San Diego, California, June 16, 2016. ©2016 Association for Computational Linguistics

course, particularly around mental health? Evidence seems to indicate that interventions to reduce stigma are occasionally effective in the short term (Thornicroft et al., 2015). As a first step in addressing this question empirically, we explore 14 of the common terms that have been the focus of a number of anti-stigma campaigns, such as 'crazy', 'mental', or 'psycho', that can be used in a derogatory or pejorative manner. We evaluate if indeed awareness of mental illnesses encourages a more restrained use of these words, either avoiding the words entirely or reducing the use of a word in its stigmatizing sense.

For data, we turn to social media, a platform used by nearly four billion people[1] worldwide. Social media platforms offer an uncensored, unscripted view of the ongoing discourse of the online generation, thus providing a source for analyzing contemporary language use. In particular for this study, we focus on public posts to Twitter.

The paper is structured as follows: we begin with a brief discussion of related work, and present our methods and motivation for gathering social media data from Twitter in a two-stage process. We then inventory the various word senses discovered in the data for each of 14 stigmatizing words related to mental health. We discuss our annotation process, beginning with finer-grained senses and moving to a coarser-grained sense inventory for comparison across the set of stigmatizing words. We show the results of word sense analysis across two different sets of social media users, demonstrating that a user's mental health awareness may be reflected in the use – or lack thereof – of stigmatizing language. Finally, we conclude the paper with a few potential applications of this technology.

2   Related Work

There has recently been an explosion in work using technology to detect and characterize various aspects of individuals with mental health disorders, particularly online (Ayers et al., 2013; Yang et al., 2010; Hausner et al., 2008) and on social media (Coppersmith et al., 2014; De Choudhury, 2013; Nguyen et al., 2014; Schwartz et al., 2013). Many social media users post about their own health conditions, including physical conditions such as can-

cer or the flu (Paul and Dredze, 2011; Dredze, 2012; Hawn, 2009), but also mental health conditions such as depression (Ramirez-Esparza et al., 2008; De Choudhury et al., 2013; Park et al., 2012), bipolar disorder (Kramer et al., 2004), schizophrenia (Mitchell et al., 2015), and a wide range of other mental health conditions (Coppersmith et al., 2015).

In contrast to this previous work, which analyzed the language use of social media users with mental health conditions, we focus on the use of language related to mental health, regardless of the social media users' mental health status. Reavley and Pilkington (2014) also examined Twitter data related specifically to stigma associated with depression and schizophrenia. Similarly, Joseph et al. (2015) analyzed the sentiment and tone in tweets containing the hashtags #schizophrenia and #schizophrenic, and compared these to tweets containing the hashtags #diabetes and #diabetic, in order to determine the difference in attitude toward an often-stigmatized illness like schizophrenia versus an un-stigmatized physical illness like diabetes. The study discovered that tweets referencing schizophrenia were twice as likely to be negative as tweets referencing diabetes, and that Twitter users were more likely to use humorous or sarcastic language in association with the adjective schizophrenic than with diabetic.

Our work has a broader scope than this previous work, in that we examine stigmatizing language related to a wide range of mental health conditions. The closest work to ours is that of Collins (2015), wherein she conducted a historical topic- and co-occurrence analysis of hashtags #insane, #psycho, '#schizo, and #nutter on Twitter. In this work, we add to this list, as described in the next section (see Table 1), and extend the analysis to include a broader examination of language use.

This work also borrows from annotation methods widely used in natural language processing. The process of annotation includes a linguistic analysis of data, the development of annotation standards or guidelines, and the manual tagging of the data with the set standards. Such annotation methods have been used in annotating data for lexical (Duffield et al., 2010), semantic (Schneider et al., 2015; Hwang et al., 2014; Hwang et al., 2010; Palmer et al., 2005), and syntactic (Marcus et al., 1994) tasks.

---

[1] http://www.statisticbrain.com/social-networking-statistics/

3   Stigmatizing Words

In this study, we focus on 14 words with the potential to stigmatize mental health, which we will refer to as *stigmatizing words*. Table 1 contains a list of the stigmatizing words used in this study.

bonkers	insane	mad	nuts	schizo
crazy	loony	mental	nutter	wacko
deranged	lunatic	nutcase	psycho	

Table 1: Stigmatizing words used for keyword search.

Starting from the 4 words 'insane', 'psycho', 'schizo', and 'nutter' as studied by Collins (2015), we extended the list by including words that are often cited as problematic terminology by various anti-stigma campaigns to arrive at our list of 14. In particular, we focused on the terminologies discussed in various blog entries, articles, or publications by National Alliance on Mental Illness (NAMI), Time to Change, and HealthyPlace[2].

4   Twitter Data

All of the data in this study comes from publicly available Twitter data collected using the Twitter API. The data was collected in two stages.

4.1   Keyword-Based Data

In the first stage, we obtained two months' (July and August 2015) worth of tweets based on a keyword search of the 14 stigmatizing words. We will refer to the set of tweets collected using this keyword-based search as the *seed set*. This collection contains over 27 million tweets. Once extracted, the seed set was then filtered to remove tweets containing the label RT (retweets) or URLs, on the assumption that such tweets often contain text not authored by the user. Tweets were also filtered to select only those marked by Twitter as English (i.e., "en" or "en-gb"). In order to exclude instances where stigmatizing words show up in the user handle (e.g., @crazygirl), user mentions (@s) were removed for the purposes of filtering. Finally, any exact-match duplicates among the set of tweets were removed for purposes of annotation. The final, filtered set consists of just over 840k tweets. Of these, 'nuts' and 'crazy' make up over

20% of the dataset, each; 'mad' is the next most frequent, at 13%, with 'psycho'; 'insane', and 'mental' following behind with 7-11% each. 'Bonkers' and 'lunatic' each comprise 3% of the data; 'nutter' and 'deranged' are less than 2% of the data, while the remaining words – 'loony', 'nutcase', 'schizo', and 'wacko' – each comprise less than 1% of the filtered seed set.

For each stigmatizing word, 100 random tweets containing the word were selected for annotation. Each selected tweet was manually analyzed to establish an inventory of types and varieties of meanings or *senses* of the words as used in the tweets (see Section 5 for further discussion). Based on the established senses, whenever a tweet was used in a clinical sense of the word, the tweet was considered to originate from a *mental health aware* (MHA) user. Users that did not have any clinical usages were considered to be *mental health unaware* (MHU) users. Table 2 provides a few example tweets for several of the stigmatizing words.

4.2   User-Based Data

The second-stage dataset, which we refer to as the *user-based set*, is constructed from tweets posted publicly by a set of users. For this dataset, we began by using the tweets annotated as MHA to extract a list of Twitter users that had minimally used mental health aware language in at least one tweet. As the tweets typically contained specific references to mental health or mental issues, we make the assumption that these users may be more sensitive to the existing stigma or prejudices towards mental health disorders. We term this set of users the MHA users.

We then extract a set of users for comparison. Generally, a comparison set would be generated based on a random selection of Twitter users. In our case, we limit that selection to users who tweeted any of the stigmatizing words from Table 1 in a non-clinical sense during the collection time period (July-August 2015) and did not use the stigmatizing words in a clinical sense during that time period, and thus do not belong to the MHA user group. We term these users the MHU users. The set of MHU users is much larger than MHA users: 686 versus 60, respectively. We additionally down-selected within the MHU set to form an age- and gender-matched comparison set, based on evidence that failing to ac-

---

[2]https://www.nami.org/,   http://www.time-to-change.org.uk/, and http://www.healthyplace.com/, respectively

"I'm fuming. How dare a TV show portray folks suffering from **mental** health issues so unfairly? As if there isn't already enough stigma around."

"this is exactly why I think JH is borderline personality disorder. seems to fit. no one wanted 2 look at lesser **mental** issue."

"I don't even score high on **schizo** symptoms and that's what bothers me most besides mood issues"

"Ha... apparently according to my **Schizo** voices (audio hallucinations) some of them went out on the piss while I was asleep"

"A lot of Americans are injured for them to portray one person as '**insane** or mentally ill' "

"If you think negatively about yourself, this should help. Im certifiably **nuts**. I know these things."

Table 2: Examples of tweets using stigmatizing words in their clinical sense.

count for age and gender can yield biased comparison groups that may skew results (Dos Reis and Culotta, 2015). To create an approximately matched comparison set, we take each user in our full MHA and MHU sets, and obtain age and gender estimates for each from the tools provided by the World Well-Being Project (Sap et al., 2014). These tools use lexica derived from Facebook data to identify demographics, and have been shown to be successful on Twitter data (Coppersmith et al., 2015). Then, in order to select the best comparison set, we selected (without replacement) the MHU user with the same gender label and closest in age to each of the MHA users.

We use a balanced dataset here for our analysis, by selecting an equal number of MHA users and comparison MHU users for our analysis. In practice and as stated above, we found approximately an order of magnitude difference between MHA and MHU users. Our selection of a balanced set enables simpler machine learning classification efforts, and helps to demonstrate the language differences between the two groups more clearly than if we had examined a dataset more representative of the population ($\sim$1/10). Our results should be taken as validation that the differences in language we observe are relevant to mental health awareness, but only one step towards applying something derived from this research as a tool in a real world scenario.

For each of the MHA users and the age- and gender-matched MHU users, we retrieved all of their most recent public tweets via the Twitter API, up to 3200 tweets.[3] Just as in the previous data collection stage, the data was filtered to select only tweets marked as English, to remove retweets and tweets containing URLs, and to remove user mentions (@s). Preprocessing of the data removed any exact-match duplicates among the filtered tweets.

From this new set of user-based tweets, we extracted each tweet containing any of the stigmatizing words. We then annotated the instances of the stigmatizing words in these extracted tweets with the senses developed in the previous stage (Section 4.1). We achieved a relatively high inter-annotator agreement rates: Cohen's kappa value of 0.74 (IAA = 86.8%) on the MHA tweets and 0.64 (IAA = 80.6%) on MHU tweets.

5   Sense Inventory for Stigmatizing Words

As mentioned in the previous section, the seed set was used to develop an inventory of fine-grained senses for each of the stigmatizing words. Instances annotated with a clinical sense were marked as *MHA tweets* and used to develop a user-based dataset. Subsequently, in order to facilitate a comparison of senses as used across stigmatizing words, the fine-grained senses were binned into coarse-grained senses. This process is detailed below.

5.1   Fine-Grained Sense Inventory

We began with the definitions provided by Merriam-Webster[4] as a basis for our initial sense inven-

---

[3] 3200 is the maximum number of historic tweets permitted by the API.

[4] http://www.merriam-webster.com/

Sense Definition	Example
Crazy	
1. irrational, crazy	"Maybe I shouldn't be revealing this **crazy** part of me..."
2. excitement	"Got the club going **crazy**!"
3. odd, unusual	"These cigar wraps are **crazy**"
4. extreme	"I miss my best friend like **crazy**."
5. intensifier	"Smh my luck has been **crazy** bad lately"
6. exclamation	"Crazy!"
7. name or label	"Codeine **crazy** goes down in some of the greatest songs ever wrote."
Mad	
1. angry, upset	"@user I'm **mad** at you for being so cute"
2. irrational, crazy	"Keep coughing like a **mad** woman"
3. extreme	"That's a **mad** show"
4. intensifier	"Why is everyone in Chile **mad** good at singing?"
5. exclamation	"**Mad**!" *(akin to "Crazy!")*
6. names or labels	"I just started thinking about a scene from **Mad** Men"
Mental	
1. clinical usage	"**Mental** health awareness is something near and dear to my heart."
2. of the mind	"Emancipate yourselves from **mental** slavery. "
3. irrational, crazy	"People are going **mental** about this lion being killed. "
Nuts	
1. irrational, crazy	"When my mom went **nuts** on my sister for playing hooky..."
2. odd, unusual	"Back to back is **nuts** but meek is about to MURDER it."
3. testicles	"Cassandra showed me her dog's **nuts**"
4. exclamation	"Aw **nuts** -_-"
5. fruit	"i don't understand why all my office's snacks have **nuts** in them."
6. 'deez nuts'	"if i had a dollar for every time i heard a kid yell "deez **nuts**" at camp i would be rich"
7. clinical use	"Why do you have you Dr's personal cell in your phone?" Uh because I'm **nuts**."
8. building parts	"The **nuts** and bolts for this will be proper implementation and effective evaluation"
Schizo	
1. irrational	"@user Total **schizo** ... I can't imagine using anything other than TweetBot."
2. clinical usage	"I was diagnosed w/addiction once, but turned out I was **schizo**. "
3. names or labels	"I added a video to a playlist **Schizo** BP2635 Brothers Pyrotechnics NEW FOR 2016"

Table 3: Examples of fine-grained sense inventory for the 5 most polysemous words of the 14 stigmatizing words analyzed.

tory. We then made two annotation passes to include missing senses, further refine existing senses, or remove senses as dictated by our annotation of the Twitter data. On average, 4 different senses were identified for the stigmatizing words, ranging from highly polysemous words with 6-8 senses like 'crazy' and 'mad' to words with 1-2 senses like 'deranged' and 'nutcase'. Table 3 shows the sense inventory for the more polysemous words in this study.

As expected, the most common sense for all of the stigmatizing words is the meaning of irrationality or a state of being "not 'right' in one's mind", in reference to a human (e.g., 'crazy' sense 1, 'mad' sense 2, or 'mental' sense 3 in Table 3). Another fairly common meaning includes the state of unusual excitement as attributed to situations (e.g., 'crazy' sense 2 or 'nuts' sense 2) or objects (e.g., 'crazy' sense 3). Note that senses that indicate that someone or something is irrational, extreme, or unusual are considered stigmatizing usages that anti-stigma campaigns highlight.

Additionally, we observe two common functional usages. First is the adverbial usages that function as intensifiers to the adjective the word precedes. For example "crazy bad" in 'crazy' sense 5 and "mad good" in 'mad' sense 4 serve to highlight or reinforce the intensity of the adjectives 'bad' and 'good', respectively. Second common functional use is the expressive usage as seen for 'crazy' sense 6, 'mad' sense 5, or 'nuts' sense 4. Rather than offering a descriptive content, these expressive serve to convey a certain emotional perspective of the speaker.[5]

Out of the 14 words, only five showed instances that were used in the clinical sense of the word : 'mental' (sense 1), 'nuts' (sense 7), 'psycho' (sense 3), 'insane' (sense 4), and 'schizo' (sense 2). These clinical senses mark the MHA tweets, from which the user-based set was generated as detailed in Section 4.2.

5.2 Coarse-Grained Sense Inventory

If we are to analyze the stigmatizing words and their senses to compare their usage in MHA tweets and MHU tweets, we will find that fine-grained senses pose a difficulty. Consider the senses in Table 3. The words 'schizo' and 'mental', for example, have three senses each, but a sense for one word does not always have a counterpart for the other. Additionally, comparison of usage between highly-polysemous 'nuts' and three-sense 'mental' would require an additional layer of analysis to bridge the differences.

In an effort to make an apples-to-apples comparison of these words, we developed a set of coarse-grained senses that can be applied to all of the stigmatizing words. Fine-grained senses were then mapped to one of five coarse-grained (CGd) senses. Table 4 shows the list of coarse-grained senses.

A.	term applied to sentient beings (often in a derogatory manner)
B.	term applied to an object, situation, or world in general
C.	**clinical usage**
D.	homonymous usage
E.	other senses

Table 4: Coarse-grained (CGd) senses for stigmatizing words.

Sense A, B and C are the relevant senses for our study. Senses A and B capture the stigmatizing sense of the word applied to sentient beings (e.g., humans, pets, etc.) and to objects or situations. Clinical or medical usages of the words are assigned to sense C. To take 'nuts' as an example, sense 1

was mapped to CGd sense A, senses 2 and 4 were mapped to CGd sense B, and sense 7 was mapped to coarse sense C.

Sense D is for homonymous usage like 'mad' sense 1 (i.e. anger in 'I'm mad at you!") or 'nuts' sense 5 (i.e. fruit in "These snacks have nuts in them"). Sense E is a miscellaneous category that includes senses unrelated to the central senses of the word (e.g., a "names and labels" senses) or instances where the sense of the word was not identifiable or unclear (e.g., "tin nuts"). In the case of 'nuts', senses 3 and 5 were mapped to CGd sense D, and senses 6 and 8 were mapped to CGd sense E.

6 MHA vs. MHU

6.1 Stigmatizing Word and Sense Use

In evaluating occurrences of stigmatizing words in MHA and MHU datasets, we find that, on the whole, the MHA users do use these words less frequently when compared to the MHU users. Table 5 shows the total count of tweets in the MHA and MHU datasets for each of the stigmatizing words.[6]

In fact, the number of MHU tweets appears to be nearly double that of MHA tweets. The sheer *lack* of the use of stigmatizing words in MHA suggests that the user's mental health awareness is likely to cause them to be more sensitive towards the stigmatization of those suffering from mental illness. Consequently, they are more likely to shy away from impulsive use of the stigmatizing words.

There are two exceptions to the observation that MHA users use stigmatizing words with less frequency. They are boldfaced in Table 5. The use of the words 'mental' and 'schizo' show higher usage of stigmatized words by the MHA set. However, if we focus on the numbers relevant to the stigmatizing senses (i.e., CGd senses A and B) the story becomes more clear. The leftmost columns of the table show that the majority of uses of the word 'mental' are in fact the clinical sense (CGd sense C). Additionally, note that the use of these words in a clinical sense by MHU users indicates that our original classification of MHU users is imperfect; by our definition, each of the MHU users producing these clinical-sense words should be classified as an MHA user. Since our seed set dataset and our user-based

---

[5]For example, "Aw nuts!" expresses certain set of emotions (e.g., regret, displeasure) as is relevant to the speaker for the immediate situation, rather than ascribing a descriptive meaning to something or someone.

[6]These counts do not include the homonymous sense D.

	Occurrences		Clinical Use	
	MHA	MHU	MHA	MHU
bonkers	2	19		
crazy	152	252		
deranged	0	12		
insane	24	54	0	1
loony	1	7		
lunatic	0	17		
mad*	22	91		
mental	267	**86**	233	45
nutcase	2	17		
nuts*	7	46	3	2
nutter	1	7		
psycho	17	34	3	0
schizo	12	**9**	9	2
total	489	631	248	50
total (all senses)	610	776		
total (A & B only)	204	503		

Table 5: Word counts of potentially-stigmatizing words in MHA and MHU tweets. An asterisk (*) indicates that the coarse-grained sense D (homonyms) for the word has been removed for this count.

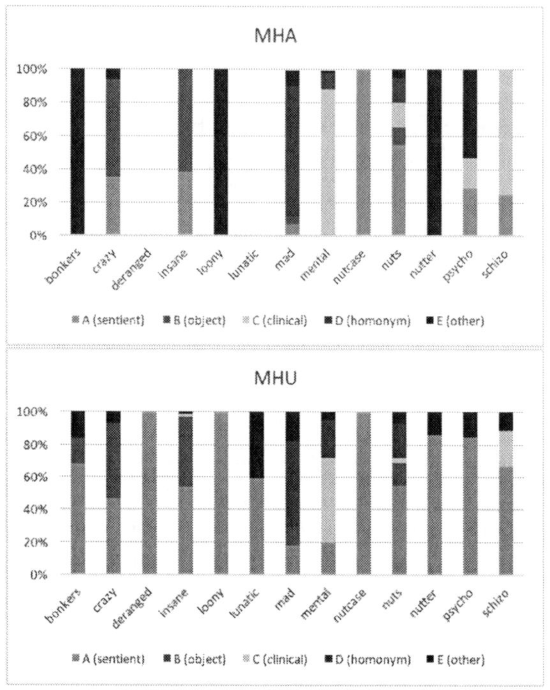

Figure 1: Visualizing coarse-grained senses for stigmatizing words as found in MHA and MHU datasets.

dataset were pulled from Twitter at different time points, approximately six months apart, our classification of MHA and MHU users could be and indeed was occasionally incorrect: MHA users might not have produced another clinical-sense stigmatizing word in the user-based dataset, and MHU users might have used such a sense, perhaps due to becoming more mental health–aware over time.

Figure 1 better visualizes the various senses of each of the stigmatizing words from each of the user groups. Consider the uses of 'mental' and 'schizo' as visualized in Figure 1 for MHA and MHU tweets. For MHA tweets, the most prominent sense of 'mental' is the clinical sense C, while the stigmatizing sense A is used very infrequently. For MHU, however, while there is a large portion of clinical sense C associated with the use of 'mental', it is not as large as that in the MHA set. Sense A also shows up with higher frequency in the MHU set. The same trend can be seen for the word 'schizo'. MHA users do not use stigmatizing sense A as often as the clinical sense C, and the reverse is true for MHU users. As it turns out, although the MHA tweets show a high use of the words 'mental' and 'schizo', most of the usage is attributed to the medical sense. The stigmatizing senses only make up 1% and 25% of the total MHA tweets for 'mental' and 'schizo', respectively, which is considerably lower than the MHU set's stigmatizing sense use, at 20% and 67% for 'mental' and 'schizo', respectively.

Beyond 'mental' and 'schizo', what Figure 1 visually captures is the prominence of the stigmatizing sense A in the MHU group. While sense A does also occur in MHA tweets, the sense is not as prevalent as in the MHU set. The only apparent counter-example in Figure 1 is that of 'nutcase': its only usage is that of sense A in the MHA data. However, note that in Table 5 there were only 2 instances of this word in use, too little data to draw a conclusion.

6.2 Visual Language Analysis

From the previous section, we learned that stigmatizing words do seem to be used differently by MHA and MHU users. In this section, we look to characterize language differences more broadly, by analyzing the set of MHA and MHU tweets as a whole. To do so, we took all of the MHA and MHU tweets gathered for the user-based dataset, extracted the tweets containing any of the 14 stigmatizing words, – all of which had been annotated for their coarse-

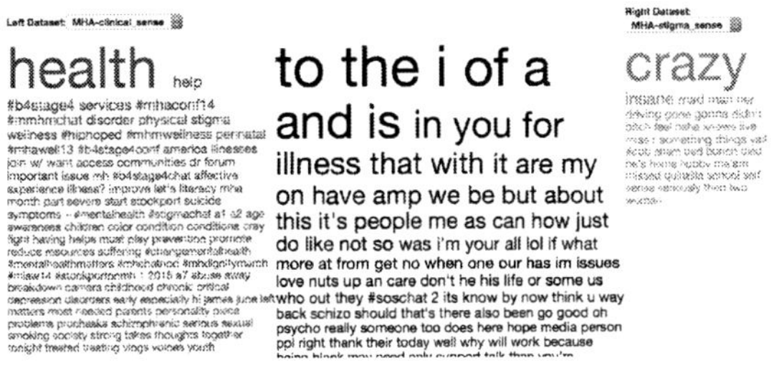

Figure 2: Vennclouds for all tweets containing the 14 stigmatizing words, as tweeted by MHA users, with words from tweets containing clinical senses of the words appearing on the left (blue text), stigmatizing senses of the words appearing on the right (red text), and the language shared by tweets containing either sense in the middle (black text).

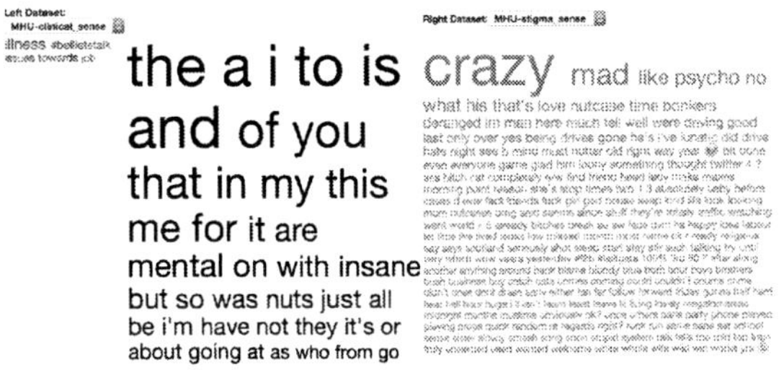

Figure 3: Vennclouds for all tweets containing the 14 stigmatizing words, as tweeted by MHU users, with words from tweets containing clinical senses of the words appearing on the left (blue text), stigmatizing senses of the words appearing on the right (red text), and the language shared by tweets containing either sense in the middle (black text).

grained (CGd) sense – and generated dynamic Vennclouds (Coppersmith and Kelly, 2014) to compare clinical-sense tweets to stigmatizing-sense tweets. Figures 2 and 3 display the resulting clouds.

From these clouds, one might note immediately that in Figure 2, the blue (leftmost) cloud is much larger than the red (rightmost), while the reverse is true in Figure 3. This simply visualizes what was previously quantified in Table 5: MHA users tend to produce more tweets containing clinical sense of the stigmatizing words, whereas MHU users tend to produce more tweets containing stigmatizing senses.

The mere presence of a blue cloud in Figure 3 demonstrates that there was some use of clinical-sense stigmatizing words from the MHU users, who therefore ought to have been categorized as MHA, as previously discussed in Section 6.1. However, on the whole, the simplistic classification of users based on clinical-sense usage held up relatively well.

Both Vennclouds show that 'crazy' was the most frequently-occurring word in stigmatized-sense tweets, shown as the largest, first word in the red (rightmost) clouds of both Figures 2 and 3, with 'mad' as the third- and second-most frequent word, respectively. In fact, these words were never used in a clinical-sense tweet by either of the user groups. This analysis shows quantitatively that, to be more aware of our own uses of stigmatizing senses, we ought to pay particular attention to these words, as the worst offenders from both groups.

The word 'health' is clearly visible as the most frequently-occurring word in the clinical-sense tweets produced by the MHA users, shown as the largest, first word in the blue (leftmost) cloud of Figure 2, with 'help', 'services', 'disorder', and 'stigma' close behind. Perhaps more interesting is the long list of hashtags that appear with high frequency in the clinical-sense tweets from the MHA users, including #b4stage4, #mhaconf14, #mmhmchat, #mhmwellness, #mhawell – all clearly related to mental health, and mental health awareness. This analysis again supports our simplistic classification of users, but additionally gives us a source we could use for another data pull. By simply looking for clinical senses of these stigmatizing words, we discovered clear communities of mental health–aware users.

7 Conclusion & Future Work

In this study we have investigated 14 common terms, used in everyday language, with the potential for stigmatizing mental illnesses in society. We were specifically interested in evaluating if awareness of mental illnesses can help discourage impulsive uses of the pejorative senses of the words. Our findings show that MHA users less frequently use stigmatizing words than MHU users, and when they do use the stigmatizing words, they use the stigmatizing senses less often than their MHU counterparts. Additionally, MHA users tend to structure their language so as to avoid applying the derogatory sense to a sentient being, and use the clinical sense of the stigmatizing word more often than MHU users. The absence of stigmatizing words or, more specifically, stigmatizing senses by MHA users suggests that the user's mental health awareness contributes to how they employ language in social media, demonstrating a degree of sensitivity towards stigmatization of those with mental illnesses.

Directions for our future work concern the improvement of methods for determining the MHA user group. Our current approach identifies MHA if they show one MHA tweet in the seed data. Unfortunately, basing whether or not a user should is MHA is based on a single tweet does not leave room for the false positive cases, where an otherwise unaware user might have tweeted a aware sounding tweet. Conversely, because the pull for seed set and user-based set were several months apart, there also may have been false negatives – MHU users that should have been classified in the user-based set as MHA users. Most immediate way to address this issue is to experiment by setting a threshold greater than one before a user is considered MHA. We will also look into taking advantage of hashtags related to mental health campaigns to identify users who are intentionally identifying themselves as a part of mental health community. Finally, we intend to also experiment with identifying users that have self-identified as having a mental condition or being a part of mental health community (Coppersmith et al., 2015) as a means of identifying the MHA group.

Another future direction of this work is in further analysis and revision of coarse-grained senses. As discussed in Section 5.1, one of the more frequent fine-grained senses we found are expressives (e.g. "Aww **nuts**!") and intensifiers (e.g. "That's **crazy** good"). These are currently grouped in with the coarse-grained sense B – one of the two stigmatizing senses, but unlike the rest of the fine-grained senses also grouped in B, these usages serve the function of expressing speaker's emotion or emphasizing a descriptive adverbial, rather than carrying a descriptive or content information. In future work, we will look into distinguishing these types of senses from others to determine if indeed these could be considered stigmatizing senses and whether or not these usages are indicative of mental health awareness.

One might imagine several uses for detecting potentially-stigmatizing language. We could use it to warn social media users that their language might been seen as stigmatizing, and offer an opportunity to re-word, similar to the "self-flagging app" mentioned in (Quinn, 2014) to detect potentially offensive or bullying language (Dinakar et al., 2012). This option provides a somewhat heavy-handed method to increase mental health awareness. The ability to automatically detect stigmatizing senses of these (and other) words might also be useful as a filter, to downweight or hide posts containing stigmatizing words, or add a warning or reporting function like Facebook's "offensive content" reporting utility, for stigmatizing language. In this way, users can choose to avoid such language, in case it might trigger negative reactions.

Finally, an automated analysis of the senses in use for potentially-stigmatizing words in everyday language might provide a method to assess whether anti-stigma campaigns are effective. Have we changed the discourse, and if so, in what ways? And, importantly, has a change in discourse resulted in easier access to care, better management of crises, and an improved quality of life for those with mental health conditions? Addressing these questions might shed light on the strengths and weaknesses of the current anti-stigma efforts, and help in guiding future work to end the stigma of mental illness.

Acknowledgments

The authors thank the anonymous reviewers for their thoughtful critiques. Kristy was partially supported in her work by the VA Office of Rural Health Program "Increasing access to pulmonary function testing for rural veterans with ALS through at home testing" (N08-FY15Q1-S1-P01346). The contents represent solely the views of the authors and do not represent the views of the Department of Veterans Affairs or the United States Government.

References

John W. Ayers, Benjamin M. Althouse, Jon-Patrick Allem, J. Niels Rosenquist, and Daniel E. Ford. 2013. Seasonality in seeking mental health information on Google. *American Journal of Preventive Medicine*, 44(5):520–525.

Brent Berlin and Paul Kay. 1991. *Basic color terms: Their universality and evolution*. Univ of California Press.

Lera Boroditsky. 2011. How language shapes thought. *Scientific American*, 304(2):62–65.

Phoebe Collins. 2015. Words will never hurt me; a study of stigmatizing language in Twitter. Via personal communication, 2015-07-12.

Glen Coppersmith and Erin Kelly. 2014. Dynamic word-clouds and Vennclouds for exploratory data analysis. In *Proceedings of the Workshop on Interactive Language Learning, Visualization, and Interfaces*, pages 22–29, Baltimore, Maryland, USA, June. Association for Computational Linguistics.

Glen Coppersmith, Mark Dredze, and Craig Harman. 2014. Quantifying mental health signals in Twitter. In *Proceedings of the ACL Workshop on Computational Linguistics and Clinical Psychology: From Linguistic Signal to Clinical Reality (CLPsych)*.

Glen Coppersmith, Mark Dredze, Craig Harman, and Kristy Hollingshead. 2015. From ADHD to SAD: Analyzing the language of mental health on Twitter through self-reported diagnoses. In *Proceedings of the 2nd Workshop on Computational Linguistics and Clinical Psychology: From Linguistic Signal to Clinical Reality (CLPsych)*, pages 1–10, Denver, Colorado, June 5. Association for Computational Linguistics.

Patrick Corrigan, Vetta Thompson, David Lambert, Yvette Sangster, Jeffrey G. Noel, and Jean Campbell. 2003. Perceptions of discrimination among persons with serious mental illness. *Psychiatric Services*.

Patrick W. Corrigan, Benjamin G. Druss, and Deborah A. Perlick. 2014. The impact of mental illness stigma on seeking and participating in mental health care. *Psychological Science in the Public Interest*, 15(2):37–70.

Munmun De Choudhury, Michael Gamon, Scott Counts, and Eric Horvitz. 2013. Predicting depression via social media. In *Proceedings of the 7th International AAAI Conference on Weblogs and Social Media (ICWSM)*.

Munmun De Choudhury. 2013. Role of social media in tackling challenges in mental health. In *Proceedings of the 2nd International Workshop on Socially-Aware Multimedia*.

Karthik Dinakar, Birago Jones, Catherine Havasi, Henry Lieberman, and Rosalind Picard. 2012. Common sense reasoning for detection, prevention, and mitigation of cyberbullying. *ACM Transactions on Interactive Intelligent Systems (TiiS)*, 2(3):18.

Virgile Landeiro Dos Reis and Aron Culotta. 2015. Using matched samples to estimate the effects of exercise on mental health from Twitter. In *Proceedings of the Twenty-Ninth AAAI Conference on Artificial Intelligence*.

Mark Dredze. 2012. How social media will change public health. *IEEE Intelligent Systems*, 27(4):81–84.

Cecily Jill Duffield, Jena D. Hwang, and Laura A. Michaelis. 2010. Identifying assertions in text and discourse: The presentational relative clause construction. In *Proceedings of Extracting and Using Constructions in Computational Linguistic Workshop held in conjunction wi th NAACL HLT 2010*, Los Angeles, California, June.

Helmut Hausner, Göran Hajak, and Hermann Spießl. 2008. Gender differences in help-seeking behavior on two internet forums for individuals with self-reported depression. *Gender Medicine*, 5(2):181–185.

Carleen Hawn. 2009. Take two aspirin and tweet me in the morning: How Twitter, Facebook, and other social media are reshaping health care. *Health Affairs*, 28(2):361–368.

Jena D. Hwang, Archna Bhatia, Claire Bonial, Aous Mansouri, Ashwini Vaidya, Nianwen Xue, and Martha Palmer. 2010. PropBank annotation of multilingual light verb constructions. In *Proceedings of the Fourth Linguistic Annotation Workshop*, pages 82–90, Uppsala, Sweden, July. Association for Computational Linguistics.

Jena D. Hwang, Annie Zaenen, and Martha Palmer. 2014. Criteria for identifying and annotating caused motion constructions in corpus data. In *Proceedings of the Ninth International Conference on Language Resources and Evaluation (LREC'14)*, Reykjavik, Iceland.

Adam J. Joseph, Neeraj Tandon, Lawrence H. Yang, Ken Duckworth, John Torous, Larry J. Seidman, and Matcheri S. Keshavan. 2015. #Schizophrenia: Use and misuse on Twitter. *Schizophrenia Research*, 165(2):111–115.

Ronald C. Kessler, Matthias Angermeyer, James C. Anthony, Ron De Graaf, Koen Demyttenaere, Isabelle Gasquet, Giovanni De Girolamo, Semyon Gluzman, Oye Gureje, Josep Maria Haro, Norito Kawakami, Aimee Karam, Daphna Levinson, Maria Elena Medina Mora, Mark A. Oakley Browne, José Posada-Villa, Dan J. Stein, Cheuk Him Adley Tsang, Sergio Aguilar-Gaxiola, Jordi Alonso, Sing Lee, Steven Heeringa, Beth-Ellen Pennell, Patricia Berglund, Michael J. Gruber, Maria Petukhova, and Somnath Chatterji. 2007. Lifetime prevalence and age-of-onset distributions of mental disorders in the World Health Organization's world mental health survey initiative. *World Psychiatry*, 6(3):168.

Adam D. I. Kramer, Susan R. Fussell, and Leslie D. Setlock. 2004. Text analysis as a tool for analyzing conversation in online support groups. In *Proceedings of the ACM Annual Conference on Human Factors in Computing Systems (CHI)*.

George Lakoff. 1990. *Women, fire, and dangerous things: What categories reveal about the mind*. Cambridge Univ Press.

Mitchell Marcus, Grace Kim, Mary Ann Marcinkiewicz, Robert Macintyre, Ann Bies, Mark Ferguson, Karen Katz, and Britta Schasberger. 1994. The Penn Treebank: Annotating predicate argument structure. In *ARPA Human Language Technology Workshop*, pages 114–119.

Bernard G. McNair, Nicole J. Highet, Ian B. Hickie, and Tracey A. Davenport. 2002. Exploring the perspectives of people whose lives have been affected by depression. *Medical Journal of Australia*, 176(Suppl)(10):S69–S76.

Margaret Mitchell, Kristy Hollingshead, and Glen Coppersmith. 2015. Quantifying the language of schizophrenia in social media. In *Proceedings of the 2nd Workshop on Computational Linguistics and Clinical Psychology: From Linguistic Signal to Clinical Reality (CLPsych)*, pages 11–20, Denver, Colorado, June. Association for Computational Linguistics.

Thin Nguyen, Dinh Phung, Bo Dao, Svetha Venkatesh, and Michael Berk. 2014. Affective and content analysis of online depression communities. *IEEE Transactions on Affective Computing*, 5(3):217–226.

Martha Palmer, Dan Guildea, and Paul Kingsbury. 2005. The Proposition Bank: An annotated corpus of semantic roles. *Computational Linguistics*, 31(1):71–105, March.

Minsu Park, Chiyoung Cha, and Meeyoung Cha. 2012. Depressive moods of users portrayed in Twitter. In *Proceedings of the ACM SIGKDD Workshop on Healthcare Informatics (HI-KDD)*.

Michael J. Paul and Mark Dredze. 2011. You are what you tweet: Analyzing Twitter for public health. In *Proceedings of the 5th International AAAI Conference on Weblogs and Social Media (ICWSM)*.

Cristina Quinn. 2014. MIT algorithm takes aim at social media cyberbullying. http://news.wgbh.org/post/mit-algorithm-takes-aim-social-media-cyberbullying. Accessed 2016-03-01.

Nairan Ramirez-Esparza, Cindy K. Chung, Ewa Kacewicz, and James W. Pennebaker. 2008. The psychology of word use in depression forums in English and in Spanish: Testing two text analytic approaches. In *Proceedings of the 2nd International AAAI Conference on Weblogs and Social Media (ICWSM)*.

Nicola J. Reavley and Pamela D. Pilkington. 2014. Use of Twitter to monitor attitudes toward depression and schizophrenia: an exploratory study. *PeerJ*, 2:e647.

Maarten Sap, Greg Park, Johannes C. Eichstaedt, Margaret L. Kern, David J. Stillwell, Michal Kosinski, Lyle H. Ungar, and H. Andrew Schwartz. 2014. Developing age and gender predictive lexica over social media. In *Proceedings of the Conference on Empirical Methods in Natural Language Processing (EMNLP)*, pages 1146–1151.

Nathan Schneider, Vivek Srikumar, Jena D. Hwang, and Martha Palmer. 2015. A hierarchy with, of, and for preposition supersenses. In *Proceedings of the 9th Linguistic Annotation Workshop*, pages 112–123, Denver, Colorado, USA, June. Association for Computational Linguistics.

H. Andrew Schwartz, Johannes C. Eichstaedt, Margaret L. Kern, Lukasz Dziurzynski, Richard E. Lucas, Megha Agrawal, Gregory J. Park, Shrinidhi K. Lakshmikanth, Sneha Jha, Martin E. P. Seligman, and Lyle H. Ungar. 2013. Characterizing geographic variation in well-being using tweets. In *Proceedings of the 8th International AAAI Conference on Weblogs and Social Media (ICWSM)*.

Substance Abuse and Mental Health Services Administration. 2014. Substance abuse and mental health services administration. In *Results from the 2013 National Survey on Drug Use and Health: Mental Health Findings, NSDUH Series H-49, HHS Publication No. (SMA) 14-4887*. Substance Abuse and Mental Health Services Administration, Rockville, MD.

Graham Thornicroft, Nisha Mehta, Sarah Clement, Sara Evans-Lacko, Mary Doherty, Diana Rose, Mirja Koschorke, Rahul Shidhaye, Claire O'Reilly, and Claire Henderson. 2015. Evidence for effective interventions to reduce mental-health-related stigma and discrimination. *The Lancet*.

World Health Organization. 2011. *The World Health Report 2001 – Mental Health: New Understanding, New Hope*. Geneva: World Health Organization.

Albert C. Yang, Norden E. Huang, Chung-Kang Peng, and Shih-Jen Tsai. 2010. Do seasons have an influence on the incidence of depression? The use of an internet search engine query data as a proxy of human affect. *PLOS ONE*, 5(10):e13728.

The language of mental health problems in social media

George Gkotsis[1,†,*], Anika Oellrich[1,†], Tim JP Hubbard[2], Richard JB Dobson[1,3]
Maria Liakata[4], Sumithra Velupillai[1,5], Rina Dutta[1]
[1]King's College London, IoPPN, London, SE5 8AF, UK
[2]King's College London, Department of Medical & Molecular Genetics, London, SE1 9RT
[3]Farr Institute of Health Informatics Research, London, WC1E 6BT, UK
[4]University of Warwick, Department of Computer Science, Warwick, CV4 7AL, UK
[5]School of Computer Science and Communication, KTH, Stockholm
[†] Authors contributed equally to this work.
[*] Corresponding author. E-mail: george.gkotsis@kcl.ac.uk.

Abstract

Online social media, such as Reddit, has become an important resource to share personal experiences and communicate with others. Among other personal information, some social media users communicate about mental health problems they are experiencing, with the intention of getting advice, support or empathy from other users. Here, we investigate the language of Reddit posts specific to mental health, to define linguistic characteristics that could be helpful for further applications. The latter include attempting to identify posts that need urgent attention due to their nature, e.g. when someone announces their intentions of ending their life by suicide or harming others. Our results show that there are a variety of linguistic features that are discriminative across mental health user communities and that can be further exploited in subsequent classification tasks. Furthermore, while negative sentiment is almost uniformly expressed across the entire data set, we demonstrate that there are also condition-specific vocabularies used in social media to communicate about particular disorders. Source code and related materials are available from: `https://github.com/gkotsis/reddit-mental-health`.

1 Introduction

Mental illnesses are estimated to account for 11% to 27% of the disability burden in Europe (Wykes et al., 2015) and mental and substance use disorders are the leading cause of years lived with disability worldwide (Whiteford et al., 2013). Our knowledge about these mental health problems is still more limited than for many physical conditions, as sufferers may relapse even after successful treatment or exhibit resistance to different treatments. Most mental health conditions begin early, disrupt education (Kessler et al., 1995) and may persist over a lifetime, causing disability when those affected would normally be at their most productive (Kessler and Frank, 1997). For example, Patel and Knapp (1997) estimated the aggregate costs of all mental disorders in the United Kingdom at 32 billion (1996/97 prices), 45% of which was due to lost productivity (Patel and Knapp, 1997). The global burden of mental and substance use disorders increased by 376% between 1990 and 2010 (Whiteford et al., 2013) which means it is an international public health priority to effectively prevent and treat mental health issues.

In the UK, 17% of adults experience a subthreshold common mental disorder (McManus et al., 2009) and up to 30% of individuals with non-psychotic common mental disorders have subthreshold psychotic symptoms (Kelleher et al., 2012) showing that a large proportion of mental illness is unrecognised, but nevertheless has a significant impact upon people's lives. Those people with conditions that meet criteria for diagnosis are treated in primary care or by mental health professionals.

Proceedings of the 3rd Workshop on Computational Linguistics and Clinical Psychology: From Linguistic Signal to Clinical Reality, pages 63–73,
San Diego, California, June 16, 2016. ©2016 Association for Computational Linguistics

Studies consistently show that between 50-60% of all individuals with a serious mental illness receive treatment for their mental health problem at any given time (Kessler et al., 2001).

However, most of the pathology tracking and improvement assessment is done through questionnaires, e.g. the Personal Health Questionnaire 9 (PHQ9) for depression (Kroenke and Spitzer, 2002), and require a subjective comment by the patient, e.g. "How many days have you been bothered with little interest or pleasure in doing things in the past two weeks?". As with every personal judgement, the responses are influenced by the environment in which the person has been asked, the relationship to the clinician and even the stigma attached to depression (Malpass et al., 2010). While there are aims to integrate real-time reporting into a patient's life (Ibrahim et al., 2015), these are still based on set questionnaires and may not fit with the main concerns of a patient.

Social media, such as Twitter[1], Facebook[2] and Reddit[3], have become an accepted platform to communicate about life circumstances and experiences. A specific example of social media in the context of illness is PatientsLikeMe (Wicks et al., 2010). PatientsLikeMe has been developed to enable people suffering from an illness to exchange information with others with the same condition, e.g. to find alternative treatment opportunities. It has been shown that the support received in such online communities can be empowering by engendering self-respect and a feeling of being in control of the situation (Barak et al., 2008). Hence, social media constitutes a tremendous resource for better understanding diseases from a patient perspective.

Social media data has recently been recognised as one of the resources to gather knowledge about mental illnesses (Coppersmith et al., 2015a; De Choudhury et al., 2013; Kumar et al., 2015). For example, Twitter data has been used to develop classifiers to recognise depression in users (De Choudhury et al., 2013) and to classify Twitter users who have attempted suicide from those who have not and from those who are clinically depressed (Coppersmith et al., 2015b). Furthermore, data col-

lected from Reddit pertaining to suicidal ideation could demonstrate the existence of the Werther effect (suicide attempts and completions after media depiction of an individual's suicide) (Kumar et al., 2015). Coppersmith and colleagues used Twitter data to determine language features that could be used to classify Twitter users into suffering from mental health problems and unaffected individuals (Coppersmith et al., 2015a). However, while the authors could identify features that allows the classification between healthy and unhealthy Twitter users, they also note that language differences in communicating about the different mental health problem remains an open question. Similarly, Mitchell et al. (2015) used Twitter data to separate users affected by schizophrenia from healthy individuals by automatically identifying characteristic language features for schizophrenia (Mitchell et al., 2015). Both the latter approaches rely on the Linguistic Inquiry and Word Count (LIWC) (Tausczik and Pennebaker, 2010), but Mitchell et al. also covers features such as Latent Dirichlet Allocation and Brown Clustering. Very recently and concurrently with our own work, De Choudhury and colleagues have shown that linguistic features can be used to predict the likelihood of individuals transitioning from posting about depression and other mental health issues on Reddit to suicidal ideation (De Choudhury et al., 2016). This work showed the ability to make causal inferences on the basis of language usage and employed a small subset of the mental health groups on Reddit.

Following on from the promise that such work holds, our goal was to study language features that are characteristic for individual mental health conditions using **large scale** Reddit data. We anticipate that our findings can be used to assist in separating posts pertaining to different mental health problems and for various language-based applications involving the better understanding of mental health conditions. Reddit is particularly suitable for such research as it has an enormous user base[4], posts and comments are topic-specific and the data is publicly available. We focussed on subreddits (communities where users can post/comment in relation to a specific topic, e.g. suicide ideations)

---

[1]https://twitter.com/?lang=en
[2]https://en-gb.facebook.com/
[3]https://www.reddit.com/

[4]According to https://en.wikipedia.org/wiki/Reddit, Reddit had 234M unique users with 542M monthly visitors as of 2015

of the Reddit data dump[5] that address the following mental health problems: Addiction, Anxiety, Asperger's, Autism, Bipolar Disorder, Dementia, Depression, Schizophrenia, self harm and suicide ideation. These conditions are commonly encountered by mental health practitioners and contribute significantly to treatment costs. We aimed to identify linguistic characteristics that are specific to any of the mental illnesses covered and can be used for text classification tasks. The investigated characteristics include lexical as well as syntactic features, the uniqueness of vocabularies, and the expression of sentiment and happiness. Our results suggest that there are linguistic features that are discriminative of the user communities used in this study. Furthermore, applying a clustering method on subreddits, we could show that subreddits mostly contain a topic-specific vocabulary. Moreover, we could also highlight that there are differences in the way that sentiment is expressed in each of the subreddits. Source code and related materials are available from: `https://github.com/gkotsis/reddit-mental-health`.

2 Methods and Materials

As our aim was to define linguistic characteristics specific to mental health problems, we downloaded the Reddit data and extracted relevant posts and comments. These were then further investigated with respect to specific linguistic features, e.g. sentence structure or unique vocabularies, to determine characteristics for subsequent classification tasks. The data set as well as the methods employed are described in the following subsections.

2.1 Social media data from Reddit

Reddit is a social media network, where registered users can post requests to a broader community. Posts are hosted in topic-specific fora, so called *subreddits*. Subreddits can be created by users based on the subject they are interested in to communicate. All users can freely join any number of subreddits and participate in discussions. This means that the posts are sent to a community potentially

knowledgeable or at least interested in the topic. We used this Reddit feature, to determine subreddits targetting specific mental health problems.

For this purpose, we filtered the entire downloaded data set for subreddits targeting any of the 10 as relevant identified diseases. The entire data set as obtained was separated into posts and comments, and we preserved this separation so that analysis could be executed on either posts, comments or both combined. Posts are initial textual statements that initiate a communication with other users. Comments are replies to posts and are organised in a tree-like structure. Both posts and comments can be written be anyone, and even the Reddit user that wrote the initial post can comment on it. We note here that the number of users, posts and comments varied substantially between subreddits (see Table 1). To refer to sets of both posts and comments (total also in Table 1), we use the term "communication" in the following sections.

Table 1: Numbers of posts, comments, ratio of comments over posts, and the total of posts and comments (called "communications") for each mental health-related subreddit included in this study. Numbers are totalled across all subreddits in the last row of this table. Extrema for each column are highlighted with a purple coloured background.

subreddit	#posts	#comments	#comments/#posts	#total
Anxiety	57,523	289,441	5.03	346,964
BPD	11,880	77,091	6.49	88,971
BipolarReddit	14,954	151,588	10.14	166,542
BipolarSOs	814	4,623	5.68	5,437
OpiatesRecovery	8,651	87,038	10.06	95,689
StopSelfHarm	4,626	24,224	5.24	28,850
addiction	4,360	6,319	1.45	10,679
aspergers	15,053	202,998	13.49	218,051
autism	9,470	52,090	5.50	61,560
bipolar	25,868	198,408	7.67	224,276
cripplingalcoholism	38,241	503,552	13.17	541,793
depression	197,436	902,039	4.57	1,099,475
opiates	56,492	906,780	16.05	963,272
schizophrenia	4,963	31,864	6.42	36,827
selfharm	12,476	68,520	5.49	80,996
SuicideWatch	90,518	619,813	6.85	710,331
Total	462,807	3,506,575	7.58	3,969,382

As shown in Table 1, the *depression* subreddit contains the largest amount of communications (1.1M), while the smallest amount is found in the *BipolarSOs* subreddit (5K). The number of posts is always smaller than the number of comments though the ratio of average number of comments per posts varies. The highest average rate of comments per posts can be seen on subreddit *opiates*, while the smallest number of replies is observed on the *addiction* subreddit.

2.2 Determining linguistic features

There are many ways to model communication. Communication in the form of language use can be characterised through a variety of feature types. Our aim is to better understand the nature and depth of the communication that takes place, and one way to do this is by the analysis of linguistic features. These features are particularly relevant in the context of mental health problems, as the abilities of the sufferer to effectively communicate can be affected by such problems (Cohen and Elvevåg, 2014). For example, someone suffering from Bipolar Disorder may suddenly write a lot, but not necessarily in a cohesive manner. In the Iowa Writers' Workshop study (Andreasen, 1987) bipolar sufferers reported that they were unable to work creatively during periods of depression or mania. During depressive episodes, cognitive fluency and energy were decreased, and during manic periods they were too distractible and disorganized to work effectively, so it would be reasonable to expect this to be reflected in their prose. Understanding these features and consequently the nature and content of the posts will allow us to better design useful classification systems and predictive models.

Through discussion, we determined an initial feature set of linguistic characteristics that draws on previously established measures of psychological relevance, such as LIWC and Coh-Metrix (Graesser et al., 2004). However, we note here that in order to not overload our initial feature set, we selected a subset of all the available possibilities. In our feature set, we included linguistic features introduced by Pitler and Nenkova (Pitler and Nenkova, 2008) and partially overlapping with those used in Coh-Metrix for predicting text quality. More specifically, we adopt features that aim at assessing the *readability* of textual content. Readability is a measurement that aims to assess the required education level for a reader to fully appreciate a certain content. The task of understanding textual content and assessing its quality encompasses various factors that are captured through the features that we also propose here (see supplemental material for more information about the implementation). A subset of these features have been used successfully to predict the answers to be marked as accepted in online Community-based Question Answering websites (Gkotsis et al., 2014).

Our first set of features pertains to the usage of specific words in documents. For instance, we look at the usage of definite articles, since we believe that definite articles are used for specific and personal communications. Similarly, we keep track of pronouns, first-person pronouns, and the ratio between them, as indicators of the degree of first-person content.

Additional features in this initial set aimed at examining text complexity. In our approach, text complexity can scale both horizontally (length, topic cohesion) and vertically (clauses, composite meanings). For the horizontal assessment, we count the number of sentences. Another set of features, which target the understanding of topic continuity and cohesion across sentences, is word overlap between adjacent sentences, either by taking into account all words, or just nouns and pronouns. For the vertical assessment, we employ the following features: a) we count the noun chunks and verb phrases (sequences of nouns and verbs, respectively) and the number of words contained within them, b) we construct the parse tree of each sentence and measure its height, and c) we count the number of subordinate conjunctions (e.g. "although", "because" etc.). A parse tree represents the syntactic structure of a sentence, and tools such as dependency or constituency parsers are readily available for utilisation, e.g. as implemented in the Python module spaCy[6].

Finally, we found that a few posts do not contain any text in their body, apart from their title. This was typically the case for posts that contained a Uniform Resource Locator (URL) to a web page of interest to the community. We believe that the ratio of the number of these posts over the total number of posts is associated with the degree of information dissemination[7], as opposed to the personal story-telling that might occur in other cases, and thus included this as an additional feature.

---

[6]https://spacy.io/

[7]For instance, we found that most URLs posted in *addiction* link to YouTube

2.3 Word-based classification to assess subreddit uniqueness

For this classification-based approach, we employed a representation based on individual words, as well as information on words that frequently co-occurred together. The aim of this task was to examine how closely aligned the vocabularies of each subreddit were, assessed via a pairwise comparison. As highlighted in Table 1, the data volume (in terms of posts and comments) differed significantly for the different subreddits. In order to compensate for the difference in size, we utilised a randomisation process by repeating the same experiment 10 times with a set of 5000 randomly drawn posts for each repeat and individually for each of the two subreddits that were compared with each other.

In order to compare the vocabularies of two subreddits with each other, we built dictionaries for each pair of subreddits, by retrieving all words and sequences of words (of length 2) occurring in one or both subreddits. We then used this list of words and frequently co-occurring words to classify posts into belonging to one of the two subreddits that are being compared and recorded the performance for each of the 10 cycles for each subreddit pair. The classification performance was then averaged across all 10 cycles to obtain a representative score for each pair of subreddits. Using this classification approach, high performance scores indicate a distinctive vocabulary while low performance scores suggest a shared vocabulary across both the subreddits. The results of this pairwise comparison are illustrated in Figure 1. More details are provided in the supplementary materials, covering the algorithm and randomisation steps.

2.4 Detecting sentiment and happiness in posts

One additional aspect that can be assessed when looking at the linguistic aspect of communications on social media is the expression of sentiment. Sentiment has been noted as a crucial indicator of how much involved someone is in a specific event (Tausczik and Pennebaker, 2010; Murphy et al., 2015), and therefore can also play a role in the expression of mental illness. Some of the conditions investigated here may have characteristic mood patterns, e.g. it is likely that someone suffering from depression will use negative sentiment and express unhappiness, while someone suffering from Bipolar Disorder may change between positive and negative mood expressions over time. However, by assessing sentiment and happiness for a large population of individuals, novel patterns for individual mental health problems may evolve.

As part of our investigation, we used two different methods, one to detect sentiment (Nielsen, 2011) and another to detect happiness (Dodds et al., 2011). Both methods, which were developed for social media studies, rely on a topic-specific dictionary. For each *post* in our subreddits, we determined the sentiment and happiness score by matching words against the dictionaries. We accumulated these scores on a per post basis and normalised it by the square root of the number of words in the post that were identified in the respective dictionary. Scores for happiness were further normalised to assign them to the same range as the values for sentiment: negative values are expressions of negative sentiment/unhappiness, positive values are expressions of positive sentiment and happiness, and a value of 0 can be seen as neutral.

We note here that while our aim is to classify both posts and comments, we limited ourselves in this task to posts only. Comments could be considered to be a source of noise, which may mask potential sentiment and happiness coming from posts, given that our data set contains a lot more comments than posts. In future work we would like to experiment with more sophisticated linguistic methods for identifying sentiment and emotion.

3 Results

After identifying the subreddits relevant to the mental health problems we were interested in, we determined linguistic features (related to content of communications) for each of the subreddits. The results of our investigations are presented in the following subsections.

3.1 Subreddits exhibit differences in linguistic features

Table 2 provides a summary of all the linguistic features for each of the 16 subreddits, that were assessed as part of this study. From this table, we see that two subreddits stand out in a number of the assessed criteria: *BiPolarSOs* and *cripplingalcoholism*. *BiPolarSOs* is a subreddit that provides support and advice to people in a relationship where either one or both partners are affected by Bipolar Disorder. Note that this means that users on this subreddit may not be affected by the disorder themselves and may result in different communications from a subreddit where only people with Bipolar Disorder are communicating. In our data set it was the smallest subreddit in terms of total number of communications (see Table 1). The subreddit *cripplingalcoholism* aims to facilitate communication between people addicted to alcohol. In the description of the subreddit, there is no emphasis on supporting each other and people can also share what they may consider positive experiences regarding their condition (e.g. "On day 8 of a bender that was supposed to end today because my boss was supposed to send me a bunch of work on Monday. She just emailed me and said she won't be sending it until Wednesday! Sweet chocolate Jesus on a bicycle, I did a jig in my jammies, cracked open a new handle of rye, and am about to take the dog on a nice drunken walk. Sobriety, I'll see you Wednesday. Maybe").

From Table 2, we see that the *BipolarSOs* subreddit not only has a higher number of first-person pronouns and a larger number of definite articles, but also that the average sentence seems to be more complex due to a high average height of the sentence parse trees, long verb clauses and a high number of subordinating conjunctions, while the average number of sentences per communication is comparable to those of the other subreddits. This suggests that people posting on this subreddit explain in detail their experience or advice. On the contrary, the *cripplingalcoholism* subreddit possesses shorter communications characterised by the lowest number of sentences per communication, the smallest maximum height of sentence trees, a low number of subordinate conjunctions and short verb clauses. Using word frequency occurrences, we also observed that here the language seems stronger than on other subreddits with the most frequently occurring word being "fuck" (details of results not provided here[8]).

The two features relating to lexical cohesion (by

means of adjacent sentences using similar words, LF10 and LF11 in Table 2), show little variation across all the 16 different subreddits. Though cohesion when only taking nouns and pronouns into consideration improves, the best value obtained is 0.22, indicating a mostly low lexical cohesion across communications on each of the subreddits. One of our longer term goals is to be able to classify posts to individual subreddits, and these scores would not be sufficiently informative for this goal due to their low variation.

3.2 Subreddit vocabulary uniqueness through classification

The word occurrence-based comparison of the subreddits was performed to better determine whether subreddits can be distinguished based on their lexical content (see supplementary material for more information). The results obtained are shown in Figure 1.

Figure 1: Heatmap of pairwise classification of posts (*only*) between subreddits. High values denote high accuracy in classification and therefore represent high discriminability in language. Low values represent low score in classification and therefore high language proximity between subreddits.

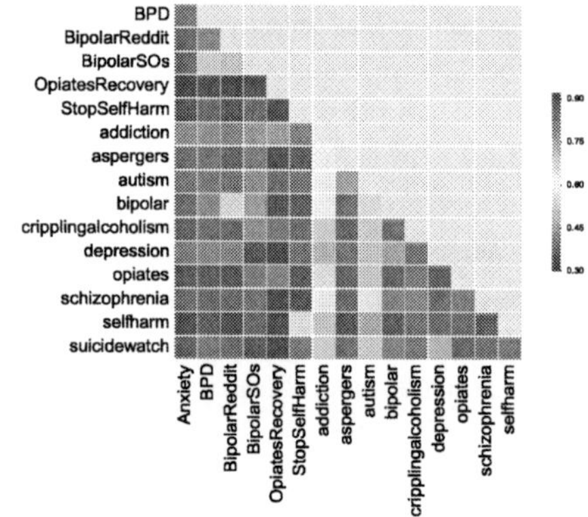

Figure 1 shows that apart from a small number of exceptions, the language of individual subreddits is discriminable, which can be further exploited for classification purposes in later stages. For example, the subreddit *OpiateRecovery* shows mostly high values, which means that the language used (based on frequency of words and word pairs) on this

---

⁸Available as a wordcloud visualisation of all subreddits at `https://github.com/gkotsis/` `reddit-mental-health/tree/master/` `wordclouds`

Table 2: Obtained results for each of the language features per subreddit. Language features investigated were: LF1 – Average number of definite article "the" in each communication; LF2 – Average number of first person pronouns; LF3 – Average number of pronouns in each communication; LF4 – Average number of noun chunks; LF5 – Average number of length of maximum verb phrase in each communication; LF6 – Average number of subordinate conjunctions; LF7 – Average value of maximum height of sentences' parse trees; LF8 – Average number of sentences in each communication; LF9 – Average ratio of number of first person pronouns over total number of pronouns; LF10 – Similarity between adjacent sentences over nouns or pronouns *only* (lexical cohesion); LF11 – Similarity between adjacent sentences over *all* words (lexical cohesion); LF12 – Ratio of posts without any body text (containing only a title and a URL) over total number of posts.

| | Not normalised features | | | | | | | | Normalised | | | |
Subreddit	LF1	LF2	LF3	LF4	LF5	LF6	LF7	LF8	LF9	LF10	LF11	LF12
Anxiety	2.24	7.67	13.13	1.85	25.68	1.43	5.95	6.51	0.54	0.19	0.18	0.10
BPD	2.23	7.98	14.28	1.83	28.32	1.48	6.14	6.63	0.54	0.20	0.18	0.09
BipolarReddit	2.14	6.49	11.54	1.84	23.91	1.44	5.98	6.15	0.54	0.18	0.18	0.01
BipolarSOs	3.53	9.68	23.06	1.99	40.52	1.49	6.67	10.12	0.40	0.17	0.17	0.04
OpiatesRecovery	2.24	6.48	11.93	1.80	23.49	1.28	5.66	6.69	0.49	0.17	0.17	0.01
StopSelfHarm	1.60	5.90	11.71	1.77	20.60	1.25	5.43	5.52	0.46	0.22	0.19	0.12
addiction	1.95	5.54	10.66	1.35	21.50	0.98	4.30	5.93	0.44	0.17	0.18	0.63
aspergers	1.94	5.12	9.69	1.72	20.76	1.53	5.88	5.06	0.53	0.17	0.18	0.12
autism	2.07	3.62	8.65	1.61	19.89	1.37	5.50	5.01	0.41	0.13	0.17	0.61
bipolar	1.86	6.16	10.62	1.73	20.82	1.31	5.53	5.67	0.56	0.18	0.17	0.15
cripplingalcoholism	0.92	2.28	4.07	1.36	8.76	0.95	4.10	3.02	0.54	0.12	0.16	0.16
depression	2.25	8.71	14.75	1.84	29.04	1.37	5.89	7.17	0.52	0.21	0.19	0.02
opiates	1.14	2.60	5.11	1.48	10.96	1.13	4.52	3.25	0.49	0.14	0.16	0.21
schizophrenia	2.13	5.96	11.15	1.80	23.74	1.45	5.82	5.85	0.50	0.18	0.18	0.13
selfharm	1.39	5.41	9.73	1.70	17.57	1.19	5.11	4.94	0.52	0.21	0.18	0.01
suicidewatch	1.96	7.10	13.44	1.85	27.85	1.29	5.74	6.73	0.46	0.22	0.19	0.03

subreddit is mostly unique. *OpiateRecovery* shows some vocabulary overlap with the *opiates* and *addiction* subreddits, which suggests that there are some shared topics on these subreddits. One of the exceptions is the subreddit *addiction*. As illustrated in the heatmap the *addiction* subreddit shows particularly low values with other subreddits such as *depression* and *suicidewatch*. This finding is not surprising as substance addiction can lead to depression and suicidal thoughts, which is expected to be also expressed in the nature of the communication. Note that the diagonal of the matrix is suppressed to reduce the matrix dimension.

Among our 16 subreddits, there are some subreddits that allude to the same mental health condition, e.g. *BipolarReddit* and *BipolarSOs* both aim to foster a community to facilitate exchange about Bipolar Disorder. While the subreddit *BipolarSOs* invites participation from users that are affected themselves or are in a relationship with someone affected by Bipolar Disorder, *BipolarReddit* is solely focussed on people suffering from this disorder. In Figure 1, we can also see that vocabularies seem to be partially shared (indicated by a lighter colour) across those subreddits addressing the same mental health prob-

lem. For example, all three subreddits relating to Bipolar Disorder (*bipolar*, *BipolarReddit* and *BipolarSOs*) show a pairwise score of ~ 0.6 as opposed to ~ 0.9 with other subreddits. Similarly, both the self-harm subreddits also share a pairwise vocabulary of ~ 0.6. Interestingly, the subreddits *autism* and *schizophrenia* also indicate a proximity of the vocabularies and further investigations are required to assess the shared vocabularies.

3.3 Sentiment/happiness expressions on subreddits

In order to assess the emotions that Reddit users express on subreddits related to mental health problems, we used two different methods: (i) to assess sentiment and (ii) to specifically assess happiness. The results obtained by both methods are shown in Figure 2. This figure illustrates that, on average, a lot of negative sentiment is expressed across the different subreddits relating to mental health problems. We can see that posts from the subreddit *Suicide-Watch* express the highest rate of negative sentiment, followed by posts from the *Anxiety* and self-harm-related subreddits.

While in the majority of cases both sentiment and

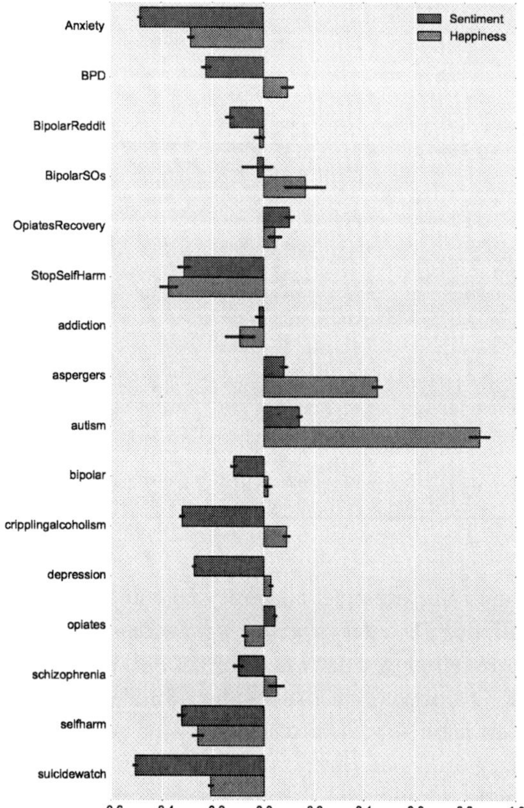

happiness expression possess the same direction (i.e. either positive or negative), in a number of subreddits this is not the case. For example, the subreddit *cripplingalcoholism* shows expressions of happiness as well as the expression of negative sentiment. As alluded to earlier, this particular subreddit includes people that see alcoholism as a lifestyle choice. Though there may be happiness expressions related to overcoming alcoholism, there are also happiness expressions relating to the glorification of alcoholism, e.g. "[...] At the bottom of this pile of clothes is a full pint! How it came to rest there I don't know, but thank you Taaka gods for your gift on this day. [...]".

Furthermore, Figure 2 shows a small number of subreddits, where posts seem to express positive sentiment. For example, the posts extracted from the subreddit *OpiatesRecovery* seem to express not only positive sentiment but also happiness. This particular subreddit aims to foster a comunity that focusses on helping each other get through opiate withdrawals and users can post their progress. While there are posts that discuss relapses, there are statements such as "[...] I'm happy to say the shivers/flashes/heebeegeebees are a lot, lot better. Not 100% gone, but gone enough. I can deal with flashes every 4-6 hours, cant deal with them every 15 minutes. [...]" to share the successes made during withdrawal. The results shown in this figure are average values, which means that subreddits that show an overall tendency to happiness and positive sentiment, may contain some posts including words of negative sentiment and unhappiness, e.g. "[...] Buying garbage from some ignorant thug to put into my fucking blood knowing how lethal it can be, but oh it couldn't happen to me. It's bizarre that after all this time of staying away I still can't fully grasp how fucking close to death I was every day. [...]" from *OpiateRecovery*.

4 Discussion

In our study, we analysed 16 different subreddits covering a range of mental health problems (see supplementary material for more details). In our selection, there are subreddits with overlapping content, e.g. *StopSelfHarm* and *selfharm*. We conducted an analysis based on a selection of linguistic features and found that most of the subreddits that are topic-unrelated, possess a unique vocabulary (in terms of words/word-pairs and the frequencies thereof) and discriminating lexical and syntactic features. We also observed differences in sentiment and happiness expressions, which can give further clues about the nature of a post.

As symptoms are shared across conditions and more so, some of the mental health problems are co-occurring (e.g. anxiety and depression), medications and treatment strategies are shared across the different illnesses, too. This, in consequence, means that part of the vocabulary and thoughts across the different subreddits are shared, making it harder to distinguish between the different subreddits and, consequently, the condition in question. Given the latter, it is even more surprising that the similarity matrix shown in Figure 1 shows a good separation of topic-specific vocabularies on subreddits.

With respect to the expression of sentiment and emotions, further work is needed. The methods applied here were developed based on Twitter data and further investigations are necessary to find the parts of the dictionary that are overlapping and an expert-guided assessment as to whether the recognised expressions are representative and meaningful in the context of mental health problems. A previous study has investigated how support is expressed in social media (Wang et al., 2015) and can be leveraged in future work to see whether similar support models hold true for the subreddits concerning mental health conditions. Moreover, the methods we have used so far are based on lexica, which lack contextual information. In future work, we plan to add more contextualised semantic methods for determining sentiment and emotions.

One limitation of the work presented here is that we did not include any subreddits that are unrelated to mental health. For example, we could have included a subreddit such as *Showerthoughts* into our subset to assess which of the features are unique to mental health problems only. However, this would require the definition of what is a truly unrelated subreddit and variety of topics so that the control set is not biased in itself. Furthermore, as our primary aim was to build a classifier that distinguishes several mental health problems based on the findings reported here, an implicit assumption is that a post is by default relevant to mental health conditions and does not need to be classified as such. Nevertheless, we plan to address this limitation in future work.

5   Conclusions

After extracting data from several subreddits pertaining to mental health problems, we investigated a subset of language features to determine discriminatory characteristics for each of the subreddits. Our results suggest that there are discriminatory linguistic features among subreddits, such as sentence complexity or vocabulary usage. We could also show that while mostly all subreddits relating to mental

health problems possess highly negative sentiment, there are a number of subreddits, where positive sentiment and happiness can be observed in posts. However, in order to determine the most discriminative features between different mental health conditions, additional work is required continuing from the results shown here. In conclusion, these results pave the way for future work on classification of posts and comments concerning a mental health condition, which in turn could allow the assignment of urgency markers to address a specific communication.

Acknowledgments

RD is supported by a Clinician Scientist Fellowship from the Health Foundation in partnership with the Academy of Medical Sciences and RD and GG are funded by the e-HOST-IT research programme. AO and RJBD would like to acknowledge NIHR Biomedical Research Centre for Mental Health, the Biomedical Research Unit for Dementia at the South London, the Maudsley NHS Foundation Trust and Kings College London. RJBD's work is also supported by awards to establish the Farr Institute of Health Informatics Research, London, from the Medical Research Council, Arthritis Research UK, British Heart Foundation, Cancer Research UK, Chief Scientist Office, Economic and Social Research Council, Engineering and Physical Sciences Research Council, National Institute for Health Research, National Institute for Social Care and Health Research, and Wellcome Trust (grant MR/K006584/1). SV is supported by the Swedish Research Council (2015-00359), Marie Sklodowska Curie Actions, Cofund, Project INCA 600398. ML would like to acknowledge the PHEME FP7 project (grant No. 611233). TJPH would like to acknowledge King's College London and the NIHR Biomedical Research Centre at Guy's and St Thomas NHS Foundation Trust.

The authors acknowledge infrastructure support from the National Institute for Health Research (NIHR). The views expressed are those of the authors and not necessarily those of the NHS, the NIHR or the Department of Health.

References

Nancy C Andreasen. 1987. Creativity and mental illness. *American Journal of Psychiatry*, 144(10):1288–1292.

Azy Barak, Meyran Boniel-Nissim, and John Suler. 2008. Fostering empowerment in online support groups. *Computers in Human Behavior*, 24(5):1867–1883.

Alex S Cohen and Brita Elvevåg. 2014. Automated computerized analysis of speech in psychiatric disorders. *Current Opinion in Psychiatry*, 27(3):203–209.

Glen Coppersmith, Mark Dredze, Craig Harman, and Kristy Hollingshead. 2015a. From adhd to sad: Analyzing the language of mental health on twitter through self-reported diagnoses. *In Proceedings of the 2015 Annual Conference of the North American Chapter of the Association for Computational Linguistics: Human Language Technologies (NAACL HLT)*, page 1.

Glen Coppersmith, Ryan Leary, Eric Whyne, and Tony Wood. 2015b. Quantifying Suicidal Ideation via Language Usage on Social Media.

Munmun De Choudhury, Michael Gamon, Scott Counts, and Eric Horvitz. 2013. Predicting Depression via Social Media. In *In Proceedings of the 2013 International AAAI Conference on Weblogs and Social Media (ICWSM)*, page 2.

Munmun De Choudhury, Emre Kiciman, Mark Dredze, Glen Coppersmith, and Mrinal Kumar. 2016. Discovering Shifts to Suicidal Ideation from Mental Health Content in Social Media. *In Proceedings of 2016 Special Interest Group on Computer-Human Interaction (SIGCHI)*.

Peter Sheridan Dodds, Kameron Decker Harris, Isabel M Kloumann, Catherine A Bliss, and Christopher M Danforth. 2011. Temporal patterns of happiness and information in a global social network: Hedonometrics and twitter. *PLOS ONE*, 6(12):e26752.

George Gkotsis, Karen Stepanyan, Carlos Pedrinaci, John Domingue, and Maria Liakata. 2014. It's all in the content: state of the art best answer prediction based on discretisation of shallow linguistic features. In *In Proceedings of the 2014 ACM conference on Web science*, pages 202–210. ACM.

Arthur C Graesser, Danielle S McNamara, Max M Louwerse, and Zhiqiang Cai. 2004. Coh-Metrix: Analysis of text on cohesion and language. *Behavior Research Methods, Instruments, & Computers*, 36(2):193–202.

Zina M Ibrahim, Lorena Fernández de la Cruz, Argyris Stringaris, Robert Goodman, Michael Luck, and Richard JB Dobson. 2015. A Multi-Agent Platform for Automating the Collection of Patient-Provided Clinical Feedback. In *In Proceedings of the 2015 International Conference on Autonomous Agents and Multiagent Systems*, pages 831–839. International Foundation for Autonomous Agents and Multiagent Systems.

Ian Kelleher, Helen Keeley, Paul Corcoran, Fionnuala Lynch, Carol Fitzpatrick, Nina Devlin, Charlene Molloy, Sarah Roddy, Mary C Clarke, Michelle Harley, et al. 2012. Clinicopathological significance of psychotic experiences in non-psychotic young people: evidence from four population-based studies. *The British Journal of Psychiatry*, 201(1):26–32.

Ronald C Kessler and Richard G Frank. 1997. The impact of psychiatric disorders on work loss days. *Psychological Medicine*, 27(04):861–873.

Ronald C Kessler, Cindy L Foster, William B Saunders, and Paul E Stang. 1995. Social consequences of psychiatric disorders, I: Educational attainment. *American Journal of Psychiatry*, 152(7):1026–1032.

Ronald C Kessler, Patricia A Berglund, Martha L Bruce, J Randy Koch, Eugene M Laska, Philip J Leaf, Ronald W Manderscheid, Robert A Rosenheck, Ellen E Walters, and Philip S Wang. 2001. The prevalence and correlates of untreated serious mental illness. *Health Services Research*, 36(6 Pt 1):987.

Kurt Kroenke and Robert L Spitzer. 2002. The PHQ-9: a new depression diagnostic and severity measure. *Psychiatric annals*, 32(9):509–515.

Mrinal Kumar, Mark Dredze, Glen Coppersmith, and Munmun De Choudhury. 2015. Detecting changes in suicide content manifested in social media following celebrity suicides. In *In Proceedings of the 26th ACM Conference on Hypertext & Social Media*, pages 85–94. ACM.

Alice Malpass, Alison Shaw, David Kessler, and Deborah Sharp. 2010. Concordance between PHQ-9 scores and patients experiences of depression: a mixed methods study. *British Journal of General Practice*, 60(575):e231–e238.

Sally McManus, Howard Meltzer, TS Brugha, PE Bebbington, and Rachel Jenkins. 2009. Adult psychiatric morbidity in England, 2007: results of a household survey.

Margaret Mitchell, Kristy Hollingshead, and Glen Coppersmith. 2015. Quantifying the language of schizophrenia in social media. *In Proceedings of the 2015 Annual Conference of the North American Chapter of the Association for Computational Linguistics: Human Language Technologies (NAACL HLT)*, page 11.

Sean M Murphy, Bernard Maskit, and Wilma Bucci. 2015. Putting Feelings into Words: Cross-Linguistic Markers of the Referential Process. *In Proceedings of the 2015 Annual Conference of the North American Chapter of the Association for Computational Linguistics: Human Language Technologies (NAACL HLT)*, page 80.

Finn Årup Nielsen. 2011. A new ANEW: Evaluation of a word list for sentiment analysis in microblogs. *arXiv preprint arXiv:1103.2903*.

A Patel and M Knapp. 1997. The cost of mental health: report to the Health Education Authority. In *Centre for Economics of Mental Health, Institute of Psychiatry London, UK Working paper*.

Emily Pitler and Ani Nenkova. 2008. Revisiting readability: A unified framework for predicting text quality. In *In Proceedings of the 2008 Conference on Empirical Methods in Natural Language Processing (EMNLP)*, pages 186–195. Association for Computational Linguistics.

Yla R Tausczik and James W Pennebaker. 2010. The psychological meaning of words: LIWC and computerized text analysis methods. *Journal of Language and Social Psychology*, 29(1):24–54.

Yi-Chia Wang, Robert E Kraut, and John M Levine. 2015. Eliciting and receiving online support: using computer-aided content analysis to examine the dynamics of online social support. *Journal of Medical Internet Research*, 17(4).

Harvey A Whiteford, Louisa Degenhardt, Jürgen Rehm, Amanda J Baxter, Alize J Ferrari, Holly E Erskine, Fiona J Charlson, Rosana E Norman, Abraham D Flaxman, Nicole Johns, et al. 2013. Global burden of disease attributable to mental and substance use disorders: findings from the Global Burden of Disease Study 2010. *The Lancet*, 382(9904):1575–1586.

Paul Wicks, Michael Massagli, Jeana Frost, Catherine Brownstein, Sally Okun, Timothy Vaughan, Richard Bradley, and James Heywood. 2010. Sharing health data for better outcomes on PatientsLikeMe. *Journal of Medical Internet Research*, 12(2):e19.

Til Wykes, Josep Maria Haro, Stefano R Belli, Carla Obradors-Tarragó, Celso Arango, José Luis Ayuso-Mateos, István Bitter, Matthias Brunn, Karine Chevreul, Jacques Demotes-Mainard, et al. 2015. Mental health research priorities for Europe. *The Lancet Psychiatry*, 2(11):1036–1042.

Exploring Autism Spectrum Disorders Using HLT

Julia Parish-Morris*, Mark Liberman°, Neville Ryant°, Christopher Cieri°, Leila Bateman*, Emily Ferguson*, Robert T. Schultz*

°Linguistic Data Consortium. University of Pennsylvania
3600 Market Street, Suite 810, Philadelphia, PA, 19104 USA

*Center for Autism Research. Children's Hospital of Philadelphia
3535 Market Street, Suite 860, Philadelphia, PA, 19104 USA

Abstract

The phenotypic complexity of Autism Spectrum Disorder motivates the application of modern computational methods to large collections of observational data, both for improved clinical diagnosis and for better scientific understanding. We have begun to create a corpus of annotated language samples relevant to this research, and we plan to join with other researchers in pooling and publishing such resources on a large scale. The goal of this paper is to present some initial explorations to illustrate the opportunities that such datasets will afford.

1 Introduction

Autism Spectrum Disorder (ASD) is a highly heterogeneous, brain-based developmental disorder affecting approximately 1.5% of the population (Christensen, 2016). Primary diagnostic indicators include impairments in social communication and reciprocity, as well as the presence of repetitive behaviors and restricted patterns of interests (American Psychiatric Association, 2013). Despite significant symptom overlap in the core domains of social communication and repetitive behaviors, individuals diagnosed with ASD can look very different from one person to the next. Clinical presentation varies substantially depending on age, context, IQ, intervention history, and presence or absence of common comorbidities such as ADHD and anxiety disorder. The heterogeneous presentation with respect to overall severity and pattern of co-occurring conditions makes research aimed at improving treatments and isolating biological mechanisms much more complicated.

The phenotypic heterogeneity of ASD contributes to conflicting research findings that paint a confusing picture in the literature. For example, depending upon the characteristics of a particular sample, groups of children with ASD can look as if they have face processing impairments or not (Weigelt, Koldewyn, & Kanwisher, 2012), perceptual processing biases or not (D'Souza, Booth, Connolly, Happé, & Karmiloff-Smith, 2015), and persistent social language differences or not (Fein et al., 2013). In response to reproducibility issues, one strategy has been to shift away from research based solely on a categorical conceptualization, such as schizophrenia, ADHD, and ASD, to a domain-based dimensional approach that cuts across traditional diagnostic categories. This approach to understanding mental disorder is explicitly encouraged by the National Institute of Mental Health through the Research Domain Criteria effort (RDoC; (Insel, 2014)). The RDoC approach is trans-diagnostic and grounded in the study of process (where there is clear or emerging support on underlying biological processes), such as specific neural systems that relate to dimensions of behavior in model systems and in humans.

Proceedings of the 3rd Workshop on Computational Linguistics and Clinical Psychology: From Linguistic Signal to Clinical Reality, pages 74–84,
San Diego, California, June 16, 2016. ©2016 Association for Computational Linguistics

A complementary approach to improve reproducibility is to focus on large sample sizes so as to be able to more easily generalize results to all individuals with autism. Most research groups lack the resources to obtain large samples, and thus pooled efforts and data sharing become key. Large samples also provide the statistical power necessary to control for a larger array of possible confounding variables. In an effort to increase data sharing and power to parse the heterogeneity of ASD, the National Institutes of Health established the National Database for Autism Research (NDAR; ("National Database for Autism Research - Home," n.d.)). This database provides de-identified data for large N secondary data analyses. However, aside from common characterization variables (see Bone, Goodwin, et al., 2014), NDAR will not have sufficient data for more specialized needs such as human language technology research.

In this paper, we describe a new opportunity for data sharing in a format designed to facilitate research on speech and language in ASD, and explore the possibilities associated with this sort of database. The Children's Hospital of Philadelphia Center for Autism Research (CAR) collected the samples analyzed here, and established a collaborative project with the University of Pennsylvania Linguistic Data Consortium (LDC). We focus on recorded conversations that took place from 2008-2015 during the course of clinical evaluations for autism.

1.1 The Autism Diagnostic Observation Schedule

The ADOS is a semi-structured, conversation- and play-based evaluation tool used by expert clinicians to help inform diagnostic decision-making. There are 4 versions of the ADOS, one of which is selected for administration based on an individual's language ability at the time of evaluation. Module 3 requires phrase speech, and includes a large section devoted to conversation. During this part of the evaluation, clinicians ask questions about social-emotional concerns. These questions are designed to elicit language or behavior that differentiates individuals with social communication difficulties from those without (e.g., "What does being a friend mean to you? Do you ever feel lonely?"). Importantly, the samples arising from this section are similar in form and content to samples used in past clinically-oriented HLT research.

One benefit of targeting language produced during the ADOS for HLT research is ubiquity; the ADOS is widely included in research-grade Gold Standard diagnostic evaluations, both inside and outside the United States, and is routinely recorded for clinical reliability purposes. Many of these audio-video recordings are associated with clinical metadata such as age, sex, clinical judgment of ASD status, autism severity metrics, IQ estimates, and social/language questionnaires, as well as genetic panels, brain scans, behavioral experiments, and infrared eye tracking. The quality of recording is variable, with a multitude of recording methods employed. A substantial number of these recordings have yet to be assembled into a large, shareable resource. We view this as a largely untapped opportunity for data sharing that could facilitate advancements in clinically oriented HLT research and autism research more broadly.

1.2 The present study

In 2013, CAR and the Linguistic Data Consortium (LDC) began a project aimed at analyzing ADOS recordings from more than 1200 toddlers, children, teens, and adults, most of which were ultimately diagnosed with ASD. These recordings are associated with rich characterization data in the form of interviews and questionnaires, cognitive and behavioral assessments, eye tracking, brain scans, and genetic tests. Our initial goal was to determine whether automated analysis of language recorded during the ADOS could predict diagnostic status, although our aims have since expanded to include identifying correlates of phenotypic variability within ASD. This second aim is particularly meaningful in the clinical domain and in our search for causes of autism; if we can accurately and objectively quantify the linguistic signal, we have a much better chance of reliably mapping it to real-world effects and to connecting it with biological mechanisms.

The current paper reports on our work-in-progress, and provides preliminary results from a cohort of 100 children. We analyze a small subset of possible lexical and acoustic features in combination with clinical measures. Our goal is to spur interest in growing and sharing valuable resources like this one.

2 Dataset

To date, our corpus includes natural language samples from 100 participants engaged in the conversation and reporting section of ADOS Module 3 (mean length of recording ~20 minutes).

2.1 Subjects

Three diagnostic groups were included: ASD (N=65, mean age: 10 years), non-ASD mixed clinical (N=18, mean age: 10.39 years), and typically developing (TD; N=17; mean age: 11.29 years). ASD is more common in males than females (Wing, 1981), and our clinical groups have more boys than girls (ASD: 75% male; non-ASD mixed clinical: 94% male; TD: 47% male). Mothers and fathers had a median post-high school educational level of 4 years (Bachelor's degree) for the ASD and non-ASD mixed clinical groups, and 2 years (Associate's degree) for the TD group. Median household income was $60,000-$99,000.

The ASD group was determined to have an autism spectrum disorder according to DSM-IV criteria after a Gold Standard evaluation that included the ADOS, cognitive testing, parent interviews, and questionnaires. After undergoing the same rigorous evaluation as their peers with ASD, the non-ASD mixed clinical group was determined not to meet diagnostic criteria. This group is highly heterogeneous, with some participants exhibiting subthreshold ASD symptoms and others diagnosed with anxiety or ADHD. Due to the small sample size of this group and the TD group, analyses should be interpreted with caution. The TD group had no reported history of ASD, no significant neurological history, no first-degree family members with ASD, and did not meet clinical cutoffs on a common ASD screener (Social Communication Questionnaire; SCQ; (Rutter, Bailey, & Lord, 2003)).

2.2 Clinical measures

Participants were administered a variety of behavioral and cognitive tests during in-person visits at the Center for Autism Research. Parents completed questionnaires about their child's social and behavioral functioning either directly before or during the visit. Means, standard deviations, and ranges are provided in Table 1.

Autism Diagnostic Observation Schedule (ADOS; (Lord et al., 2012)). In addition to providing natural language samples, the ADOS is a scored instrument. Highly trained clinicians rate various aspects of children's behavior on a scale of 0-3 (higher = more autism-like). A subset of these ratings are combined using an algorithm that results in a total score for each of two domains: social affect (SA) and repetitive behaviors/restricted interests (RRB). Three comparison scores can also be calculated, which roughly index the severity of autism symptoms for a given child overall, in the social affect domain, and in the repetitive behaviors/restricted interests domain (see Table 1).

Table 1. Means and standard deviations for cognitive test scores, clinical observation ratings, and parent questionnaires.

	ASD	Non-ASD	TD
Full-scale IQ	105.31 (14.88)	97.77 (11.01)	104.06 (14.68)
Verbal IQ	106.91 (14.41)	100.78 (12.64)	108.24 (14.07)
Nonverbal IQ	105.94 (13.95)	95.06 (10.29)	100.94 (14.24)
ADOS severity score	6.49 (2.47)	2.72 (1.56)	1.47 (0.94)
ADOS SA severity score	6.29 (2.42)	3.06 (1.92)	2.06 (1.3)
ADOS RRB severity score	7.08 (2.54)	4.72 (2.91)	2.53 (2.18)
SRS t-score	80.6 (16.46)	81.22 (17.91)	39.82 (5.05)
CCC-2 GCC	81.44 (14.13)	77.24 (14.84)	115 (8.24)
CCC-2 SIDI	-9.75 (8.07)	-5.7 (12.68)	5.4 (6.01)

Differential Abilities Scales – 2nd Edition (DAS-II; (Elliott, 2007)). Overall (full-scale) IQ, non-verbal IQ, and verbal IQ were assessed via the DAS-II. DAS-II IQ measures have a mean of 100.

Children's Communication Checklist – 2nd Edition (CCC; (Norbury, Nash, Baird, & Bishop, 2004)). The CCC-2 is a norm-referenced parent report questionnaire focused on aspects of structural and pragmatic language. The Global Communication Composite (GCC) is an overall measure of parent impressions of child communication competency, and the Social Interaction Difference Index (SIDI) score is designed to flag children in need of further evaluation for ASD or other disorders (negative scores indicate risk).

2.3 Interviews

Research reliable PhD-level clinical psychologists and/or psychology trainees administered the ADOS module 3 to all participants in quiet neutral rooms. Evaluations were videotaped using a single feed or PiP from 3 corner-mounted cameras, and audio was recorded through a ceiling microphone. After we obtained consent from participants to use their sessions for research purposes, entire video recordings were copied from their original media onto a shared file system accessible only to project members with current certifications for research on human subjects. Audio was extracted from the video stream and saved in lossless FLAC format. Except for extraction and format conversion, the data was identical to the original recording.

The ADOS is a semi-structured interview, so questions from the conversation and reporting section were occasionally spread throughout the entire interview (which lasts approximately 45-60 minutes). More often, they were clustered together in a section that lasts ~20 minutes. A knowledgeable member of study staff selected the largest chunk of continuous conversation and reporting questions for transcription and annotation.

2.4 Transcription and annotation

As described in a prior methods paper (Parish-Morris et al., 2016), transcription teams at LDC and CAR created time aligned, verbatim, orthographic transcripts of the conversation and reporting section for each participant. The LDC transcription team consisted of two junior and two senior transcribers, all college educated native speakers of American English. The junior transcribers performed segmentation of the audio files into pause groups and transcription. The senior transcribers corrected the initial transcripts and occasionally did transcription from scratch.

For this effort, LDC created a new transcription specification that resembles those used for conversational speech. The principal differences are that the current specification requires that participants be labeled only by their role (Interviewer and Participant) and that the boundaries between speech and non-speech be placed rather accurately because (inter-)turn duration is a factor of interest.

After LDC established the transcription process and pilot results were found to be promising, CAR developed a team to extend the corpus and begin evaluating inter-annotator agreement. The CAR team consists of multiple pairs of college educated native speakers of American English that transcribe the conversation and reporting section of the ADOS independently, a third more senior transcriber responsible for comparing and adjudicating the work of the first two, and a fourth transcriber who compares CAR and LDC transcripts when the latter are available, and adjudicates remaining disagreements. In this way, 4 transcribers and 2 adjudicators with complementary goals produce a "gold standard" transcript for analysis and for evaluation/training of future transcriptionists.

2.5 Quality control

LDC transcribed 52 files, and CAR transcribed 100 including independent transcriptions of the 52 that LDC transcribed. A simple comparison of word level identity between CAR's adjudicated transcripts and LDC's transcripts revealed 93.22% overlap on average, before a third adjudication resolved differences between the two. In the case of files that were transcribed by CAR only (N=48), pre-adjudication overlap in word-level comparisons between transcribers averaged 92.18%. We are confident that two or three complete transcriptions plus one or two complete adjudications has resulted in a reliable data set.

2.6 Forced alignment

Segmentations for the transcribed turns of each ADOS evaluation were produced by forced alignment using an aligner trained on all turns in the corpus. The aligner was trained with the Kaldi ASR toolkit (Povey et al., 2011) using the CMUdict lexicon with stress markings removed; pronunciations for out-of-vocabulary (OOV) words were generated with the Sequitur G2P toolkit

(Besacier, Barnard, Karpov, & Schultz, 2014) using a model trained on CMUdict. The acoustic frontend consisted of 13 mel frequency cepstral coefficient (MFCC) features extracted every 10 ms using a 25 ms Hamming window plus first and second differences; all features were normalized to zero mean and unit variance on a per-speaker basis. A standard 3-state Bakis model was used for all speech phones and a 5-state models allowing forward skips used to model non-speech phones (silence, breaths, coughs, laughter, lipsmacks, and other non-speech vocalizations), untranscribable regions, and out-of-vocabulary words (words which were not in CMUdict and for which grapheme-to-phoneme transduction failed). To improve segmentation accuracy, special 1-state boundary models were inserted at each phone transition as in Yuan et al. (2013). Acoustic modeling was performed using a deep neural network consisting of 4 layers of 512 rectified linear units with input consisting of an 11 frame context (5-1-5).

Feature extraction. In this first analysis, we focused on child features (lexical and acoustic). Planned future analyses will assess interviewer features, and integrate across both speakers to assess variables such as synchrony and accommodation.

Word choice. Prior research suggests that individuals with ASD produce idiosyncratic or unusual words more often than their typically developing peers (Ghaziuddin & Gerstein, 1996; Prud'hommeaux, Roark, Black, & Van Santen, 2011; Rouhizadeh, Prud'Hommeaux, Santen, & Sproat, 2015; Rouhizadeh, Prud'hommeaux, Roark, & van Santen, 2013; Volden & Lord, 1991); and may repeat words or phrases (van Santen, Sproat, & Hill, 2013). Using a lexical feature selection approach (Monroe, Colaresi, & Quinn, 2008), we calculated the frequency of each word in a child's transcript. We used this feature to classify samples as ASD or TD.

Disfluency. Differential use of the filler words "um" and "uh" has been found across men and women, older and younger people, and in ASD (Irvine, Eigsti, & Fein, 2016; Lunsford, Heeman, & Van Santen, 2012; Wieling et al., 2016). Here, we compared the percentage of UM relative to UM+UH across groups.

Speaking rate. In our pilot analysis, we found slower speaking rates in children with ASD vs. TD (Parish-Morris et al., 2016). We attempted to replicate this finding in a larger sample by calculating the mean duration of each word produced by participants in a speech segment (a stretch of speaking between silent pauses).

Latency to respond. Children with ASD have been reported to wait longer before responding in the course of conversation (Heeman, Lunsford, Selfridge, Black, & Van Santen, 2010). To explore this feature in our own sample, we calculated the elapsed time between clinician and child turns.

Fundamental frequency. Prior research has found that pitch variables distinguish language produced by children with ASD from language produced by typically developing children (Asgari, Bayestehtashk, & Shafran, 2013; Kiss, van Santen, Prud'hommeaux, & Black, 2012; Schuller et al., 2013). Here we compared the prosody of participants by calculating mean absolute deviation from the median (MAD) as an outlier-robust measure of dispersion in F0 distribution.

3 Preliminary analysis and results

The analyses and figures below are meant to spur interest and give a hint as to potential avenues to explore using a larger data set. A subset (N=46) of the current sample was described in a forthcoming paper (Parish-Morris et al., 2016).

3.1 Diagnostic classification

We found that word choice alone served surprisingly well to separate the ASD and TD groups. Naïve Bayes classification, using leave-one-out cross validation and weighted log-odds-ratios calculated using the "informative Dirichlet prior" algorithm of Monroe et al. (2008), correctly classified 68% of ASD patients and 100% of typical participants. Receiver Operating Characteristic (ROC) analysis revealed good sensitivity and specificity using this classification metric, with AUC=85% (Figure 1).

The 20 most "ASD-like" words in this analysis were: *{nsv}, know, he, a, now ,no , uh, well, is, actually, mhm, w-, years, eh, right, first, year, once, saw, was* (where {nsv} stands for "non-speech vocalization", meaning sounds that with no lexical counterpart, such as imitative or expressive noises). Of note, "uh" appears in this list, as does "w-", a stuttering-like disfluency.

At the other end of the scale, we found that the 20 least "ASD-like" words in this analysis were:

like, um, and, hundred, so, basketball, something, dishes, go, york, or, if, them, {laugh}, wrong, be, pay, when, friends. Here, the word "um" appears, as does the word "friends, and laughter.

Figure 1. Receiver operating characteristic on word choice separates ASD from TD.

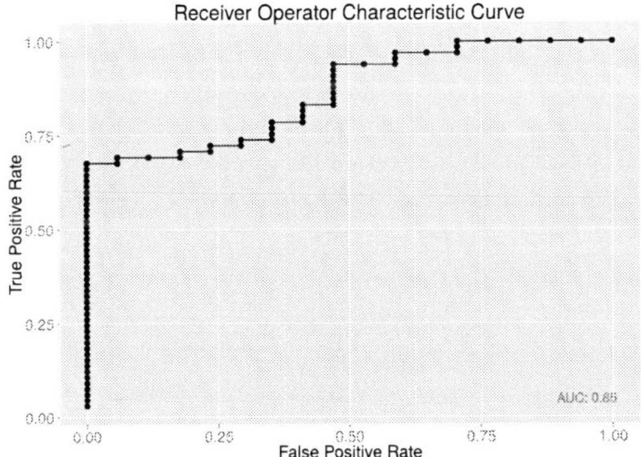

As we discuss below, many linguistic and phonetic features showed systematic differences among the diagnostic groups, and feeding combinations of these features into modern machine-learning algorithms will certainly do an even better job of classifying the participants in our dataset than a simple "bag of words" model. However, we feel that focus on classification at this stage is premature, because of the previously-referenced phenotypic diversity and uneven diagnostic group sizes in our sample. Rather, we believe that similar analysis of much larger datasets will enable us to place individuals in a space with several significant dimensions of relevant variation, rather than trying to force them into discrete categories.

3.2 Other feature differences

Disfluency. We compared rates of um production across the ASD and TD groups (um/(um+uh)). The ASD group produced UM as 61% of their filled pauses (CI: 54%-68%), while the TD group produced UM as 82% of their filled pauses (CI: 75%-88%). The minimum value for the TD group was 58.1%, and 23 of 65 participants in the ASD group fell below that value.

Given prior research showing sex differences on this variable (Wieling et al., 2016), we marked data points as originating from males or females for the purposes of visualization. Figure 2, plotting overall rate of filled pauses against the proportion of filled pauses that are UM, illustrates this interaction of sex and diagnostic category. This naturally raises the question of what other characteristics might also be correlated with these differences; and it underlines the opportunity to use data of this type to discover and explore new dimensions of relevant variation.

Figure 2. Disfluencies in the ASD and TD groups.

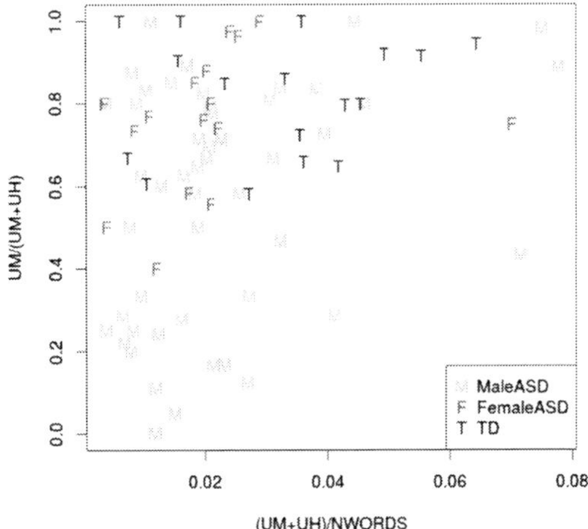

Speaking rate. A comparison of mean word duration as a function of phrase length revealed that TD participants spoke the fastest (overall mean word duration of 376 ms, CI 369-382, calculated from 6891 phrases), followed by the non-ASD mixed clinical group (mean=395 ms; CI 388-401, calculated from 6640 phrases), followed by the ASD group with the slowest speaking rate (mean=402 ms; CI: 398-405, calculated from 24276 phrases).

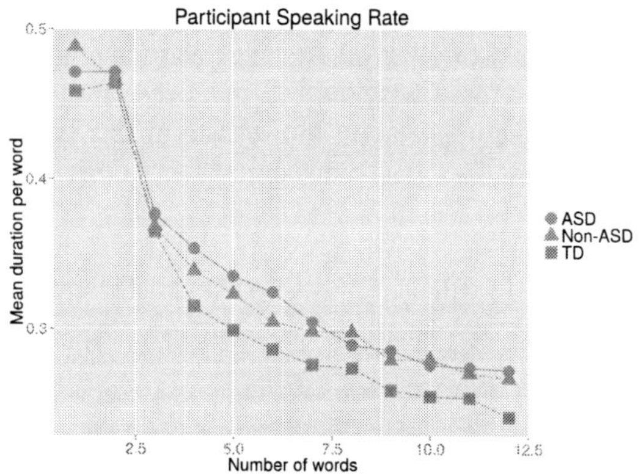

Figure 3. Mean word duration as a function of phrase length differed among all three groups.

Child latency to respond. Our analyses revealed that children with ASD were slower to respond to interviewer bids for conversation than TD participants, with children in the non-ASD mixed clinical group falling in the between.

Figure 4: Cumulative distribution of response latencies for three diagnostic categories.

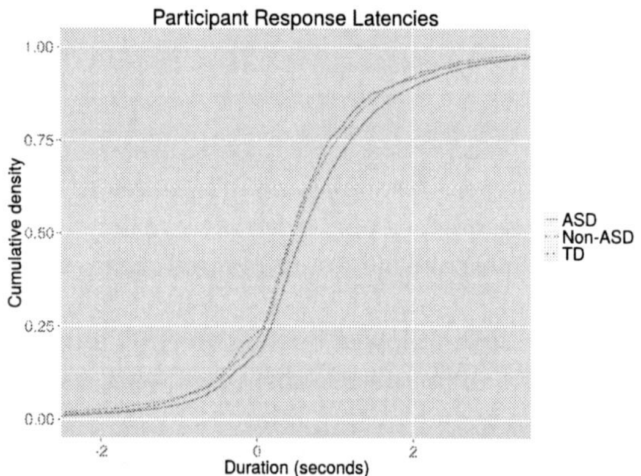

Fundamental Frequency. To compare the prosody of participants we examined an outlier-robust measure of dispersion in their F0 distribution: mean absolute deviation from the median (MAD). F0 contours were extracted for every ADOS session using an implementation of the Kaldi pitch tracking algorithm (Gharemani et al. 2014) using a 10 ms step, 10 ms analysis window width, and search range of 50 to 600 Hz, with all frames identified as belonging to a voiced phone in the forced alignment retained. After then dropping frames from speech segments (as defined in Sec-

tion 2.7) of duration less than 500 ms and and longer than 5 seconds, F0 values were transformed from Hz to semitones using the 5th percentile of each speaker as the base, which served as input for computation of MAD. As depicted in the box-and-whisker plot in Figure 5, MAD values for F0 are both higher and more variable within the ASD and non-ASD mixed clinical group than the TD group (ASD: median: 1.99, IQR: 0.95; non-ASD: median: 1.95, IQR: 0.80; TD: median: 1.47, IQR: 0.26).

Figure 5: Median absolute deviation from median F0 in semitones relative to speaker's 5th percentile.

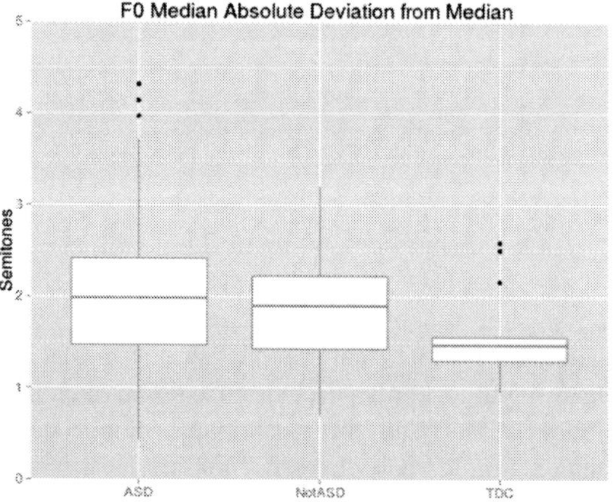

3.3 Correlations with clinical and demographic measures

Our relatively large group of 65 children with ASD offered an opportunity to examine within-group correlations. Due to space constraints, we focus on disfluency and response latency. Future analyses with a larger sample will explore these relationships in TD and non-ASD mixed clinical participants.

Disfluency. We explored relationships between the percent of um/uh disfluencies that were "um", and age/sex/IQ. No significant relationships were found with age or IQ (full-scale, verbal, or nonverbal). As suggested by Figure 2, we found significant sex differences in "um" fillers. Males with ASD filled pauses with "um" instead of "uh" at significantly lower rates (M=56%) than females with ASD (M=75%; Welch's t=-3.20, p=.003). This finding mirrors sex differences found in larger samples of typically developing adults (Wieling et al., 2016). More "um" use was also associated with lower ADOS severity scores (Spearman's Rho=-.25, *p*=.045; males and females did not differ on autism severity), but parent ratings of social and communication competence as measured by the CCC-2 were unrelated to "um" use. This discrepancy could be due to the nature of the prolonged observation on the part of parents (judgments are based on years of observation, during which time parents may become used to their child's disfluencies) versus the short, time-constrained observations of clinicians.

Child latency to respond. The mean length of transitions from interviewer to participant did not correlate with age or any measure of IQ, nor did it differ by participant sex. It did, however, correlate positively with overall ADOS calibrated severity scores (Pearson's r =.28, *p*=.02). An examination of subscale severity scores suggests some measure of specificity; the social communication severity score of the ADOS correlated with response latency (Pearson's r=.31, *p*=.01), while the repetitive behaviors/restricted interests severity score did not (Pearson's r =.04, *p*=.73). As in the case of disfluencies, response latency did not correlate with parent reports of social communication competence.

3.4 Discussion

Our preliminary exploration of this new data set indicates that word choice produced during ADOS evaluations can be used to differentiate children with ASD from typically developing children with good sensitivity and specificity. Using a variety of features, including word choice, inter-turn pause length, and fundamental frequency, we were able to characterize the linguistic signal at a highly granular level. Importantly, we not only found that these features discriminate groups, but also showed that certain features also correlate with clinical presentation. This relationship suggests language-clinical connections that inform personalized approaches to social communication intervention.

Classification sensitivity and specificity using word choice went down relative to prior work with a smaller pilot sample (AUC: 92%; (Parish-Morris et al., 2016)). This may be due to at least two factors that underline the need for a larger corpus than the one we have at present. First, we increased the variability of our ASD sample by adding more het-erogeneous participants. Our first pilot sample consisted of carefully selected "clean" groups of children with classic ASD and typically developing controls, whereas the extension reported here was much more realistic and clinically unclear (e.g., we included ASD participants with a milder phenotype or clinical comorbidities). Second, participants in our first pilot groups were individually matched on a variety of characteristics (age, IQ, sex, parent education, income). Our extended sample tripled our ASD sample, did not increase our TD sample significantly, and did not match individually. It is unusual for TD participants to be administered the ADOS evaluation in most labs, partly due to the expensive and time-consuming nature of the assessment. Large, comparable samples from TD participants are essential to research in this area, and will require efforts to improve accessibility and reduce cost in future studies.

4 Future directions

4.1 New sources, more participants

The ASD sample reported here is large relative to much prior work, but our analyses were nonetheless constrained by smaller comparison groups. We are actively annotating additional ASD samples from past studies conducted at the Center for Autism Research, collecting new data from an expanded age range in our lab (including preschoolers and adults), and seeking out collaborators who wish to contribute language samples to this collection. (Due to privacy laws, final transcripts and audio recordings from this and all other collections must be carefully wiped of personally identifiable information prior to sharing, a process that is currently underway for the present sample.) In particular, we are searching for diverse, well-phenotyped samples enriched for typically developing participants, participants with non-ASD clinical diagnoses, and females with ASD.

Fewer girls than boys are diagnosed with ASD (Christensen, 2016), and they have been historically understudied. Significant linguistic features interact with sex, however (e.g., differences in the use of disfluencies such as um/uh), making this variable especially important to study. We aim to build a cohort of samples from females with and without ASD, to explore the effects of sex-diagnosis interactions on language features.

One immediate goal for our team is to begin telephone collection of ADOS-like samples. Research-grade ADOS recordings, while retrospectively ubiquitous, are not inexpensive or easy to obtain. At present, participants and families must meet with a highly trained clinician, often traveling long distances to do so. We are in the process of developing a protocol that can be administered over the telephone, with relatively untrained conversational partners. We aim to explore the relative classification and characterization value of this method versus rigorous lab-based ADOS recordings.

4.2 Interviewer Analysis

Our current analysis is far from comprehensive. Most notably, we constrained our analyses to child features. Given that the ADOS evaluation is a conversation, it is essential to analyze interviewer speech and language characteristics as well (Bone et al., 2012; Bone, Lee, Black, et al., 2014; Bone, Lee, Potamianos, & Narayanan, 2014). Future analysis plans include assessing dynamic relationships between interviewer and child features over the course of the evaluation.

4.3 Additional types of annotation

We saw interesting patterns in the use of UM and UH emerge in the present analysis, and in the list of the most ASD-associated words, we saw one example of a fluent self-correction, namely the partial word *w-*. This suggests that a more comprehensive annotation of disfluencies, including their semantic, morpho-syntactic, phonetic, and prosodic affinities, would be informative.

Word frequencies were surprisingly diagnostic – perhaps the frequency of syntactic and semantic word categories will also be interesting, including things like parts of speech, negations, and contractions. It is likely to be worthwhile to distinguish the semantic categories of referents, e.g. to individuals, groups, places, and so on. Various other semantic categories may also be interesting – concreteness of reference, span of co-reference relations, definiteness and indefiniteness, and so on.

We saw some signal in simple counts of turn length and speech-segment length – it is plausible that we would learn more from an analysis of syntactic features such as clause length, depth of embedding, frequency of various sorts of modification, etc. Modern analysis techniques can make it relatively cheap to get high-quality analyses of this type.

We could multiply examples almost indefinitely. Our main point in starting the list is that when we have a large body of sharable data of this type, then researchers with new ideas can add their own layers of annotation and explore the resulting patterns. Modern techniques for tagging, parsing, and other sorts of analysis will make such explorations increasingly efficient – as long as a large body of appropriate data is available.

Acknowledgments

This project was supported by an Autism Science Foundation Postdoctoral Fellowship awarded to J. Parish-Morris (Mentors: R.T. Schultz, M. Liberman, C. Cieri), by the NICHD funded Intellectual and Developmental Research Center grant (# U54 HD86984, M Yudkoff, PI), a grant from the Pennsylvania Department of Health (SAP # 4100047863) to R. Schultz and by NIMH RC1MH08879 (R. Schultz, PI). We gratefully acknowledge all the children and families that participated in our research, as well as the clinicians, staff, and students that collected/compiled data at the Center for Autism Research.

References

American Psychiatric Association. (2013). *Diagnostic and Statistical Manual of Mental Disorders, 5th Edition: DSM-5* (5 edition). Washington, D.C: American Psychiatric Publishing.

Asgari, M., Bayestehtashk, A., & Shafran, I. (2013). Robust and accurate features for detecting and diagnosing autism spectrum disorders. In *INTERSPEECH* (pp. 191–194). Retrieved from http://www.cslu.ogi.edu/~zak/is13-autism.pdf

Besacier, L., Barnard, E., Karpov, A., & Schultz, T. (2014). Automatic speech recognition for under-resourced languages: A survey. *Speech Communication*, *56*, 85–100. http://doi.org/10.1016/j.specom.2013.07.008

Bone, D., Black, M. P., Lee, C.-C., Williams, M. E., Levitt, P., Lee, S., & Narayanan, S. (2012). Spontaneous-Speech Acoustic-Prosodic Features of Children with Autism and the Interacting Psychologist. In *INTERSPEECH*. Retrieved from http://sail.usc.edu/~dbone/Bone_spontaneousProsody_ADOS_IS2012.pdf

Bone, D., Goodwin, M. S., Black, M. P., Lee, C.-C., Audhkhasi, K., & Narayanan, S. (2014). Applying Machine Learning to Facilitate Autism Diagnostics: Pitfalls and Promises. *Journal of Autism and Developmental Disorders*. http://doi.org/10.1007/s10803-014-2268-6

Bone, D., Lee, C.-C., Black, M. P., Williams, M. E., Lee, S., Levitt, P., & Narayanan, S. (2014). The Psychologist as an Interlocutor in Autism Spectrum Disorder Assessment: Insights From a Study of Spontaneous Prosody. *Journal of Speech Language and Hearing Research*, *57*(4), 1162. http://doi.org/10.1044/2014_JSLHR-S-13-0062

Bone, D., Lee, C.-C., Potamianos, A., & Narayanan, S. (2014). An Investigation of Vocal Arousal Dynamics in Child-Psychologist Interactions using Synchrony Measures and a Conversation-based Model. In *Fifteenth Annual Conference of the International Speech Communication Association*. Retrieved from https://mazsola.iit.unimiskolc.hu/~czap/letoltes/IS14/IS2014/PDF/AUTHOR/IS140377.PDF

Christensen, D. L. (2016). Prevalence and Characteristics of Autism Spectrum Disorder Among Children Aged 8 Years—Autism and Developmental Disabilities Monitoring Network, 11 Sites, United States, 2012. *MMWR. Surveillance Summaries*, *65*. Retrieved from http://www.cdc.gov/mmwr/volumes/65/ss/ss6503a1.htm

D'Souza, D., Booth, R., Connolly, M., Happé, F., & Karmiloff-Smith, A. (2015). Rethinking the concepts of "local or global processors": evidence from Williams syndrome, Down syndrome, and Autism Spectrum Disorders. *Developmental Science.* http://doi.org/10.1111/desc.12312

Elliott, C. D. (2007). Differential Ability Scales®-II - DAS-II. San Antonio, TX: Harcourt Assessment. Retrieved from http://www.pearsonclinical.com/education/products/100000468/differential-ability-scales-ii-das-ii.html

Fein, D., Barton, M., Eigsti, I.-M., Kelley, E., Naigles, L., Schultz, R. T., … Tyson, K. (2013). Optimal outcome in individuals with a history of autism: Optimal outcome in individuals with a history of autism. *Journal of Child Psychology and Psychiatry*, *54*(2), 195–205. http://doi.org/10.1111/jcpp.12037

Ghahremani, P., BabaAli, B., Povey, D., Ried hammer, K., Trmal, J., & Khudanpur, S. (2014, May). A pitch extraction algorithm tuned for automatic speech recognition. In *IEEE ICASSP 2014.*

Ghaziuddin, M., & Gerstein, L. (1996). Pedantic speaking style differentiates Asperger Syndrome from High-Functioning Autism.

Heeman, P. A., Lunsford, R., Selfridge, E., Black, L., & Van Santen, J. (2010). Autism and interactional aspects of dialogue. In *Proceedings of the 11th Annual Meeting of the Special Interest Group on Discourse and Dialogue* (pp. 249–252). Association for Computational Linguistics. Retrieved from http://dl.acm.org/citation.cfm?id=1944551

Insel, T. R. (2014). The NIMH research domain criteria (RDoC) project: precision medicine for psychiatry. *American Journal of Psychiatry*, *171*(4), 395–397.

Irvine, C. A., Eigsti, I.-M., & Fein, D. A. (2016). Uh, Um, and Autism: Filler Disfluencies as Pragmatic Markers in Adolescents with Optimal Outcomes from Autism Spectrum Disorder. *Journal of Autism and Developmental Disorders*, *46*(3), 1061–1070. http://doi.org/10.1007/s10803-015-2651-y

Kiss, G., van Santen, J. P., Prud'hommeaux, E. T., & Black, L. M. (2012). Quantitative Analysis of Pitch in Speech of Children with Neurodevelopmental Disorders. In *INTERSPEECH*. Retrieved from http://20.210-193-52.unknown.qala.com.sg/archive/archive_papers/interspeech_2012/i12_1343.pdf

Lord, C., Rutter, M., DiLavore, P. S., Risi, S., Gotham, K., & Bishop, S. L. (2012). Autism diagnostic observation schedule, second edition (ADOS-2). Torrance, CA: Western Psychological Services.

Lunsford, R., Heeman, P. A., & Van Santen, J. P. (2012). Interactions Between Turn-taking Gaps, Disfluencies and Social Obligation. In *INTERSPEECH* 2012.

Monroe, D. L., Colaresi, M. P., & Quinn, K. M. (2008). Fightin' Words: Lexical Feature Selection and Evaluation for Identifying the Content of Political Conflict. *Political Analysis*, *16*(4), 372–403.

National Database for Autism Research - Home. (n.d.). Retrieved April 7, 2016, from https://ndar.nih.gov/

Norbury, C. F., Nash, M., Baird, G., & Bishop, D. (2004). Using a parental checklist to identify diagnostic groups in children with communication impairment: a validation of the Children's Communication Checklist--2. *International Journal of Language & Communication Disorders / Royal College of Speech & Language Therapists*, *39*(3), 345–364. http://doi.org/10.1080/13682820410001654883

Parish-Morris, J., Cieri, C., Liberman, M., Bateman, L., Ferguson, E., & Schultz, R. T. (2016). Building Language Resources for Exploring Autism Spectrum Disorders. *Proceedings of the Language Resources and Evaluation Conference 2016.*

Povey, D., Ghoshal, A., Boulianne, G., Burget, L., Glembek, O., Goel, N., … others. (2011). The Kaldi speech recognition toolkit. In *IEEE 2011 workshop on automatic speech recognition and understanding.* IEEE Signal Processing Society. Retrieved from http://infoscience.epfl.ch/record/192584

Prud'hommeaux, E. T., Roark, B., Black, L. M., & Van Santen, J. (2011). Classification of atypical language in autism. In *Proceedings of the 2nd Workshop on Cognitive Modeling and Computational Linguistics* (pp. 88–96), ACL.

Rouhizadeh, M., Prud'Hommeaux, E., Santen, J. V., & Sproat, R. (2015). Measuring idiosyncratic interests in children with autism. Presented at the 53rd Annual Meeting of the Association for Computational Linguistics and the 7th International Joint Conference on Natural Language Processing of the Asian Federation of Natural Language Processing, ACL-IJCNLP 2015.

Rouhizadeh, M., Prud'hommeaux, E. T., Roark, B., & van Santen, J. P. (2013). Distributional semantic models for the evaluation of disordered language. In *HLT-NAACL* (pp. 709–714). Citeseer.

Rutter, M., Bailey, A., & Lord, C. (2003). SCQ: The Social Communication Questionnaire. Los Angeles, CA: Western Psychological Services. Retrieved from https://www.wpspublish.com/store/Images/Downloads/Product/SCQ_Manual_Chapter_1.pdf

Schuller, B., Steidl, S., Batliner, A., Vinciarelli, A., Scherer, K., Ringeval, F., … others. (2013). The INTERSPEECH 2013 computational paralinguistics challenge: social signals, conflict, emotion, autism.

van Santen, J. P. H., Sproat, R. W., & Hill, A. P. (2013). Quantifying Repetitive Speech in Autism Spectrum Disorders and Language Impairment: Repetitive speech in ASD and SLI. *Autism Research*, *6*(5), 372–383. http://doi.org/10.1002/aur.1301

Volden, J., & Lord, C. (1991). Neologisms and idiosyncratic language in autistic speakers. *Journal of Autism and Developmental Disorders*, *21*(2), 109–130. http://doi.org/10.1007/BF02284755

Weigelt, S., Koldewyn, K., & Kanwisher, N. (2012). Face identity recognition in autism spectrum disorders: A review of behavioral studies. *Neuroscience & Biobehavioral Reviews*, *36*(3), 1060–1084. http://doi.org/10.1016/j.neubiorev.2011.12.008

Wieling, M., Grieve, J., Bouma, G., Fruehwald, J., Coleman, J., & Liberman, M. (2016). Variation and change in the use of hesitation markers in Germanic languages. *Language Dynamics and Change, Forthcoming.*

Wing, L. (1981). Sex ratios in early childhood autism and related conditions. *Psychiatry Research*, *5*(2), 129–137.

Yuan, J., Ryant, N., Liberman, M., Stolcke, A., Mitra, V., & Wang, W. (2013). Automatic phonetic segmentation using boundary models. In *INTERSPEECH 2013.*

Generating Clinically Relevant Texts:
A Case Study on Life-changing Events

Mayuresh Oak[1], Anil K. Behera[3], Titus P. Thomas[1], Cecilia Ovesdotter Alm[2],
Emily Prud'hommeaux[2], Christopher Homan[3], Raymond Ptucha[1]

[1]Kate Gleason College of Engineering
[2]College of Liberal Arts
[3]Golisano College of Computing and Information Sciences
Rochester Institute of Technology
Rochester, NY 14623, USA
{mso4106[†]|akb2701[†]|tpt7797[†]|coagla[†]|emilypx[†]|cmh[ξ]|rwpeec[†]
[†]@rit.edu [ξ]@cs.rit.edu

Abstract

The need to protect privacy poses unique challenges to behavioral research. For instance, researchers often can not use examples drawn directly from such data to explain or illustrate key findings. In this research, we use data-driven models to synthesize realistic-looking data, focusing on discourse produced by social-media participants announcing life-changing events. We comparatively explore the performance of distinct techniques for generating synthetic linguistic data across different linguistic units and topics. Our approach offers utility not only for reporting on qualitative behavioral research on such data, where directly quoting a participant's content can unintentionally reveal sensitive information about the participant, but also for clinical computational system developers, for whom access to realistic synthetic data may be sufficient for the software development process. Accordingly, the work also has implications for computational linguistics at large.

1 Introduction

Behavioral research using personal data, such as that from social media or clinical studies, must continually balance insights gained with respect for privacy. Ethical and legal demands also come into play. De-identification involves removing information such as named entities, address-specific information and social security numbers. However, naive approaches are often prone to privacy attacks. Such de-identified data will often still contain information that, when combined with other data from different resources, can point to the individual who generated it. For example, if a de-identified dataset contains detailed demographic information, it could then be possible to extract a small list of people matching this information and to identify a specific person using other, publicly available data.

One approach that strikes a good balance is to synthesize realistic-looking data with the same statistical properties as actual data. Our contribution is to compare different techniques for synthesizing behavioral data. Specifically, we explore this problem in a case study with social media texts that involve social media participants making announcements about life-changing events, which are personal in nature and which also may affect, positively or negatively, a person's well-being.

Two immediate applications to clinical research that motivate this approach are: *qualitative results reporting involving textual data* and *data access issues for software development purposes*. Neither readers of scientific reports nor software developers need access to the original data as long as realistic looking synthetic data is available.

2 Related Work

In the clinical setting, data privacy is important. *Anonymization* aims to ensure that data is untraceable to an original user, whereas *de-identification* may allow the data to be traced back to a user with third-party information.

Szarvas et al. (2007) developed a model for anonymizing personal health information (PHI) from discharge records. The model identifies PHIs

Proceedings of the 3rd Workshop on Computational Linguistics and Clinical Psychology: From Linguistic Signal to Clinical Reality, pages 85–94,
San Diego, California, June 16, 2016. ©2016 Association for Computational Linguistics

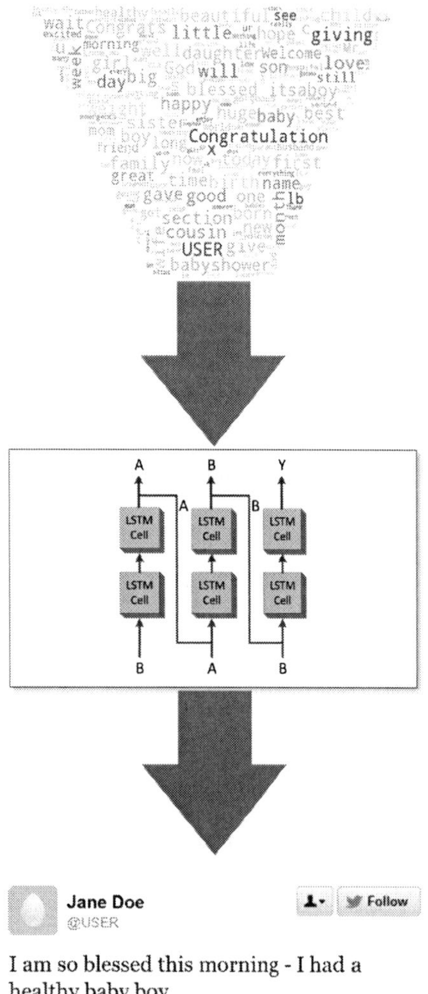

Figure 1: Top level view of the proposed anonymization system. Data is fed to a model which here is a character-based Long-Short Term Memory (LSTM). The LSTM generates new tweets based on the input data.

in several steps and labels all entities which can be tagged from the text structure. It then queries for additional PHI phrases in the text with help from tagged PHI entities.

Bayardo and Agrawal (2005) present improved k-anonymity methods and provide efficient algorithms for data dimensionality reduction. However, even if information such as names of people or providers or quasi-identifiers (QIs) are removed, there are still ways to compare the de-identified data with other records having these identifiers.

In contrast to traditional anonymization and de-identification methods, generation of synthetic data can handle various aspects of hiding individuals, by aggregating and severing data from individual users, yet maintaining the statistical properties of the data used to train generation models. For this paper we explore several forms of data generation, using social media (Twitter) data about life-changing events as a case study. For example, Twitter data has been used for studying important life-changing events (De Choudhry et al., 2013; Li et al., 2014). Other studies present methods for anonymizing Twitter datasets. Terrovitis et al. (2008) model social media as an undirected, unlabeled graph which does retain privacy of social media users. Daubert et al. (2014) discuss the different methods for anonymization of Twitter data. However, there is a lack of work that addresses synthetic data creation using machine generation models.

This paper compares traditional statistical language models and Long Short Term Memory (LSTM) models to learn models from a training set of Twitter data to generate synthetic tweets. LSTMs are recurrent neural networks designed to learn both long and short term temporal sequences. These networks were introduced by Hochreiter and Schmidhuber (1997), with several improvements over the years, the most common of which include individual gating elements (Graves and Schmidhuber, 2005). LSTMs have been shown to perform at state-of-the-art levels for many tasks, including handwriting recognition and generation, language modeling, and machine translation (Greff et al., 2015).

3 Data

Twitter is a microblogging platform used by people to post about their lives. If harnessed properly, tweets can be used for analysis and research of behavioral patterns as well as in studying health information.

We collected tweets using Twitter's streaming API along with customized query strings. These queries targeted the life-changing events of *birth*, *death*, *marriage*, and *divorce*. The tweet collection process suggested that users were more likely to share joyful news about marriage and birth, and

Table 1: Birth patterns

birth of baby/brother/son/daughter/brother/sister
parents of baby/son/daughter/boy/girl/angel
arrival of baby/brother/son/daughter/sister/angel
just gave birth to baby/son/daughter/boy/girl
weigh/weighing #Number lbs/pounds
its a boy/girl
pregnant/c-section

Table 2: Marriage patterns

I'm/we are getting/sister/brother/mother married
friend/uncle/aunt is getting married
I/we/sister/brother/friend/uncle/aunt got married

Table 3: Death patterns

RIP mom/mama/dad/father/grandmother/brother/
RIP grandpa/grandfather/sister/friend
he/mom/mama/dad/father passed away
grandfather/grandpa/grandma passed away
brother/sister/friend passed away

less likely to share difficult news about death and divorce. Tweets on divorce were particularly scarce, so this event was ignored as the study continued.

The pool of tweets came from a collection of tweets from a mid-sized city in the US North East in 2013 as well as streaming tweets irrespective of location from early 2016. Roughly 18 million tweets were collected, including tweets for the three aforementioned categories of birth, death, and marriage. Only the text of the tweets was utilized for this study.

After inspecting the data, we formulated a set of lexical keywords, phrases and regular expressions to collect tweets by category. These reflected topical patterns, such as announcements of marriage or birth in the family, the weight of the newborn baby or whether it is a girl or a boy, or the passing of a friend or family member. Table 1 shows the patterns used to extract tweets about *birth*. Similarly, Table 2 shows the patterns for *marriage*, and Table 3 for *death*. We attempted to remove tweets about celebri-

ties, TV shows, news stories, and jokes. After filtering, we selected and hand-annotated for each category a set of 2000 tweets. For comparison's sake we also chose randomly 2000 (unlabeled) tweets from the data, and call this the *general* category. Note that any tweet could be present in this category, including those from the first three categories.

We replaced Twitter usernames with the token *@USER*, while URL links, retweets, and emoticons were replaced with the keywords *URL*, *RT*, and *EMOT*, respectively. We removed the pound signs from hashtags to make it look more like general written language and to reduce the dictionary size of the word-based language models.

For the character-based models, we performed the following further steps. We separated each character in the input data by a space and replaced the usual space characters with *<space>*. We considered the tags introduced in the earlier pre-processing phase (e.g. - *@USER*) to be unique characters. On output, we replaced all space characters with the null string and replace the space tag *<space>* with the space character.

Tables 4 through 6 show samples of collected tweets.

Table 4: Birth tweets

She gave birth to the baby aww congrats loulou @USER
birth of Baby Tyler (They picked my baby name suggestion)

Table 5: Death tweets

my grandpa passed away today All I hope is that things get better
@USER my grandma passed away

Table 6: Marriage tweets

me and @USER just got married
we getting married

4 Methods

4.1 Long-Short Term Memory

Recurrent neural networks (RNN) are popular models that have shown great potential in many natural language processing (NLP) tasks. LSTMs (Hochreiter and Schmidhuber, 1997; Graves and Schmidhuber, 2005) are a specific subset of RNNs that have been modified to be especially good at conditioning on both long and short term temporal sequences. LSTMs modify the standard design of neural networks in several ways: they eliminate the strict requirement that neurons only connect to other neurons in succeeding layers (adding recurrence), convert the standard neuron into a more complex *memory cell*, and add non-linear gating units which serve to govern the information flowing out of and recursively flowing back into the cell (Greff et al., 2015). The memory cell differentiates itself from a simple neuron by including the ability to remember its state over time; this coupled with gating units gives the LSTM the ability to recognize important long-term dependencies while simultaneously forgetting unimportant collocations.

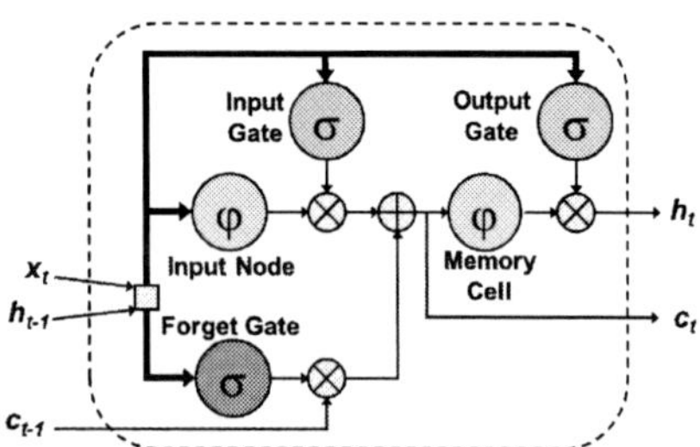

Figure 2: A single LSTM memory block. The three gates govern the input node and memory cell to allow long term memory. The function φ is the *tanh* function and the function σ is the *sigmoid* function.

The LSTM we use here, as implemented by Karpathy (2015) modifies the original architecture by removing *peephole connections*. The intuitive understanding of the components in an LSTM memory block can be summarized as:

1. **Input node**: Also known as input modulation gate or new memory gate, takes the input and the past hidden state to summarize the new input in light of the past context from h_{t-1}.

2. **Input gate**: Also known as write gate, takes the input and the past hidden state to determine the importance of the current input as it effects the cell.

3. **Forget gate**: Also known as reset gate, takes the input and the past hidden state and gives the provision for the hidden layer to discard or forget the historical data.

4. **Output gate**: Takes the input and the past hidden state and determines what parts of the cell output c_t need to be present in the new hidden state h_t for the next timestep.

5. **Memory cell**: Takes advice from the forget gate and governed Input Node to determine the usefulness of the previous memory c_{t-1} to produce the new memory c_t.

The functionality above describes only how a *single* LSTM memory block works, analogous to a single neuron in a regular neural network. To create an LSTM which learns, hundreds of these blocks are combined in a single layer (analogous to hundreds of nodes in a hidden layer), with the hidden output, h_t, c_t of one block feeding into the input of another. Further complexity (and learning power) is added by including multiple layers of LSTM memory blocks. The final output of LSTM memory blocks (or inputs from one layer to the next) are provided by calculating $y_t = W_y f(h_t)$, where W_y is an output weight matrix to learn and $f(\cdot)$ is an activation function which can vary depending on use case.

The input, x_t, to an LSTM memory block differs depending on implementation and use case. When using LSTMs for NLP, the input can be word or character-based. The LSTM used in this research (Karpathy, 2015), takes as input a vector representing an individual data item (character/word) and predicts the most probable data item given the current data item and the LSTM's previous states. Training, therefore, is done by taking an example sequence of data items, predicting the next data item using the current weights, calculating the difference between what was predicted and what should have been predicted, and back propagating this difference to update the weights. All LSTM models were trained for 500 epochs and sequence length of 50, where the sequence length is the length of time the LSTM cell is unrolled per iteration. Two LSTM layers were used to train the model on the input data. Each LSTM layer had 512 hidden nodes. Language generation can be performed after training, in which the LSTM is given either a starting sequence of data items (or it calculates the most probable sequence to start with), and then generates new data items based on its own predictions in previous time steps.

4.2 Standard N-gram Language Models

In order to demonstrate the particular utility of LSTMs for generating realistic tweets, the output of our character- and word-based LSTM methods was compared to that of standard n-gram backoff language models. Such models are widely used to model the probability of word sequences for many NLP applications, including machine translation, automatic speech recognition, and part-of-speech tagging. The SRI Language Modeling Toolkit (SRILM) was used to build 4-gram word- and character-based language models (Stolcke, 2002). Using these models, we then generate synthetic tweets using the OpenGRM Ngram library (Roark et al., 2012).

4.3 Experimental Design

For each event category, we divided the dataset of 2000 tweets into 1800 training and 200 testing instances. We used the machine translation quality metric BLEU (Papineni et al., 2002) to measure the similarity between machine generated tweets and the held out tests sets. For each model, we generated ten sets of 200 tweets. We calculated BLEU scores (without the brevity penalty) using the full 200-tweet test set as the reference for each candidate tweet and report the average of the BLEU scores of all ten sets of tweets generated by a given model.

To gain further insight into the effectiveness of the machine generated data, we asked human annotators to evaluate the generated tweets. We selected 800 tweets by randomly sampling: 400 human generated tweets (100 from each category), and 400 machine generated tweets. The 400 machine gener-

Table 7: Mean BLEU scores and their standard deviation over ten generated test sets of 200 tweets per model, by topic, model, and linguistic unit.

Topic	Model		BLEU
Birth	LSTM	char	**34.61** ±2.53
		word	32.36 ±2.21
	LM	char	12.15 ±0.63
		word	32.01±0.96
Marriage	LSTM	char	31.14±2.30
		word	26.22±0.77
	LM	char	12.54±1.08
		word	**32.26**±0.96
Death	LSTM	char	**20.16**±2.78
		word	17.84±9.45
	LM	char	6.04±0.62
		word	16.93±0.67
General	LSTM	char	40.55±4.27
		word	17.62±2.17
	LM	char	5.46±0.60
		word	**44.74**±1.33

ated tweets consisted of 25 tweets for each combination of model (LM-char, LM-word, LSTM-char, LSTM-word) and category (*birth*, *marriage*, *death*, *general*). For each tweet, the annotators indicated if they thought the tweet was generated by a human or machine, and they rated the quality of the tweet on the basis of syntax and semantics. Also, they indicated which topic category they thought the tweet belonged to.

5 Results

BLEU, a measure of n-gram precision widely used to evaluated machine translation output, was used to objectively evaluate the similarity between the human-generated tweets and the synthetic tweets produced by our models. Table 7 shows the BLEU scores for each combination of topic, model, and linguistic unit. The character-based LSTM models and the word-based LM models both perform very strongly, with each reporting the highest BLEU score in two of the four topics. We further note that the character-based LSTM always outperforms the word-based LSTM. Although it might be surprising that a character-based model would produce higher values for a word n-gram precision metric such as

Table 8: The percent of instances where the four human annotators (A1 - A4) were deceived into thinking a synthetic tweet was human generated. The values in bold are the best performing models for each category by annotator. (*B = birth, D = death , M = marriage , B = general*).

Model	A1				A2				A3				A4			
	B	*D*	*M*	*G*	*B*	*D*	*M*	*G*	*B*	*D*	*M*	*G*	*B*	*D*	*M*	*G*
LM-char	14	0	0	0	14	0	20	0	40	52	28	16	16	8	8	12
LM-word	18	8	21	10	18	8	50	**40**	**80**	**80**	**88**	**72**	32	32	**48**	44
LSTM-char	**45**	25	**44**	0	36	**25**	**56**	22	60	72	68	64	**40**	**44**	40	**44**
LSTM-word	33	**38**	30	**11**	**44**	**25**	40	11	76	72	48	44	36	36	24	28

BLEU, we suspect this is due to the fact that the large feature space of the word-based model in combination with the relatively small number of training tweets (roughly 1800) is not optimal for learning an LSTM model.

5.1 Human evaluation

A randomized set of 800 tweets, both real and synthetic, from all four topic categories was submitted to a panel of annotators (co-authors). Each annotator was asked to decide whether the tweet was real

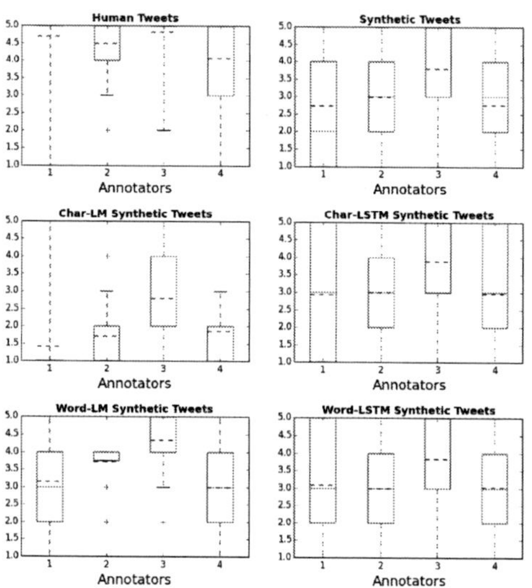

Figure 4: Semantics score by annotator. Higher scores suggest more satisfactory generation of semantic contents (median = red line, mean = dashed line).

(i.e., produced by a human) or synthetic (i.e., generated by one of the LSTM or n-gram language models). Each tweet was also rated in terms of its syntax and semantics on a five point Likert scale. In addition, the annotators were asked to select the intended topic category (*birth, death, marriage,* or *general*) of the tweet.

Figure 5 shows the ability of human annotators to accurately identify a tweet's topic. In general, the annotators were able to identify the topic of the human tweets, with the weakest performance in the *general* category. Identifying the intended topic of the synthetic tweets was more challenging for the

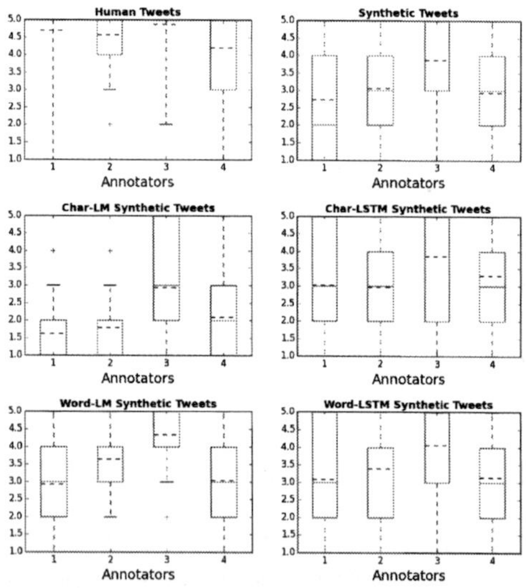

Figure 3: Syntax score by annotator. Higher scores suggest more satisfactory generation of syntactic structures (median = red line, mean = dashed line).

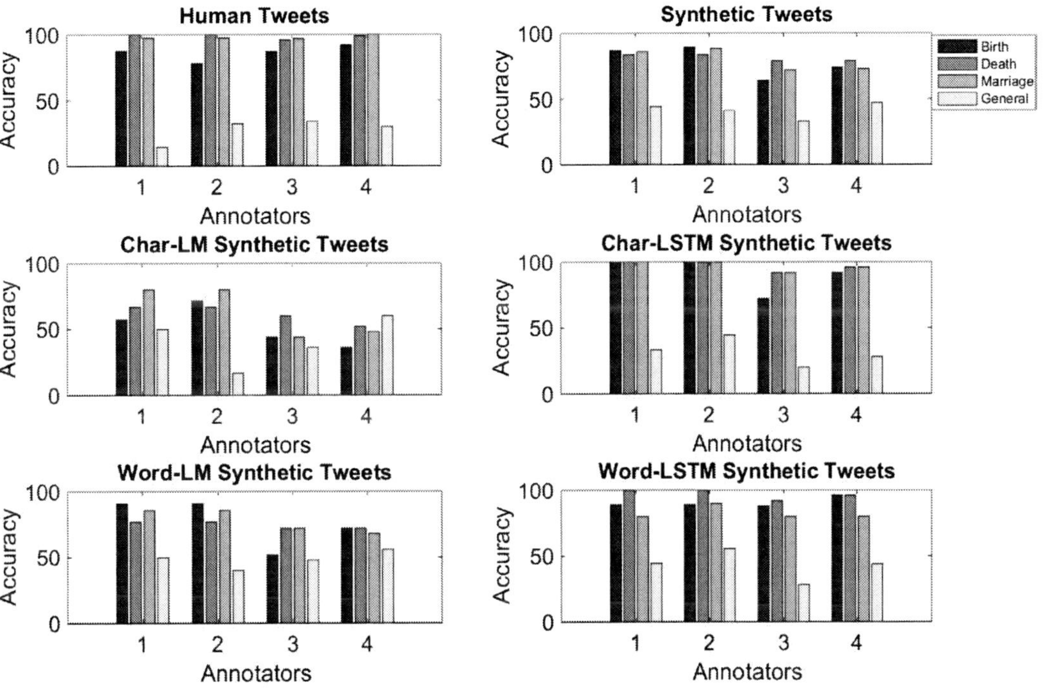

Figure 5: Ability of four human annotators (A1 - A4) to predict the topic category of the data from which a tweet was generated, per model. The top left panel reflects results for human-composed tweets, whereas the top right panel shows results across synthetic tweets, corresponding to the four models in subsequent panels. (Dark blue = *birth* , light blue = *death* , green = *marriage* , yellow = *general*).

annotators, but accuracy was quite high in all topics other than *general*. We note that the *general* category was not filtered to remove tweets that could have belonged to the other topics, which could explain this discrepancy.

Figures 3 and 4 show the distribution of each annotator's syntax and semantics scores for each model. These boxplots show that there was significant variance in the annotators' evaluation of the syntactic and semantic quality of the tweets. We note, however, that the models yielding the highest BLEU scores, char-LSTM and word-LM, tended to receive more favorable scores for syntactic and semantic quality. The character-based LM model, whose BLEU scores were significantly lower than other models, consistently received the most unsatisfactory evaluation of syntactic and semantic quality by all four annotators. It also seems that the LSTM models produce output that is more consistent in its

semantic and syntactic quality, with smaller annotator to annotator variance than the LM models.

With regard to Figure 5, Annotators 1 and 2 rated 283 (selected randomly) tweets, while Annotators 3 and 4 rated all 800 tweets; and with regard to Figures 3, 4, and Table 8, all annotators rated 283 tweets. Annotators 1 and 2 have an academic background in linguistics, while the other two annotators do not have prior linguistic training, perhaps explaining why annotators 1 and 2 generally were better able to identify the topic category. Annotators 1 and 2 tended to have similar distributions of semantic and syntactic quality scores across models, which again is likely related to their previous training in linguistics and linguistic annotation. Annotator 4 may have been less forgiving about non-standard language use in the human-composed tweets, while annotator 3 was more tolerant of the syntax and semantics of machine-generated tweets.

Table 9: Synthetic tweets marked as human generated by all four annotators.

Congrats to @USER and her husband on the birth of their son Welcome to the Cyclone family, Eally Kinglan URL URL (***Char LSTM Generated***)
@USER congratulations on birth of your son,20 days,ago,URL (***Word LM Generated***)
@USER @USER @USER,looks like we're getting hitched in June URL (***Word LM Generated***)
Im getting married in 17 days death (***Char LSTM Generated***)
RT @USER rip grandma 2 8 16 (***Word LM Generated***)

Table 10: Synthetic tweets marked as synthetic by all four annotators.

RT @USER The new part prigials give birth to bely son Junt and I'm delined a hape proud (***Char LSTM Generated***)
I'm so sorry for your loss and world harry gotting to my funeral it was without URL (***Word LM Generated***)

Table 8 shows the percent of instances a human annotator marked a synthetic tweet as human generated. Table 9 shows some of the tweets that were generated by language models but were identified by all four annotators as human generated. A few example tweets that were correctly identified by all four annotators as synthetic tweets are displayed in Table 10.

6   Conclusion

We have discussed generating synthetic data in the context of readers of scientific reports or software developers. In addition, one potential clinical application might be to apply this to patient transcripts so that they could be shown to other patients suffering from similar problems, e.g., for anonymized virtual group therapy. Such an approach might be especially useful in rural and developing regions, where clinical resources are sparse. Anonymization of data in research is often necessary to protect patient or user identity. This research explores data-driven models to generate realistic-looking discourse with the same statistical properties as a training corpus. Specifically, this research explores the synthetic generation of tweets, contrasting LM and LSTM models, character-based and word-based linguistic units, and the topic categories of birth, death, and marriage. Based on the results from objective BLEU scores and subjective human evaluation, the word-based LM and char-based LSTM models performed well, deceiving annotators 41 and 43 percent of the time on average into thinking a synthetic tweet was human generated. This research shows promising evidence that the synthetic generation of user data may be preferred to existing techniques of naive anonymization which can potentially lead to user identification through combination of demographic data mining and ancillary metadata.

References

Puneet Agarwal, Rajgopal Vaithiyanathan, Saurabh Sharma, and Gautam Shroff. 2012. {Catching the Long-Tail: Extracting Local News Events from Twitter}. *Proceedings of the Sixth International AAAI Conference on Weblogs and Social Media.*

Roberto J Bayardo and Rakesh Agrawal. 2005. Data privacy through optimal k-anonymization. In *Data Engineering, 2005. ICDE 2005. Proceedings. 21st International Conference on*, pages 217–228. IEEE.

Edward Benson, Aria Haghighi, and Regina Barzilay. 2011. Event discovery in social media feeds. In *Proceedings of the 49th Annual Meeting of the Association for Computational Linguistics: Human Language Technologies-Volume 1*, pages 389–398. Association for Computational Linguistics.

Deepayan Chakrabarti and Kunal Punera. 2011. Event Summarization Using Tweets. *ICWSM*, 11:66–73.

J. Daubert, L. Bock, P. Kikirasy, M. Muhlhauser, and M. Fischer. 2014. Twitterize: Anonymous Microblogging. In *Computer Systems and Applications (AICCSA), 2014 IEEE/ACS 11th International Conference on*, pages 817–823, Nov.

Munmun De Choudhry, Scott Counts, and Eric Horvitz. 2013. Major life changes and behavioral markers in social media: Case of childbirth. In *Proceedings of the 16th ACM Conference on Computer Supported Cooperative Work (San Antonio, TX, USA, Feb 23-27, 2013). CSCW 2013.* ACM.

Munmun De Choudhury, Scott Counts, and Eric Horvitz. 2013. Major life changes and behavioral markers in social media: case of childbirth. In *Proceedings of the*

2013 conference on Computer supported cooperative work, pages 1431–1442. ACM.

Barbara Di Eugenio, Nick Green, and Rajen Subba. 2013. Detecting life events in feeds from twitter. In *2013 IEEE Seventh International Conference on Semantic Computing*, pages 274–277. Ieee.

Jeffrey Donahue, Lisa Anne Hendricks, Sergio Guadarrama, Marcus Rohrbach, Subhashini Venugopalan, Kate Saenko, and Trevor Darrell. 2015. Long-term recurrent convolutional networks for visual recognition and description. In *Proceedings of the IEEE Conference on Computer Vision and Pattern Recognition*, pages 2625–2634.

Lilian Edwards and Andrea M Matwyshyn. 2013. Twitter (R) evolution: privacy, free speech and disclosure. In *Proceedings of the 22nd international conference on World Wide Web companion*, pages 745–750. International World Wide Web Conferences Steering Committee.

Rumi Ghosh, Tawan Surachawala, and Kristina Lerman. 2011. Entropy-based classification of'retweeting'activity on twitter. *arXiv preprint arXiv:1106.0346*.

Alex Graves and Jürgen Schmidhuber. 2005. Framewise phoneme classification with bidirectional LSTM and other neural network architectures. *Neural Networks*, 18(5):602–610.

Klaus Greff, Rupesh Kumar Srivastava, Jan Koutník, Bas R Steunebrink, and Jürgen Schmidhuber. 2015. LSTM: A Search Space Odyssey. *arXiv preprint arXiv:1503.04069*.

Sepp Hochreiter and Jürgen Schmidhuber. 1997. Long short-term memory. *Neural computation*, 9(8):1735–1780.

Andrej Karpathy and Li Fei-Fei. 2015. Deep visual-semantic alignments for generating image descriptions. In *Proceedings of the IEEE Conference on Computer Vision and Pattern Recognition*, pages 3128–3137.

Andrej Karpathy. 2015. Char-RNN: Multi-layer recurrent neural networks (LSTM, GRU, RNN) for character-level language models in torch. `https://github.com/karpathy/char-rnn`. Accessed: 2015-07-17.

Ninghui Li, Tiancheng Li, and Suresh Venkatasubramanian. 2007. t-closeness: Privacy beyond k-anonymity and l-diversity. In *Data Engineering, 2007. ICDE 2007. IEEE 23rd International Conference on*, pages 106–115. IEEE.

Jiwei Li, Alan Ritter, Claire Cardie, and Eduard H Hovy. 2014. Major Life Event Extraction from Twitter based on Congratulations/Condolences Speech Acts. In *EMNLP*, pages 1997–2007.

Shirin Nilizadeh, Apu Kapadia, and Yong-Yeol Ahn. 2014. Community-enhanced de-anonymization of online social networks. In *Proceedings of the 2014 ACM SIGSAC Conference on Computer and Communications Security*, pages 537–548. ACM.

Kishore Papineni, Salim Roukos, Todd Ward, and Wei-Jing Zhu. 2002. BLEU: a method for automatic evaluation of machine translation. In *Proceedings of the 40th annual meeting on association for computational linguistics*, pages 311–318. Association for Computational Linguistics.

Rene Pickhardt, Thomas Gottron, Martin Körner, Paul Georg Wagner, Till Speicher, and Steffen Staab. 2014. A generalized language model as the combination of skipped n-grams and modified kneser-ney smoothing. *arXiv preprint arXiv:1404.3377*.

Jacob Ratkiewicz, Michael Conover, Mark Meiss, Bruno Gonçalves, Alessandro Flammini, and Filippo Menczer. 2011. Detecting and Tracking Political Abuse in Social Media. In *ICWSM*.

Brian Roark, Richard Sproat, Cyril Allauzen, Michael Riley, Jeffrey Sorensen, and Terry Tai. 2012. The OpenGrm open-source finite-state grammar software libraries. In *Proceedings of the ACL 2012 System Demonstrations*.

Takeshi Sakaki, Makoto Okazaki, and Yutaka Matsuo. 2010. Earthquake Shakes Twitter Users: Real-time Event Detection by Social Sensors. In *Proceedings of the 19th International Conference on World Wide Web*, WWW '10, pages 851–860, New York, NY, USA. ACM.

Pierangela Samarati and Latanya Sweeney. 1998. Generalizing data to provide anonymity when disclosing information. In *PODS*, volume 98, page 188.

Priya Sidhaye and Jackie Chi Kit Cheung. 2015. Indicative Tweet Generation: An Extractive Summarization Problem? *Proceedings of the 2015 Conference on Empirical Methods in Natural Language Processing*, pages 138–147.

Amardeep Singh, Divya Bansal, and Sanjeev Sofat. 2014. An approach of privacy preserving based publishing in twitter. In *Proceedings of the 7th International Conference on Security of Information and Networks*, page 39. ACM.

Richard Socher, Milad Mohammadi, and Rohit Mundra. Spring 2015. Cs 224d: Deep learning for NLP. http://cs224d.stanford.edu/lecture_notes/LectureNotes4.pdf.

Andreas Stolcke. 2002. SRILM – An Extensible Language Modeling Toolkit. In *Proceedings of the International Conference on Spoken Language Processing*, volume 2, pages 901–904.

György Szarvas, Richárd Farkas, and Róbert Busa-Fekete. 2007. State-of-the-art anonymization of medical records using an iterative machine learning framework. *Journal of the American Medical Informatics Association*, 14(5):574–580.

Manolis Terrovitis, Nikos Mamoulis, and Panos Kalnis. 2008. Privacy-preserving anonymization of set-valued data. *Proceedings of the VLDB Endowment*, 1(1):115–125.

Tsung-Hsien Wen, Milica Gasic, Nikola Mrksic, Pei-Hao Su, David Vandyke, and Steve Young. 2015. Semantically conditioned lstm-based natural language generation for spoken dialogue systems. *arXiv preprint arXiv:1508.01745*.

Jian Xu, Wei Wang, Jian Pei, Xiaoyuan Wang, Baile Shi, and Ada Wai-Chee Fu. 2006. Utility-based Anonymization Using Local Recoding. In *Proceedings of the 12th ACM SIGKDD International Conference on Knowledge Discovery and Data Mining*, KDD '06, pages 785–790, New York, NY, USA. ACM.

Don't Let Notes Be Misunderstood: A Negation Detection Method for Assessing Risk of Suicide in Mental Health Records

George Gkotsis[1], Sumithra Velupillai[1,2], Anika Oellrich[1],
Harry Dean[1], Maria Liakata[3] and Rina Dutta[1]
[1] IoPPN, King's College London
`firstname.lastname@kcl.ac.uk`
[2] School of Computer Science and Communication, KTH, Stockholm
[3] Department of Computer Science, University of Warwick
`m.liakata@warwick.ac.uk`

Abstract

Mental Health Records (MHRs) contain free-text documentation about patients' suicide and suicidality. In this paper, we address the problem of determining whether grammatic variants (inflections) of the word "suicide" are affirmed or negated. To achieve this, we populate and annotate a dataset with over 6,000 sentences originating from a large repository of MHRs. The resulting dataset has high Inter-Annotator Agreement (κ 0.93). Furthermore, we develop and propose a negation detection method that leverages syntactic features of text[1]. Using parse trees, we build a set of basic rules that rely on minimum domain knowledge and render the problem as binary classification (affirmed vs. negated). Since the overall goal is to identify patients who are expected to be at high risk of suicide, we focus on the evaluation of positive (affirmed) cases as determined by our classifier. Our negation detection approach yields a recall (sensitivity) value of 94.6% for the positive cases and an overall accuracy value of 91.9%. We believe that our approach can be integrated with other clinical Natural Language Processing tools in order to further advance information extraction capabilities.

1 Introduction

Suicide is a leading cause of death globally. Approximately 10% of people report having suicidal thoughts at some point in their lives (Nock et al., 2013) and each year 0.3% of the general population

---

[1] `https://github.com/gkotsis/negation-detection`

make a suicide attempt (Borges et al., 2010). Mental disorders (particularly depression, substance abuse, schizophrenia and other psychoses) are associated with approximately 90% of all suicides (Arsenault-Lapierre et al., 2004). Assessment of suicide risk is therefore routine practice for clinicians in mental health services, but it is notoriously inaccurate as well as time-consuming (Ryan et al., 2010). Although individual risk factors associated with suicide have been reported in depth (e.g. Steeg et al., 2016), integrating them into an algorithm to analyse signatures of suicidality has been beset with difficulties.

Clinicians document the progress of mental health patients in Mental Health Records (MHRs), predominantly using free text, with sparse structured information. This poses new and interesting challenges for clinical Natural Language Processing (NLP) tool development that could assist in identifying which patients are most at risk of suicide, and when (Haerian et al., 2012; Westgate et al., 2015). Developing a classifier to identify times of greatest risk for suicide at an individual patient level (Kessler et al., 2015; Niculescu et al., 2015) would assist in targeting suicide prevention strategies to those patients who are most vulnerable (Mann et al., 2005). Negation can be used to denote absence or inversion of concepts. As a linguistic feature it can play a prominent role in monitoring both symptom context and risk in psychological conditions (Chu et al., 2006). For instance, one study found that almost 50% of the clinical concepts in narrative reports were negated (Chapman et al., 2001).

In this paper, we address the long-term goal of de-

Proceedings of the 3rd Workshop on Computational Linguistics and Clinical Psychology: From Linguistic Signal to Clinical Reality, pages 95–105,
San Diego, California, June 16, 2016. ©2016 Association for Computational Linguistics

veloping improved information retrieval systems for clinicians and researchers, with a specific focus on suicide risk assessment. To achieve this, we focus on the problem of determining negation concerning mentions of suicide. Clinical concepts are most often defined as nouns ("suicide") or noun phrases ("suicide ideation"), and a negation detection algorithm needs to model the surrounding context to correctly ascertain whether the concept is negated or not ("patient has never expressed any suicidal ideation" vs. "patient expressing suicidal ideation").

Modelling the surrounding context of words can be done in different ways. Our work is motivated by the advances in Probabilistic Context Free Grammar Parsers (PCFGs), which allow us express widely generalisable negation patterns in terms of restrictions on constituents. A solution to negation detection that uses different aspects of linguistic structure can provide richer and more informative features. As a next step we want to extend our work and extract other important features from MHRs, such as the statements in the form of subject-predicate-object, temporal characteristics or degree of suicidality.

We propose an automated method for determining negation in relation to documented suicidality in MHRs. Our negation detection algorithm relies on syntactic information and is applied and evaluated on a manually annotated corpus of sentences containing mentions of *suicide*, or inflections thereof, from a repository of mental health notes. Our paper makes the following contributions:

- we create an annotated dataset containing over 6,000 sentences with mentions of suicide (affirmed or negated),

- we propose a new method for incorporating syntactic information for automatically determining whether a mention of interest is affirmed or negated.

To our knowledge, no previous research has addressed the problem of negation detection in the domain of MHRs and suicidality.

2 Related Work

Negation detection has long been recognized as a crucial part of improved information extraction system development in the biomedical and clinical NLP research community (Morante and Sporleder, 2010), as negated concepts alter the meaning of what is extracted. In general, successful approaches have relied on terminological resources defining negation keywords, concepts, and other rules for determining negation values (lexicon- and rule-based), or based on machine learning methods, where models have been built based on large sets of manually annotated training examples (Meystre et al., 2008). In both cases, manually annotated corpora are needed for training, developing and evaluation. Systems are usually evaluated by calculating precision (positive predictive value) and recall (sensitivity).

One of the earliest, and still widely used, negation detection algorithms is NegEx, which determines whether or not a specified target concept is negated by searching for predefined lexical negation (e.g. *not*), pseudonegation (*no increase*) and conjunction (*except*) cues surrounding the concept (6 words before and after). On a test set of 1000 discharge summary sentences (1235 concepts), NegEx resulted in 84.5% precision and 77.8% recall (Chapman et al., 2001). The NegEx algorithm has also been extended to handle further semantic modifiers (e.g. uncertainty, experiencer) and a wider surrounding context with improved results (overall average precision 94%, recall 92%) when evaluated on 120 reports of six different types (Harkema et al., 2009), and to also perform document-level classifications including semantic modifiers (Chapman et al., 2011).

Lexical approaches relying on surface features are limited in that the *linguistic* relation between the target term and the negation is not captured. NegFinder (Mutalik et al., 2001) is a system that, in addition to defining lexical cues, uses a context free grammar parser for situations where the distance between a target term and negation is far. This approach resulted in 95.7% recall and 91.8% precision when evaluated on 1869 concepts from 10 documents. Syntactic parsers can provide a richer representation of the relationship between words in a sentence, which has been utilised also for negation detection solutions. For instance, DepNeg (Sohn et al., 2012) rely on the syntactic context of a target concept and negation cue, which improved negation detection performance, in particular for reducing the number of false positives (Type I errors) on a test set of 160 Mayo clinical notes (96.6% precision,73.9% recall). Similarly, DEEPEN (Mehrabi et al., 2015) adds a step after applying NegEx on clinical notes. Syntactic information from a dependency parse tree is then used in a number of rules to determine the final negation value, resulting in precision of 89.2-96.6% and recall of 73.8-96.3% on two different clinical datasets and three different types of clinical concepts.

Machine learning approaches have also been applied to the negation detection problem with success. These approaches rely on the access to training data, which has been provided within the framework of shared tasks such as the 2010 i2b2 challenge (Uzuner et al., 2011) for clinical text, the BioScope (Vincze et al., 2008) corpus in the CoNLL-2010 shared task for biomedical research articles as well as clinical text, the ShARe corpus (Pradhan, Sameer and Elhadad, Noémie and South, Brett R and Martinez, David and Christensen, Lee and Vogel, Amy and Suominen, Hanna and Chapman, Wendy W and Savova, Guergana, 2015) in the ShARe/CLEF eHealth and SemEval challenges, and the GENIA corpus (Kim et al., 2003) in the BioNLP'09 shared task.

A comprehensive study on current state-of-the-art negation detection algorithms and their performance on different corpora is presented by Wu et al (2014). As is concluded in this study, none of the existing state-of-the-art systems are guaranteed to work well on a new domain or corpus, and there are still open issues when it comes to creating a generalizable negation detection solution.

3 Proposed framework

Two main stages were employed in this study: 1) data collection and creation of a MHR corpus with annotations of concepts marked as negated or affirmed, and 2) the development of our proposed methodology to detect negations for the purpose of assessing risk of suicide from MHRs[2]. Figure 1 provides an overview of the workflow we employed in this study. We discuss these stages in detail below.

3.1 Dataset and annotation

Pseudonymised and de-identified mental health records of all patients (both in and outpatients) from the Clinical Record Interactive Search (CRIS) database were used (Perera et al., 2016). CRIS has records from the South London and Maudsley NHS Foundation Trust (SLaM), one of the largest mental health providers in Europe. SLaM covers the Lambeth, Southwark, Lewisham and Croydon boroughs in South London. CRIS has full ethical approval as a database for secondary analysis (Oxford REC C, reference 08/H0606/71+5) under a robust, patient-led and externally approved governance structure. Currently, CRIS contains mental health records for around 226K patients, and approximately 18.6 million documents with free text. Out of these documents, 783K contain at least one mention of "suicid*" (111K patients). Monitoring suicide risk is an important task for mental health teams, and therefore use of the term "suicid*" was expected to be common.

The annotation task was defined on a concept-level: each target concept ("suicid*") in a sentence was to be marked as either *negative* (negated mention, e.g."denies suicidal thoughts") or *positive* (affirmed mention, e.g."patient with suicidal thoughts")[3]. In clinical narratives, there are cases where this distinction is not necessarily straightforward. For instance, in a sentence like "low risk of suicide based on current mental state", a clinician may be inclined to interpret this as *negated* (this is not a patient at risk of suicide), while a linguistic interpretation would be that this is *not negated* (there is no linguistic negation marker in this example). In this study, the annotators were asked to focus on linguistic negation markers, and disregard clinical interpretations, in order to create a well-defined and unambiguously annotated corpus. They were also instructed to annotate mentions of suicide regardless of whether comments concerned the patient, their family member or a friend.

A collection of 5000 randomly selected MHRs was extracted, divided (segmented) into individual sentences, keeping only sentences containing the target concept. This resulted in a corpus of *6066*

---

[2]The source code for our tool is available at `https://github.com/gkotsis/negation-detection`.

[3]Annotators were also allowed to assign the value "Irrelevant" for uncertain or otherwise problematic cases.

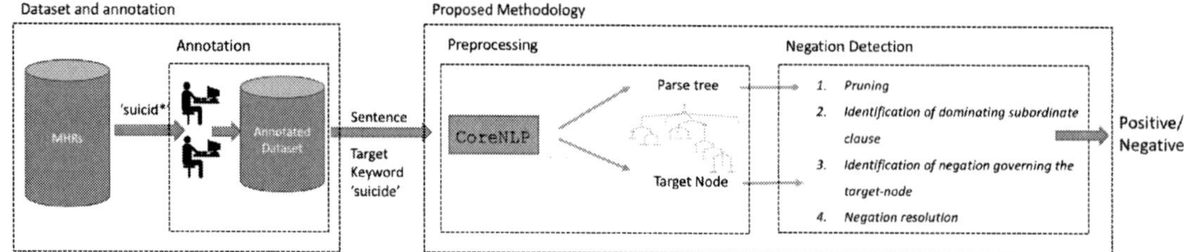

Figure 1: Workflow illustration. Two main stages were employed: 1) data extraction and annotation for corpus creation, and 2) development of the proposed methodology for negation resolution.

sentence-instances.

One annotator (domain expert) annotated the entire corpus. To assess the feasibility and estimate the upper performance levels that could be expected from an automated system, we employed a double-annotation procedure on a portion of the corpus. We calculated the Inter-Annotator Agreement (IAA) in order to examine if the task is well-defined. A randomly selected subset (1244 sentences, >20% of the corpus) was given to a second annotator (NLP researcher) to calculate IAA.

The IAA analysis showed that our annotators agreed on 97.9% of the instances (Cohen's κ 0.93, agreement over 1218 sentences). From this result, we concluded that: 1) the annotation task was indeed defined in an unambiguous way and was well-understood by humans, and 2) there are still some cases that are inherently difficult to assess, due to a degree of ambiguity, which is to be expected in real-world settings. The final corpus contains 2941 sentences annotated as positive (affirmation of suicide) and 3125 annotated as negative (i.e. suicide negated, 48.5% - 51.5% positive to negative ratio).

3.2 Proposed method for negation detection

Our proposed methodology consisted of two steps: 1) preprocessing and formatting the data, and 2) execution of the negation resolution task.

3.2.1 Preprocessing

Each sentence was preprocessed in order to prepare the input for the negation resolution algorithm in a suitable format: a syntactic representation (parse tree) and the target token ("suicide").

Our proposed methodology makes use of *constituency-based parse trees*. A constituency tree is a tree that categorises nodes as grammatical constituents (e.g. NP, VP) using the Penn Treebank tagset (Marcus et al., 1993). Nodes are classified either as leaf nodes with terminal categories (such as noun, verb, adjective etc.) or interior nodes with non-terminal categories (e.g. verb phrase, sentence etc.). Therefore, constituency trees are quite expressive and provide us with rich information concerning the roles of elements and chunks of elements found in written natural language. In this study, we used the Probabilistic Context Free Grammar (PCFG) parser that is built into the Stanford Core NLP toolkit (Klein and Manning, 2003), a variant on the probabilistic CKY algorithm, which produces a constituency parse tree representation for each sentence. As will become clear in the sections below, we found constituency parse trees particularly useful in modelling global grammatical constraints on the scope of negation and in the context of surface mentions of the word "suicide". Such constraints would have been harder to express using dependency parsers, although we do plan to incorporate dependency triples in future analysis.

In addition, the target token was also searched for in the sentence tree, in a reduced form (by applying stemming) in order to identify all possible inflections of the word "suicide".

3.2.2 Negation resolution algorithm

Similar to other approaches, we reduced the problem of negation resolution to the problem of identifying the *scope of negation*. The basic premise of scope-based negation resolution algorithms is that a list of negation words (or phrases) is provided. In this study, we defined a list of 15 negation cues[4] based on an initial manual analysis of the data. Once

---

[4]See supplement for the complete list.

a negation cue is found in the syntactic tree, a scope-based algorithm attempts to mark the concept that is affected by this negation word.

Our approach starts from the target-node ("suicide") and *traverses* the tree moving upwards and visiting nodes of the tree accordingly. The function and role of each node-element in relation to negation resolution during this traversal is then considered through a set of operations:

- *Pruning* refers to the removal of interior nodes that are not expected to have an impact on the final output. Figure 2 shows an example of tree pruning. Node pruning occurs when two conditions are met: a) a node is tagged with subordinate conjunctions or clause-related Treebank categories, and b) the node and none of its children contain the target node. After pruning, the remainder of the tree is further processed.

- *Identification of the dominating subordinate clause* is an action that also results in the removal of selected nodes, but with an important difference: it leads to the generation of a new *subtree*. During pruning, once a node is considered irrelevant, *all* of its children are removed. Here, the aim is to isolate the target node from higher level nodes that do not propagate the negation to the lower levels of the tree, hence leading to a new *subtree*. For a node to be considered a root candidate in the new tree, it has to be classified as a "subordinate clause" (SBAR) and the subtree must contain the target node. Figure 3 illustrates an example of this operation, where the highlighted segment shows the nodes that are *not* participating in the formation of the new tree. The new tree is kept and used for further processing in the subsequent steps.

- *Identification of negation governing the target-node* aims to deal with tree structures, such as conjunctions, where negations can be propagated to the target node. Intuitively, the traversal continues upwards as long as the initial context remains the same. If a sentence ("S") is found, a stopping condition is met and only the node-child of the stopping node is examined. In this context, the algorithm will flag the target node as negated regardless of the negation

words counted (at least one negation stopword must be present, see final step below for counting negations). If a negation word is found, its *relative* position with regards to the target node is considered. When the negation word is to the *left* of the target node, the target is considered negated. This approach allows us to capture cases of potential ambiguity. Figure 4 contains an example where the negation word is contained in a sibling noun phrase (NP), to the left of the target NP.

- *Negation resolution* is the last operation that is applied on the final version of the tree, after the previous operations have been executed. This step simply counts the number of negation words in the tree. If the number is odd, the algorithm predicts a "negative" value, else it returns "positive". This counting step allows us to take into account cases where multiple negations are propagated to the target node and are cancelling each other.

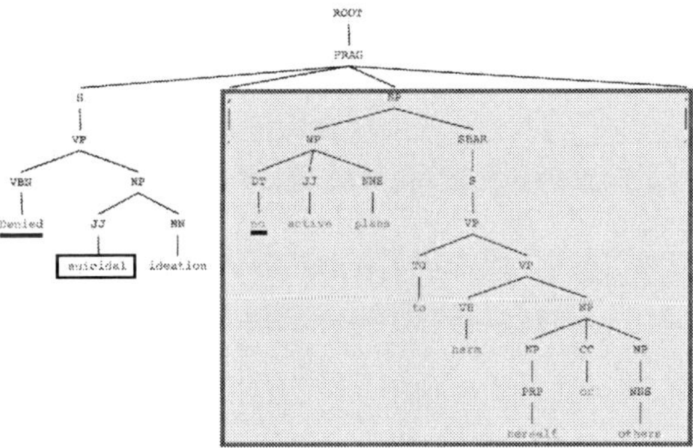

Figure 2: An example of pruning. The highlighted fragment is considered to be out of the scope of the target-node ("suicidal") and is therefore removed.

3.2.3   Evaluation metrics

We evaluate results with precision (positive predictive value), recall (sensitivity), F-measure (harmonic mean of precision and recall) and accuracy (correct classifications over all classifications). We also compare our algorithm against two other, openly available, lexical negation resolution approaches: pyConTextNLP (Chapman et al., 2011)[5]

---

[5]available by pip install.

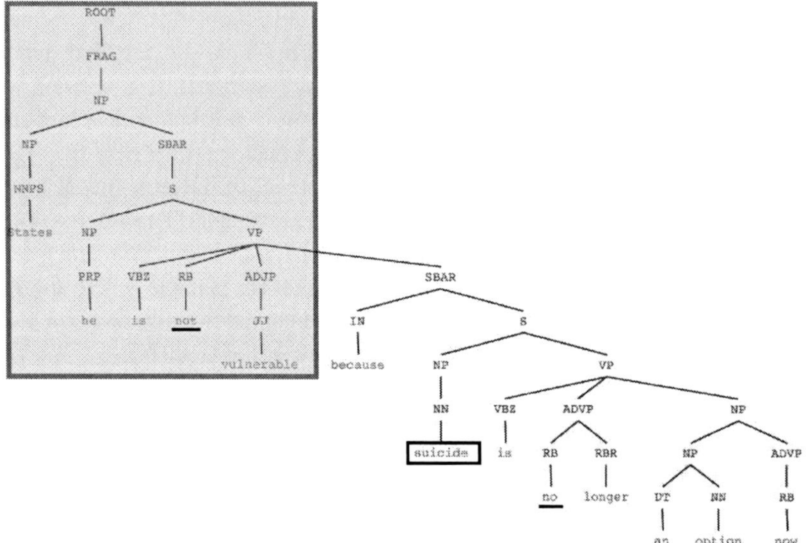

Figure 3: An example of a dominating subordinate clause. The highlighted fragment shows the nodes that are not included in the formation of the new tree.

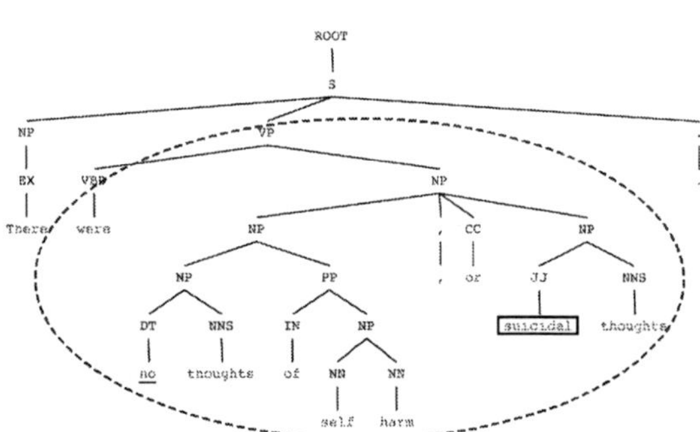

Figure 4: An example of a governing node. The highlighted verb phrase governs the target-node ("suicidal") and also exhibits ellipsis.

and the NegEx (Chapman et al., 2001) 2009 python implementation[6]. Since these approaches depend on lists of negation and termination cues, we compare results with three configurations: 1) NegEx as obtained from the online code repository, 2) pyConTextNLP with the negation and termination cues from configuration 1 (pyConTextNLP-N), and 3) pyConTextNLP with the negation and termination cues created for our proposed approach (pyConTextNLP-O).

Furthermore, we provide a more detailed performance analysis with regards to the length (in words) of a sentence, since the syntactic parses are more error-prone for longer sentences (lower accuracy and time-out requests).

4 Negation detection results

Our study focusses on assessing the risk of suicide based on information contained in mental health records. Since the overall goal is to identify patients who are expected to be at high risk of suicide, we focus on the evaluation of *positive* (affirmed) cases as determined by our classifier, i.e. cases without negation or where the negation does

---

[6]https://storage.googleapis.com/
google-code-archive-downloads/v2/code.
google.com/negex/negex.python.zip

not govern the target keyword ("suicide"). These affirmed cases are where, according to the clinician, patients have entered into a heightened state of risk (risk assessment), they must be re-assessed and have their suicide risk updated frequently like a time-dependent "weather forecast" (Bryan and Rudd, 2006). Short-term risk assessments, like weather forecasts, are much more accurate than longer-term assessments (Simon, 1992).

Table 1 presents the confusion matrix for our classifier when compared with the manual annotations. In addition, the numbers as obtained from pyConTextNLP, when installed and used with the NegEx lexicon (pyConTextNLP-N), are shown in brackets. The table shows that both classifiers produce few Type I (false positive) and II (false negative) errors. Our proposed approach manages to correctly identify more positive/affirmed cases (2782 vs. 2733), albeit at a higher cost compared to pyConTextNLP-N (more false positives, 331 vs. 172). On the other hand, our proposed solution identifies fewer negative cases (i.e. 159 instances wrongly identified as negative vs. 208). In summary, pyConTextNLP-N has a higher bias towards negative instances, which results in lower recall for the positive instances, but higher accuracy overall.

<table>
<tr><td rowspan="6" style="writing-mode: vertical-lr">Prediction</td><td></td><td colspan="2" align="center">Class</td></tr>
<tr><td></td><td>Positive</td><td>Negative</td></tr>
<tr><td>Positive</td><td>2782 (2733)</td><td>331 (172)</td></tr>
<tr><td>Negative</td><td>159 (208)</td><td>2794 (2953)</td></tr>
<tr><td>Total</td><td>2941</td><td>3125</td></tr>
</table>

Table 1: Confusion matrix: Manually annotated (Class) vs. predicted (Prediction) instances from our proposed algorithm. Numbers in brackets report on pyContextNLP-N (negation lexicon from NegEx).

Table 2 reports on the precision, recall, F-Measure and accuracy for the positive (affirmed) cases when using the four different negation resolution systems and configurations[7]. Results are overall very similar, and very high, except perhaps for pyContextNLP-O (83.2% accuracy) which demonstrates how important the lexical resources and definitions are for improved performance. This also means that the high results for our proposed approach is promising, as

---
[7]Note that in our evaluation we have not selected a specific tool as a baseline.

there is less need for manual creation and curation of lexical resources. Furthermore, this result also reflects characteristics of this data: mentions of suicide in mental health records are negated in a fairly consistent and unambiguous way.

	P	R	FM	A
NegEx	93.4	92.1	92.8	93
pyConTextNLP-N	**94.1**	92.9	**93.5**	**93.7**
pyConTextNLP-O	80.7	86	83.2	83.2
Proposed	89.4	**94.6**	91.9	91.9

Table 2: Results for negation resolution using different tools: NegEx, PyConTextNLP with negation and termination cues from the original NegEx code (pyConTextNLP-N), PyConTextNLP with negation and termination cues from our proposed approach (pyConTextNLP-O), and our proposed approach (Proposed). Precision (P), Recall (R), F-Measure (FM) and Accuracy (A) report on the case of positive/affirmed instances.

Although the overall results are high, there are some aspects that could be studied further, for instance the effect of preprocessing. There are a few instances where the sentence chunking failed, which poses a severe challenge for the syntactic analysis. Figure 5 presents the cumulative word count of sentence instances. The vast majority of the instances contain less than 50 words, but there are a few instances where a "sentence" contains more than 300 words. These long sentences turned out to be complete documents. Clinical text is known for being noisy and hard to correctly tokenise in many cases, and instead of removing these cases, we decided to keep them so as to have a closer to real-world assessment of the efficiency of our methodology.

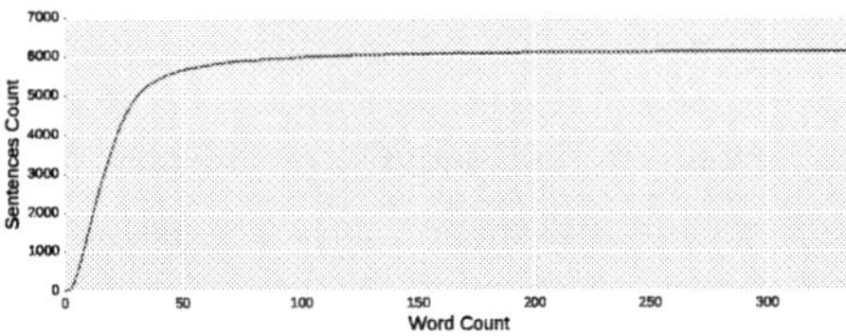

Figure 5: Cumulative word count of sentences in our dataset.

Furthermore, to understand the effect of keeping incorrectly tokenised sentences, we studied the performance of our proposed tool based on sentence length (as defined by word count). Figure 6 presents the mean cumulative accuracy of our algorithm with regards to the word count of the sentences. The figure shows that the system performance is significantly higher for shorter sentences. This performance slowly declines as lengthier sentences are included[8].

5 Discussion and Future Work

The corpus that we have created for this study is, to our knowledge, the first of its kind, and also of a considerable size[9]. At the same time, for the annotation process, decisions were made that introduce some limitations in our study design (e.g. linguistic focus, target concepts). Hence, the results presented in this work are generalisable but are, to a certain degree, overestimating clinical reality, real world applicability and generalisability. Despite these limitations, we believe that our analysis of the dataset sheds light in the broad area of suicide risk assessment from MHRs.

Furthermore, our proposed negation resolution approach is competitive when compared to state-of-the-art tools. In particular, it performs slightly better for correctly classifying positive/affirmed mentions as opposed to negated mentions. This is a welcomed outcome, since in our use case we aim to focus on patients at risk for suicidal behaviour. Additionally, an early observation concerning its performance is that our tool is better for cases of short, simple and properly punctuated text, which is something that could be addressed by better writing support in MHR systems, and by the authors of health record notes. Small, incremental changes in the documentation creation process can increase the quality of the clinical NLP tools' output considerably.

Comparing our results to previous research is not straightforward, since we are using a new corpus and we study negation resolution on a new domain. However, in general, our results are very promising and in line with, or above, previously reported results on negation detection. For instance, NegEx, when applied on a variety of corpora and use cases, has resulted in precision ranging from 84.5% – 94% (Chapman et al., 2001; Harkema et al.,

2009). When compared to approaches that also incorporate syntactic information in the negation resolution algorithm, both DepNeg (Sohn et al., 2012) and DEEPEN (Mehrabi et al., 2015) report high overall results when evaluated on different types of clinical corpora, in particular for reducing false positives (i.e. overgenerating predictions of negation). However, DEEPEN is biased to the performance of NegEx, whereas our proposed approach is completely standalone. Furthermore, previous research studies report results with an emphasis on performance on negation detection, not on detecting affirmed instances, which is a crucial issue in our case.

There are several areas in which we plan to extend this work. As already discussed, negation detection tools can exhibit a drop in performance when applied on different corpora (Wu et al., 2014). In our approach, the dictionary of negation keywords is much smaller compared to other approaches. We believe that this feature is a sign that our method is robust and can be generalisable. We intend to evaluate the approach on other datasets – clinical as well as other text types, e.g. biomedical articles and abstracts, to assess the generalisability of our proposed system. Moreover, our approach to use parse trees allows us to extend our work and extract further semantic and syntactic layers of information. In particular, we plan to focus on the extraction of statements (e.g. in the form of subject-predicate-object), the identification of temporal characteristics as well as the extraction of the degree of suicidality. Most importantly, we also plan to use this algorithm for suicide risk modelling. We already have a cohort study in progress, where this system will be central to the model.

6 Conclusions

Free text found in Mental Health Records (MHRs) is a rich source of information for clinicians. In this paper, we focus on the problem of suicide risk assessment by studying mentions of suicide in MHRs. To that end, we 1) produced and presented a new corpus of MHRs annotated for negation or affirmation of mentions of suicidality, with high Inter-Annotator Agreement, and 2) developed an algorithm for negation resolution relying on constituency parse tree information. The results of our study confirm the

---

[8]In Figure 6, notice that we have clipped the X-axis to show sentences of up to 80 words. The plotted line converges to the overall mean accuracy of 91.9, as reported in Table 2.

[9]Access to this material is, however, restricted by IRB approval and data access protocols.

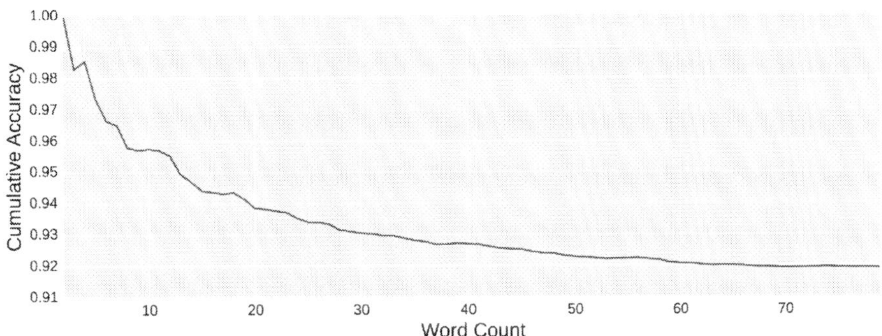

Figure 6: Mean cumulative accuracy on sentences containing up to N words using our proposed negation resolution algorithm.

prominence of negation in MHRs and justify the need for developing a negation detection mechanism. Our approach is competitive when compared to lexical negation resolution algorithms, and performs better for correctly classifying affirmed mentions. Finally, our negation detection algorithm can be applied on different datasets, and can be extended in order to extract more semantics.

Acknowledgments

RD is supported by a Clinician Scientist Fellowship from the Health Foundation in partnership with the Academy of Medical Sciences. RD, GG and HD are funded by the e-HOST-IT research programme. SV is supported by the Swedish Research Council (2015-00359) and the Marie Skłodowska Curie Actions, Cofund, Project INCA 600398. AO would like to acknowledge NIHR Biomedical Research Centre for Mental Health, the Biomedical Research Unit for Dementia at the South London, the Maudsley NHS Foundation Trust and Kings College London. ML would like to acknowledge the PHEME FP7 project (grant No. 611233).

The data resource is funded by the National Institute for Health Research (NIHR) Biomedical Research Centre and Dementia Biomedical Research Unit at South London and Maudsley NHS Foundation Trust and King's College London.

References

Geneviève Arsenault-Lapierre, Caroline Kim, and Gustavo Turecki. 2004. Psychiatric diagnoses in 3275 suicides: a meta-analysis. *BMC Psychiatry*, 4:37.

Guilherme Borges, Matthew K Nock, Josep M Haro Abad, Irving Hwang, Nancy A Sampson, Jordi Alonso, Laura Helena Andrade, Matthias C Angermeyer, Annette Beautrais, Evelyn Bromet, Ronny Bruffaerts, Giovanni de Girolamo, Silvia Florescu, Oye Gureje, Chiyi Hu, Elie G Karam, Viviane Kovess-Masfety, Sing Lee, Daphna Levinson, Maria Elena Medina-Mora, Johan Ormel, Jose Posada-Villa, Rajesh Sagar, Toma Tomov, Hidenori Uda, David R Williams, and Ronald C Kessler. 2010. Twelve-month prevalence of and risk factors for suicide attempts in the world health organization world mental health surveys. *Journal of Clinical Psychology*, 71(12):1617–28, Dec.

Craig J Bryan and M David Rudd. 2006. Advances in the assessment of suicide risk. *Journal of Clinical Psychology*, 62(2):185–200.

Wendy W Chapman, Will Bridewell, Paul Hanbury, Gregory F. Cooper, and Bruce G. Buchanan. 2001. A simple algorithm for identifying negated findings and diseases in discharge summaries. *Journal of Biomedical Informatics*, 34(5):301 – 310.

B.E. Chapman, S. Lee, H.P. Kang, and W.W. Chapman. 2011. Document-level classification of CT pulmonary angiography reports based on an extension of the ConText algorithm. *Journal of Biomedical Informatics*, 44(5):728–737.

David Chu, John N Dowling, and Wendy W Chapman. 2006. Evaluating the effectiveness of four contextual features in classifying annotated clinical conditions in emergency department reports. In *AMIA Annual Symposium Proceedings*, pages 141–145. American Medical Informatics Association.

Krystl Haerian, Hojjat Salmasian, and Carol Friedman. 2012. Methods for identifying suicide or suicidal ideation in EHRs. In *AMIA Annual Symposium Proceedings*, pages 1244–1253. American Medical Informatics Association.

Henk Harkema, John N. Dowling, Tyler Thornblade, and Wendy W. Chapman. 2009. ConText: An algorithm for determining negation, experiencer, and temporal status from clinical reports. *Journal of Biomedical Informatics*, 42(5):839 – 851. Biomedical Natural Language Processing.

Ronald C Kessler, Christopher H Warner, Christopher Ivany, Maria V Petukhova, Sherri Rose, Evelyn J Bromet, Millard Brown, Tianxi Cai, Lisa J Colpe, Kenneth L Cox, et al. 2015. Predicting suicides after psychiatric hospitalization in US Army soldiers: the Army Study to Assess Risk and Resilience in Servicemembers (Army STARRS). *JAMA Psychiatry*, 72(1):49–57.

J-D Kim, Tomoko Ohta, Yuka Tateisi, and Jun'ichi Tsujii. 2003. Genia corpus—a semantically annotated corpus for bio-textmining. *Bioinformatics*, 19(suppl 1):i180–i182.

Dan Klein and Christopher D Manning. 2003. Accurate unlexicalized parsing. In *Proceedings of the 41st Annual Meeting on Association for Computational Linguistics-Volume 1*, pages 423–430. Association for Computational Linguistics.

J John Mann, Alan Apter, Jose Bertolote, Annette Beautrais, Dianne Currier, Ann Haas, Ulrich Hegerl, Jouko Lonnqvist, Kevin Malone, Andrej Marusic, et al. 2005. Suicide prevention strategies: A systematic review. *JAMA*, 294(16):2064–2074.

Mitchell P Marcus, Mary Ann Marcinkiewicz, and Beatrice Santorini. 1993. Building a Large Annotated Corpus of English: The Penn Treebank. *Computational linguistics*, 19(2):313–330.

Saeed Mehrabi, Anand Krishnan, Sunghwan Sohn, Alexandra M. Roch, Heidi Schmidt, Joe Kesterson, Chris Beesley, Paul Dexter, C. Max Schmidt, Hongfang Liu, and Mathew Palakal. 2015. DEEPEN: A negation detection system for clinical text incorporating dependency relation into NegEx. *Journal of Biomedical Informatics*, 54:213–219.

S M Meystre, G K Savova, K C Kipper-Schuler, and J F Hurdle. 2008. Extracting information from textual documents in the electronic health record: a review of recent research. *IMIA Yearbook*, (1):128–144.

Roser Morante and Caroline Sporleder, editors. 2010. *Proceedings of the Workshop on Negation and Speculation in Natural Language Processing*. University of Antwerp, Uppsala, Sweden, July.

P.G. Mutalik, A. Deshpande, and P.M. Nadkarni. 2001. Use of general-purpose negation detection to augment concept indexing of medical documents: a quantitative study using the UMLS. *JAMIA*, 8(6):598–609.

AB Niculescu, DF Levey, PL Phalen, H Le-Niculescu, HD Dainton, N Jain, E Belanger, A James, S George, H Weber, et al. 2015. Understanding and predicting suicidality using a combined genomic and clinical risk assessment approach. *Molecular Psychiatry*, 20(11):1266–1285.

Matthew K Nock, Jennifer Greif Green, Irving Hwang, Katie A McLaughlin, Nancy A Sampson, Alan M Zaslavsky, and Ronald C Kessler. 2013. Prevalence, correlates, and treatment of lifetime suicidal behavior among adolescents: Results from the national comorbidity survey replication adolescent supplement. *JAMA Psychiatry*, 70(3):300–310.

Gayan Perera, Matthew Broadbent, Felicity Callard, Chin-Kuo Chang, Johnny Downs, Rina Dutta, Andrea Fernandes, Richard D Hayes, Max Henderson, Richard Jackson, et al. 2016. Cohort profile of the South London and Maudsley NHS Foundation Trust Biomedical Research Centre (SLaM BRC) Case Register: current status and recent enhancement of an Electronic Mental Health Record-derived data resource. *BMJ Open*, 6(3):e008721.

Pradhan, Sameer and Elhadad, Noémie and South, Brett R and Martinez, David and Christensen, Lee and Vogel, Amy and Suominen, Hanna and Chapman, Wendy W and Savova, Guergana. 2015. Evaluating the state of the art in disorder recognition and normalization of the clinical narrativet. *JAMIA*, 22(1):143–154.

Christopher Ryan, Olav Nielssen, Michael Paton, and Matthew Large. 2010. Clinical decisions in psychiatry should not be based on risk assessment. *Australasian Psychiatry*, 18(5):398–403.

RI Simon. 1992. Clinical risk management of the suicidal patient. *Clinical psychiatry and the Law. 2nd ed. American Psychiatric Press*, pages 259–96.

Sunghwan Sohn, Stephen Wu, and Christopher G Chute. 2012. Dependency parser-based negation detection in clinical narratives. *AMIA Summits on Translational Science*, 2012:1–8.

Sarah Steeg, Matthew Haigh, Roger T Webb, Nav Kapur, Yvonne Awenat, Patricia Gooding, Daniel Pratt, and Jayne Cooper. 2016. The exacerbating influence of hopelessness on other known risk factors for repeat self-harm and suicide. *Journal of affective disorders*, 190:522–528.

Özlem Uzuner, Brett R South, Shuying Shen, and Scott L DuVall. 2011. 2010 i2b2/VA challenge on concepts, assertions, and relations in clinical text. *JAMIA*, 18(5):552–556.

V. Vincze, G. Szarvas, R. Farkas, G. Móra, and J. Csirik. 2008. The BioScope corpus: biomedical texts annotated for uncertainty, negation and their scopes. *BMC Bioinformatics*, 9(11):1–9.

Christine Leonard Westgate, Brian Shiner, Paul Thompson, and Bradley V Watts. 2015. Evaluation of Veterans' Suicide Risk With the Use of Linguistic Detection Methods. *Psychiatric services*, 66(10):1051.

Stephen Wu, Timothy Miller, James Masanz, Matt Coarr, Scott Halgrim, David Carrell, and Cheryl Clark. 2014. Negation's Not Solved: Generalizability Versus Optimizability in Clinical Natural Language Processing. *PLoS ONE*, 9(11):e112774.

Exploratory Analysis of Social Media Prior to a Suicide Attempt

Glen Coppersmith
Qntfy
glen@qntfy.com

Kim Ngo
Qntfy, University of Notre Dame
kim@qntfy.com

Ryan Leary
Qntfy
ryan@qntfy.com

Anthony Wood
Qntfy
tony@qntfy.com

Abstract

Tragically, an estimated 42,000 Americans died by suicide in 2015, each one deeply affecting friends and family. Very little data and information is available about people who attempt to take their life, and thus scientific exploration has been hampered. We examine data from Twitter users who have attempted to take their life and provide an exploratory analysis of patterns in language and emotions around their attempt. We also show differences between those who have attempted to take their life and matched controls. We find quantifiable signals of suicide attempts in the language of social media data and estimate performance of a simple machine learning classifier with these signals as a non-invasive analysis in a screening process.

1 Introduction

Mental health poses a sizable challenge by any metric. An estimated 1 in 4 Americans will contend with a mental health condition in a given year (National Institutes of Health, 2013). Around 1% of people die by suicide, 2.7% attempt suicide, 3.1% make a plan for suicide, and 9.2% are challenged with suicidal ideation (Nock et al., 2008). Tragically, this means roughly 4.8 million Americans alive today will die by suicide, placing suicide among the top ten leading causes of death in the United States (Sullivan et al., 2013). Worldwide, it is the leading cause of death for women age 15-19 and the second leading cause of death for teenagers (World Health Organization and others, 2014). What's worse, the rates of suicide seem to be increasing, up 28% in the civilian population of the United States between 1999 and 2010 (Sullivan et al., 2013).

Despite the magnitude of the challenge posed by suicide, we have a relatively sparse understanding of what precisely gives rise to suicide risk. To prevent suicides, we need a better understanding of the underlying phenomena relating to both the immediate risk of suicide (or *acute suicidal risk*) and the long term risks. For both cases, data is extremely sparse, never in real time, and subject to some bias. Few objective measures exist to measure outcomes, and those that do exist tend to have poor temporal resolution (measured in weeks or months) and are labor intensive. Optimizing intervention efficacy or policy-level strategies is difficult without such data.

Here we explore a novel dataset of social media data from users who have attempted to take their own life. This kind of data has not previously been available in sufficient quantities or at this granularity, so we provide broad intuition and interpretation of trends, rather than testing specific hypotheses. Our primary contributions are: [1] We find quantifiable signals of suicide, with sufficient performance and scalability to warrant consideration as part of a screening process. [2] We provide intuition about the data via simple visualizations of linguistic content of users prior to a suicide attempt. [3] We use automatic emotion classification to uncover interesting patterns in the emotional composition of posts made by users in the time around a suicide attempt. [4] Where possible, we tie these phenomena back to existing psychological research. This paper deliberately only scratches the surface of the possible insight encoded in data related to suicide attempts.

106

Proceedings of the 3rd Workshop on Computational Linguistics and Clinical Psychology: From Linguistic Signal to Clinical Reality, pages 106–117,
San Diego, California, June 16, 2016. ©2016 Association for Computational Linguistics

Quantifying Mental Health: Thanks to the use of vital signs like temperature and blood pressure, cross correlation of various easy-to-observe symptoms and the rapid measurement of blood chemistry, the diagnosis of physical illness has improved radically since 1900. Mental and behavioral healthcare has not benefited in the same way from binary diagnostics. In part, this may be because physical health conditions manifest irrespective of whether the patient is in a diagnostic healthcare setting, while mental health conditions manifest when a person interacts with the rest of their world, making measurement in a laboratory difficult. Social media may seem, at first, to be a strange data source for studying mental health, but there are myriad quantifiable signals within social media that capture how a person interacts with their world. We suggest that data collected in the "white space" between visits with healthcare professionals may be part of a rigorous, scalable, and quantified diagnostic approach to mental and behavioral illness. Language, in particular, has proven to be a potent lens for the analysis of mental health, as evidenced by the wide usage of the Linguistic Inquiry Word Count (Tausczik and Pennebaker, 2010; Pennebaker et al., 2007; Pennebaker et al., 2001) and the depth of publications at the Computational Linguistics and Clinical Psychology workshops (Resnik et al., 2014; Mitchell et al., 2015a; Hollingshead and Ungar, 2016).

Mental Health through Social Media: Social media data is necessarily stored in formats conducive to analysis via computer. This allows for larger sample sizes and higher frequency than anything ever before possible. Collecting the ordinary language of thousands of users over weeks, months or years has become trivial in comparison to the paper based analysis methods of the past.

Work examining mental health conditions that affect a large number of people has proliferated, especially depression (Coppersmith et al., 2015b; Schwartz et al., 2014; Resnik et al., 2013; De Choudhury et al., 2013a; De Choudhury et al., 2013b; Rosenquist et al., 2010; Ramirez-Esparza et al., 2008; Chung and Pennebaker, 2007). Similarly, common psychological phenomena, like personality factors and psychological well-being are now well-studied through emprical analysis of social media data (Schwartz et al., 2013b; Park et al., 2015; Schwartz et al., 2013a). These approaches and survey methods were sufficient to support analysis of relatively common conditions, but are not as effective for rarer ones.

Coppersmith et al. (2014a) introduced methods for examining public data which allowed for more scalable creation of data sets, thus permitting the examination of rarer conditions. Post traumatic stress and schizophrenia are two examples of conditions significantly rarer than depression, whose analysis are possible by these techniques (Coppersmith et al., 2014b; Mitchell et al., 2015b). Suicide and suicidal ideation were more difficult to obtain data for, but some population-level analysis was enabled by anonymous suicide help fora (Kumar et al., 2015; Kiciman et al., 2016). Additionally, Robertson et al. (2012) investigated the role that social media has in suicide clusters (among people in disparate geographies connected online).

At the individual level, techniques similar in nature to Coppersmith et al. (2014a) can provide social media data for users prior to a suicide attempt of sufficient size to allow linguistic analysis (Coppersmith et al., 2015c; Wood et al., 2016). Coppersmith et al. (2015c) was able to automatically separate users who would attempt to end their life from neurotypical controls and further tie signals explicitly back to the psychometrically validated Linguistic Inquiry Word Count categories and existing psychological theories. Furthermore, they found slight but measurable differences between those who would attempt to end their life and those challenged by depression without suicidal ideation. The operative question has been: are there quantifiable markers in an individual's social media content that indicate their current or future risk of acute suicidal crisis?

Biases: The existing methods for assessing the events surrounding suicidal crisis resulting in a suicide attempt are heavily susceptible to recall bias and context bias (Shiffman et al., 2008). People are more likely to remember negatively charged information when they are in a negative mood (Clark and Teasdale, 1982), as when asked to reconstruct information about a suicide attempt. The available information about the events leading up to a suicide attempt are generally based on the self report of peo-

I'm so glad I survived my suicide attempt to see the wedding today.
I was so foolish when I was young, so many suicide attempts!
I have been out of touch since I was hospitalized after my suicide attempt last week.
It's been half a year since I attempted suicide, and I wish I had succeeded
I'm going to go commit suicide now that the Broncos won... #lame
It is going to be my financial suicide, but I NEEEEEEEEEED those shoes.

Figure 1: Fictitious example tweets of genuine statements of a suicide attempt (top), genuine statements indicating a time (middle) and disingenuous statements (bottom).

ple who survived one or more attempts or the reconstructions of events provided by friends or family members after a traumatic loss. All of these issues pose serious problems for accurate recall, compounded by the effects of biases. Contrastively, social media streams are biased in other ways, often towards self presentation, but recorded in the moment.

Often, treatment progress is assessed using weekly or monthly questionnaires or interviews that require retrospection on the part of the patient. However, retrospective self-report measures are notoriously context dependent and highly influenced by momentary accessible information. Furthermore, the commonly reported tendency toward "backfilling" that often happens when written journals are employed in a therapeutic context is worth noting (Stone et al., 2003). When a patient is asked to keep a paper journal in the space between office visits, they frequently backfill the entries just prior to their appointment from (biased) memory, to please their therapist or appear compliant. Thus, several weeks of mood journaling may be compiled in the waiting area before their visit rather than as they naturally occur. All of these issues pose a problem for reconstructing events surrounding suicidal crisis and make wider generalizations more challenging, bording on speculative. Ideally, analysis of personal social media data in conjunction with more traditional methods may offset the short comings of each method in isolation.

2   Data

We examine data from people who **publicly** state on Twitter that they have tried to take their own life, and provide enough evidence for the casual observer to determine the date of their suicide attempt. Specifically, we have 554 users who stated that they attempted to take their life, 312 of which give an in-

dication of when their latest attempt was. The exact date of their attempt was available for 163 users, and 125 of them had data available prior to the date of their attempt. We do not include any users who have marked their profile as *private*, and for each user we examine only their **public** data, which does **not** include any direct messages or deleted posts.

For each user, a human annotator examined their tweets and verified that [1] the user's statement of attempting to take their life appeared genuine[1] [2] the user is speaking about their own suicide attempt, and [3] that the suicide attempt could be localized in time. See Figure 1 for example tweets.

We estimate the age and gender of each user who attempted to take their life to provide aggregate demographic information from the users in the dataset (see Figure 2) and to allow us to directly control for variability due to age and gender in our analysis. Demographic estimates were derived from the authored content of each user via lexica magnanimously provided by the World Well-Being Project (Sap et al., 2014). Though imperfect (91.9% accuracy for gender, $r = 0.83$ correlation for age), these estimates are informative in aggregate. Notably, there are significantly more women in our data than men, and almost all users are between the age of 15 and 29. This indicates that we do not have a representative sample of the demographics on Twitter, with polling indicating that 37% of adults aged 18 to 29 and 12% of those in middle age are on Twitter (Duggan et al., 2015). Since the older demographic, also at risk for suicide, does not show up in our sample, it suggests that we are primarily capturing the youth at risk for suicide, perhaps because they are more likely to discuss the subject openly.

---

[1]Previously, annotators have shown high agreement for differentiating between genuine and disingenuous statements involving mental health conditions, $\kappa = 0.77$ (Coppersmith et al., 2015c).

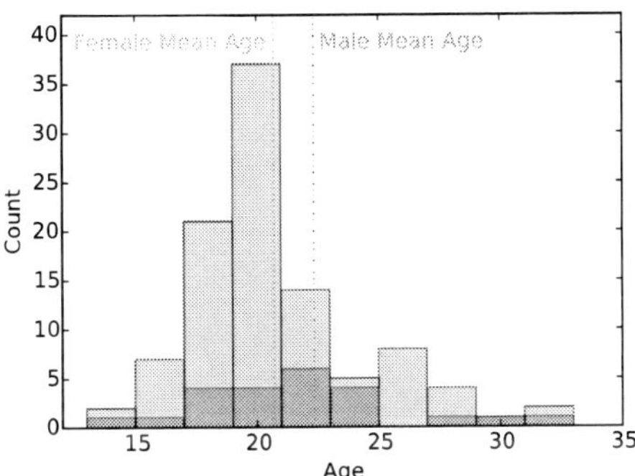

Figure 2: Histogram of the ages of users who attempted to take their life. Females are in green, and males in blue. The mean age of each gender is denoted by vertical lines.

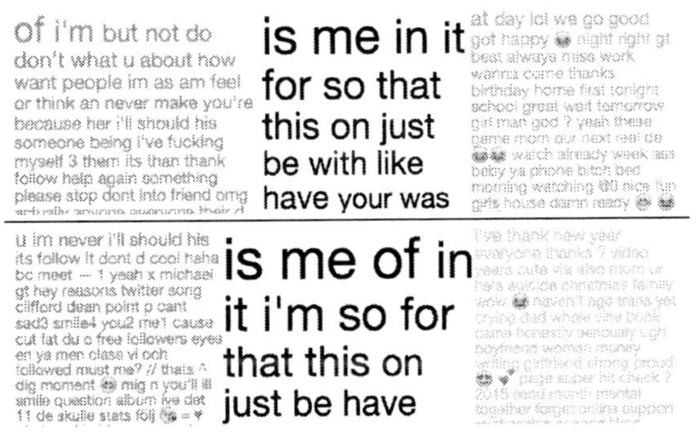

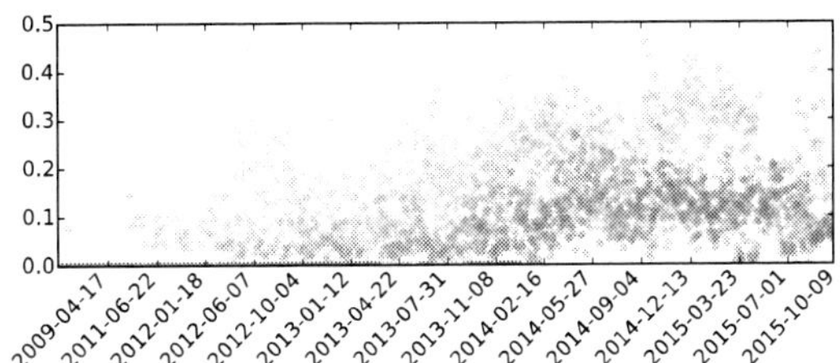

Figure 3: Vennclouds visualizing the differences in language usage between the groups examined here. The top cloud compares users who attempt to take their life (left) with neurotypicals (right). The bottom compares users who attempt to take their life prior to (left) and after (right) their attempt. Larger words occur more frequently in the corpus.

For each user who has attempted to take their life, we draw an age- and gender-matched control from a large pool of random English users. We find a user of the same estimated gender and the smallest difference in esitmated age. It is likely that 4-8% of these (assumed) neurotypical control users have or will try to take their life, given the rates of suicide attempts in the population (Nock et al., 2008). This contamination will only serve to weaken our models and obscure trends. We make no attempt to remedy this and the results should be treated as lower bounds.

3 Exploration of Language Data

First, we visualize the linguistic differences in our populations via simple and straightforward methods

Figure 4: Proportion of tweets containing an emoji (y-axis), by date (x-axis). Neurotypicals in green, users prior to their suicide attempt in blue and after their attempt in red.

to provide intuition about the sort of information available and glean insight as to how this data might relate to existing psychological theory. In all cases, we compare (1) users who have tried to take their life to their matched neurotypical controls and (2) users prior to and after they attempt to take their life.

Vennclouds: Figure 3 show Vennclouds comparing word usage in our populations. As explanation, consider the top Venncloud which compares users prior to their attempt to take their life (left) with neurotypicals (right). This examines language at the level of *tokens*, which here is either a single word, emoticon, or symbol. Each token can only show up once in the visualization, so if the token is used with higher probability by neurotypical users, it is displayed on the right. If it is used with higher probability by users who tried to take their life (only examining data prior to that attempt), it is displayed on the left. Tokens that occur with approximately the same probability are displayed in the middle. For a more detailed description, see Coppersmith and Kelly (2014). A few interesting phenomena emerge from this simple analysis: [1] neurotypicals use emoticons and emoji with much higher probability than a user prior to a suicide attempt (also see Figure 4), [2] users are more likely to talk about suicide *after* an attempt than before it, [3] users prior to a suicide attempt use more self-focused language, replicating similar findings in those challenged with depression (Chung and Pennebaker, 2007; Coppersmith et al., 2014a; Coppersmith et al., 2015a), [4] users prior to a suicide attempt are more likely to employ automatic means of tracking their followers (as most uses of the token "followers" are from the automatic output of these applications).

Figure 4 indicates that neurotypicals (green) use

emoticons and emoji with a higher frequency than those who attempt suicide, before (blue) or after (red) that attempt. For each day where we have at least 10 tweets, we calculate the proportion of tweets for each group that contains an emoticon or an emoji. Interestingly, neurotypicals and people who attempt suicide seem to adopt emoji around the same time, starting in 2012, but neurotypicals use them more.

4   Methods

We are primarily concerned with drawing two comparisons here. First, what observable differences exist between users who attempt to take their life and the rest of the (neurotypical) population? Second, what observable differences exist between users prior to and after a suicide attempt?

Preprocessing: The processing of unedited language data prior to the application of any machine learning or visualization techniques often have significant effects on the outcome. Here, for each tweet we replace all usernames in the text with the single token "@", and replace all URLs with the single token "*". For example "Check out `https://OurDataHelps.org` powered by @Qntfy ! :)" would be "Check out * powered by @ ! :)" after preprocessing. All emoticons and emoji remain intact and are treated as single characters. While many types of linguistic analysis examine the content and topics of documents, we are equally interested in content and context. Here, we diverge from most natural language processing, which often dismiss many very frequently used words as uninteresting, and remove them from analysis (sometimes referred to as "filler" or "stop" words). Previous work has demonstrated (and frequently replicated) that some of these words (e.g., first person and third person pronouns) hold psychological meaning, and thus should be included in analysis (Pennebaker, 2011; Chung and Pennebaker, 2007). Likewise, lemmatizing or stemming words may also remove information about how the author experiences the world, such as whether their language is future- or past-focused.

Character Language Models: For classification, we prefer simple, straightforward methods that pro-

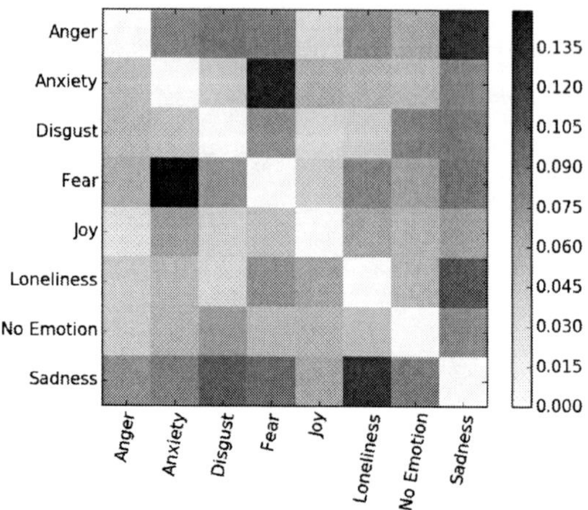

Figure 5: Confusion matrix for emotion classifier, denoting the proportion of tweets from the emotion on the row that are misclassified as the emotion on the column. Diagonals (representing correct classifications) have been removed to better illustrate the misclassifications. Thus, *sadness* is most frequently misclassified as *loneliness* while *fear* and *anxiety* are most confusable.

vide scores at a per-tweet level. Here, we use character n-gram language models followed by logistic regression via scikit-learn (Pedregosa et al., 2011). These models are particularly appropriate for social media given their robustness to creative spelling, missing spaces, and other eccentricities that result from short, unedited text (Coppersmith et al., 2014b; McNamee and Mayfield, 2004). We use character n-grams up to length 5 (so tokens might include "suici" and "uicid"). Spaces, punctuation, emoticons, emoji, and generic username and url tokens ("@" and "*" respectively) are included as characters. Logistic regression allows us to learn how strongly each of these character n-gram tokens are associated with the populations examined. We use this method to: **[1]** compare those who attempted to take their life against neurotypicals, **[2]** compare language before and after a suicide attempt, and **[3]** n-way classification of emotions. All performance measures are calculated via 10-fold cross validation.

Emotional States: To estimate emotional states from social media posts, we collected a novel corpus with automatically induced emotion labels, as inspired by Mohammad (2012). These methods might be used to detect emotional states that indicate high risk for suicidal crisis. Detection of hypomanic states (associated with multiple attempts) (Bryan et al., 2008) and elevated levels of guilt or shame have been found among some populations at risk for suicide (Ray-Sannerud et al., 2012). Hashtags provide implicit labels of emotion (excluding any tweet that also has #SARCASM or #JK) – a tweet that contains #ANGER is labeled *anger*, but not one that contains #ANGER #SARCASM. We diverged from past work and focused on emotions more directly related to suicide and psychological phenomena, as well as an automatically-induced *no emotion* category. We used up to 40,000 tweets from each label, selected from a random Twitter sample collected during 2015. For each tweet, we removed the hashtag label from the text, and trained a character n-gram language model.

Inclusion of a *no emotion* label calls for a slightly more complicated training procedure, as these training tweets were selected simply because they lacked an explicit emotional hashtag. Many of the tweets in this category do express an emotion. Creating *no emotion* training data using tweets that lack an explicit emotion hashtag results in the *no emotion* label being particularly contaminated by tweets expressing emotions. This, in turn leads the classifier to frequently misclassify emotional tweets as having *no emotion*. This would skew the performance of the classifier when used beyond training and skew the estimates of accuracy of the classifier (since many tweets labeled and evaluated as *no emotion* actually have emotional content). Thus, we employ semi-supervised learning to decrease the effect of this contamination: We train the model once with 40k random tweets we label as *no emotion*, then use this initial model to score each of a second set of *no emotion* tweets. Any tweet in this second set of ostensibly *no emotion* tweets that is classified by the inital model as having any emotion is removed, since it is likely to be a contaminating emotion-bearing tweet. A random (second) subset of 40k tweets are then selected from those that remain. The model we use for analysis is trained with this cleaner (second) set of 40k *no emotion* tweets.

Emotion classification from statements in isolation is a very difficult task, even for humans, as evidenced by low inter-annotator agreement (e.g., 47% agreement between three annotators in Purver and

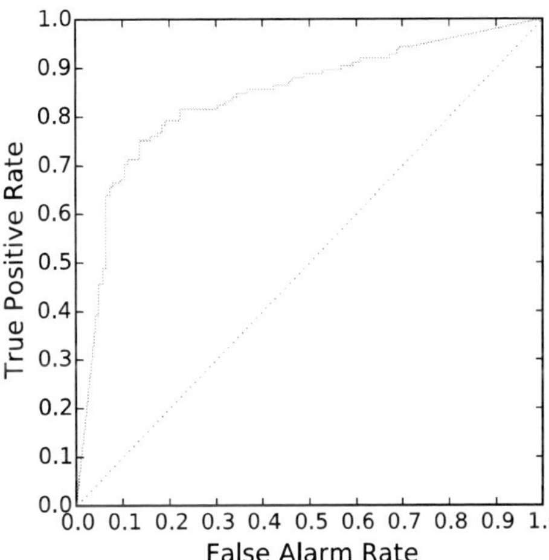

Figure 6: ROC curve for separating users who attempted to take their life from matched neurotypicals.

Battersby (2012)). Additionally, the emotions that are conveyed are also often mixed, making a single label insufficiently descriptive. For further analysis of performance and errors of the emotion classifier, see the Technical Appendix.

Briefly, we assessed classification accuracy of this 8-way classifier with 10-fold cross validation, with a resulting F1 of 53. While not directly comparable, reported state of the art results for 2- and 6-way classification range between 45 and 65 (though some treat the task as a multi-level classification problem, *emotion-detection* followed by *emotion-discrimination*, reporting F1 separately and further complicating comparisons) (Mohammad and Kiritchenko, 2015; Purver and Battersby, 2012). The confusion matrix for all the emotions examined can be found in Figure 5.

5 Results

We demonstrate that quantifiable signals relevant to suicide can be found in social media data with simple analysis, then put them in the context of performance in a realistic setting. We use techniques conducive to introspection to facilitate comparison with existing psychological literature.

Quantifiable Signals: To find quantifiable signals of suicide risk, we build character n-gram language models to separate users who have attempted to take their life from their matched neurotypicals. Specifically, we examine only data prior to each user's suicide attempt. A ROC curve denoting the tradeoff between false alarms (neurotypical users misidentified as at risk to take their life) and true hits (users who will attempt to take their life, identified as such) can be seen in Figure 6.

For a single point of performance for comparison, note that at roughly 10% false alarms, we correctly identfy about 70% of those who will try to take their life. Extrapolating from this likely performance in the real world is not entirely straightforward, but a worthy exercise. We can assume that in our neurotypical population of 15-29 year olds, 4-8% of users will (or have) tried to take their life (Nock et al., 2008; Kann et al., 2014). Thus, the size of the neurotypical population is likely to be more than ten times the size of the at-risk population.

If we were to use this simple method to screen 1000 people aged 15-29, we would expect 40-80 of them (4-8%) to attempt to take their life at some point in time. For simplicity, we will use 6% or 60 users. If we were to randomly select users for additional screening, we would expect that 6% of them will go on to try to take their life – a hit rate of 6%. Straightforward application of the example operating point to 1000 person population would be expected to yield 42 (70% of 60) at risk individuals and 94 (10% of 940) neurotypical flagged for additional screening – a hit rate of 30%.

Our sample of neurotypicals are likely contaminated by users who have or will attempt to take their life, so our estimates of false-alarms may be inflated due to this contamination. In the best-case scenario, these at-risk neurotypical users were flagged correctly, so we reduce our false alarm estimates accordingly. Thus an upper-bound on our performance would be if we consider that 6% of the neurotypical population is currently classified as false alarms, but are actually true hits. Factoring them out would yield a false alarm rate of just 4%, so this optimistic operating point would identify the same 42 at-risk people as above, and 38 (4% of 940) neurotypical users for additional screening – a hit rate of 58%.

In sum, a screening tool for people aged 15-29 based on these simple methods could identify a group for additional screening for which between 30 and 60% would be at risk for a suicide attempt.

While more optimization remains to be done, this strongly suggests that technology-assisted screening is within the realm of the possible.

Emotional Posts: We scored each tweet with an emotion classifier, and examined the relative composition of each user's tweets by week, for three months on either side of a user's suicide attempt. Figure 7 shows the percentage of each user's tweets each week that contained a given emotion. Time (by week) on the x-axis and percentage of tweets with that emotion on the y-axis. The day of the suicide attempt and the week following it are included at $x = 0$, indicated by the dotted vertical line. The colored dot indicates the median percentage across all users who attempted to take their life, and the error bars indicate one standard deviation above and below the median. The equivalent median from the neurotypical population is included as a solid horizontal line, with one and two standard errors above and below indicated by dashed and dotted horizontal lines respectively. The median emotional percentage of the users who attempted to take their life for the three months prior to a suicide attempt is indicated by a colored horizontal line left of 0. Similarly, for the three months after the attempt.

Since our analysis is largely exploratory, and not hypothesis-driven, it behooves us to take results that might otherwise be considered statistically significant with a higher degree of skepticism. A reasonable guideline for interpreting these plots to account for the many comparisons made is to consider differences where the error bars are entirely non-overlapping. While other more subtle differences may exist, they should be the subject of more principled and hypothesis-driven experiments. With that lens, some stark differences remain.

Interestingly, while users appear to have a markedly higher incidence of tweets tagged with *anger* and *sadness* prior to the attempt, they fall to levels more in line with neurotypicals after an attempt. A few weeks prior to the suicide attempt there is a marked increase in the percentage of *sadness* tweets and then a noticeable increase in *anger* and *sadness* the week following the suicide attempt (to include the day of the attempt). Some examples of tweets from the day of the suicide attempt and tagged as *anger* or *sadness* are shown in Figure 8,

My parents admitted they ignore my mental health, I am so pissed off now. I'm only good for being a verbal punching bag. Why can't I find my damn pills so I can just fucking overdose?
I listed reasons I should die and reasons I should not die. I had no reasons not to die. I found 7 reasons to die. two people next to each other in the same room can be in totally separate places, one of the saddest truths I'm totally pathetic even the scars from my attempts are pathetic

Figure 8: Example tweets labeled with *anger* (top) and *sadness* (bottom) from the day of a suicide attempt.

as an illustration of what signals may be driving that change. In some of these tweets, the depth of emotion is more complex than is captured by these simplistic labels – some indicate that the author is angry at themselves and the situation they find themselves in, perhaps in line with the *guilt* and *shame* found by Bryan et al. (2013).

Contrasting *anger* and *sadness*, the percentage of *fear* and *disgust* tweets appear in line with neurotypicals prior to their attempt, yet they decrease to levels below neurotypicals after the attempt. They also appear to have a consistently lower amount of tweets that convey *loneliness*, which decreases further after their attempt. There are a number of apparent single-week shifts away from neurotypical or away from the users who have attempted to take their life, though drawing conclusions on any of them would be prematurely speculative. These should serve as grist for more directed studies in the future. No interesting trends were observed for *anxiety* so it was omitted for brevity.

People who attempt to take their life tend to have a higher overall proportion of tweets estimated to be emotional, and that proportion tends to *increase* after their attempt. Intriguingly, this finding seems (at first blush) at odds with the results from the Vennclouds and Figure 4, where users who attempted suicide used emoticons and emoji less frequently than neurotypicals. Taken together, these might indicate that though users who attempt suicide express more emotion, they do so with words rather than emoticons or emoji – perhaps suggesting a depth of emotion that are not adequately served by the vast array of emoji.

Volume: Finally, some interesting changes in the overall volume of activity are illustrated in Figure 9. Users who attempt to take their life generate tweets at a level higher than neurotypicals prior to their attempt, but after their attempt appear to return to lev-

els commensurate with neurotypicals. One possible explanation for this might be an implicit or explicit call for help, though deeper analysis is certainly required.

6 Caveats and Limitations

When drawing conclusions from this work, there are some caveats and limitations to keep in mind, any of which may affect the generalizability of the findings – all suggesting future, more controlled studies. All the people investigated here survived their suicide attempt, so there may be systematic differences between those in our dataset and those who die by suicide. Similarly, we have no verification of the attempts of these users, though the data has face validity with existing research on suicide. The data explored here is primarily from women aged 15-29. While this is a group at elevated risk for suicide, their behavior, motivations, and stressors are likely significantly different from other at-risk groups (e.g., transgendered individuals or middle-aged males). Furthermore, these users self identify and present themselves as challenged with a highly stigmatized issue in a very public manner. It is clear this is a subpopulation separate from neurotypical controls. We cannot be sure, however, exactly how different this population might be from the larger cohort who has attempted to take their life.

7 Conclusion

The caveats above notwithstanding, we have provided an empirical analysis of the language usage of people prior to a suicide attempt, to be used as grist for further exploration and research. Ideally, even these simple analyses can provide a foundation for non-invasive screening and interventions to prevent suicides. However, significant challenges exist in applying this technology broadly in ways that preserve privacy and maintain a high standard of care

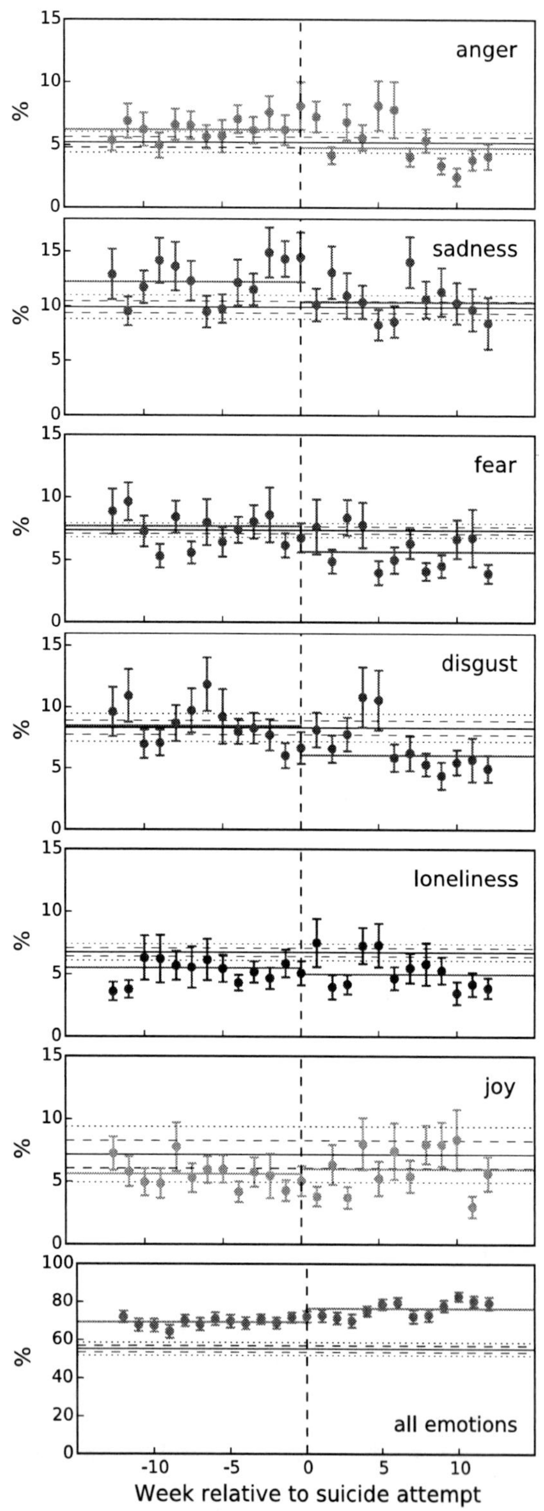

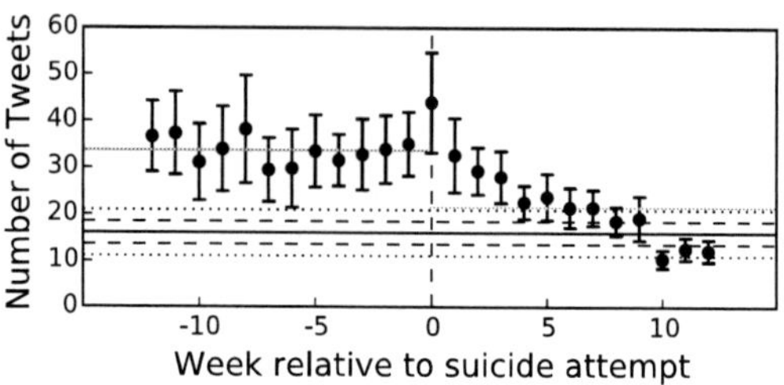

Figure 9: Volume of tweets from users who tried to take their life (dots), surrounding their suicide attempt. All features of the plot are equivalent to those in Figure 7.

using limited clinical resources. Despite the potential lives saved, the general population may not be amenable to its use given the perceived cost to privacy, as reaction to the Samaritan's Radar[2], suggests. However, **opt-in** continual analysis of social media data may be a reasonable method for ecological momentary assessment and for monitoring psychological and behavioral state over time. For further discussion of the ethics, privacy, and practical considerations around interventions using this kind of technology, see Wood et al. (2016).

Suicide is a large and looming challenge, claiming a tragic number of lives each year. Given the societal stigma, discrimination, and prejudice associated with it, finding data to better understand the risk of suicide has been a consistent challenge. Our analysis here suggests some future directions for exploration, along with providing some quantified insight into the phenomena of acute suicidal risk. It is a small but important step towards improved outcomes and lives saved.

Acknowledgments

The authors would like to thank April Foreman, Bart Andrews, Bill Schmitz and the #SPSM community for their continued intellectual and emotional contributions to the improvement and empowerment of suicide prevention. We would also like to thank the anonymous reviewers for improving the quality of this manuscript, and the organizers of CLPsych for their contributions to this research community.

[2]http://www.samaritans.
org/how-we-can-help-you/
supporting-someone-online/
samaritans-radar

Figure 7: Emotion-labeled tweets from users who tried to take their life.

References

Craig J Bryan, Leigh G Johnson, M David Rudd, and Thomas E Joiner. 2008. Hypomanic symptoms among first-time suicide attempters predict future multiple attempt status. *Journal of clinical psychology*, 64(4):519–530.

Craig J Bryan, Chad E Morrow, Neysa Etienne, and Bobbie Ray-Sannerud. 2013. Guilt, shame, and suicidal ideation in a military outpatient clinical sample. *Depression and anxiety*, 30(1):55–60.

Cindy Chung and James Pennebaker. 2007. The psychological functions of function words. *Social Communication*.

David M Clark and John D Teasdale. 1982. Diurnal variation in clinical depression and accessibility of memories of positive and negative experiences. *Journal of abnormal psychology*, 91(2):87.

Glen Coppersmith and Erin Kelly. 2014. Dynamic word-clouds and Vennclouds for exploratory data analysis. In *Association for Computational Linguistics Workshop on Interactive Language Learning and Visualization*, June.

Glen Coppersmith, Mark Dredze, and Craig Harman. 2014a. Quantifying mental health signals in Twitter. In *Proceedings of the ACL Workshop on Computational Linguistics and Clinical Psychology*.

Glen Coppersmith, Craig Harman, and Mark Dredze. 2014b. Measuring post traumatic stress disorder in Twitter. In *Proceedings of the 8th International AAAI Conference on Weblogs and Social Media (ICWSM)*.

Glen Coppersmith, Mark Dredze, Craig Harman, and Kristy Hollingshead. 2015a. From ADHD to SAD: Analyzing the language of mental health on Twitter through self-reported diagnoses. In *Proceedings of the Workshop on Computational Linguistics and Clinical Psychology: From Linguistic Signal to Clinical Reality*, Denver, Colorado, USA, June. North American Chapter of the Association for Computational Linguistics.

Glen Coppersmith, Mark Dredze, Craig Harman, Kristy Hollingshead, and Margaret Mitchell. 2015b. CLPsych 2015 shared task: Depression and PTSD on Twitter. In *Proceedings of the Shared Task for the NAACL Workshop on Computational Linguistics and Clinical Psychology*.

Glen Coppersmith, Ryan Leary, Eric Whyne, and Tony Wood. 2015c. Quantifying suicidal ideation via language usage on social media. In *Joint Statistics Meetings Proceedings, Statistical Computing Section*. JSM.

Munmun De Choudhury, Scott Counts, and Eric Horvitz. 2013a. Social media as a measurement tool of depression in populations. In *Proceedings of the 5th ACM International Conference on Web Science*.

Munmun De Choudhury, Michael Gamon, Scott Counts, and Eric Horvitz. 2013b. Predicting depression via social media. In *Proceedings of the 7th International AAAI Conference on Weblogs and Social Media (ICWSM)*.

Maeve Duggan, Nicole B Ellison, Cliff Lampe, Amanda Lenhart, and Mary Madden. 2015. Social media update 2014. *Pew Research Center*, 19.

Kristy Hollingshead and Lyle Ungar, editors. 2016. *Proceedings of the Workshop on Computational Linguistics and Clinical Psychology: From Linguistic Signal to Clinical Reality*. North American Association for Computational Linguistics, San Diego, California, USA, June.

Laura Kann, Steve Kinchen, et al. 2014. Youth risk behavior surveillance – united states, 2013.

Emre Kiciman, Mrinal Kumar, Glen Coppersmith, Mark Dredze, and Munmun De Choudhury. 2016. Discovering shifts to suicidal ideation from mental health content in social media. In *Proceedings of the SIGCHI Conference on Human Factors in Computing Systems*. ACM.

Mrinal Kumar, Mark Dredze, Glen Coppersmith, and Munmun De Choudhury. 2015. Detecting changes in suicide content manifested in social media following celebrity suicides. In *Proceedings of the 26th ACM conference on Hypertext and hypermedia*. ACM.

Paul McNamee and James Mayfield. 2004. Character n-gram tokenization for European language text retrieval. *Information Retrieval*, 7(1-2):73–97.

Margaret Mitchell, Glen Coppersmith, and Kristy Hollingshead, editors. 2015a. *Proceedings of the Workshop on Computational Linguistics and Clinical Psychology: From Linguistic Signal to Clinical Reality*. North American Association for Computational Linguistics, Denver, Colorado, USA, June.

Margaret Mitchell, Kristy Hollingshead, and Glen Coppersmith. 2015b. Quantifying the language of schizophrenia in social media. In *Proceedings of the Workshop on Computational Linguistics and Clinical Psychology: From Linguistic Signal to Clinical Reality*, Denver, Colorado, USA, June. North American Chapter of the Association for Computational Linguistics.

Saif M. Mohammad and Svetlana Kiritchenko. 2015. Using hashtags to capture fine emotion categories from tweets. *Computational Intelligence*, 31(2):301–326.

Saif Mohammad. 2012. #emotional tweets. In **SEM 2012: The First Joint Conference on Lexical and Computational Semantics – Volume 1: Proceedings of the main conference and the shared task, and Volume 2: Proceedings of the Sixth International Workshop on Semantic Evaluation (SemEval 2012)*, pages 246–255,

Montréal, Canada, 7-8 June. Association for Computational Linguistics.

National Institute of Mental Health National Institutes of Health. 2013. Statistics: Any disorder among adults. http://www.nimh.nih.gov/statistics/1ANYDIS_ADULT.shtml. [Online; accessed 2013-03-05].

Matthew K Nock, Guilherme Borges, Evelyn J Bromet, Jordi Alonso, Matthias Angermeyer, Annette Beautrais, Ronny Bruffaerts, Wai Tat Chiu, Giovanni De Girolamo, Semyon Gluzman, et al. 2008. Cross-national prevalence and risk factors for suicidal ideation, plans and attempts. *The British Journal of Psychiatry*, 192(2):98–105.

Gregory Park, H Andrew Schwartz, Johannes C Eichstaedt, Margaret L Kern, Michal Kosinski, David J Stillwell, Lyle H Ungar, and Martin EP Seligman. 2015. Automatic personality assessment through social media language. *Journal of personality and social psychology*, 108(6):934.

Fabian Pedregosa, Gaël Varoquaux, Alexandre Gramfort, Vincent Michel, Bertrand Thirion, Olivier Grisel, Mathieu Blondel, Peter Prettenhofer, Ron Weiss, Vincent Dubourg, Jake Vanderplas, Alexandre Passos, David Cournapeau, Matthieu Brucher, and Matthieu Perrot Édouard Duchesnay. 2011. scikit-learn: Machine learning in Python. *The Journal of Machine Learning Research*, 12:2825–2830.

James W. Pennebaker, Martha E. Francis, and Roger J. Booth. 2001. *Linguistic inquiry and word count: LIWC2001*. Erlbaum Publishers, Mahwah, NJ.

James W. Pennebaker, Cindy K. Chung, Molly Ireland, Amy Gonzales, and Roger J. Booth. 2007. *The development and psychometric properties of LIWC2007*. LIWC.net, Austin, TX.

James W. Pennebaker. 2011. The secret life of pronouns. *New Scientist*, 211(2828):42–45.

Matthew Purver and Stuart Battersby. 2012. Experimenting with distant supervision for emotion classification. In *Proceedings of the 13th Conference of the European Chapter of the Association for Computational Linguistics*, EACL '12, pages 482–491, Stroudsburg, PA, USA. Association for Computational Linguistics.

Nairan Ramirez-Esparza, Cindy K. Chung, Ewa Kacewicz, and James W. Pennebaker. 2008. The psychology of word use in depression forums in English and in Spanish: Testing two text analytic approaches. In *Proceedings of the 2nd International AAAI Conference on Weblogs and Social Media (ICWSM)*.

Bobbie N Ray-Sannerud, Diana C Dolan, Chad E Morrow, Kent A Corso, Kathryn E Kanzler, Meghan L Corso, and Craig J Bryan. 2012. Longitudinal outcomes after brief behavioral health intervention in an integrated primary care clinic. *Families, Systems, & Health*, 30(1):60.

Philip Resnik, Anderson Garron, and Rebecca Resnik. 2013. Using topic modeling to improve prediction of neuroticism and depression. In *Proceedings of the Conference on Empirical Methods in Natural Language Processing (EMNLP)*, pages 1348–1353.

Philip Resnik, Rebecca Resnik, and Margaret Mitchell, editors. 2014. *Proceedings of the Workshop on Computational Linguistics and Clinical Psychology: From Linguistic Signal to Clinical Reality*. Association for Computational Linguistics, Baltimore, Maryland, USA, June.

Lindsay Robertson, Keren Skegg, Marion Poore, Sheila Williams, and Barry Taylor. 2012. An adolescent suicide cluster and the possible role of electronic communication technology. *Crisis*.

J. Niels Rosenquist, James H. Fowler, and Nicholas A. Christakis. 2010. Social network determinants of depression. *Molecular psychiatry*, 16(3):273–281.

Maarten Sap, Greg Park, Johannes C. Eichstaedt, Margaret L. Kern, David J. Stillwell, Michal Kosinski, Lyle H. Ungar, and H. Andrew Schwartz. 2014. Developing age and gender predictive lexica over social media. In *Proceedings of the Conference on Empirical Methods in Natural Language Processing (EMNLP)*, pages 1146–1151.

H. Andrew Schwartz, Johannes C. Eichstaedt, Margaret L. Kern, Lukasz Dziurzynski, Richard E. Lucas, Megha Agrawal, Gregory J. Park, Shrinidhi K. Lakshmikanth, Sneha Jha, Martin E. P. Seligman, and Lyle H. Ungar. 2013a. Characterizing geographic variation in well-being using tweets. In *Proceedings of the 8th International AAAI Conference on Weblogs and Social Media (ICWSM)*.

H. Andrew Schwartz, Johannes C. Eichstaedt, Margaret L. Kern, Lukasz Dziurzynski, Stephanie M. Ramones, Megha Agrawal, Achal Shah, Michal Kosinski, David Stillwell, Martin E. P. Seligman, and Lyle H. Ungar. 2013b. Personality, gender, and age in the language of social media: The open-vocabulary approach. *PLOS ONE*, 8(9).

H. Andrew Schwartz, Johannes Eichstaedt, Margaret L. Kern, Gregory Park, Maarten Sap, David Stillwell, Michal Kosinski, and Lyle Ungar. 2014. Towards assessing changes in degree of depression through Facebook. In *Proceedings of the ACL Workshop on Computational Linguistics and Clinical Psychology*.

Saul Shiffman, Arthur A Stone, and Michael R Hufford. 2008. Ecological momentary assessment. *Annu. Rev. Clin. Psychol.*, 4:1–32.

Arthur A Stone, Saul Shiffman, Joseph E Schwartz, Joan E Broderick, and Michael R Hufford. 2003.

Patient compliance with paper and electronic diaries. *Controlled clinical trials*, 24(2):182–199.

E Sullivan, Joseph L Annest, F Luo, TR Simon, and LL Dahlberg. 2013. Suicide among adults aged 35–64 years, united states, 1999–2010. *Center for Disease Control and Prevention, Morbidity and Mortality Weekly Report*.

Yla R. Tausczik and James W. Pennebaker. 2010. The psychological meaning of words: LIWC and computerized text analysis methods. *Journal of Language and Social Psychology*, 29(1):24–54.

Anthony Wood, Jessica Shiffman, Ryan Leary, and Glen Coppersmith. 2016. Discovering shifts to suicidal ideation from mental health content in social media. In *Proceedings of the SIGCHI Conference on Human Factors in Computing Systems*. ACM.

World Health Organization et al. 2014. *Preventing suicide: A global imperative*. World Health Organization.

CLPsych 2016 Shared Task: Triaging content in online peer-support forums

David N. Milne and **Glen Pink** and **Ben Hachey** and **Rafael A. Calvo**
University of Sydney
NSW 2006, Australia
{david.milne,glen.pink,ben.hachey,rafael.calvo}@sydney.edu.au

Abstract

This paper introduces a new shared task for the text mining community. It aims to directly support the moderators of a youth mental health forum by asking participants to automatically triage posts into one of four severity labels: *green, amber, red* or *crisis*. The task attracted 60 submissions from 15 different teams, the best of whom achieve scores well above baselines. Their approaches and results provide valuable insights to enable moderators of peer support forums to react quickly to the most urgent, concerning content.

1 Introduction

When facing tough times, the best support often comes from someone who has been through similar experiences (Pfeiffer et al., 2011). Forums are a simple way to facilitate such peer-support online, but when they involve vulnerable people and sensitive subject matter they require careful cultivation. There is growing evidence that online peer-support without professional input has limited effectiveness (Kaplan et al., 2011), and Kummervold et al. (2002) obtained almost unanimous feedback from forum users that professionals should actively participate or offer a safety net of passive monitoring.

The need for human moderation raises concerns of cost and scalability. This provides opportunity for text mining and NLP to augment human moderators by allowing them to focus on the individuals and posts that most urgently require their attention. For example, affect detection could locate emotionally charged posts (Calvo and D'Mello, 2010), and

Yin et al. (2009) could identify malicious users. For the domain of mental health, De Choudhury et al. (2013) could prioritize clinically depressed individuals, and O'Dea et al. (2015) could help moderators respond quickly to suicidal ideation.

There has recently been a great deal of research that mines social media texts for mental health, but most have been isolated investigations. This paper introduces a new shared task for researchers to collaborate on and concretely compare what does and does not work. It releases a dataset of forum posts that have been manually annotated with how urgently they require a moderator's attention.

To our knowledge, the only other shared task involving social media and mental health is Coppersmith et al. (2015), who aim to detect depression and PTSD on Twitter. Other shared tasks have used data that is easier to de-identify: Pestian et al. (2012) focus on emotion detection within anonymized suicide notes, while Pradhan et al. (2014) and their predecessors focus on making clinical records easier to digest and understand.

The remainder of the paper is structured as follows. The next section describes ReachOut: an online community of Australian youth that provides both data and motivation. Section 3 describes the dataset extracted from these forums and the annotation process. Section 4 summarizes the methods and common themes of participating teams, and Section 5 contains their results. Our use of public yet sensitive data raises complex ethics issues that are addressed in Section 6. The final section describes some of the opportunities and challenges that remain unexplored and invites readers to participate.

Proceedings of the 3rd Workshop on Computational Linguistics and Clinical Psychology: From Linguistic Signal to Clinical Reality, pages 118–127,
San Diego, California, June 16, 2016. ©2016 Association for Computational Linguistics

2 The ReachOut forums

ReachOut.com is an Australian non-profit established in 1996 to support young people. It offers on-line resources about everyday topics like family, school and friendships, as well as more difficult issues such as alcohol and drug addition, gender identity, sexuality, and mental health concerns. About 1 in 3 young people in Australia are aware of the site (Metcalf and Blake, 2013), and it received about 1.8 million visitors in 2014 (Millen, 2014). In a survey conducted in 2013, approximately 77% of visitors reported experiencing high or very high levels of psychological distress, which indicates that the site is reaching people in need (Metcalf and Blake, 2013). 46% of these distressed visitors reported feeling more likely to access (for the first time) professional support after their visit.

Much of this success is due to the strong on-line community that has developed around ReachOut, thanks to a lively peer-support forum. This offers a safe, supportive environment for 14-25 year-olds to anonymously share their personal experiences.

Maintaining this environment and ensuring it remains a positive place to be requires a great deal of effort. ReachOut employs several senior moderators full-time, and also recruits and trains new young people each year as volunteer peer moderators. Collectively, this *Mod Squad* listens out for anything that might require attention, responding when needed with encouragement, compassion and links to relevant resources. In extreme cases they will occasionally redact content that is overly distressing or triggering, or where the author has jeopardized their own safety and anonymity. There is an escalation process to follow when forum members might be at risk of harm. Not all of the moderators' actions are so dire however; often they step in to congratulate someone for making progress, or simply to keep conversation flowing and build rapport.

3 Data and annotation

The ReachOut Triage Shared Task dataset consists of 65,024 forum posts written between July 2012 and June 2015. The data is structured in XML and preserves all metadata such as when the post was made, who authored it, and where it fits in the navigational structure of boards, threads, replies and quotes. We discuss the ethical considerations of using such sensitive yet public data in Section 6.

The vast majority posts are left unannotated, to provide a testbed for unsupervised and semi-supervised approaches such as topic modelling, co-training and distant supervision. A subset of 1,227 posts were manually annotated by three separate judges (the first three authors of the paper) using a semaphore pattern to indicate how urgently they require a moderators attention:

- **Crisis** indicates that the author (or someone they know) is in imminent risk of being harmed, or harming themselves or others. Such posts should be prioritized above all others.

- **Red** indicates that a moderator should respond to the post as soon as possible.

- **Amber** indicates that a moderator should address the post at some point, but they need not do so immediately.

- **Green** identifies posts that do not require direct input from a moderator, and can safely be left for the wider community of peers to respond to.

The annotation task began with the judges discussing the first ∼200 posts and arriving at a collective decision for each, guided by an informal annotation and triage criteria provided by Reachout. At that point the judges were able to formalize their decision process into the flowchart shown in Figure 1. This illustrates some of the complexity and subjectivity involved in the task: the judges (and future algorithms) have to consider both the textual content of the post and the sentiment behind it (e.g. that a post is *red* because it describes *current distress*), and also the trajectory of how authors follow up on their own previous concerning posts (e.g. that a post is *amber* because a prior situation has not worsened, but is also not entirely resolved).

Within the annotation system, posts were always viewed in the full context of how they were found in the live forum, rather than as an independent chunk of text. Posts were annotated against the flowchart to capture both the semaphore annotation and a more detailed sub-annotation. They could also be annotated as *ambiguous* if they fell outside the logic provided by the flowchart.

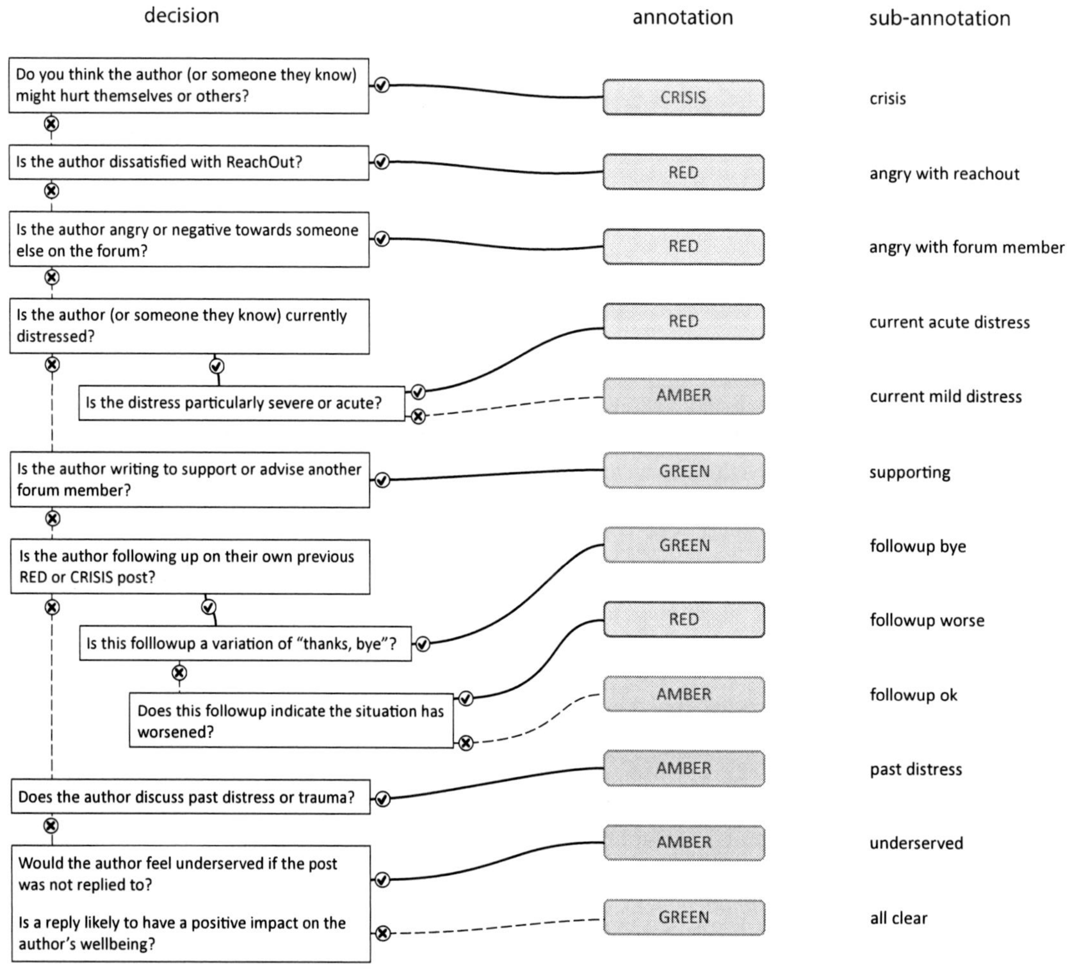

Figure 1: The triage annotation decision tree

After settling on this decision tree, the judges annotated each of the remaining posts independently. Inter-annotator agreement was then measured over these posts, excluding 22 that had been labelled as *ambiguous* by at least one of the judges. Over 977 cases (and four possible labels), the three judges achieved a Fleiss's Kappa of 0.706 and pairwise Cohen's Kappa scores ranging between 0.674 and 0.761. Viera and Garrett (2005) would interpret this as substantial agreement. Finally the judges met in person to resolve any remaining disagreements and ambiguous cases and arrive at a consensus.

Table 1 shows the final distribution of labels across the annotated portion of the dataset, and how

	train	%	test	%
crisis	39	4	1	0
red	110	12	27	11
amber	249	26	47	19
green	549	58	166	69
total	947		280	

Table 1: Distribution of labels across training and testing data.

it was split into 947 posts for training and 280 for testing. The posts were not stratified or distributed randomly, but were instead split on a particular date (the 28th of May 2015). Consequently the distribution of labels across the two sets is not entirely even, which makes the task somewhat more challenging and realistic. It also ensures that features can be extracted from the behaviour leading up to each post without accidentally contaminating training data with testing data.

4 Shared task submissions

Teams were given roughly 4 weeks from being provided with the training data to submitting test results. Teams were permitted to submit a maximum of 5 runs. We received 60 submissions from the 15 teams participating in the task. In this section we look at the various approaches to the task, and what techniques were and were not successful. First we briefly describe the top-performing approaches, and then summarise techniques used across systems.

4.1 Top systems

The top three systems achieved similar performance via very different approaches.

Kim et al. (2016) base their approach on SGD classifiers with a small feature space, varying several different aspects of implementation. There features consist of only TF-IDF weighted unigrams, and post embeddings using sent2vec (Le and Mikolov, 2014). Their best run was an ensemble of three classifiers which, in contrast to other teams, were trained on the 12 sub-annotation labels (e.g. *current acute distress*) as opposed to the 4 coarse labels. They find that this substantially increases *red* recall and *amber* precision, this suggests a better assignment of labels around the *red/amber* boundary. They incorporate a classifier which make sentence-level predictions, summing the distributions across sentences to select the label for a post.

Malmasi et al. (2016) implement a meta-classifier approach. Base linear SVM classifiers are constructed from a larger feature space than the other top-performing systems, they generate these base classifiers for both the target posts as well as preceding and following posts. These base classifiers are in turn used to train a meta-classifier, which is extended to a Random Forest of meta-classifiers. They find that Random Forests outperform SVMs at the meta-classifier level, but there is some performance variation between classifiers which they expect is due to the randomness inherent in training Random

Forests. Despite the lower result, their RBF-kernel SVM meta-classifier still performs well, suggesting robustness of this approach.

Brew (2016) experiment with leveraging unlabelled data, but their baseline RBF-kernel SVM achieves a better score than any of their more elaborate approaches. Features used were TF-IDF weighted unigrams and bigrams, author type, post kudos, and whether a post is the first in its thread. They provide analysis in their system description paper, one observation is that the official metric may give unstable results which happen to overly benefit their implementation in this instance. Accuracy results in Section 5 may support this, as the accuracy of this system is slightly below the other top systems, but even across unofficial metrics this is still one of the top-performing approaches.

4.2 General approaches

Systems generally used a logistic regression or SVM classifier, or an ensemble of these classifiers. Most systems learned coarse-level labels only and used a relatively straightforward learning setup.

Successful approaches use several different types of features: as well as features derived from post content, we find systems include features derived from post metadata and larger forum structure.

4.2.1 Post content features

Systems extract typical features from post subjects and body text. Most systems preprocess the text to handle HTML entities, and extract unigram and bigram features, potentially using lemmatised tokens. Better performing systems weight these n-grams with TD-IDF (Kim et al., 2016; Brew, 2016), or incorporate embeddings. Top-performing (Malmasi et al., 2016) make use of further n-gram features, adding character n-grams, token skip-grams and POS n-grams to the above.

Lexicons, particularly the Linguistic Inquiry and Word Count (Pennebaker et al., 2015) lexicon, are used as measure of emotion (Cohan et al., 2016) and sentiment (Malmasi et al., 2016). Cohan et al. (2016) additionally leverage DepecheMood (Staiano and Guerini, 2014) to identify emotions associated with a post, and the MPQA subjectivity lexicon (Wilson et al., 2005) to distinguish between objective and subjective posts. In particular, Cohan et al. (2016) apply these lexicons to the final sentence in a post, in an effort to capture the final mental state of the user, particularly where it relates to self-harm in lengthy posts that do not otherwise indicate self-harm. Zirikly et al. (2016) use the NRC Word-Emotion Association Lexicon (Mohammad and Turney, 2013) for emotion-word features.

Cohan et al. (2016) generate LDA topics of each post. Amiri et al. (2016) generate 30 topics over the full ReachOut.com corpus as well as the `reddit.com/r/Depression` subreddit. They then similarly use post topics as features.

Some approaches incorporate sentiment techniques into classification. Zirikly et al. (2016) label sentences with sentiment, using CoreNLP (Manning et al., 2014), and use counts of each sentiment as features, Shickel and Rashidi (2016) make use of sentiment labelling in a similar way. Almeida et al. (2016) add sentiment dictionaries.

Semi-structural features are included by Zirikly et al. (2016). One simple feature is the count of user names mentioned in posts. Other features capture repeated syntax, such as a popular thread that asks users to systematically turn negatives into positives. Deeper syntactic features are included by Malmasi et al. (2016), as are Brown cluster features. Wang et al. (2016) make explicit use of emoticons.

4.2.2 Post metadata features

Participants made only limited use of post metadata. Author ranking (the role of the author on the site) and kudos were the most used elements; followed by times posts were created and edited, the thread and board they belong to, and the number of times they are viewed.

4.2.3 Forum structure features

Most systems made little use of forum structure and hierarchy other than using thread ID as a simple feature. Malmasi et al. (2016) make use of posts before and after the target post; Pink et al. (2016) use post reply chains as a source of features; and a number of systems generate features from posts in context or aggregated features, such as the number of posts in a thread (Cohan et al., 2016). Brew (2016) add a feature which indicates whether a post is the first in a thread, which may be a useful straightforward feature, given how the data was annotated.

Most systems do not consider unlabelled posts. As mentioned, Cohan et al. (2016) and Amiri et al. (2016) build LDA models over the data. Zirikly et al. (2016) experiment with a semi-supervised SVM.

5 Results

In this section we only consider the best run for all teams. Readers are encouraged to refer to the individual system description papers for results of all runs.

5.1 Metric

The official metric for the shared task is macro-averaged F-score, because it gives more weight to the infrequent yet more critical labels than a micro-average. Identifying a metric that appropriately targets downstream requirements is difficult, particularly as desired recall is different across labels: a lower precision may acceptable for a higher recall *crisis* labelling, but not for *amber*. Brew (2016) provide some analysis of the stability of this metric. We note that ordering results by accuracy produces a fairly similar ordering.

5.2 Official results

The official scores are listed Table 2. It additionally reports scores gained by treating *crisis*, *red* and *amber* as a single *flagged* label against *green*, and by treating *crisis* and *red* as a single *urgent* label against *amber* and *green*. The participants' top systems are compared against to a straightforward baseline system that uses unigrams and bigrams as features, and a default scikit-learn (Pedregosa et al., 2011) logistic regression classifier.

Results are close across different approaches: three teams tie for first place, the next two teams are behind by only a few instances. The median is 0.34.

We note that the *crisis* label only occurs once in the test data and none of the systems successfully detected it. This has a large impact on the official macro-average metric; for example, if we disregard this label from Kim et al. (2016), the score would be 0.63. Fortunately all systems suffer the same disadvantage so the relative comparisons remain fair, although it is possible that systems optimised for *crisis* labels may have been slightly disadvantaged. We expect that a more sophisticated evaluation metric is required to handle this minimally represented class:

team	official	acc	flagged	flagged acc	urgent	urgent acc
Kim et al. (2016)	**0.42**	**0.85**	0.85	**0.91**	0.62	0.91
Malmasi et al. (2016)	**0.42**	0.83	**0.87**	**0.91**	0.64	**0.93**
Brew (2016)	**0.42**	0.79	0.78	0.85	**0.69**	**0.93**
Cohan et al. (2016)	0.41	0.80	0.81	0.87	0.67	0.92
Desmet et al. (2016)	0.40	0.80	0.80	0.87	0.62	0.92
Opitz (2016)	0.37	0.79	0.76	0.85	0.50	0.91
Zirikly et al. (2016)	0.36	0.77	0.78	0.85	0.60	0.90
Rey-Villamizar et al. (2016)	0.34	0.77	0.79	0.86	0.51	0.89
Pink et al. (2016)	0.33	0.78	0.73	0.85	0.48	0.90
Asgaria et al. (2016)	0.32	0.79	0.76	0.86	0.40	0.90
Amiri et al. (2016)	0.31	0.73	0.68	0.80	0.50	0.90
Wang et al. (2016)	0.30	0.73	0.76	0.83	0.48	0.89
Almeida et al. (2016)	0.29	0.74	0.68	0.82	0.51	0.88
Shickel and Rashidi (2016)	0.23	0.76	0.79	0.86	0.09	0.83
Franco-Penya and Sanchez (2016)	0.13	0.42	0.58	0.60	0.36	0.75
baseline	0.31	0.78	0.75	0.86	0.38	0.89

Table 2: Official results for the CLPsych 2016 shared task. *official* is crisis, red and amber macro-averaged F-score, *acc* is accuracy, *flagged* is crisis + red + amber, *urgent* is crisis + red (against amber + green). Top results are bolded.

team	crisis	red	amber	green
Kim	0.00	**0.65**	0.61	**0.94**
Malmasi	0.00	0.58	**0.69**	0.93
Brew	0.00	**0.65**	0.61	0.88
Cohan	0.00	0.59	0.64	0.90
Desmet	0.00	0.57	0.63	0.90
Opitz	0.00	0.48	0.62	0.89
Zirikly	0.00	0.51	0.58	0.89
Rey-Villamizar	0.00	0.43	0.58	0.90
Pink	0.00	0.49	0.49	0.89
Asgaria	0.00	0.41	0.56	0.90
Amiri	0.00	0.44	0.48	0.85
Wang	0.00	0.36	0.55	0.87
Almeida	0.00	0.40	0.48	0.87
Shickel	0.00	0.10	0.59	0.90
Franco-Penya	0.00	0.16	0.24	0.62
baseline	0.00	0.39	0.53	0.90

Table 3: Per-label F-scores for each run in Table 2.

if any system had correctly labelled the one *crisis* instance with reasonable precision, it would likely drastically outperform other systems.

For the best run of each team, we evaluate on each label and include the results in Table 3. Generally, systems perform well on *green*, and a substantial portion of performance is reliant on the *red/amber* decision. The is reflected in the *flagged* result in Table 2, sorting by this column would result in a substantially different ordering.

Many of the top-performing approaches are no-

tably different, however there are some interesting comparisons that can be made. Both Kim et al. (2016) and Brew (2016) are successful with only a small feature space. The latter system demonstrates that it is useful to consider not just the usual n-grams, but also custom features such as author type, kudos, and whether a post is first in the thread. It is interesting that the top teams achieved similar results. A larger exploration of the feature space may help identify those that are most useful.

Overall, the scarcity of crisis posts made full labelling a difficult task. However, the teams were able to achieve good scores for the *flagged* and *urgent* binary classification problems. These are promising results for supporting ReachOut's moderators.

6 Ethical considerations

In this paper we have built a shared task around publicly available data. Even though the data is already freely accessible, it needs to be treated with care and respect because it involves sensitive subject matter. The process of obtaining consent to release it to the research community was by no means straightforward. In this section we describe some of the questions and concerns that were raised in discussions with our own ethics committee, in the hope that they might be helpful to other researchers undertaking similar work. These discussions were guided by the Australian National Statement on Ethical Conduct in Human Research; obviously each researcher should seek out the corresponding legislation relevant to them (which may differ from our own), and follow recommendations of relevant authorities.

6.1 What is the potential for harm, and how can it be minimized?

The National Statement describes a balance between benefit and risk; that any risk of harm must be offset or justified by likely benefits (either for the participants themselves or the wider community). We identified three groups of participants to whom this annotation and release of data might cause harm: to the researchers who annotated the data, to the researchers with whom the data is shared, and to the people who authored the content.

The first two groups were easily catered for, by ensuring that the researchers were aware of the potentially distressing and triggering nature of the content, and providing appropriate access to care (i.e. location-specific helplines).

The third group is of much greater concern. While these forum members have already shared their data publicly, our annotations serve to single out the most distressed and vulnerable individuals among them. Disclosing their identities could cause serious distress, and may undermine their willingness to seek help in future. Fortunately these forum members are instructed by ReachOut to keep themselves safe and anonymous, and the moderators described in Section 2 respond to and actively redact any identifying information that is inadvertently shared.

To further protect this anonymity, participating researchers were restricted from contacting contacting individuals within the dataset (i.e. via the forums), cross-referencing individuals with the dataset against any other datasets or social media accounts, or making any other attempt to identify individuals. They were also not permitted to publish any portion of the dataset (e.g. example posts) other than summary statistics, or share it with anyone else. Future users of the dataset will have the same restrictions.

6.2 Should the data be redacted?

Another possible strategy for minimising potential harm is to redact the data to remove any identifying information. This is difficult to do for public social media data, because any structure or terms that remain can be searched on and compared to reconstruct it. Counter-intuitively, the more accessible data is, the more difficult it is to share safely.

Zimmer (2010) provides a cautionary tale in which private Facebook data was shared inadvertently, despite researchers' honest efforts to protect it. The previous CLPsych shared task (Coppersmith et al., 2015) provides another example of a dataset that remains re-identifiable despite redaction. It gathered tweets from participants who self-indicated that they were suffering from depression and post-traumatic stress, and redacted them by hashing usernames and any other readily identifiable information. And yet, for many individuals there likely remains enough text to cross-reference against twitter archives. Consequently recipients of this data had to sign a privacy agreement stating they would make no attempt to re-identify them.

A safer example is Sumner et al. (2012), who shared a dataset of twitter profiles matched to self-reported ratings for the *big five* personality traits and the *dark triad* of anti-social personality traits. Here the data is more aggressively redacted by only retaining basic statistics and frequencies of terms found in the Linguistic Inquiry and Word Count (LIWC) lexicon. This obviously limits researchers to using only a narrow set of predefined features.

Another strategy would be to encode all content such that researchers could count the relative frequencies of all terms without being able to read or understand them. This allows greater freedom than Sumner et al. but is still very limiting. For example, researchers would not be able to cross-reference terms against external vocabularies or bootstrap other sources of data (Section 4.2.1), or even perform their own lemmatisation. It would also make error analysis difficult if not impossible.

In summary, it does not seem possible to render public data truly non-identifiable without greatly hindering research. Fortunately our ethics committee felt that the anonymous nature of the ReachOut forums provided good protection of privacy. Their key remaining concern was that forum members might be identifiable if they reuse user names from other forms of social media. This motivated some of the restrictions described in Section 6.1.

6.3 Should consent be obtained?

Ideally any research involving human participants should be done with their full knowledge and consent. However, this dataset involves hundreds of distinct authors, to reduce the risk that the resulting algorithms would become over-fitted to any individuals writing style. Consequently obtaining consent individually for each participant would require an impractical investment of time. Additionally, our only means of contact would be via the forum, which is a place where many participants are only active for a short period of time to ask a specific question and then move on. Consequently, a great deal of valuable data would have been lost if we required consent from each individual participant.

Fortunately, the National Statement provides provisions for waiving the need for disclosure and consent when it is impractical to obtain it. For brevity, we will not exhaustively list all of the relevant requirements, but will instead focus on those that are particularly relevant for this research:

The first requirement is that *involvement in the research carries no more than low risk to participants*. As explained previously, the main risk here is the potential disclosure of sensitive information about the participants. Fortunately, the largely anonymous nature of ReachOut combined with the restrictions placed on researchers meant that this risk of disclosure was minimal.

Another pertinent requirement is that *there is no known or likely reason for thinking that participants would not have consented if they had been asked*. Given that the forum data is already widely shared and requires no special privileges to browse it, we argued that the participants appear to be comfortable allowing anyone to read their posts, as long as they can remain anonymous. Our focus then has been to ensure this anonymity is kept intact.

One last requirement is that *the benefits from the research justify any risks of harm associated with not seeking consent*. To our minds, this raises an obligation for the research to be more than merely an interesting text classification problem; that it must lead to something that is of direct benefit to the users and moderators of ReachOut. Consequently we are now working to build an accurate classifier from the insights gained during the shared task, and have in-

tegrated an early version of this triage system into the moderators suite of tools (Calvo et al., 2016). This system is already helping moderators respond quickly to urgent forum posts, and we hope to make it much more accurate in the near future.

7 Conclusions and future work

The CLPsych 2016 shared task was an interesting and difficult one. It asked participants to tackle the complex and somewhat subjective problem of prioritizing posts on a mental health forum, and elicited a broad array of algorithms and techniques.

The quantity and quality of participation has been excellent, and the organisers would like to thank teams for their engagement. The top performing teams performed well above the baseline, and made substantial progress on the task.

Participants were given limited time to hone their algorithms, so we hope they continue their work. There are many facets of the data still to explore, such as modelling the history and mental state of users, capturing structural and temporal data from the forum hierarchy, and further leveraging unlabelled data with semi-supervised or distantly supervised techniques. We will continue to work on and support this task and will be integrating ideas into the system used by ReachOut's moderators.

We invite interested researchers to join us on this challenging and worthwhile problem[1].

Acknowledgments

The authors thank ReachOut.com for providing the setting for the shared task; Kristy Hollingshead and Lyle Ungar for hosting and supporting the task at CLPsych; and participants for contributing to making this a successful task.

This research is funded by the Young and Well Cooperative Research Centre, an Australian-based international research centre that unites young people with researchers, practitioners, innovators and policy-makers from over 70 partner organisations. Together we explore the role of technology in young people's lives, and how it can be used to improve the mental health and wellbeing of young people aged 12-25. The Young and Well CRC is established

---

[1]Researchers can apply for access to the ReachOut triage dataset at `http://bit.ly/triage-dataset`

under the Australian Government's Cooperative Research Centres Program. Calvo is supported by an Australian Research Council Future Fellowship.

References

Hayda Almeida, Marc Queudot, and Marie-Jean Meurs. 2016. Automatic Triage of Mental Health Online Forum Posts: CLPsych 2016 System Description. In *Proceedings of the 3rd Workshop on Computational Linguistics and Clinical Psychology: From Linguistic Signal to Clinical Reality*, San Diego, California, USA, June 16.

Hadi Amiri, Hal Daumé III, Meir Friedenberg, and Philip Resnik. 2016. The University of Maryland CLPsych 2016 Shared Task System. In *Proceedings of the 3rd Workshop on Computational Linguistics and Clinical Psychology: From Linguistic Signal to Clinical Reality*, San Diego, California, USA, June 16.

Ehsaneddin Asgaria, Soroush Nasiriany, and Mohammad R.K. Mofrad. 2016. Textual Analysis and Automatic Triage of Posts in a Mental Health Forum. In *Proceedings of the 3rd Workshop on Computational Linguistics and Clinical Psychology: From Linguistic Signal to Clinical Reality*, San Diego, California, USA, June 16.

Chris Brew. 2016. Classifying ReachOut posts with a radial basis function SVM. In *Proceedings of the 3rd Workshop on Computational Linguistics and Clinical Psychology: From Linguistic Signal to Clinical Reality*, San Diego, California, USA, June 16.

Rafael A Calvo and Sidney D'Mello. 2010. Affect detection: An interdisciplinary review of models, methods, and their applications. *IEEE Transactions on Affective Computing*, 1(1):18–37.

Rafael A Calvo, Sazzad M Hussain, David N Milne, Kjartan Nordbo, Ian Hickie, and Peter Danckwerts. 2016. Augmenting Online Mental Health Support Services. In Daniela Villani, editor, *Integrating Technology in Positive Psychology Practice*, chapter 4, pages 82–103. IGI Global.

Arman Cohan, Sydney Young, and Nazli Goharian. 2016. Triaging Mental Health Forum Posts. In *Proceedings of the 3rd Workshop on Computational Linguistics and Clinical Psychology: From Linguistic Signal to Clinical Reality*, San Diego, California, USA, June 16.

Glen Coppersmith, Mark Dredze, Craig Harman, Kristy Hollingshead, and Margaret Mitchell. 2015. CLPsych 2015 shared task: Depression and PTSD on Twitter. In *Proceedings of the 2015 Conference of the North American Chapter of the Association for Computational Linguistics Human Language Technologies (NAACL HLT 2015)*, page 31.

Munmun De Choudhury, Michael Gamon, Scott Counts, and Eric Horvitz. 2013. Predicting Depression via Social Media. In *ICWSM*, page 2.

Bart Desmet, Gilles Jacobs, and Véronique Hoste. 2016. LT3 shared task submission. In *Proceedings of the 3rd Workshop on Computational Linguistics and Clinical Psychology: From Linguistic Signal to Clinical Reality*, San Diego, California, USA, June 16.

Hector-Hugo Franco-Penya and Liliana Mamani Sanchez. 2016. Predicting on-line users in psychological need on Reach out forums. In *Proceedings of the 3rd Workshop on Computational Linguistics and Clinical Psychology: From Linguistic Signal to Clinical Reality*, San Diego, California, USA, June 16.

Katy Kaplan, Mark S. Salzer, Phyllis Solomon, Eugene Brusilovskiy, and Pamela Cousounis. 2011. Internet peer support for individuals with psychiatric disabilities: A randomized controlled trial". *Social Science & Medicine*, 72(1):54–62.

Sunghwan Mac Kim, Yufei Wang, Stephen Wan, and Cecile Paris. 2016. Data61-CSIRO systems at the CLPsych 2016 Shared Task. In *Proceedings of the 3rd Workshop on Computational Linguistics and Clinical Psychology: From Linguistic Signal to Clinical Reality*, San Diego, California, USA, June 16.

Per E Kummervold, Deede Gammon, Svein Bergvik, Jan-Are K Johnsen, Toralf Hasvold, and Jan H Rosenvinge. 2002. Social support in a wired world: use of online mental health forums in Norway. *Nordic journal of psychiatry*, 56(1):59–65.

Quoc V. Le and Tomas Mikolov. 2014. Distributed Representations of Sentences and Documents. In *Proceedings of the 31th International Conference on Machine Learning, ICML 2014, Beijing, China, 21-26 June 2014*, volume 32 of *JMLR Proceedings*, pages 1188–1196.

Shervin Malmasi, Marcos Zampieri, and Mark Dras. 2016. Predicting Post Severity in Mental Health Forums. In *Proceedings of the 3rd Workshop on Computational Linguistics and Clinical Psychology: From Linguistic Signal to Clinical Reality*, San Diego, California, USA, June 16.

Christopher D. Manning, Mihai Surdeanu, John Bauer, Jenny Finkel, Steven J. Bethard, and David McClosky. 2014. The Stanford CoreNLP natural language processing toolkit. In *Association for Computational Linguistics (ACL) System Demonstrations*, pages 55–60.

Atari Metcalf and Victoria Blake. 2013. ReachOut.com Annual User Survey Results. http://about.au.reachout.com/

wp-content/uploads/2015/01/ReachOut.
com-Annual-User-Survey-2013.pdf.
Accessed:2016-04-02.

Doug Millen. 2014. ReachOut Annual Report 2013/2014. http://about.au.reachout.com/us/annual-reports-financials. Accessed:2016-04-02.

Saif M. Mohammad and Peter D. Turney. 2013. Crowdsourcing a Word-Emotion Association Lexicon. *Computational Intelligence*, 29(3):436–465.

Bridianne O'Dea, Stephen Wan, Philip J Batterham, Alison L Calear, Cecile Paris, and Helen Christensen. 2015. Detecting suicidality on Twitter. *Internet Interventions*, 2(2):183–188.

Juri Opitz. 2016. System Description. In *Proceedings of the 3rd Workshop on Computational Linguistics and Clinical Psychology: From Linguistic Signal to Clinical Reality*, San Diego, California, USA, June 16.

Fabian Pedregosa, Gaël Varoquaux, Alexandre Gramfort, Vincent Michel, Bertrand Thirion, Olivier Grisel, Mathieu Blondel, Peter Prettenhofer, Ron Weiss, Vincent Dubourg, Jake Vanderplas, Alexandre Passos, David Cournapeau, Matthieu Brucher, Matthieu Perrot, and Édouard Duchesnay. 2011. Scikit-learn: Machine Learning in Python. *J. Mach. Learn. Res.*, 12:2825–2830, November.

James W Pennebaker, Ryan L Boyd, Kayla Jordan, and Kate Blackburn. 2015. The Development and Psychometric Properties of LIWC2015. *UT Faculty/Researcher Works*.

John P Pestian, Pawel Matykiewicz, Michelle Linn-Gust, Brett South, Ozlem Uzuner, Jan Wiebe, Kevin B Cohen, John Hurdle, and Christopher Brew. 2012. Sentiment analysis of suicide notes: A shared task. *Biomedical informatics insights*, 5(Suppl. 1):3.

Paul N. Pfeiffer, Michele Heisler, John D. Piette, Mary A.M. Rogers, and Marcia Valenstein. 2011. Efficacy of peer support interventions for depression: a meta-analysis. *General Hospital Psychiatry*, 33(1):29–36.

Glen Pink, Will Radford, and Ben Hachey. 2016. Classification of mental health forum posts. In *Proceedings of the 3rd Workshop on Computational Linguistics and Clinical Psychology: From Linguistic Signal to Clinical Reality*, San Diego, California, USA, June 16.

Sameer Pradhan, Noémie Elhadad, Wendy Chapman, Suresh Manandhar, and Guergana Savova. 2014. SemEval-2014 task 7: Analysis of clinical text. In *Proceedings of the 8th International Workshop on Semantic Evaluation (SemEval 2014)*, Dublin, Ireland, August.

Nicolas Rey-Villamizar, Prasha Shrestha, Thamar Solorio, Farig Sadeque, Steven Bethard, and Ted Pedersen. 2016. Semi-supervised CLPsych 2016 Shared Task System Submission. In *Proceedings of the 3rd Workshop on Computational Linguistics and Clinical Psychology: From Linguistic Signal to Clinical Reality*, San Diego, California, USA, June 16.

Benjamin Shickel and Parisa Rashidi. 2016. Automatic Triage of Mental Health Forum Posts for the CLPsych 2016 Shared Task. In *Proceedings of the 3rd Workshop on Computational Linguistics and Clinical Psychology: From Linguistic Signal to Clinical Reality*, San Diego, California, USA, June 16.

Jacopo Staiano and Marco Guerini. 2014. Depeche Mood: a Lexicon for Emotion Analysis from Crowd Annotated News. In *Proceedings of the 52nd Annual Meeting of the Association for Computational Linguistics (Volume 2: Short Papers)*, pages 427–433, Baltimore, Maryland, June. Association for Computational Linguistics.

Chris Sumner, Alison Byers, Rachel Boochever, and Gregory J Park. 2012. Predicting dark triad personality traits from twitter usage and a linguistic analysis of tweets. In *Machine Learning and Applications (ICMLA), 2012 11th International Conference on*, volume 2, pages 386–393. IEEE.

Anthony J Viera and Joanne M Garrett. 2005. Understanding interobserver agreement: the kappa statistic. *Family Medicine*, 37(5):360–363.

Chen-Kai Wang, Hong-Jie Dai, Chih-Wei Chen, Jitendra Jonnagaddala, and Nai-Wen Chang. 2016. Combining Multiple Classifiers Using Global Ranking for ReachOut.com Post Triage. In *Proceedings of the 3rd Workshop on Computational Linguistics and Clinical Psychology: From Linguistic Signal to Clinical Reality*, San Diego, California, USA, June 16.

Theresa Wilson, Janyce Wiebe, and Paul Hoffmann. 2005. Recognizing Contextual Polarity in Phrase-level Sentiment Analysis. In *Proceedings of the Conference on Human Language Technology and Empirical Methods in Natural Language Processing*, HLT '05, pages 347–354, Stroudsburg, PA, USA. Association for Computational Linguistics.

Dawei Yin, Zhenzhen Xue, Liangjie Hong, Brian D Davison, April Kontostathis, and Lynne Edwards. 2009. Detection of harassment on web 2.0. *Proceedings of the Content Analysis in the WEB*, 2:1–7.

Michael Zimmer. 2010. "But the data is already public": on the ethics of research in Facebook. *Ethics and information technology*, 12(4):313–325.

Ayah Zirikly, Varun Kumar, and Philip Resnik. 2016. The GW/UMD CLPsych 2016 Shared Task System. In *Proceedings of the 3rd Workshop on Computational Linguistics and Clinical Psychology: From Linguistic Signal to Clinical Reality*, San Diego, California, USA, June 16.

Data61-CSIRO systems at the CLPsych 2016 Shared Task

Sunghwan Mac Kim[1], Yufei Wang[2]*, Stephen Wan[1] and Cécile Paris[1]
[1]Data61, CSIRO, Sydney, Australia
[2]School of Information Technology and Electrical Engineering,
The University of Queensland, Brisbane, Australia
`Mac.Kim@csiro.au, Yufei.Wang1@uq.net.au,`
`Stephen.Wan@csiro.au, Cecile.Paris@csiro.au`

Abstract

This paper describes the Data61-CSIRO text classification systems submitted as part of the CLPsych 2016 shared task. The aim of the shared task is to develop automated systems that can help mental health professionals with the process of triaging posts with ideations of depression and/or self-harm. We structured our participation in the CLPsych 2016 shared task in order to focus on different facets of modelling online forum discussions: (i) vector space representations; (ii) different text granularities; and (iii) fine- versus coarse-grained labels indicating concern. We achieved an F1-score of 0.42 using an ensemble classification approach that predicts fine-grained labels of concern. This was the best score obtained by any submitted system in the 2016 shared task.

1 Introduction

The aim of the shared task is to research and develop automatic systems that can help mental health professionals with the process of triaging posts with ideations of depression and/or self-harm. We structured our participation in the CLPsych 2016 shared task in order to focus on different facets of modelling online forum discussions: (i) vector space representations (TF-IDF vs. embeddings); (ii) different text granularities (e.g., sentences vs posts); and (iii) fine-versus coarse-grained (FG and CG respectively) labels indicating concern.

(i) For our exploration of vector space representations, we explored the traditional TF-IDF feature

representation that has been widely applied to NLP. We also investigated the use of post embeddings, which have recently attracted much attention as feature vectors for representing text (Zhou et al., 2015; Salehi et al., 2015). Here, as in other related work (Guo et al., 2014), the post embeddings are learned from the unlabelled data as features for supervised classifiers. (ii) Our exploration of text granularity focuses on classifiers for sentences as well as posts. For the sentence-level classifiers, a post is split into sentences as the basic unit of annotation using a sentence segmenter. (iii) To explore the granularity of labels indicating concern, we note that the data includes a set of 12 FG labels representing factors that assist in deciding on whether a post is concerning or not. These are in addition to 4 CG labels.

We trained 6 single classifiers based on different combinations of vector space features, text granularities and label sets. We also explored ensemble classifiers (based on these 6 single classifiers), as this is a way of combining the strengths of the single classifiers. We used one of two ensemble methods: majority voting and probability scores over labels. We submitted five different systems as submissions to the shared task. Two of them were based on single classifiers, whereas the remaining three systems used ensemble-based classifiers. We achieved an F1-score of 0.42 using an ensemble classification approach that predicts FG labels of concern. This was the best score obtained by any submitted system in the 2016 shared task.

The paper is organised as follows: Section 2 briefly discusses the data of the shared task. Section 3 presents the details of the systems we sub-

---

This work was performed while Yufei was at CSIRO.

Proceedings of the 3rd Workshop on Computational Linguistics and Clinical Psychology: From Linguistic Signal to Clinical Reality, pages 128–132,
San Diego, California, June 16, 2016. ©2016 Association for Computational Linguistics

mitted. Section 4 then shows experimental results. Finally, we summarise our findings in Section 5.

2 Data

The dataset used in the shared task is a collection of online posts crawled from a mental health forum, ReachOut.com[1], collected by the shared task annotators, who then labelled each discussion post with one of 4 CG labels: *Green*, *Amber*, *Red* and *Crisis*, describing how likely a post is to require the attention of a mental health professional. Each post is also annotated with one of 12 FG labels, which are mapped deterministically to one of the 4 CG labels according to the relationships presented in Table 1 (which also provides the frequencies of these relationships). For instance, a post labelled with *Red* could be labelled with one of 4 FG labels: *angryWithForumMember*, *angryWithReachout*, *currentAcuteDistress* and *followupWorse*. As can be seen in the table, the dataset is imbalanced since it contains more *Green* labelled posts than any other post.

The corpus consists of 65,024 posts, and it is subdivided into labelled (947) and unlabelled data (64,077). The final test data contains an extra 241 forum posts. Each post is provided in an XML file and each post file contains metadata, such as the number of "likes" a post received from the online community. The shared task requires each submitted system to predict a label for each of test posts.

In addition to the post data, the data set contains anonymised metadata about post authors, which indicates whether authors were affiliated with ReachOut, either as a community moderator or a site administrator. Specifically, this metadata contains anonymised author IDs and their forum ranking. In total, there were 1,640 unique authors and 20 author rankings on the forums. Each author has one of the 20 rankings. 7 ranking types indicate ReachOut affiliated, whereas 13 author ranking types represent a member of the general public.

3 Systems Description

3.1 Text Pre-processing

We performed several text pre-processing steps prior to feature extraction in order to reduce the noisiness

[1] http://forums.au.reachout.com/

CG label	Frequency	FG label	Frequency
Green	549	allClear	367
		followupBye	16
		supporting	166
Amber	249	underserved	34
		currentMildDistress	40
		followupOk	165
		pastDistress	10
Red	110	angryWithForumMember	1
		angryWithReachout	2
		currentAcuteDistress	87
		followupWorse	20
Crisis	39	crisis	39

Table 1: CG and FG label sets. Their frequencies represent the number of posts in the labelled dataset.

of the original forum posts. We removed HTML special characters, non-ASCII characters and stop words, and all tokens were lower-cased. We used NLTK (Bird et al., 2009) to segment sentences for the sentence-level classifiers, producing 4,305 sentences from the 947 posts.

3.2 Features

We used two types of feature representations for the text: TF-IDF and post embeddings. The TF-IDF feature vectors of unigrams were generated from the labelled dataset, whereas the embeddings were obtained using both labelled and unlabelled dataset using sent2vec (Le and Mikolov, 2014). We obtained the embeddings for the whole post directly instead of combining the embeddings for the individual words of the post due to the superior performance of document embeddings (Sun et al., 2015; Tang et al., 2015).

In our preliminary investigations, we explored various kinds of features such as bi- and trigrams, metadata from the posts (such as the number of views of a post or the author's affiliation with ReachOut) and orthographic features (for example, the presence of emoticons, punctuation, etc.), but we did not obtain any performance benefits with respect to intrinsic evaluations on the training data.

3.3 Classifiers

For the text classifiers, we trained a MaxEnt model using scikit-learn's SGDClassifier (Pedregosa et al., 2011) with the log loss function and a learning rate of 0.0001 as our classifier for all experiments. In the training phrase, the weights of SGDClassifier are optimised using stochastic gradient descent (SGD) through minimising a given loss function, and L2 regularisation is employed to avoid overfitting. The log loss function in SGDClassifier allows us to obtain the probability score of a label at prediction time.

We developed classifiers for two granularities of text: (i) entire posts, and (ii) sentences in posts. For the latter, we post-processed the predicted sentence-level labels to produce post-level labels (to be consistent with the shared task). We obtained distributions of probabilities for the label sets for each sentence, and then summed the distributions for all sentences in a post. This provided a final distribution of probabilities for labels for a post. The label with the highest probability was then taken as the inferred label for the post.

To perform the post-processing steps above, we used the distributions for labels produced by the MaxEnt model. That is, the model can be used to provide estimates for the probabilities of:

- CG labels given a post, $P(CG\ label|post)$;
- CG labels given a sentence, $P(CG\ label|sentence)$;
- FG labels given a post, $P(FG\ label|post)$; and
- FG labels given a sentence, $P(FG\ label|sentence)$.

We also developed classifiers for the CG and FG label sets. In the case of the FG set, we again performed post-processing steps to produce CG labels. In this case, we deterministically reduced the predicted 12 labels to the 4 CG labels, using the mapping presented in Table 1.

This allowed us to experiment with different combinations of the 3 facets, described in Section 1. We built 6 classifiers based on the combination of the configurations described so far as follows:

C1. post-level TF-IDF classifier using 4 labels
C2. post-level embedding classifier using 4 labels
C3. sentence-level TF-IDF classifier using 4 labels
C4. post-level TF-IDF classifier using 12 labels
C5. post-level embedding classifier using 12 labels
C6. sentence-level TF-IDF classifier using 12 labels

3.4 Ensembles

One reason why the ensemble approaches may work well is that, even if a classifier does not pick the correct label, the probabilities for all labels can still be taken as input to the ensemble approach. For example, although a classifier may have chosen a la-

System	Training results	Official test results
Post-tfidf-4labels	0.25	0.39
Sent-tfidf-12labels	0.35	0.37
Ensb-6classifiers-mv	**0.37**	0.37
Ensb-3classifiers-4labels-prob	0.35	0.35
Ensb-3classifiers-12labels-prob	**0.37**	**0.42**

Table 2: F1 results for 5-fold cross-validation on training data and the official test results from the shared task.

bel incorrectly, the correct label could have had the second highest probability score, which when combined with information from other classifiers may lead to the correct label being assigned.

As mentioned in Section 1, the outputs of the ensemble models were produced using one of two ensemble methods: majority voting and probability scores over labels. In the majority voting method, each classifier votes for a single label, and the label with highest number of votes is selected for the final decision. The second ensemble method uses an estimate of the posterior probability for each label from individual classifiers, and the label with highest sum of probabilities is chosen for the final prediction. Neither ensemble method requires any parameter tuning.

3.5 Submitted Systems

Five different systems were adopted for our submissions to the shared task. Two were based on a single MaxEnt classifier, whereas the remaining three systems used ensemble-based classifiers. The two single classifiers were as follows:

1. a single classifier C1 (*Post-tfidf-4labels*)
2. a single classifier C6 (*Sent-tfidf-12labels*)

And the three ensemble classifiers are:

3. an ensemble classifier combining all six C1-C6 by majority voting (*Ensb-6classifiers-mv*)
4. an ensemble classifier combining C1, C2, C3 by posterior probabilities (*Ensb-3classifiers-4labels-prob*)
5. an ensemble classifier combining C4, C5, C6 by posterior probabilities (*Ensb-3classifiers-12labels-prob*)

The *Post-tfidf-4labels* system uses a standard approach predicting 4 CG labels with respect to posts using TF-IDF feature representation. The *Sent-tfidf-12labels* system predicts 12 fined-grained labels for sentences using the same feature representation method. The *Ensb-6classifiers-mv* system combines all judgements of the six MaxEnt classifiers described in Section 3.3 through majority voting. The

System	F1	Accuracy	Filter F1	Filter Accuracy
Post-tfidf-4labels	0.39	0.81	0.82	0.88
Sent-tfidf-12labels	0.37	0.80	0.81	0.88
Ensb-6classifiers-mv	0.37	0.83	0.81	0.90
Ensb-3classifiers-4labels-prob	0.35	0.82	0.80	0.89
Ensb-3classifiers-12labels-prob	**0.42**	**0.85**	**0.85**	**0.91**

Table 3: Results for the test set. The filter decides whether the label of a forum post is *green* or not (non-green vs. green).

		P	R	F1
Ensb-3classifiers-4labels-prob	Amber	**0.60**	0.57	0.59
	Red	0.69	**0.33**	0.45
	Crisis	0.00	0.00	0.00
Ensb-3classifiers-12labels-prob	Amber	**0.71**	0.53	0.61
	Red	0.68	**0.63**	0.65
	Crisis	0.00	0.00	0.00

Table 4: Comparison results on the test dataset in terms of precision, recall and F1.

remaining two systems, *Ensb-3classifiers-4labels-prob* and *Ensb-3classifiers-12labels-prob*, use the sum of label probabilities estimated from individual classifiers to select the most probable label. The main difference between the two systems is the estimation of probability scores in different level of label granularities (CG labels vs. FG labels).

4 Experimental Results

In this section, we present two evaluation results: the cross-validation results and the final test results. We performed 5-fold cross-validation on the training set (947 labelled posts). We also report the shared task evaluation scores for the five systems on the test set of 214 posts. These are shown in Table 2 where scores are computed for three labels: *Amber*, *Red* and *Crisis* (but not Green), since this is the official evaluation metric in the shared task.

We observe that two of the ensemble systems (*Ensb-6classifiers-mv* and *Ensb-3classifiers-12labels-prob*) show higher F1-scores than the others in the cross-validation experiments. In particular, *Ensb-3classifiers-12labels-prob* performs best both in the cross-validation experiment (0.37) and the main competition (0.42).

Somewhat surprisingly, the first system, *Post-tfidf-4labels*, gave us an F1-score of 0.39 on the test data, while its F1-score was the lowest in the cross-validation experiment. This result indicates that good performance is possible on the test dataset using a "textbook" TF-IDF classifier but further investigation is required to understand why the official test result differs from our cross-validation result.

Table 3 shows the superior performance of the *Ensb-3classifiers-12labels-prob*, with respect to the other systems in terms of F1 and accuracy. It achieved the highest accuracy (0.85) for the three labels. Furthermore, it is a robust system for identifying the non-concerning label, *Green*.

It is interesting to see that the F1-score was improved by performing the hard classification task of 12 labels compared to 4-label classification. We compare the performance of the *Ensb-3classifiers-4labels-prob* and *Ensb-3classifiers-12labels-prob* systems on the test data per label, as shown in Table 4 to shed light on why the 12-labelling system has superior performance. Both systems were unable to detect any *Crisis*-labelled posts. A notable difference between the two systems is that the *Ensb-3classifiers-12labels-prob* system produces significantly higher recall (0.63) than the *Ensb-3classifiers-4labels-prob* system (0.33). In addition, the *Ensb-3classifiers-12labels-prob* system has a higher precision for finding *Amber* posts. These results consequently led to overall better F1 as shown in Table 3, and suggest that identifying *Green* and *Amber* posts for a user-in-the-loop scenario may be one way to help moderators save time in triaging posts.

5 Conclusion

We applied single and ensemble classifiers to the task of classifying online forum posts based on the likelihood of a mental health professional being required to intervene in the discussion. We achieved an F1-score of 0.42 with a system that combined post and sentence-level classifications through probability scores to produce FG labels. This was the best score obtained by any submitted system in the 2016 shared task. The experimental results suggest that identifying *Green* and *Amber* posts for a user-in-the-loop scenario may be one way to help moderators save time in triaging posts.

Acknowledgments

We would like to thank the organisers of the shared task for their support.

References

Steven Bird, Ewan Klein, and Edward Loper. 2009. *Natural Language Processing with Python*. O'Reilly Media, Inc., 1st edition.

Jiang Guo, Wanxiang Che, Haifeng Wang, and Ting Liu. 2014. Learning sense-specific word embeddings by exploiting bilingual resources. In *Proceedings of COLING 2014, the 25th International Conference on Computational Linguistics: Technical Papers*, pages 497–507, Dublin, Ireland, August. Dublin City University and Association for Computational Linguistics.

Quoc Le and Tomas Mikolov. 2014. Distributed representations of sentences and documents. In Tony Jebara and Eric P. Xing, editors, *Proceedings of the 31st International Conference on Machine Learning (ICML-14)*, pages 1188–1196. JMLR Workshop and Conference Proceedings.

Fabian Pedregosa, Gaël Varoquaux, Alexandre Gramfort, Vincent Michel, Bertrand Thirion, Olivier Grisel, Mathieu Blondel, Peter Prettenhofer, Ron Weiss, Vincent Dubourg, Jake Vanderplas, Alexandre Passos, David Cournapeau, Matthieu Brucher, Matthieu Perrot, and Édouard Duchesnay. 2011. Scikit-learn: Machine learning in python. *J. Mach. Learn. Res.*, 12:2825–2830, November.

Bahar Salehi, Paul Cook, and Timothy Baldwin. 2015. A word embedding approach to predicting the compositionality of multiword expressions. In *Proceedings of the 2015 Conference of the North American Chapter of the Association for Computational Linguistics: Human Language Technologies*, pages 977–983, Denver, Colorado, May–June. Association for Computational Linguistics.

Fei Sun, Jiafeng Guo, Yanyan Lan, Jun Xu, and Xueqi Cheng. 2015. Learning word representations by jointly modeling syntagmatic and paradigmatic relations. In *Proceedings of the 53rd Annual Meeting of the Association for Computational Linguistics and the 7th International Joint Conference on Natural Language Processing (Volume 1: Long Papers)*, pages 136–145, Beijing, China, July. Association for Computational Linguistics.

Duyu Tang, Bing Qin, and Ting Liu. 2015. Document modeling with gated recurrent neural network for sentiment classification. In *Proceedings of the 2015 Conference on Empirical Methods in Natural Language Processing*, pages 1422–1432, Lisbon, Portugal, September. Association for Computational Linguistics.

Guangyou Zhou, Tingting He, Jun Zhao, and Po Hu. 2015. Learning continuous word embedding with metadata for question retrieval in community question answering. In *Proceedings of the 53rd Annual Meeting of the Association for Computational Linguistics and the 7th International Joint Conference on Natural Language Processing (Volume 1: Long Papers)*, pages 250–259, Beijing, China, July. Association for Computational Linguistics.

Predicting Post Severity in Mental Health Forums

Shervin Malmasi[1,2]   **Marcos Zampieri**[3,4]   **Mark Dras**[1]
[1]Macquarie University, Sydney, NSW, Australia
[2]Harvard Medical School, Boston, MA 02115, USA
[3]Saarland University, Germany
[4]German Research Center for Artificial Intelligence, Germany
{first.last}@mq.edu.au, marcos.zampieri@dfki.de

Abstract

We present our approach to predicting the severity of user posts in a mental health forum. This system was developed to compete in the 2016 Computational Linguistics and Clinical Psychology (CLPsych) Shared Task. Our entry employs a meta-classifier which uses a set of of base classifiers constructed from lexical, syntactic and metadata features. These classifiers were generated for both the target posts as well as their contexts, which included both preceding and subsequent posts. The output from these classifiers was used to train a meta-classifier, which outperformed all individual classifiers as well as an ensemble classifier. This meta-classifier was then extended to a Random Forest of meta-classifiers, yielding further improvements in classification accuracy. We achieved competitive results, ranking first among a total of 60 submitted entries in the competition.

1 Introduction

Computational methods have been widely used to extract and/or predict a number of phenomena in text documents. It has been shown that algorithms are able to learn a wide range of information about the authors of texts as well. This includes, for example, the author's native language (Gebre et al., 2013; Malmasi and Dras, 2015a), age and gender (Nguyen et al., 2013), and even economic conditions such as income (Preoţiuc-Pietro et al., 2015). These tasks are often considered to be a part of a broader natural language processing task known as authorship profiling (Rangel et al., 2013).

More recently, such approaches have been applied to investigating psychological factors associated with the author of a text. For practical purposes most of the applications that deal with clinical psychology use social media data such as *Twitter, Facebook*, and online forums (Coppersmith et al., 2014). Examples of health and psychological conditions studied using texts and social media are: suicide risk (Thompson et al., 2014), depression (Schwartz et al., 2014), autism (Tanaka et al., 2014; Rouhizadeh et al., 2015), and schizophrenia (Mitchell et al., 2015).

In this paper we propose an approach to predict the severity of posts in a mental health online forum. Posts were classified into for levels of severity (or urgency) represented by the labels *green, amber, red*, and *crisis* according to indication of risky or harmful behavior by users (e.g. self-harm, suicide, etc.). This kind of classification task serves to provide automatic triage of user posts in order to help moderators of forums and related online communities to respond to urgent posts. Our approach competed in the CLPsych 2016 shared task and achieved the highest accuracy among submitted systems.

2 Task and Data

The dataset of the CLPsych shared task was compiled from the *ReachOut.com*[1] forums. *ReachOut.com* is an online youth mental health service that provides information, tools and support to young people aged 14-25.

The corpus consists of a total 65,024 posts formatted in XML and including metadata (e.g. time stamp, thread, post id, user id, etc.). Each post in

---

[1]http://au.reachout.com/

133

Proceedings of the 3rd Workshop on Computational Linguistics and Clinical Psychology: From Linguistic Signal to Clinical Reality, pages 133–137,
San Diego, California, June 16, 2016. ©2016 Association for Computational Linguistics

the labeled sets was manually annotated with a label representing how urgent a post should be handled by one of the *ReachOut.com* moderators.

Data Sets	Posts
Labeled Train	977
Labeled Test	250
Unlabeled	63,797
Total	65,024

Table 1: CLPsych Corpus Divided by Data Set

According to the shared task organizers, these labels were attributed according to the following criteria:

- Green: a moderator does not need to prioritize addressing this post.

- Amber: a moderator needs to look at this and assess if there are enough responses and support from others or if they should reply.

- Red: a moderator needs to look at this as soon as possible and take action.

- Crisis: the author (or someone they know) might hurt themselves or others (a red instance that is of urgent importance).

Participating systems should be trained to predict these labels, with evaluation on the test set.

3 Feature Extraction

We used three categories of features: lexical, syntactic, and metadata features. These features and our preprocessing method are outlined here.

3.1 Preprocessing

The following preprocessing was performed on the texts: HTML removal was performed, with links and anchor text being preserved. Smileys and emoticons were converted to text tags, e.g. #SmileySad and #SmileyHappy. Quotes from previous posts (e.g. the one being replied to) were also removed so as not to mix features from distinct messages.[2]

---

[2]This was facilitated by the fact that such quotations were labeled as such using the HTML blockquote tag.

3.2 Lexical Features

We represent words in the texts using different features based on characters, word forms and lemmas. We summarize the lexical features used in our system as follows:

- **Character n-grams:** we extracted n-grams of order 2–8.

- **Word n-grams:** words were represented as 1–3 grams.

- **Word skip-grams:** To capture the longer distance dependencies not covered by word n-grams we also used word skip-grams as described in Guthrie et al. (2006). We extract 1, 2 and 3-skip word bigrams.

- **Lemma n-grams:** we used a lemmatized version of the texts and extract lemma n-grams of order 1–3.

- **Word Representations:** To increase the generalizability of our models we used word representation features based on Brown clustering as a form of semi-supervised learning. This was done using the method described by Malmasi et al. (2015a). We used the clusters generated by Owoputi et al. (2013). They collected From 56 million English tweets (837 million tokens) and used it to generate 1,000 hierarchical clusters over 217 thousand words.

3.3 Syntactic Features

We used a set of (morpho-)syntactic features for deeper linguistic analysis, using the Stanford CoreNLP system for extracting these. The intuition is that structural or syntactic patterns present in posts might reveal relevant information regarding the psychological condition of writers.

- **Part-of-Speech (POS) n-grams:** these features rely on POS annotation and they are used to represent morphosyntactic patterns. We use POS tags modeled as 1–3 grams.

- **Dependencies:** we use dependency relations between constituents of sentences as features. They provide good indication of syntactic patterns in the data.

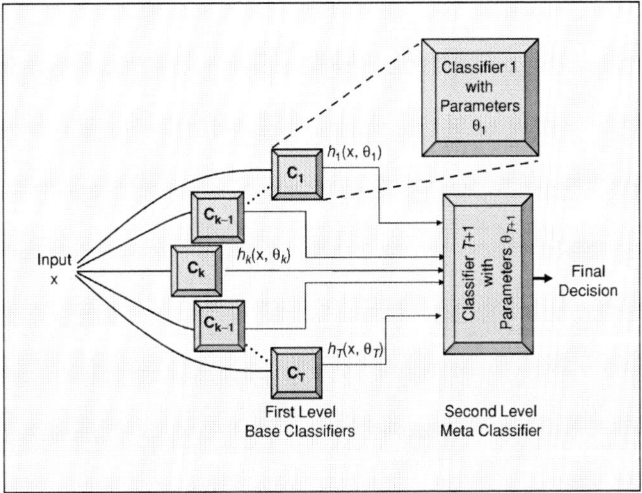

Figure 1: An illustration of a meta-classifier architecture. Image reproduced from Polikar (2006).

- **Production Rules:** similar to dependency relations, production rules capture the overall structure of grammatical constructions.

3.4 Metadata and Other Features

Finally, the third type of features used in our system relies on metadata. We used two feature groups taking advantage of the information present in the corpus about the forum itself and the user.

- **Board ID:** The forum is divided into individual boards according to topic. The ID of the board to which a post belongs is used as a feature.

- **User details:** The user information of a post's author, including the number of posts and affiliation status were used as features. This helps with the correct classification of messages from moderators and veteran users.

- **Subject:** The subjects of the postings were too short and unvaried for training a classifier. Instead, we applied the LIWC lexicon (Pennebaker et al., 2015) as a proxy measure of the subject's sentiment. These lexicon features were used to train a classifier.

3.5 Feature Contexts

Our features were extracted from several contexts, including the post itself in isolation, the last 1-2 recent posts by the author, the last 2-5 recent posts in the thread and the next 1-2 posts by the author (where available).

4 Methodology and Systems

We employed a meta-classifier for our entry, also referred to as classifier stacking. A meta-classifier architecture is generally composed of an ensemble of base classifiers that each make predictions for all of the input data. Their individual predictions, along with the gold labels are used to train a second-level meta-classifier that learns to predict the label for an input, given the decisions of the individual classifiers. This setup is illustrated in Figure 1. This meta-classifier attempts to learn from the collective knowledge represented by the ensemble of local classifiers. The first step in such an architecture is to create the set of base classifiers that form the first layer. We describe this process below.

4.1 Ensemble Construction

Our ensemble was created using linear Support Vector Machine classifiers.[3] We used the features listed in Section 3 to create our ensemble of classifiers. A single classifier was trained for each feature type and context, resulting in an ensemble of over 100 classifiers. Each classifier predicts every input and assigns a continuous output to each of the possible labels.

---

[3]Linear SVMs have proven effective in many text classification tasks (Malmasi and Dras, 2014; Malmasi et al., 2015b; Malmasi and Dras, 2015b).

Run	Official Score	Accuracy	F-score (NG vs. G)	Accuracy (NG vs. G)	Rank
Run 1	0.37	0.80	0.83	0.89	11th
Run 2	0.38	0.80	0.83	0.89	9th
Run 3	**0.42**	0.83	**0.87**	**0.91**	1st
Run 4	**0.42**	**0.84**	**0.87**	**0.91**	1st
Run 5	0.40	0.82	0.85	0.90	6th

Table 2: Official CLPsych scores. Best results in bold. Rankings are out of the 60 systems submitted.

Classifiers ensembles have proven to be an efficient and robust alternative in other text classification tasks such as language identification (Malmasi and Dras, 2015a), grammatical error detection (Xiang et al., 2015), and complex word identification (Malmasi et al., 2016).

4.2 Meta-classifier

For our meta-classifier, We experimented with three algorithms: Random Forests of decision trees, a linear SVM just like our base classifiers and a Radial Basis Function (RBF) kernel SVM. The inputs to the meta-classifier are the continuous outputs from each base SVM classifier in our ensemble, along with the original gold label. For the Random Forest classifiers, the final label is selected through a plurality voting process across all decision trees in the forest.

All were found to perform well, but the linear SVM was was outperformed by its RBF-kernel counterpart. This could be because the RBF-kernel SVM is more suitable for data with a smaller number of features such as here and can provide non-linear decision boundaries. Accordingly, we did not use the linear SVM for our entry due to the 5 run limit.

4.3 Systems

Using the methods described so far, we created five different systems for the CLPsych shared task:

- **System 1:** Our first system used the RBF-kernel SVM meta-classifier.

- **Systems 2–5:** The other four systems were based on Random Forests. This is because we noted some performance variation between different Random Forest classifiers, likely due to the randomness inherent to the algorithm.

5 Results

Submissions were evaluated on the unlabeled test set. The official evaluation metric is the F-score over all non-green labels. The results obtained by our 5 systems are shown in in Table 2. We report the official score by the organizers and the ranking among all submitted systems. According to the the organizers a total of 60 runs were submitted.

The meta-classifier approach proved to be robust and appropriate for this task. We observed that all five runs submitted were ranked in the top half of the table (four of them in the top 10). Systems 3 and 4 were ranked first according to the official score, achieving 84% accuracy for all four classes and 91% accuracy in discriminating between *green* and *non-green* posts.

The Random Forest meta-classifiers all outperformed their SVM counterpart. The differences in results among the four different Random Forest classifiers highlights the randomness that is inherent to their training.

6 Conclusion and Future Work

We presented an approach to predict severity of posts in a mental health forum. We proposed the use of a meta-classifier and three types of features based on words, syntax, and metadata presented in Section 3. We submitted five runs to the CLPsych shared task and all of them were ranked in the top half of the table. Our best system achieved 84% accuracy for all four classes and 91% accuracy in discriminating between *green* and *non-green* posts. Our approach was ranked first in the shared task.

Acknowledgments

The authors would like to thank the organizers for proposing this interesting shared task.

References

Glen Coppersmith, Mark Dredze, and Craig Harman. 2014. Quantifying mental health signals in twitter. In *Proceedings of the Workshop on Computational Linguistics and Clinical Psychology*.

Binyam Gebrekidan Gebre, Marcos Zampieri, Peter Wittenburg, and Tom Heskes. 2013. Improving native language identification with tf-idf weighting. In *Proceedings of the BEA Workshop*.

David Guthrie, Ben Allison, Wei Liu, Louise Guthrie, and Yorick Wilks. 2006. A closer look at skip-gram modelling. In *Proceedings of LREC*.

Shervin Malmasi and Mark Dras. 2014. Chinese Native Language Identification. In *Proceedings of EACL*.

Shervin Malmasi and Mark Dras. 2015a. Language identification using classifier ensembles. In *Proceedings of the LT4VarDial Workshop*.

Shervin Malmasi and Mark Dras. 2015b. Multilingual Native Language Identification. In *Natural Language Engineering*.

Shervin Malmasi, Hamed Hassanzadeh, and Mark Dras. 2015a. Clinical Information Extraction using Word Representations. In *Proceedings of the Australasian Language Technology Workshop (ALTA)*, pages 66–74, Sydney, Australia, 12.

Shervin Malmasi, Eshrag Refaee, and Mark Dras. 2015b. Arabic Dialect Identification using a Parallel Multidialectal Corpus. In *PACLING 2015*, pages 209–217.

Shervin Malmasi, Mark Dras, and Marcos Zampieri. 2016. LTG at SemEval-2016 Task 11: Complex Word Identification with Classifier Ensembles. In *Proceedings of SemEval*.

Margaret Mitchell, Kristy Hollingshead, and Glen Coppersmith. 2015. Quantifying the language of schizophrenia in social media. In *Proceedings of the 2nd Workshop on Computational Linguistics and Clinical Psychology*.

Dong-Phuong Nguyen, Rilana Gravel, RB Trieschnigg, and Theo Meder. 2013. "how old do you think i am?" a study of language and age in twitter. In *Proceedings of ICWSM*.

Olutobi Owoputi, Brendan O'Connor, Chris Dyer, Kevin Gimpel, Nathan Schneider, and Noah A Smith. 2013. Improved part-of-speech tagging for online conversational text with word clusters. In *Proceedings of NAACL*.

James W Pennebaker, Ryan L Boyd, Kayla Jordan, and Kate Blackburn. 2015. The Development and Psychometric Properties of LIWC2015. *UT Faculty/Researcher Works*.

Robi Polikar. 2006. Ensemble based systems in decision making. *Circuits and Systems Magazine, IEEE*, 6(3):21–45.

Daniel Preoţiuc-Pietro, Svitlana Volkova, Vasileios Lampos, Yoram Bachrach, and Nikolaos Aletras. 2015. Studying user income through language, behaviour and affect in social media. *PloS one*, 10(9).

Francisco Rangel, Efstathios Stamatatos, Moshe Moshe Koppel, Giacomo Inches, and Paolo Rosso. 2013. Overview of the author profiling task at PAN 2013. In *Proceedings of CLEF*.

Masoud Rouhizadeh, Richard Sproat, and Jan van Santen. 2015. Similarity measures for quantifying restrictive and repetitive behavior in conversations of autistic children. In *Proceedings of the 2nd Workshop on Computational Linguistics and Clinical Psychology*.

H. Andrew Schwartz, Johannes Eichstaedt, Margaret L. Kern, Gregory Park, Maarten Sap, David Stillwell, Michal Kosinski, and Lyle Ungar. 2014. Towards assessing changes in degree of depression through facebook. In *Proceedings of the Workshop on Computational Linguistics and Clinical Psychology*.

Hiroki Tanaka, Sakriani Sakti, Graham Neubig, Tomoki Toda, and Satoshi Nakamura. 2014. Linguistic and acoustic features for automatic identification of autism spectrum disorders in children's narrative. In *Proceedings of the Workshop on Computational Linguistics and Clinical Psychology*.

Paul Thompson, Craig Bryan, and Chris Poulin. 2014. Predicting military and veteran suicide risk: Cultural aspects. In *Proceedings of the Workshop on Computational Linguistics and Clinical Psychology*.

Yang Xiang, Xiaolong Wang, Wenying Han, and Qinghua Hong. 2015. Chinese grammatical error diagnosis using ensemble learning. In *Proceedings of the NLP-TEA Workshop*.

Classifying ReachOut posts with a radial basis function SVM

Chris Brew
Thomson Reuters Corporate Research and Development
1 Mark Square
London EC2A 4EG, UK
`Chris.Brew@tr.com`

Abstract

The ReachOut clinical psychology shared task challenge addresses the problem of providing an automatic triage for posts to a support forum for people with a history of mental health issues. Posts are classified into `green`, `amber`, `red` and `crisis`. The non-green categories correspond to increasing levels of urgency for some form of intervention. The Thomson Reuters submissions arose from an idea about self-training and ensemble learning. The available labeled training set is small (947 examples) and the class distribution unbalanced. It was therefore hoped to develop a method that would make use of the larger dataset of unlabeled posts provided by the organisers. This did not work, but the performance of a radial basis function SVM intended as a baseline was relatively good. Therefore, the report focuses on the latter, aiming to understand the reasons for its performance.

1 Introduction

The ReachOut clinical psychology shared task challenge addresses the problem of providing an automatic triage for posts to a support forum for people with a history of mental health issues. Posts are classified into `green,amber,red` and `crisis`. The non-green categories correspond to increasing levels of urgency for some form of intervention, and can be regarded as positive. `Green` means "all clear", no need for intervention. Table 1 includes manually-created examples of posts from each class.[1]

---

[1]These are made-up examples, for reasons of patient confidentiality. They are also much shorter than typical posts.

Class	Example
green	sitting in my armchair listening to the birds
amber	Not over that old friendship.
red	What's the point of talking to anyone?
crisis	Life is pointless. Should call psych.

Table 1: Examples of possible posts

The entry from Thomson Reuters was planned to be a system in which an ensemble of base classifiers is followed by a final system combination step in order to provide a final answer. But this did not pan out, so we report results on a baseline classifier. All of the machine learning was done using `scikit-learn` (Pedregosa et al., 2011). The first step, shared between all runs, was to split the labeled data into a training partition of 625 examples (`Train`) and two development sets (`Dev_test1` and `Dev_test2`) of 161 examples each. There were two development sets only because of the plan to do system combination. This turns out to have been fortunate. All data sets were first transformed into `Pandas` (McKinney, 2010) data-frames for convenient onward processing. When the test set became available, it was similarly transformed into the test data-frame (`Test`).

The first submitted run was an RBF SVM, intended as a strong baseline. This run achieved a better score than any of the more elaborate approaches, and, together with subsequent analysis, sheds some light on the nature of the task and the evaluation metrics used.

Proceedings of the 3rd Workshop on Computational Linguistics and Clinical Psychology: From Linguistic Signal to Clinical Reality, pages 138–142,
San Diego, California, June 16, 2016. ©2016 Association for Computational Linguistics

2 An RBF-based SVM

This first run used the standard `scikit-learn` (Pedregosa et al., 2011) SVM[2], with a radial basis function kernel. `scikit-learn` provides a grid search function that uses stratified cross-validation to tune the classifier parameters.

The RBF kernel is:

$$K(x, x') = e^{-\gamma ||x - x'||^2}$$

where $\gamma = \frac{1}{2\sigma^2}$ and the objective function is:

$$\min \frac{1}{2} ||w||^2 + C \sum_i \xi_i$$

where $||w||^2$ is the ℓ_2-norm of the separating hyperplane and ξ_i is an indicator variable that is 1 when the ith point is misclassified. The C parameter affects the tradeoff between training error and model complexity. A small C tends to produce a simpler model, at the expense of possibly underfitting, while a large one tends to fit all training data points, at the expense of possibly overfitting. The approach to multi-class classification is the "one versus one" method used in (Knerr et al., 1990). Under this approach, a binary classifier is trained for each pair of classes. The winning classifier is determined by voting.

2.1 Features

The features used were:

- single words and 2-grams weighted with scikit-learn's TFIDF vectorizer,using a vocabulary size limit ($|V|$) explored by grid search. The last example post would, *inter alia*, have a feature for 'pointless' and another for 'call psych'

- a feature representing the author type provided by ReachOut's metadata. This indicates whether the poster is a ReachOut staff member, an invited visitor, a frequent poster, or one of a number of other similar categories.

- a feature providing the kudos that users had assigned to the post. This is a natural number reflecting the number of 'likes' a post has attracted.

---

[2] A Python wrapper for LIBSVM (Chang and Lin, 2011)

| | Counts | | | |
	dev_test1	dev_test2	test	train
green	92	95	166	362
amber	47	38	47	164
red	14	23	27	73
crisis	8	5	**1**	26

| | Percentages | | | |
	dev_test1	dev_test2	test	train
green	57.14%	59.00%	68.88%	57.92%
amber	29.19%	23.60%	19.50%	26.24%
red	8.69%	14.29%	11.20%	11.68%
crisis	4.97%	3.11%	**0.41%**	4.16%

Table 2: Class distribution for training, development and test sets.

- a feature indicating whether the post being considered was the first in its thread. This is derived from the thread IDs and post IDs in each post.

2.2 Datasets, class distributions and evaluation metrics

Class distributions We have four datasets: the two sets of development data, the main training set and the official test set distributed by the organisers. Table 2 shows the class distributions for the three evaluation sets and the training set are different. In particular, the final test set used for official scoring has only one instance of the `crisis` category, when one might expect around ten. Of course, none of the teams knew this at submission time. The class distributions are always imbalanced, but it is a surprise to see the extreme imbalance in the final test set.

Evaluation metrics The main evaluation metric used for the competition is a macro-averaged F1-score restricted to `amber`, `red` and `crisis`. This is very sensitive to the unbalanced class distributions, since it weights all three positive classes equally. A classifier that correctly hits the one positive example for `crisis` will achieve a large gain in score relative to one that does not. Micro-averaged F1, which simply counts true positives, false positives and false negatives over all the positive classes, might have proven a more stable target. An alternative is the multi-class Matthews correlation coefficient (Gorodkin, 2004). Or, since the labels are really ordinal, similar to a Likert scale, quadratic weighted kappa (Vaughn and Justice, 2015) could be used.

2.3 Grid search with unbalanced, small datasets

Class weights Preliminary explorations revealed that the classifier was producing results that over-represented the 'green' category. To rectify this, the grid search was re-done using a non-uniform class weight vector of 1 for 'green' and 20 for 'crisis','red' and 'amber'. The effect of this was to increase by a factor of 20 the effective classification penalty for the three positive classes. The grid search used for the final submission set γ=0.01, C at 15 logarithmically spaced locations between 1 and 1000 inclusive, all vocabulary size limits in $\{10, 30, 100, 300, 1000, 3000, 10000\}$ and assumed that author type, kudos and first in thread were always relevant and should always be used. The scoring metric used for this grid search was mean accuracy. The optimal parameters for this setting were estimated to be: C=51.79, $|V|$=3000.

The role of luck in feature selection This classifier is perfect on the training set, suggesting overfitting (see section 4 for a deeper dive into this point). Classification reports for the two development sets are shown in table 3. After submission a more complete grid search was conducted allowing for the possibility of excluding the author type, kudos and first in thread features. All but kudos were excluded. Comparing using `Dev_test1` the second classifier would have been chosen, but using `Dev_test2` we would have chosen the original. The major reason for this difference is that the second classifier happened to correctly classify one of the 8 examples for `crisis` in `Dev_test1`, but missed all the five examples of that class in `Dev_test2`. In fact, on the actual test set, the first classifier is better. The choice to tune on `Dev_test1` was arbitrary, and fortunate. The choice not to consider turning off the metadata features was a pure accident. Tuning via grid search is challenging in the face of small training sets and unbalanced class distributions, and in

this case would have led the classifier astray.

Once optimal parameters had been selected, the classifier was re-trained using on the concatenation of `Train`, `Dev_test1` and `Dev_test2`, and predictions were generated for `Test`.

3 Results on official test set

Table 4 contains classification reports for the class-weighted version that was submitted and a non-weighted version that was prepared after submission. The source of the improved official score achieved by the class-weighted version is a larger F-score on the `red` category, at the expense of a smaller score on the `green` category, which is not one of the positive categories averaged in the official scoring metric.

Dev_test1

class	precision	recall	f1-score	support
green	0.88	0.93	0.91	92
amber	0.73	0.64	0.68	47
red	0.29	0.43	0.34	14
crisis	1.00	0.12	0.22	8

Dev_test2

class	precision	recall	f1-score	support
green	0.81	0.95	0.87	95
amber	0.59	0.50	0.54	38
red	0.53	0.39	0.45	23
crisis	0.00	0.00	0.00	5

Table 3: Classification reports for `Dev_test1` and `Dev_test2`.

Test (using class weights)

class	precision	recall	f1-score	support
green	**0.93**	**0.84**	**0.88**	166
amber	0.51	0.74	0.61	47
red	**0.73**	**0.59**	**0.65**	27
crisis	0.00	0.00	0.00	1

Test (no class weights)

class	precision	recall	f1-score	support
green	**0.89**	**0.94**	**0.91**	166
amber	0.58	0.64	0.61	47
red	**0.71**	0.37	**0.49**	27
crisis	0.00	0.00	0.00	1

Table 4: Classification reports for `Test` with and without class weights.

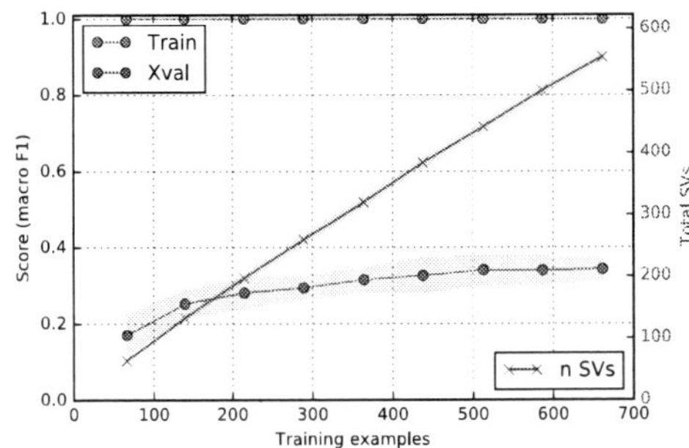

Figure 1: Learning curve (macro F1) (left) and number of support vectors (right)

4 Analysis

The left axis of figure 1 shows how the performance changes as a function of the number of examples used. This graph uses the parameter settings and class weights from the main submission (i.e $|V|$=3000, C=51.79, γ=0.01). The lower curve (green) shows the mean and standard deviation of the official score for test sets selected by cross-validation. The upper curve (red) shows performance on the (cross-validated) training set, which is always at ceiling. The right axis corresponds to the blue curve in the middle of figure 1 and indicates the number of support vectors used for various sizes of training set. Almost every added example is being catered for by a new support vector, suggesting overfitting. There is just a little generalisation for the green class, almost none for the others. Figure 2 shows the variation in macro-F1 with C and γ. The scoring function for grid search is the official macro-averaged F1 restricted to non-green classes, in contrast to the average accuracy used elsewhere. The optimal value selected by this cross-validation is C=64 and γ=0.0085. This is roughly the same as C=51.79, γ=0.01 chosen by cross-validation on average accuracy.

5 Discussion

The ReachOut challenge is evidently a difficult problem. The combination of class imbalance and an official evaluation metric that is very sensitive to performance on sparsely inhabited classes means that the overall results are likely to be unstable.

It is not obvious what metric is the best fit for the

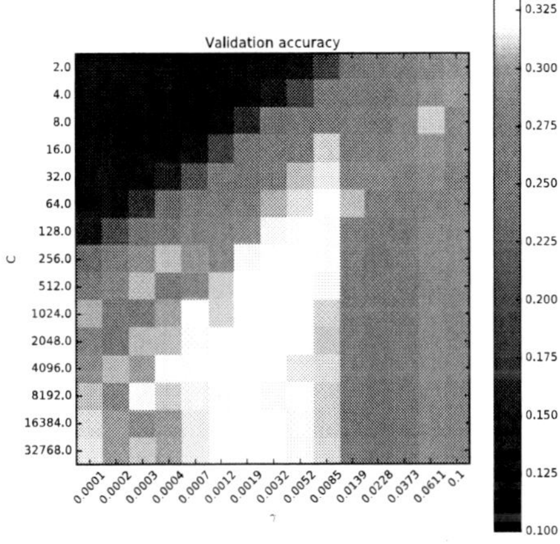

Figure 2: Heat map of variation of macro-F1 as a function of γ and C (with $|V|$=3000)

therapeutic application, because the costs of misclassification, while clearly non-uniform, are difficult to estimate, and the rare classes are intuitively important. It would take a detailed clinical outcome study to determine exactly what the tradeoffs are between false positives, false negatives and misclassifications within the positive classes.

The labeled data set, while of decent size, and representative of what can reasonably be done by annotators in a small amount of time, is not so large that the SVM-based approach, with the features used, has reached its potential. The use of the class weight vector does appear to be helpful in improving the official score by trading off performance on the red label against a small loss of performance on the green label.

Acknowledgments

Thanks to Tim Nugent for advice on understanding and visualizing SVM performance, and to Jochen Leidner and Khalid-Al-Kofahi for providing resources, support and encouragement. Thanks to all members of the London team for feedback and writing help.

References

Chih-Chung Chang and Chih-Jen Lin. 2011. LIBSVM: A library for support vector machines. *ACM Transactions on Intelligent Systems and Technology*, 2:27:1–27:27. Software available at `http://www.csie.ntu.edu.tw/~cjlin/libsvm`.

J. Gorodkin. 2004. Comparing two K-category assignments by a K-category correlation coefficient. *Computational Biology and Chemistry*, 28:367374.

Stefan Knerr, Léon Personnaz, and Gérard Dreyfus. 1990. Single-layer learning revisited: a stepwise procedure for building and training a neural network. In *Neurocomputing*, pages 41–50. Springer.

Wes McKinney. 2010. Data structures for statistical computing in python. In Stéfan van der Walt and Jarrod Millman, editors, *Proceedings of the 9th Python in Science Conference*, pages 51 – 56.

F. Pedregosa, G. Varoquaux, A. Gramfort, V. Michel, B. Thirion, O. Grisel, M. Blondel, P. Prettenhofer, R. Weiss, V. Dubourg, J. Vanderplas, A. Passos, D. Cournapeau, M. Brucher, M. Perrot, and E. Duchesnay. 2011. Scikit-learn: Machine learning in Python. *Journal of Machine Learning Research*, 12:2825–2830.

David Vaughn and Derek Justice. 2015. On the direct maximization of quadratic weighted kappa. *CoRR*, abs/1509.07107.

Triaging Mental Health Forum Posts

Arman Cohan, Sydney Young and **Nazli Goharian**
Information Retrieval Lab
Department of Computer Science
Georgetown University
{arman, nazli}@ir.cs.goergetown.edu, sey24@georgetown.edu

Abstract

Online mental health forums provide users with an anonymous support platform that is facilitated by moderators responsible for finding and addressing critical posts, especially those related to self-harm. Given the seriousness of these posts, it is important that the moderators are able to locate these critical posts quickly in order to respond with timely support. We approached the task of automatically triaging forum posts as a multiclass classification problem. Our model uses a supervised classifier with various features including lexical, psycholinguistic, and topic modeling features. On a dataset of mental forum posts from ReachOut.com[1], our approach identified critical cases with a F-score of over 80%, showing the effectiveness of the model. Among 16 participating teams and 60 total runs, our best run achieved macro-average F1-score of 41% for the critical categories (The best score among all the runs was 42%).

1 Introduction

Social media such as Twitter, Facebook, Tumblr and online forums provide a platform for people seeking social support around various psychological and health problems. Analysis of social media posts can reveal different characteristics about the user, including their health and well-being (Paul and Dredze, 2011). Information exchange through social media concerning various health challenges has been extensively studied (Aramaki et al., 2011; Lampos and Cristianini, 2012; Yates et al., 2014; De Choudhury and De, 2014; Parker et al., 2015; Yates et al., 2016). Prior research has also studied social media to analyze and characterize mental health problems. Coppersmith et al. (2014) provided quantifiable linguistic information about signals of mental disorders in Twitter. Schwartz et al. (2014)

---

[1] http://forums.au.reachout.com/

analyzed Facebook status updates to build a model for predicting the degree of depression among users. Topic modeling approaches have been also investigated in automatic identification of depression from social media (Resnik et al., 2015).

Apart from prior work in general linguistic analysis for identifying mental disorders, there have been some efforts to investigate self-harm communications in social media (Won et al., 2013; Jashinsky et al., 2014; Thompson et al., 2014; Gunn and Lester, 2015; Sueki, 2015). In these works, large scale analysis of Twitter posts have been performed to identify correlations of self-harm language with actual suicide rates. On the individual level, Burnap et al. (2015) used an ensemble classification approach to classify tweets into suicide related topics such as reporting of suicide, memorial and social support. De Choudhury et al. (2016) analyzed a collection of posts from Reddit to characterize the language of suicide related posts and to predict shifts from discussion of mental health content to expression of suicidal ideation.

Compared to Twitter and Facebook which are general purpose social platforms, online mental health forums are virtual communities that are more focused on mental health issues. In these forums, users provide help and support for one another along with forum moderators. An example of such forums is ReachOut.com, which is an online youth mental health service providing information, tools and support to young people aged 14-25. Similar to many other mental health support forums, ReachOut.com provides methods for communicating anonymously about mental issues and seeking help and guidance from trained moderators. There are sometimes posts that indicate signs of self-harm. These posts need to be prioritized and attended to by the moderators as soon as possible to prevent potential harm to the at-risk user.

We propose an approach to identify forum posts

Proceedings of the 3rd Workshop on Computational Linguistics and Clinical Psychology: From Linguistic Signal to Clinical Reality, pages 143–147,
San Diego, California, June 16, 2016. ©2016 Association for Computational Linguistics

indicating signs of self-harm; furthermore, we focus on triaging the posts based on the criticality of the content. We approach this task as a multiclass classification problem. We utilize a regularized logistic regression classifier with various sets of features extracted from the post and its context in the thread. The features include lexical, psycholinguistic and topic modeling features. In CLPsych 2016 shared task, among 60 total submitted runs by all participants, our approach achieved above median results for all of our submitted runs which shows the effectiveness of our approach. Furthermore, our best run achieved the F-1 score of 0.41 for critical categories while the best score over all the runs were 0.42.

2   Identifying self-harm posts

We identify mental health forum posts that indicate signs of self-harm and also triage these posts. The posts showing no ideation of harm are labeled as green, while the other posts are labeled as amber, red, and crisis based on their criticality. We approach this task as a multiclass classification problem. We extract lexical, contextual, psycholinguistic and topic modeling features to train the classifier.

2.1   Features

Lexical features   We examine several lexical features for indications of the user's mental health. The Linguistic Inquiry Word Count (LIWC) (Pennebaker et al., 2015) is a psycholinguistic lexicon that quantifies the mental state of an individual in terms of attributes. As it contains close to 100 attributes, we experiment with different subsets to identify the most relevant measures. We identify the affective attributes subset of LIWC as the most helpful features, which include positive emotion, negative emotion, anxiety, anger, sadness, and swear.

To further quantify the emotions associated with a forum post, we use DepecheMood (Staiano and Guerini, 2014), which is a lexicon of 37k entries. In this lexicon, each expressions is assigned a relevance probability to each of the following 8 dimensions of emotions: fear, amusement, anger, annoy, apathy, happiness, inspiration and sadness. The final emotion distribution of each post is computed by sum of the probabilities for individual terms in the post divided by the total number of terms in the post. In addtion to the probabilities associated with each of the emotions, we also consider the dominant emotion as a separate feature. To distinguish between the subjective and objective forum posts, we utilize the MPQA subjectivity lexicon (Wilson et al., 2005). Each term in the lexicon has a prior polarity value of "positive", "negative", or "neutral". We assign +1 to positive, -1 to negative, and 0 to neutral. The final subjectivity feature of a post is the sum of all individual subjectivity values divided by the total number of terms in the post.

Inspection of the forum posts reveals that in many cases the critical posts consist of a lengthy post body which does not indicate any signals of self-harm. However, the author changes the tone eventually and ends the posts with a sentence that indicates signs of potential self-harm. Therefore, to also account for the final mental state of the user, we consider features extracted from the last sentence separately. Specifically, we extract subjectivity and LIWC affective features of the last sentence. To account for variations of the mental state of the user throughout the post, we also consider the variance of sentence level emotions as a separate feature.

Contextual Features   During analysis, it became evident that to understand some of the posts completely, one needs to also consider the rest of conversation in the corresponding thread. Thus, we also extracted features that would provide context for the post. We consider the author's prior posts in the thread, as well as the surrounding (previous and next) posts by other users. We also considered the subject of the thread as a separate feature.

Textual Statistics   We examine two types of textual statistics for each post. We categorize each thread based on the number of posts (n) in the thread: $n \leq 5$, $5 < n \leq 10$, $10 < n \leq 20$, $20 < n \leq 50$, $50 < n$. We also consider the frequency of certain seed words within the post that would signal the most serious posts. The seed word list contain "want to die", "harm[ing] myself", and "suicid[e/al]".

Topic modeling   Topic modeling has been previously shown to be effective for identification of mental health problems (Resnik et al., 2015). Therefore, we utilize topic models for mapping each post to a set of predefined number of topics. We use LDA to extract the topics associated with each post. We infer the topics by training the LDA model on the entire ReachOut forum dataset.

Run	Features	Boost
1	body, author's posts, subject, emotion, thread length, LIWC (affective, female) , and seed terms.	C +.2
2	body, author's posts, emotion, thread length, LIWC (affective, female, negate), and seed terms	C +.3 R +.2 A +.1
3	body, author's posts, emotion, thread length, LIWC (affective, female, negate), seed terms, and last sentence	C +.3 R +.2

Table 1: The feature sets for each of the runs and the boosting values of Crisis (C), Red (R) and Amber (A) categories.

2.2 Classification

We experimented with several classification algorithms including SVMs with linear and rbf kernels, Random Forests, Adaboost and Logistic Regression. We also experimented with ensemble of these classifiers. Logistic regression with L1 regularization provided the best results based on 4 fold cross validation on the training set. We noticed that the classifier's recall for critical categories was quite low especially in cases of "crisis". This is expected given the low number of training posts in the critical categories. To improve the recall, we boost the prediction probabilities of the classifier for the critical categories by a constant value. We conducted a full grid search on the boosting values for each categories and based on the results on the training set, we selected two of the boosting settings for the final runs.

3 Experimental setup

The data provided by the CLPsych 2016 Shared Task consists of forum posts from Reachout.com, a mental health forum for individuals between 14-25 years old. The data contains 1,188 annotated posts with triage labels. 947 of these posts were provided for training, while 241 posts were withheld for testing. The class breakdown of the 947 training labeled posts is 39 crisis, 110 red, 249 amber, and 549 green.

The official evaluation metric for the shared task is macro-averages of F1-scores for the crisis, red, and amber categories. We also report macro-average of F1-scores and accuracy for the non-green versus the green class labels. We use stratified 4-fold cross-validation on the training dataset of 947 posts. The baseline is a classifier with unigram bag-of-words features from the body of the posts.

4 Results and discussion

We evaluated different settings of features and classifiers discussed in Section 2; we then selected the

Macro Average	NG		NG vs. G	
	F1	Acc	F1	Acc
Run 1	0.38	0.78	**0.82**	**0.88**
Run 2	0.33	0.75	0.80	0.86
Run 3	**0.41**	**0.80**	0.81	0.81

Table 2: Official results of the submitted runs on the test set. NG: Non-Green, G: Green, F1: F1-Score, Acc: Accuracy

Run	Crisis(1)			Red(27)			Amber(47)			Avg
	P	R	F1	P	R	F1	P	R	F1	
1	0	0	0	**62.50**	55.56	58.82	50.00	63.83	56.07	38.30
2	0	0	0	50.00	51.85	50.91	45.45	53.19	49.02	33.31
3	0	0	0	59.26	**59.26**	**59.26**	**58.93**	**70.21**	**64.08**	**41.11**

Table 3: Breakdown of Precision (P), Recall (R) and F1-Score (F1) on test set by category. The number in front of each category shows the number of gold occurrences in each category.

settings that resulted in the best non-green macro-average F1-score as our final submitted runs (Table 1). The official results of our submitted runs are presented in Table 2. The breakdown of the results by category is presented in Table 3. Our third run achieved the highest results with 0.41 non-green average F-score (The best performance among all participants was 0.42). We were not able to identify the only instance of the crisis category correctly, hence the F-score of 0 for crisis. The detailed results of each run on the training set based on 4-fold stratified cross-validation is shown in Table 4 and the breakdown by category is illustrated in Table 5. Interestingly, while the three of the runs show comparable results on the training set (above 47%), on the test set, variation is larger. The third run, which added the context of the last sentence of the post, had the highest performance. Contrary to our expectations, the second run, which had performed the best with the training dataset showed the lowest performance with the unseen test data. This could be due to the drift caused by boosting the amber category, as also reflected in lower F-score in this category.

4.1 Feature analysis

Table 6 displays the impact of various extracted features compared with the baseline model. Overall, most of the features had a positive impact on the model's performance. The features whose addition resulted in the highest score increase are the contextual features of all the author's posts in the thread, posts not by the author in the thread, and the affective attributes and polarity of the last sentence of

	NG		NG vs. G	
	F1	Acc	F1	Acc
Baseline	36.71	86.67	75.21	81.62
Run 1	47.47	89.02	85.30	88.17
Run 2	47.67	88.38	86.12	88.60
Run 3	47.12	88.21	85.60	88.28

Table 4: Results on the training set (stratified 4-fold cross-validation). NG: Non-Green, G: Green. F1: F1-Score, Acc: Accuracy

	Crisis			Red			Amber		
	P	R	F1	P	R	F1	P	R	F1
Baseline	53.85	17.95	26.92	37.31	22.73	28.25	58.04	52.21	54.97
Run 1	33.33	20.53	25.40	52.00	47.27	49.52	68.75	66.27	67.48
Run 2	32.26	25.64	28.57	45.45	50.00	47.62	70.04	63.86	66.81
Run 3	30.30	25.64	27.78	47.06	50.91	48.91	68.78	61.04	64.68

Table 5: Results breakdown by category (training set).

the post. The linguistic features and textual statistics both improved and detracted from the performance of the classifier.

Once examining the effects of features individually, we experimented with feature combinations. Table 7 displays the building steps of our highest performing models. Feature combinations that did not result in improvements are not displayed due to space limitation. We observe that adding helpful features generally improves the results. Interestingly, while thread length alone with body decreased the non-green F1 score, when used in combination with the LIWC affective attributes, the performance improved.

Error analysis revealed that many of false negatives in critical cases include longer posts having a general positive/neutral tone. In such posts, when there is a small section indicating self-harm, the post becomes critical. However, when considering features from the entire post, the effect of that small section fades away. We tried to tackle this problem by considering affective sentence level features and expanding seed words, but it did not result in improvements. Limited training data in the critical categories hinders learning the optimal decision boundary in a high-dimensional feature space. This can be observed by looking at the performance breakdown by category (Table 5). We observe that the F-score for the crisis category is the lowest ($\sim 28\%$), then the red category ($\sim 48\%$) and finally the amber category ($\sim 67\%$). This trend among the categories is in line with the number of training examples in each category (39 crisis, 110 red and 249 amber). Since the number of features are relatively large, small

Macro Average	NG		NG v. G	
	F1	Acc	F1	Acc
Body (Baseline)	36.71	86.67	75.21	81.62
Body+all LIWC	33.23	86.20	78.34	82.89
Body+thread length	34.19	86.39	75.57	81.84
Body+subject	36.47	86.94	77.57	83.21
Body+subjectivity	36.56	86.55	76.19	82.05
Body+LIWC female	36.84	86.62	75.00	81.41
Body+affective	36.88	86.52	76.71	82.37
Body+LIWC negate	37.19	86.73	75.81	81.94
Body+emotion	37.01	86.69	74.79	81.20
Body+time	37.04	86.66	75.61	81.94
Body+seeds	37.07	86.73	75.61	81.94
Body+topics	37.61	86.84	75.85	82.05
Body+last sentence	37.62	86.79	76.69	82.15
Body+surrounding posts	40.30	87.86	83.00	86.38
Body+author's posts	41.13	88.21	82.65	86.17

Table 6: Feature analysis by adding individual features to the body. NG: Non-Green; G: Green; F1: F1-Score, Acc: Accuracy

Feature Combination	NG		NG v. G	
	F1	Acc	F1	Acc
Body (Baseline)	36.71	86.67	75.21	81.62
+ affective	36.88	86.52	76.71	82.37
+ thread length	38.31	86.45	76.84	82.37
+ emotion	38.52	86.55	76.52	82.05
+ author's posts	44.81	89.05	84.5	87.65
+ LIWC female	44.93	88.81	84.77	87.86
+ LIWC negate	45.37	88.77	84.5	87.65
+ seeds	46.39	88.88	85.19	88.17

Table 7: Feature analysis for combined features. NG: Non-Green; G: Green; F1: F1-Score, Acc: Accuracy

number of training data limits learning the optimal decision boundary. On the other hand, when we try to reduce the feature space dimensionality, we are not capturing the characteristics that distinguish between the categories. Therefore, we argue that having more data in the critical categories would results in improvements in the absolute F-score measures.

5   Conclusions

We approached automated triaging of mental health forum posts as a multiclass classification problem by using various sets of features. The most effective features for this task proved to be the psycholinguistic, contextual and sentence level affective features. In addition, boosting the classifier predictions for the critical categories resulted in further improvements. All of our submitted runs achieved above median results among 16 participating teams and our best run, obtained non-green F-1 score of 41% (while the best overall result was 42%). The absolute measure of F1-scores for individual critical classes indicates that there is much room for future research in the analysis and classification of mental forum posts.

146

References

Eiji Aramaki, Sachiko Maskawa, and Mizuki Morita. 2011. Twitter catches the flu: Detecting influenza epidemics using Twitter. In *Proceedings of the Conference on Empirical Methods in Natural Language Processing*, EMNLP '11, pages 1568–1576, Stroudsburg, PA, USA. Association for Computational Linguistics.

Pete Burnap, Walter Colombo, and Jonathan Scourfield. 2015. Machine classification and analysis of suicide-related communication on Twitter. In *Proceedings of the 26th ACM Conference on Hypertext & Social Media*, pages 75–84. ACM.

Glen Coppersmith, Mark Dredze, and Craig Harman. 2014. Quantifying mental health signals in Twitter. In *Proceedings of the Workshop on Computational Linguistics and Clinical Psychology: From Linguistic Signal to Clinical Reality*, pages 51–60.

Munmun De Choudhury and Sushovan De. 2014. Mental health discourse on reddit: Self-disclosure, social support, and anonymity. In *International AAAI Conference on Web and Social Media*, ICWSM '14. AAAI.

Munmun De Choudhury, Emre Kiciman, Mark Dredze, Glen Coppersmith, and Mrinal Kumar. 2016. Discovering shifts to suicidal ideation from mental health content in social media. In *Proceedings of the 34rd Annual ACM Conference on Human Factors in Computing Systems*, CHI '16, New York, NY, USA. ACM.

John F Gunn and David Lester. 2015. Twitter postings and suicide: An analysis of the postings of a fatal suicide in the 24 hours prior to death. *Suicidologi*, 17(3).

Jared Jashinsky, Scott H Burton, Carl L Hanson, Josh West, Christophe Giraud-Carrier, Michael D Barnes, and Trenton Argyle. 2014. Tracking suicide risk factors through Twitter in the US. *Crisis*.

Vasileios Lampos and Nello Cristianini. 2012. Nowcasting events from the social web with statistical learning. *ACM Transactions on Intelligent Systems and Technology*, 3(4):72:1–72:22, September.

Jon Parker, Andrew Yates, Nazli Goharian, and Ophir Frieder. 2015. Health-related hypothesis generation using social media data. *Social Network Analysis and Mining*, 5(1):1–15.

Michael J Paul and Mark Dredze. 2011. You are what you tweet: Analyzing Twitter for public health. *International AAAI Conference on Web and Social Media*, 20:265–272.

James W Pennebaker, Ryan L Boyd, Kayla Jordan, and Kate Blackburn. 2015. The development and psychometric properties of liwc2015. *UT Faculty/Researcher Works*.

Philip Resnik, William Armstrong, Leonardo Claudino, Thang Nguyen, Viet-An Nguyen, and Jordan Boyd-Graber. 2015. Beyond LDA: Exploring supervised topic modeling for depression-related language in Twitter. In *Proceedings of the 2nd Workshop on Computational Linguistics and Clinical Psychology: From Linguistic Signal to Clinical Reality*, pages 99–107, Denver, Colorado, June 5. Association for Computational Linguistics.

H. Andrew Schwartz, Johannes Eichstaedt, Margaret L. Kern, Gregory Park, Maarten Sap, David Stillwell, Michal Kosinski, and Lyle Ungar. 2014. Towards assessing changes in degree of depression through facebook. In *Proceedings of the Workshop on Computational Linguistics and Clinical Psychology: From Linguistic Signal to Clinical Reality*, pages 118–125, Baltimore, Maryland, USA, June. Association for Computational Linguistics.

Jacopo Staiano and Marco Guerini. 2014. Depeche mood: a lexicon for emotion analysis from crowd annotated news. In *Proceedings of the 52nd Annual Meeting of the Association for Computational Linguistics*, pages 427–433, Baltimore, Maryland, June. Association for Computational Linguistics.

Hajime Sueki. 2015. The association of suicide-related Twitter use with suicidal behaviour: a cross-sectional study of young internet users in Japan. *Journal of affective disorders*, 170:155–160.

Paul Thompson, Craig Bryan, and Chris Poulin. 2014. Predicting military and veteran suicide risk: Cultural aspects. In *Proceedings of the Workshop on Computational Linguistics and Clinical Psychology: From Linguistic Signal to Clinical Reality*, pages 1–6, Baltimore, Maryland, USA, June. Association for Computational Linguistics.

Theresa Wilson, Janyce Wiebe, and Paul Hoffmann. 2005. Recognizing contextual polarity in phrase-level sentiment analysis. In *Proceedings of the Conference on Human Language Technology and Empirical Methods in Natural Language Processing*, HLT '05, pages 347–354, Stroudsburg, PA, USA. Association for Computational Linguistics.

Hong-Hee Won, Woojae Myung, Gil-Young Song, Won-Hee Lee, Jong-Won Kim, Bernard J Carroll, and Doh Kwan Kim. 2013. Predicting national suicide numbers with social media data. *PloS one*, 8(4):e61809.

Andrew Yates, Jon Parker, Nazli Goharian, and Ophir Frieder. 2014. A framework for public health surveillance. In *Language Resources and Evaluation*, LREC '14, pages 475–482.

Andrew Yates, Nazli Goharian, and Ophir Frieder. 2016. Learning the relationships between drug, symptom, and medical condition mentions in social media. In *International AAAI Conference on Web and Social Media*, ICWSM '16. AAAI.

Mental Distress Detection and Triage in Forum Posts: The LT3 CLPsych 2016 Shared Task System

Bart Desmet and **Gilles Jacobs** and **Véronique Hoste**
LT3, Language and Translation Technology Team
Department of Translation, Interpretation and Communication
Ghent University
Groot-Brittanniëlaan 45, 9000 Ghent, Belgium
bart.desmet@ugent.be, gillesm.jacobs@ugent.be, veronique.hoste@ugent.be

Abstract

This paper describes the contribution of LT3 for the CLPsych 2016 Shared Task on automatic triage of mental health forum posts. Our systems use multiclass Support Vector Machines (SVM), cascaded binary SVMs and ensembles with a rich feature set. The best systems obtain macro-averaged F-scores of 40% on the full task and 80% on the green versus alarming distinction. Multiclass SVMs with all features score best in terms of F-score, whereas feature filtering with bi-normal separation and classifier ensembling are found to improve recall of alarming posts.

1 Introduction

The 2016 ACL Workshop on Computational Linguistics and Clinical Psychology included a shared task focusing on triage classification in forum posts from ReachOut.com, an online service for youth mental health issues. The aim is to automatically classify an unseen post as one of four categories indicating the severity of mental distress. ReachOut staff has annotated a corpus of posts with *crisis/red/amber/green* semaphore labels that indicate how urgently a post needs moderator attention.

The system described in this paper is based on a suicidality classification system intended for Dutch social media (Desmet and Hoste, 2014). Therefore, we approach the current mental distress triage task from a suicide detection standpoint.

2 Related Work

Machine learning and natural language processing have already shown potential in modelling and de-tecting suicidality in the arts (Stirman and Pennebaker, 2001; Mulholland and Quinn, 2013) and in electronic health records (Haerian et al., 2012). However, work on computational approaches to the automatic detection of suicidal content in online user-generated media is scarce.

One line of research focuses on detecting suicidality in individuals relying on their post history: Huang et al. (2007) aim to identify Myspace.com bloggers at risk of suicide by means of a keyword-based approach using a manually collected dictionary of weighted suicide-related terms. Users were ranked by pattern-matching keywords on their posts. This approach suffered from low precision (35%) and the data does not allow to measure recall, i.e. the number of actually suicidal bloggers that are missing from the results. Similarly, Jashinsky et al. (2014) manually selected keywords by testing search queries linked to various risk factors in a user's Twitter profile. In order to validate this search approach, users posting tweets that match the suicide keywords were grouped by US state for trend analysis. The proportion of at-risk tweeters vs. control-group tweeters were strongly correlated with the actual state suicide rates. While this methodology yields a correct proportion of at-risk users, it is unclear how many of those tweets are false positives and how many at-risk tweets are missing.

Going beyond a keyword-based approach, Guan et al. (2015) performed linear regression and random forest machine learning for Chinese Weibo.com microbloggers. Suicidality labels were assigned to users in the data set by means of an online psychological evaluation survey. As classification features

Proceedings of the 3rd Workshop on Computational Linguistics and Clinical Psychology: From Linguistic Signal to Clinical Reality, pages 148–152,
San Diego, California, June 16, 2016. ©2016 Association for Computational Linguistics

they took social media profile metadata and psychometric linguistic categories in a user's post history. Results showed that Linear Regression and Random Forest classifiers obtain similar scores with a maximum of 35% F-score (23% precision and 79% recall) being the highest performance.

As in the CLPsych 2016 Shared Task, another line of research aims to classify suicidality on the post level, rather than the level of user profiles. Desmet and Hoste (2014) proposed a detection approach using machine learning with a rich feature set on posts in the Dutch social media platform Netlog. Their corpus was manually annotated by suicide intervention experts for suicide relevance, risk and protective factors, source origin, subject of content, and severity. Two binary classification tasks were formulated: a relevance task which aimed to detect posts relevant to suicide, and a threat detection task to detect messages that indicate a severe suicide risk. For the threat detection task, a cascaded setup which first filters irrelevant messages with SVM and then predicts the severity with k-Nearest Neighbors (KNN) performed best: 59.2% F-score (69.5% precision and 51.6% recall). In general, both KNN and SVM outperform Naive Bayes and SVM was more robust to the inclusion of bad features. The system presented in this paper is for the most part an extension and English adaptation of this suicidal post detection pipeline.

3 System Overview

We investigated a supervised classification-based approach to the mental distress triage task using SVMs. Below, we describe the data and features that were used, and the way classifiers were built, optimized and combined.

3.1 Data

Labeled data sets: 1/8th of the manually annotated training data was sampled as a held-out development set ($n = 118$ with at least 4 instances of each class), the remainder ($n = 829$) was used for training. In the results section, we also report on the held-out test set ($n = 241$).

Reddit background corpus: In order to perform terminology extraction and topic modelling, we collected domain-relevant text from Reddit.com, a predominantly English social news and bulletin board website. We used the title and body text from all opening posts in mental health and suicide-related boards posted between 2006 and 2014, resulting in a 82.7 million token corpus of over $270,000$ posts. The selected boards mainly contain user-generated discussion on mental health, depression, and suicidal thoughts, similar to the ReachOut forums.

Tokenization and preprocessing: All textual data was tokenized and lower-cased to reduce variation. For topic modelling, emoji and punctuation were removed. Pattern (De Smedt and Daelemans, 2012) was used for lemmatization.

3.2 Features

We aimed to develop a rich feature set that focused on lexical and semantic information, with fine-grained and more abstract representations of content. Some syntactic and non-linguistic features were also included.

Bag-of-words features: We included binary token unigrams, bigrams and trigrams, along with character trigrams and fourgrams. The latter provide robustness to the spelling variation typically found in social media.

Term lists: Domain-specific multiword terms were derived from the Reddit background corpus, using the TExSIS terminology extraction tool (Macken et al., 2013). One list was based on suicide-specific boards (*/r/SuicideWatch* and */r/suicidenotes*, 2884 terms), the other included terms only found in other mental health boards (1384 terms).

Lexicon features: We computed positive and negative opinion word ratio and overall post sentiment using both the MPQA (Wilson et al., 2005) and Hu and Liu's (2004) opinion lexicons. We added positive, negative and neutral emoji counts based on the BOUNCE emoji sentiment lexicon (Kökciyan et al., 2013). We also included the relative frequency of all 64 psychometric categories in the Linguistic Inquiry and Word Count (LIWC) dictionary (Pennebaker et al., 2007). LIWC features have proven useful in (Stirman and Pennebaker, 2001) for modelling suicidality in literary works. Furthermore, we included diminisher, intensifier, negation, and "allness" lexica because of their significance in suicide notes analysis (Osgood and Walker, 1959; Gottschalk and Gleser, 1960; Shapero, 2011).

Topic models: Using the gensim topic modelling library (Řehůřek and Sojka, 2010) we trained several LDA (Blei et al., 2003) and LSI (Deerwester et al., 1990) topic models with varying granularity ($k = 20, 50, 100, 200$). A similarity query was done on each model resulting in two feature groups: k topic similarity scores and the average similarity score. This should allow the classifier to learn which latent topics are relevant for the task, and to what extent the topics align with the ones in the Reddit background corpus. In line with Resnik et al. (2015), we used topic models to capture latent semantic and syntactic structure in the mental health domain. However, we did not include supervised topic models.

Syntactic features: Two binary features were implemented indicating whether the imperative mood was used in a post and whether person alternation occurred (i.e. combinations of first and second person pronouns).

Post metadata: We furthermore included several non-linguistic features based on a post's metadata: the time of day a post was made (expressed in three-hour blocks), the board in which it was posted, whether the post includes a subject line or a URL, the role of the author and whether he or she is a moderator, whether the post is the first in a thread, whether there are (moderator) reactions or kudos (i.e. thumbs-up votes).

When applied to the training data, this resulted in 59 feature groups and $107,852$ individual features, the majority of which were bag-of-words features (almost 96%).

3.3 Classifiers

Using SVMs, we tested three different approaches to the problem of correctly assigning the four triage labels to the forum posts. We considered detection of posts with a high level of alarm (*crisis* or *red*) to be the priority. Where possible, recall of the priority labels was promoted, since false negatives are most problematic there.

With **multiclass SVMs**, one model is used to predict all four labels at once. We hypothesized that distinguishing green from non-green posts would require different information than detecting the more alarming categories. We therefore also tested cascades of three **binary SVMs**, in which each classifier predicts a higher level of alarm: green vs. rest; red or crisis vs. rest; and crisis vs. rest. The binary results are combined in a way that the label with the highest level of alarm is assigned. This essentially sacrifices some precision on lower-priority classes for better high-priority recall.

Finally, we tested **ensembles** of various multiclass and binary systems. Predictions were combined with two voting methods: normal majority voting (reported as *ensemble-majority*), and crisis-priority voting (*ensemble-priority*) where the most alarming label with at least 2 votes is selected.

3.4 Optimization

Typically, the performance of a machine learning algorithm is not optimal when it is used with all implemented features and with the default algorithm settings. SVMs are known to perform well in the presence of irrelevant features, but dimensionality reduction can still be beneficial for classification accuracy and resource usage. In this section, we describe the methods we tested for feature selection and hyperparameter optimization.

With **feature filtering**, a metric is used to determine the informativeness of each feature, given the training data. Yang (1997) found that Information Gain (IG) allows aggressive feature removal with minimal loss in accuracy. Forman (2003) corroborates this finding, but remarks that IG is biased towards the majority class, unlike the Bi-Normal Separation (BNS) metric, which typically achieves better minority class recall. In the results, we compare both filtering methods (*-ig* and *-bns*) to no filtering (*-nf*). IG was applied with a threshold of 0.005 (92-97% reduction), BNS with threshold 3 (79-93% reduction for binary tasks, no multiclass support).

We also applied **wrapped optimization**, where combinations of selected feature groups and hyperparameters are evaluated with SVM using three-fold crossvalidation. Exhaustive exploration of all combinations was not possible, so we used genetic algorithms to approximate an optimal solution (Desmet et al., 2013). In the results section, all reported systems have been optimized for feature group and hyperparameter selection, except for *multiclass-unopt* (baseline without filtering or optimization) and *multiclass-hyper* (only hyperparameter optimization, no feature filtering or selection).

4 Results and discussion

In Table 4, we report the four-label classification results of all systems. Most systems perform well in comparison to the shared task top score of 42% macro-averaged F-score, with the *multiclass-nf* submission scoring highest at 40%. This indicates that the implemented features and approach are within the current state of the art.

system	dev		test	
	F	acc	F	acc
multiclass-unopt	0.00	0.64	0.00	0.69
multiclass-hyper	0.36	0.75	0.41	0.80
multiclass-nf *	0.50	0.75	0.40	0.80
multiclass-ig	0.36	0.74	0.35	0.78
binary-nf *	0.39	0.69	0.36	0.74
binary-ig	0.36	0.75	0.32	0.77
binary-bns *	0.38	0.64	0.19	0.54
ensemble-majority *	0.54	0.79	0.35	0.77
ensemble-priority *	0.51	0.75	0.37	0.78

Table 1: Results for four-label classification (F = macro-averaged F-score, acc = accuracy). The 5 systems submitted for the shared task are indicated with an asterisk.

Arguably, macro-averaged F-score is a harsh metric for this task: it treats the three alarming categories as disjunct, although confusion between those classes can be high and the distinction may not matter much from a usability perspective. Since the test set only contained one *crisis* instance, failing to detect it effectively limits the ceiling for macro-averaged F-score to 67%. This partly explains the low scores in Table 4. For comparison, we list F-score, precision and recall for the *green* vs. *alarming* distinction in Table 4. Alarming posts can be detected with $F = 80\%$ and recall up to 89% (*ensemble-priority*).

system	dev				test			
	F	P	R	acc	F	P	R	acc
multicl-unopt	0.00	0.00	0.00	0.64	0.00	0.00	0.00	0.69
multicl-hyper	0.76	0.78	0.74	0.83	0.78	0.77	0.79	0.86
multicl-nf	0.75	0.76	0.74	0.82	0.80	0.77	0.84	0.87
multicl-ig	0.78	0.77	0.79	0.84	0.76	0.75	0.77	0.85
binary-nf	0.72	0.70	0.74	0.79	0.79	0.72	0.88	0.85
binary-ig	0.81	0.78	0.84	0.86	0.75	0.75	0.76	0.85
binary-bns	0.73	0.62	0.88	0.76	0.63	0.50	0.87	0.68
ensemble-maj	0.82	0.79	0.86	0.86	0.77	0.73	0.81	0.85
ensemble-prior	0.77	0.67	0.91	0.81	0.80	0.73	0.89	0.86

Table 2: Results for binary classification: *green* vs. all other classes (F = F-score, P = precision, R = recall, acc = accuracy)

We tested three classifier configurations, and find that a multiclass approach performs as well as or better than more complex systems. On the development data, ensemble systems perform best, although this is not confirmed by the four-label test results, possibly due to paucity of *crisis* instances. It appears that ensembles are a sensible choice especially if recall is important. This may be due to the inclusion of the high-recall *binary-bns* cascade, the low precision of which is offset by ensemble voting. Overall, the aim of improving recall with cascaded and ensemble classifiers seems to have been effective: compared to multiclass systems, they all favour recall over precision more, both on development and test data.

The unoptimized *multiclass-unopt* acts as a majority baseline that always predicts *green*, indicating that hyperparameter optimization is essential. Feature selection, on the other hand, does not yield such a clear benefit. On the held-out test data, the *nf* systems consistently outperform their *ig* and *bns* counterparts in terms of F-score. On the development data, feature filtering has a positive effect on recall, particularly when BNS is applied. In summary, the applied feature selection techniques are sometimes successful in removing the bulk of the features without harming performance, although the results suggest that they may remove too many or cause overfitting.

5 Conclusion

This paper discussed an SVM-based approach to the CLPsych 2016 shared task. We found that our systems performed well within the state of the art, with macro-averaged F-scores of 40% on the full task, and 80% for the distinction between green and alarming posts, suggesting that confusion between the three alarming classes is high. Multiclass systems performed best, but ensemble classifiers and feature filtering with BNS perform comparably and are better suited when high recall is required.

Acknowledgments

We would like to thank the organizers for an interesting shared task. This work was carried out in the framework of AMiCA (IWT SBO-project 120007), funded by the Flemish government agency for Innovation by Science and Technology (IWT).

References

David Blei, Andrew Ng, and Michael Jordan. 2003. Latent dirichlet allocation. *the Journal of machine Learning research*, 3:993–1022.

Tom De Smedt and Walter Daelemans. 2012. Pattern for python. *The Journal of Machine Learning Research*, 13(1):2063–2067.

Scott Deerwester, Susan Dumais, George Furnas, Thomas Landauer, and Richard Harshman. 1990. Indexing by latent semantic analysis. *Journal of the American society for information science*, 41(6):391.

Bart Desmet and Véronique Hoste. 2014. Recognising suicidal messages in dutch social media. In *9th International Conference on Language Resources and Evaluation (LREC)*, pages 830–835.

Bart Desmet, Véronique Hoste, David Verstraeten, and Jan Verhasselt. 2013. Gallop documentation. *LT3 Technical report*, pages 13–03.

George Forman. 2003. An extensive empirical study of feature selection metrics for text classification. *The Journal of machine learning research*, 3:1289–1305.

Louis Gottschalk and Goldine Gleser. 1960. An analysis of the verbal content of suicide notes. *British Journal of Medical Psychology*, 33(3):195–204.

Li Guan, Bibo Hao, Qijin Cheng, Paul SF Yip, and Tingshao Zhu. 2015. Identifying chinese microblog users with high suicide probability using internet-based profile and linguistic features: Classification model. *JMIR mental health*, 2(2):17.

Krystl Haerian, Hojjat Salmasian, and Carol Friedman. 2012. Methods for identifying suicide or suicidal ideation in EHRs. In *AMIA Annual Symposium Proceedings*, volume 2012, pages 1244–1253. American Medical Informatics Association.

Minqing Hu and Bing Liu. 2004. Mining and summarizing customer reviews. In *Proceedings of the tenth ACM SIGKDD international conference on Knowledge discovery and data mining*, pages 168–177. ACM.

Yen-Pei Huang, Tiong Goh, and Chern Li Liew. 2007. Hunting suicide notes in web 2.0-preliminary findings. In *Multimedia Workshops, 2007. ISMW'07. Ninth IEEE International Symposium on*, pages 517–521. IEEE.

Jared Jashinsky, Scott Burton, Carl Hanson, Josh West, Christophe Giraud-Carrier, Michael Barnes, and Trenton Argyle. 2014. Tracking suicide risk factors through Twitter in the US. *Crisis*, 35(1):51–59.

Nadin Kökciyan, Arda Çelebi, Arzucan Özgür, and Suzan Üsküdarl. 2013. BOUNCE: Sentiment Classification in Twitter using Rich Feature Sets. In *Second Joint Conference on Lexical and Computational Semantics (*SEM): Proceedings of the Seventh International Workshop on Semantic Evaluation (SemEval 2013)*, volume 2, pages 554–561, Atlanta, Georgia, USA, June. Association for Computational Linguistics.

Lieve Macken, Els Lefever, and Veronique Hoste. 2013. Texsis: bilingual terminology extraction from parallel corpora using chunk-based alignment. *Terminology*, 19(1):1–30.

Matthew Mulholland and Joanne Quinn. 2013. Suicidal tendencies: The automatic classification of suicidal and non-suicidal lyricists using nlp. In *IJCNLP*, pages 680–684.

Charles Osgood and Evelyn Walker. 1959. Motivation and language behavior: A content analysis of suicide notes. *The Journal of Abnormal and Social Psychology*, 59(1):58.

James Pennebaker, Roger Booth, and Martha Francis. 2007. Liwc2007: Linguistic inquiry and word count. *Austin, Texas: liwc. net.*

Radim Řehůřek and Petr Sojka. 2010. Software Framework for Topic Modelling with Large Corpora. In *Proceedings of the LREC 2010 Workshop on New Challenges for NLP Frameworks*, pages 45–50, Valletta, Malta, May. ELRA.

Philip Resnik, William Armstrong, Leonardo Claudino, and Thang Nguyen. 2015. The university of maryland clpsych 2015 shared task system. *NAACL HLT 2015*, pages 54–60.

Jess Jann Shapero. 2011. *The language of suicide notes*. Ph.D. thesis, University of Birmingham.

Shannon Wiltsey Stirman and James W. Pennebaker. 2001. Word use in the poetry of suicidal and nonsuicidal poets. *Psychosomatic Medicine*, 63(4):517–522.

Theresa Wilson, Janyce Wiebe, and Paul Hoffmann. 2005. Recognizing contextual polarity in phrase-level sentiment analysis. In *Proceedings of the conference on human language technology and empirical methods in natural language processing*, pages 347–354. Association for Computational Linguistics.

Yiming Yang and Jan Pedersen. 1997. A comparative study on feature selection in text categorization. In *ICML*, volume 97, pages 412–420.

Text Analysis and Automatic Triage of Posts in a Mental Health Forum

Ehsaneddin Asgari[1] and **Soroush Nasiriany**[2] and **Mohammad R.K. Mofrad**[1]

Departments of Bioengineering[1] and Electrical Engineering and Computer Science[2]
University of California, Berkeley
Berkeley, CA 94720, USA
`asgari@ischool.berkeley.edu, snasiriany@berkeley.edu, mofrad@berkeley.edu`

Abstract

We present an approach for automatic triage of message posts in ReachOut.com mental health forum, which was a shared task in the 2016 Computational Linguistics and Clinical Psychology (CLPsych). This effort is aimed at providing the trained moderators of ReachOut.com with a systematic triage of forum posts, enabling them to more efficiently support the young users aged 14-25 communicating with each other about their issues. We use different features and classifiers to predict the users' mental health states, marked as green, amber, red, and crisis. Our results show that random forests have significant success over our baseline mutli-class SVM classifier. In addition, we perform feature importance analysis to characterize key features in identification of the critical posts.

1 Introduction

Mental health issues profoundly impact the well-being of those afflicted and the safety of society as a whole (Üstün et al., 2004). Major effort is still needed to identify and aid those who are suffering from mental illness but doing so in a case by case basis is not practical and expensive (Mark et al., 2005). These limitations inspired us to develop an automated mechanism that can robustly classify the mental state of a person. The abundance of publicly available data allows us to access each person's record of comments and message posts online in an effor to predict and evaluate their mental health.

1.1 Shared Task Description

The CLPsych 2016 Task accumulates a selection of 65,514 posts from ReachOut.com, dedicated to providing a means for members aged 14-25 to express their thoughts in an anonymous environment. These posts have all been selected from the years 2012 through 2015. Of these posts, 947 have been carefully analyzed, and each assigned a label: green (the user shows no sign of mental health issues), amber (the user's posts should be reviewed further to identify any issues), red (there is a very high likelihood that the user has mental health issues), and crisis (the user needs immediate attention). These 947 posts-label pairs represent our train data. We then use the train data to produce a model that assigns a label to any generic post. A separate selection of 241 posts are dedicated as the test data, to be used to evaluate the accuracy of the model.

2 Methods

Our approach for automatic triage of posts in the mental health forum, much like any other classification pipeline, is composed of three phases: feature extraction, selection of learning algorithm, and validation and parameter tuning in a cross validation framework.

2.1 Feature extraction

Feature extraction is one of the key steps in any machine learning task, which can significantly influence the performance of learning algorithms (Bengio et al., 2013). In the feature extraction phase we extracted the following information from the given XML files of forum posts: author, the authors rank-

153

Proceedings of the 3rd Workshop on Computational Linguistics and Clinical Psychology: From Linguistic Signal to Clinical Reality, pages 153–157,
San Diego, California, June 16, 2016. ©2016 Association for Computational Linguistics

ing in the forum, time of submission and editing, number of likes and views, the body of the post, the subject, the thread associated to the post, and changeability of the text. For the representation of textual data (subject and body) we use both tf-idf and the word embedding representation of the data (Mikolov et al., 2013b; Mikolov et al., 2013a; Zhang et al., 2011). Skip-gram word embedding which is trained in the course of language modeling is shown to capture syntactic and semantic regularities in the data (Mikolov et al., 2013c; Mikolov et al., 2013a). For the purpose of training the word embeddings we use skip-gram neural networks (Mikolov et al., 2013a) on the collection of all the textual data (subject/text) of 65,514 posts provided in the shared task. In our word embedding training, we use the word2vec implementation of skip-gram (Mikolov et al., 2013b). We set the dimension of word vectors to 100, and the window size to 10 and we sub-sample the frequent words by the ratio $\frac{1}{10^3}$. Subsequently, to encode a body/subject of a post we use tf-idf weighted sum of word-vectors in that post (Le and Mikolov, 2014). The features are summarized in Table 1. To ensure being inclusive in finding important features, stop words are not removed.

2.2 Automatic Triage

The Random Forest (RF) classifier (Breiman, 2001) is employed to predict the users mental health states (green, red, amber, and crisis) from the posts in the ReachOut forum. A random forest is an ensemble method based on use of multiple decision trees (Breiman, 2001). Random forest classifiers have several advantages, including estimation of important features in the classification, efficiency when a large proportion of the data is missing, and efficiency when dealing with a large number of features (Cutler et al., 2012); therefore random forests fit our problem very well. The validation step is conducted over 947 labeled instances, in a 10xFold cross validation process. Different parameters of random forests, including the number of trees, the measure of split quality, the number of features in splits, and the maximum depth are tuned using cross-validation. In this work, we use Scikit implementation of Random Forests (Pedregosa et al., 2011).

Our results on the training set show that incorpo-

ration of unlabeled data in the training using label propagation by means of nearest-neighbor search does not increase the classification accuracy. Therefore, the unlabeled data is not incorporated in the training.

For the comparison phase, we consider multiclass Support Vector Machine classifier (SVM) with radial basis function kernel as a baseline method (Cortes and Vapnik, 1995; Weston and Watkins, 1998).

3 Results

Our results show that random forests have significant success over SVM classifiers. The 4-ways classification accuracies are summarized in Table 3. The evaluations on the test set for the random forest approach are summarized in Table 3.

3.1 Important Features

Random Forests can easily provide us with the most relevant features in the classification (Cutler et al., 2012; Breiman, 2001). Random Forest consists of a number of decision trees. In the training procedure, it can be calculated how much a feature decreases the weighted impurity in a tree. The impurity decrease for each feature can be averaged and normalized over all trees of the ensemble and the features can be ranked according to this measure (Breiman et al., 1984; Breiman, 2001). We extracted the most discriminative features in the automatic triage of the posts using mean decrease impurity for the best Random Forest we obtained in the cross-validation (Breiman et al., 1984).

Our results shows that from the top 100 features, $\frac{88}{100}$ were related to the frequency of particular words in the body of the post, $\frac{4}{100}$ were related to the posting/editing time (00:00 to 23:00) and the day in the month (1st to 31th), $\frac{4}{100}$ were indication of the author and author ranking, $\frac{2}{100}$ were related to the frequency of words in the subject, $\frac{1}{100}$ was the number of views, and $\frac{1}{100}$ was the number of likes a post gets.

The top 50 discriminative features, their importance, and their average values for each class are provided in Table 3.1. We have also presented the inverse document frequency (IDF) to identify how

Features Extracted from ReachOut forum posts		
Feature	Description	Length
Author	One hot representation of unique authors in 65755 posts.	1605
Ranking of the author	One hot representation of the author category.	25
Submission time	Separated numerical representations of year, day, month, and the hour that a post is submitted to the forum.	4
Edit time	Separated numerical representations of year, day, month, and the hour that a post is edited in the forum.	4
Likes	The number of likes a post gets.	1
Views	The number of times a post is viewed by the forum users.	1
Body	Tf-idf representation of the text in the body of the post.	55758
Subject	Tf-idf representation of the text in the subject of the post.	3690
Embedded-Body	Embedding representation of the text in the body of the post.	100
Embedded-Subject	Embedding representation of the text in the subject of the post.	100
Thread	One hot representation of the thread of the post.	3910
Read only	If the post is readonly.	1

Table 1: List of features that have been used in the automatic triage of ReachOut forum posts

Classifiers / Features	Random Forest Classifier	SVM Classifier
Tf-idf features	$71.28\% \pm 2.9\%$	$42.2\% \pm 3.1\%$
Embedding features	$71.26\% \pm 4.0\%$	$42.2\% \pm 4.0\%$

Table 2: The average 4-ways classification accuracies in 10xFold cross-validation for the random forest and support vector machine classifiers tuned for the best parameters on two different sets of features. Embedding features refer to use of embeddings for the body and the subject instead of tf-idf representations.

Methods	Accuracy	Non-green vs . green accuracy
Random Forest & tf-idf features	79%	86%
Random Forest & embedding features	78%	86%

Table 3: The results of evaluation over 241 test data points.

much information each word has encoded within the collection of posts (Robertson, 2004). Many interesting patterns can be observed in the word usage of each class. For example, the word 'feel' significantly more often occurs in the red and crisis posts. Surprisingly, there were some stop-words among the most important features. For instance, words 'to' and 'not', on average occur in green posts $\frac{1}{2}$ of times of non-green posts. Another example is the usage of the word 'me', which occurs more frequently in non-green posts. Furthermore, the posts with more 'likes' are less likely to be non-green.

Subject: As indicated in Table 3.1 posts which have word 're' in their subjects are more likely to belong to the green class.

Time: As shown in Figure 1 and Table 3.1 the red posts on average are submitted on a day closer to the end of the month. In addition, the portion of red and crisis message posts in the interval of 5 A.M. to 7 A.M. was much higher than the green and amber posts.

4 Conclusion

In this work, we explored the automatic triage of message posts in a mental health forum. Using Random Forest classifiers we obtain a higher triage accuracy in comparison with our baseline method, i.e. a mutli-class support vector machine. Our results showed that incorporation of unlabeled data did not increase the classification accuracy of Random Forest, which could be due to the fact that Random Forests themselves are efficient enough in dealing with missing data points (Cutler et al., 2012). Furthermore, our results suggest that employing full vocabularies would be more discriminative than using sentence embedding. This could be interpreted as the importance of occurrence of particular words rather than particular concepts. In addition, taking advantage of the capability of Random Forest in the estimation of important features in classification, we explored the most relevant features contributing in the automatic triage.

Acknowledgments
Fruitful discussions with Meshkat Ahmadi, Mohsen Mahdavi, and Mohammad Soheilypour are gratefully acknowledged.

Rank	Feature	Importance	IDF	Green Average value	Amber Average value	Red Average value	Crisis Average value
1	body: you	0.068	0.004	16.912 ± 24.13	3.941 ± 10.238	2.728 ± 7.077	2.432 ± 8.605
2	body: to	0.059	0.012	4.948 ± 5.739	8.964 ± 6.83	9.408 ± 7.265	9.552 ± 7.666
3	subject: re	0.053	0.03	3.904 ± 1.871	3.6 ± 1.843	3.246 ± 2.637	2.802 ± 2.112
4	$\#oflikes$	0.027	-	0.749 ± 1.104	0.353 ± 0.882	0.155 ± 0.453	0.154 ± 0.489
5	body: just	0.021	0.007	2.632 ± 6.332	6.69 ± 8.962	8.349 ± 9.697	8.702 ± 9.992
6	body: feeling	0.02	0.009	0.884 ± 3.463	2.527 ± 7.216	4.227 ± 9.606	3.188 ± 5.812
7	body: don	0.02	0.008	1.407 ± 4.523	3.998 ± 7.302	4.996 ± 7.599	9.074 ± 13.873
8	body: me	0.019	0.006	2.73 ± 6.471	7.848 ± 10.056	9.321 ± 11.432	8.264 ± 8.207
9	$\#ofviews$	0.016	-	96.016 ± 53.53	95.372 ± 50.9	92.158 ± 53.715	113.735 ± 56.293
10	body: know	0.016	0.007	1.55 ± 4.957	3.976 ± 7.806	4.863 ± 7.615	8.218 ± 11.262
11	body: want	0.015	0.008	0.548 ± 2.587	3.253 ± 7.431	3.875 ± 8.172	5.29 ± 8.699
12	body: anymore	0.013	0.013	0.063 ± 0.734	0.523 ± 2.578	2.594 ± 5.881	4.709 ± 9.327
13	body: do	0.013	0.007	1.987 ± 5.58	4.339 ± 7.226	4.741 ± 7.275	6.123 ± 8.322
14	body: and	0.011	0.009	5.629 ± 6.389	7.953 ± 7.687	10.007 ± 7.579	6.749 ± 5.905
15	body: negative	0.011	0.012	0.117 ± 1.354	1.184 ± 4.354	2.583 ± 6.404	4.446 ± 8.769
16	body: it	0.01	0.007	6.89 ± 9.562	10.607 ± 10.575	9.079 ± 9.527	7.56 ± 8.055
17	post hour (1-24)	0.01	-	9.922 ± 4.325	9.474 ± 4.135	9.118 ± 4.585	8.615 ± 4.159
18	body: my	0.01	0.007	5.137 ± 8.414	9.722 ± 10.703	10.303 ± 10.178	7.928 ± 10.775
19	body: the	0.01	0.011	4.744 ± 5.5	6.667 ± 6.064	5.95 ± 5.578	6.513 ± 6.729
20	body: for	0.01	0.008	4.418 ± 7.1	3.894 ± 5.61	3.274 ± 5.427	6.135 ± 5.89
21	body: about	0.009	0.008	1.646 ± 4.452	3.567 ± 5.711	2.11 ± 4.567	2.149 ± 4.574
22	body: so	0.009	0.008	3.387 ± 6.759	4.95 ± 7.102	7.57 ± 9.347	5.02 ± 7.942
23	body: this	0.009	0.008	2.624 ± 5.609	2.849 ± 5.489	5.302 ± 5.768	5.046 ± 6.633
24	post day (1-7)	0.009	-	15.25 ± 8.407	15.719 ± 8.625	15.3 ± 8.907	17.436 ± 8.217
25	edit day (1-7)	0.009	-	15.25 ± 8.407	15.719 ± 8.625	15.3 ± 8.907	17.436 ± 8.217
26	body: can	0.009	0.006	3.436 ± 7.302	4.297 ± 6.909	6.333 ± 7.913	12.029 ± 12.095
27	body: but	0.008	0.006	3.588 ± 6.988	7.376 ± 9.226	5.354 ± 7.634	8.245 ± 10.021
28	body: not	0.008	0.007	2.274 ± 5.459	5.037 ± 8.02	4.504 ± 7.172	3.901 ± 6.398
29	body: get	0.008	0.006	1.672 ± 4.627	3.552 ± 6.559	4.505 ± 8.02	4.35 ± 8.532
30	edit hour (1-24)	0.008	-	9.922 ± 4.325	9.474 ± 4.135	9.118 ± 4.585	8.615 ± 4.159
31	$author_x$	0.007	-	0.149 ± 0.357	0.072 ± 0.259	0.264 ± 0.443	0.308 ± 0.468
32	body: that	0.007	0.007	4.244 ± 7.687	5.513 ± 7.665	4.905 ± 7.357	3.875 ± 6.288
33	body: of	0.006	0.008	3.954 ± 5.989	4.902 ± 6.235	5.014 ± 5.904	5.425 ± 6.389
34	body: when	0.005	0.008	1.689 ± 4.25	2.998 ± 5.77	2.779 ± 5.249	2.871 ± 4.733
35	body: even	0.005	0.008	0.993 ± 3.499	1.513 ± 4.099	2.699 ± 5.337	4.37 ± 8.633
36	body: have	0.005	0.005	4.081 ± 7.854	6.196 ± 8.662	6.415 ± 8.511	5.191 ± 7.057
37	body: cant	0.005	0.013	0.033 ± 0.764	0.693 ± 4.004	1.589 ± 4.911	0.25 ± 1.091
38	body: all	0.005	0.006	1.866 ± 5.437	3.487 ± 6.37	3.691 ± 7.05	2.804 ± 6.987
39	subject: into	0.004	0.187	0.099 ± 0.511	0.391 ± 0.941	0.838 ± 1.249	0.728 ± 1.201
40	body: what	0.004	0.008	1.813 ± 4.463	2.725 ± 4.901	2.778 ± 4.744	2.577 ± 5.045
41	body: everything	0.004	0.01	0.262 ± 1.903	0.64 ± 2.8	1.726 ± 4.957	1.376 ± 3.576
42	body: $username_x$	0.004	0.016	1.096 ± 4.881	1.394 ± 5.164	0.938 ± 3.523	1.608 ± 4.565
43	body: in	0.004	0.009	3.467 ± 6.878	3.311 ± 4.559	4.241 ± 5.246	3.175 ± 4.247
44	body: feel	0.004	0.007	1.477 ± 4.989	3.145 ± 6.323	5.187 ± 8.689	3.746 ± 6.598
45	body: try	0.004	0.009	0.683 ± 3.816	1.465 ± 4.957	1.46 ± 3.793	1.902 ± 4.574
46	body: anything	0.004	0.007	0.541 ± 3	1.602 ± 4.745	2.195 ± 5.751	4.237 ± 10.067
47	body: am	0.004	0.008	1.162 ± 5.241	1.655 ± 4.619	2.523 ± 5.922	1.642 ± 4.584
48	body: at	0.004	0.007	2.033 ± 5.47	3.349 ± 6.469	3.661 ± 6.051	4.058 ± 6.735
49	body: with	0.004	0.01	2.029 ± 4.01	3.189 ± 5.024	2.679 ± 3.776	1.591 ± 2.872
50	body: safe	0.004	0.012	0.342 ± 2.802	0.163 ± 1.801	0.662 ± 3.339	2.907 ± 6.549

Table 4: The 50 most discriminative features of posts and their mean values for each class of green, amber, red, and crisis, which are ranked according to their feature importance. For the words we have also provided their IDF.

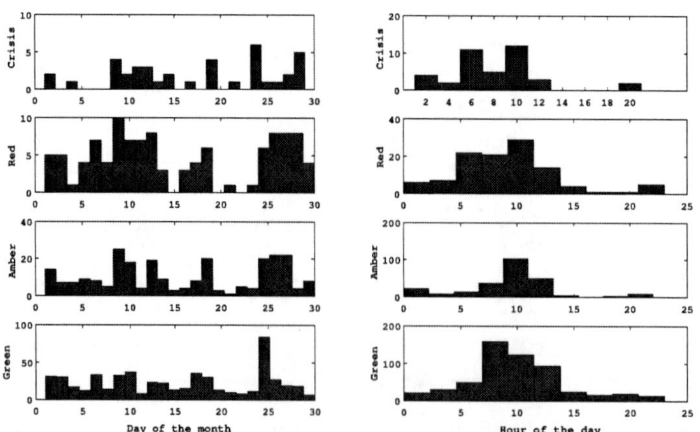

Figure 1: Histogram of message posting time distribution for each mental health state (crisis, red, amber, and green). The left plots show distribution of posts in days of the month (1-31) and the right plots show the distribution of the hours of the day.

References

Yoshua Bengio, Aaron Courville, and Pierre Vincent. 2013. Representation learning: A review and new perspectives. *Pattern Analysis and Machine Intelligence, IEEE Transactions on*, 35(8):1798–1828.

Leo Breiman, Jerome Friedman, Charles J Stone, and Richard A Olshen. 1984. *Classification and regression trees*. CRC press.

Leo Breiman. 2001. Random forests. *Machine learning*, 45(1):5–32.

Corinna Cortes and Vladimir Vapnik. 1995. Support-vector networks. *Machine learning*, 20(3):273–297.

Adele Cutler, D Richard Cutler, and John R Stevens. 2012. Random forests. In *Ensemble Machine Learning*, pages 157–175. Springer.

Quoc V Le and Tomas Mikolov. 2014. Distributed representations of sentences and documents. *arXiv preprint arXiv:1405.4053*.

Tami L Mark, Rosanna M Coffey, Rita Vandivort-Warren, Hendrick J Harwood, et al. 2005. Us spending for mental health and substance abuse treatment, 1991-2001. *Health Affairs*, 24:W5.

Tomas Mikolov, Kai Chen, Greg Corrado, and Jeffrey Dean. 2013a. Efficient estimation of word representations in vector space. *arXiv preprint arXiv:1301.3781*.

Tomas Mikolov, Ilya Sutskever, Kai Chen, Greg S Corrado, and Jeff Dean. 2013b. Distributed representations of words and phrases and their compositionality. In *Advances in neural information processing systems*, pages 3111–3119.

Tomas Mikolov, Wen-tau Yih, and Geoffrey Zweig. 2013c. Linguistic regularities in continuous space word representations. In *HLT-NAACL*, pages 746–751.

Fabian Pedregosa, Gaël Varoquaux, Alexandre Gramfort, Vincent Michel, Bertrand Thirion, Olivier Grisel, Mathieu Blondel, Peter Prettenhofer, Ron Weiss, Vincent Dubourg, et al. 2011. Scikit-learn: Machine learning in python. *The Journal of Machine Learning Research*, 12:2825–2830.

Stephen Robertson. 2004. Understanding inverse document frequency: on theoretical arguments for idf. *Journal of documentation*, 60(5):503–520.

TB Üstün, Joseph L Ayuso-Mateos, Somnath Chatterji, Colin Mathers, and Christopher JL Murray. 2004. Global burden of depressive disorders in the year 2000. *The British journal of psychiatry*, 184(5):386–392.

Jason Weston and Chris Watkins. 1998. Multi-class support vector machines. Technical report, Citeseer.

Wen Zhang, Taketoshi Yoshida, and Xijin Tang. 2011. A comparative study of tf* idf, lsi and multi-words for text classification. *Expert Systems with Applications*, 38(3):2758–2765.

The UMD CLPsych 2016 Shared Task System: Text Representation for Predicting Triage of Forum Posts about Mental Health

Meir Friedenberg, Hadi Amiri, Hal Daumé III, Philip Resnik
Department of Computer Science,UMIACS
University of Maryland, College Park
meir@terpmail.umd.edu, {hadi,hal3f,resnik}@umd.edu

Abstract

We report on a multiclass classifier for triage of mental health forum posts as part of the CLPsych 2016 shared task. We investigate a number of document representations, including topic models and representation learning to represent posts in semantic space, including context- and emotion-sensitive feature representations of posts.

1 Introduction

The 2016 CLPsych Shared Task focused on automatic triage of posts from ReachOut.com, an anonymous online mental health site for young people that permits peer support and dissemination of mental health information and guidance. Peer support and volunteer services like ReachOut, Koko,[1] and Crisis Text Line[2] offer new and potentially very important ways to help serve mental health needs, given the challenges many people face in obtaining access to mental health providers and the astronomical societal cost of mental illness (Insel, 2008). In such settings, however, it is essential that moderators be able to quickly and accurately identify posts that require intervention from trained personnel, e.g., where there is potential for harm to self or others. This shared task aimed to make progress on that problem by advancing technology for automatic triage of forum posts. In particular, the task involved prediction of categories for ReachOut posts, with the four categories, {*crisis*, *red*, *amber*, *green*}, indicating how urgently the post needs attention.

---

[1]itskoko.com

[2]crisistextline.org

2 Systems Overview

Following Resnik et al. (2015), the core of our system is classification via multi-class support vector machines (SVMs) with a linear kernel. We explore topic models as well as context- and emotion-sensitive representations of posts, together with baseline bag of words representations, as features for our model.

2.1 Baseline Lexical Features

We considered bag of words and bag of bigrams in conjunction with TF-IDF and binary weighting schemes of these represenations and stopword removal. Our preliminary experiments with development data suggested that binary weighted bag of words features with stopword removal were an effective baseline; we refer to this feature set simply as BOW.

2.2 Topic Models

We use Latent Dirichlet Allocation (LDA) (Blei et al., 2003) to create a 30-topic model on the entire ReachOut corpus (including labeled, unlabeled, and test data), as well as posts from the Reddit.com /r/Depression forum, yielding document (forum post) topic probability posteriors as features. The inclusion of the test data among the inputs to LDA can be thought of as a transductive approach to model generation for this shared task aiming to take maximal advantage of available data, although this would prevent post-by-post processing in a real-world setting.

Proceedings of the 3rd Workshop on Computational Linguistics and Clinical Psychology: From Linguistic Signal to Clinical Reality, pages 158–161,
San Diego, California, June 16, 2016. ©2016 Association for Computational Linguistics

System #	Description
1	BOW
2	BOW + Context-Sensitive Representations
3	Emotion-Sensitive Representations (Euclidean distance)
4	BOW + Topic Posteriors (LDA)
5	BOW + Topic Posteriors + Emotion-Sensitive Representations (Cosine similarity)

Table 1: System Features and Runs

2.3 Context-Sensitive Representation

We obtain context-sensitive representations of an input post by concatenating the average word embedding of the input post with its "context" information (represented by low dimensional vectors) and passing the resulting vector to a basic autoencoder (Hinton and Salakhutdinov, 2006). We obtain context vectors for posts via non-negative matrix factorization (NMF) where the disttribution of an input post over the topics in the dataset is used as its context vector. We use the pre-trained 300-dimensional word embeddings provided by `Word2Vec`.[3]

Formally, we use NMF to identify context information for input posts as follows. Given a training dataset with n posts, i.e., $\mathbf{X} \in \mathbb{R}^{v \times n}$, where v is the size of a global vocabulary and the scalar k is the number of topics in the dataset, we learn the topic matrix $\mathbf{D} \in \mathbb{R}^{v \times k}$ and a context matrix $\mathbf{C} \in \mathbb{R}^{k \times n}$ using the following sparse coding algorithm:

$$\min_{\mathbf{D},\mathbf{C}} \quad \|\mathbf{X} - \mathbf{DC}\|_F^2 + \mu\|\mathbf{C}\|_1, \qquad (1)$$
$$s.t. \quad \mathbf{D} \succeq 0, \ \mathbf{C} \succeq 0,$$

where each column in $\mathbf{C}$ is a sparse representation of an input over all topics and can be used as context information for its corressponding input post. Note that we obtain the context of test instances by transforming them according to the fitted NMF model on training data. We believe combining test and training data (as discussed above) will further improve the quality of our context vectors.

We concatenate the average word embeddings and context vectors of input posts and pass them to a basic deep autoencoder (Hinton and Salakhutdinov, 2006) with three hidden layers. The hidden representations produced by the autoencoder will be used as context-sensitive representations of inputs and considered as features in our system.

2.4 Emotion-Sensitive Representation

The emotion-sensitive representation of an input post is obtained by computing the distance (Euclidean distance or cosine similarity) between the average word embedding of the input post with nine categories of emotion words. The emotion categories that we consider are

> *anger, disgust, sadness, fear, guilt, interest, joy, shame, surprise,*

where each category has a designated word, e.g. "anger", and its 40 nearest neighbor words in embedding space according to Euclidean distance. For example, the category for *anger* contains "anger" along with related words like "resentment", "fury", "frustration", "outrage", "disgust", "indignation", "dissatisfaction", "discontentment", etc.[4] Using the Euclidean distance or cosine similarity between average word embedding of the input post with the embedding of each emotion word yields 311 features for the classifier, one per emotion-word category ignoring the emotion words that were removed.

2.5 Classifier Details

In our experiments we used multi-class SVM classifiers with a linear kernel. Specifically, we used the python scikit-learn module (Pedregosa et al., 2011), which interfaces with the widely-used libsvm.[5] We employed a one-vs-one decision function, and used the 'balanced' class_weight option to set class weights to be inversally proportional to their frequency in the training data.[6] All other parameters were set to their default values.

---

[4] We also manually verified the nearest neighbor words to ensure that they correctly represent their corresponding categories, and remove words that appear in at least two categories with opposite sentiment orientation.

[5] scikit-learn.org/stable/modules/generated/sklearn.svm. SVC.html

[6] One-vs-one beat one-vs-all in preliminary experimentation.

---

[3] `code.google.com/p/word2vec`.

Specific feature combinations for our systems are reported in Table 1 and were selected based on development data. While our main criterion for choosing what features to use was Macro-Averaged F-Score, System 3 (emotion-sensitive representations) was selected primarily because of its superior performance on red prediction. Given the importance of red and crisis prediction in this context, we found this system interesting and consider its relative success at red prediction to be worthy of further exploration.

2.6 Data Preparation

Preprocessing: We performed the same basic preprocessing on all posts, including removing URLs and non-ascii characters, unescaping HTML, and expansion of contractions. We also lemmatized the tokens.

Data Splits: As per the suggestion in the shared task description, we set aside the last 250 posts of the training data as development data. Our primary use of the development data was in system development and selecting feature combinations. We also removed one post each from the training and development data as they did not appear to us to have significant linguistic content.

3 Results

Tables 2 and 3 show the performance of our submitted systems on development and test data respectively. Table 4 presents the effects of different feature combinations on development data performance, which we used to select our systems for submission.

Test data performance is noticeably worse for all five of our systems than development data performance. A non-negligible part of that seems to be our performace on crisis recall - the fact that there is only one crisis post in the test data set implies that when our system incorrectly labels that post an F-Score of 0 is necessarily averaged in. Evaluating why all five of our systems predict a green label for the crisis post seems like a worthwhile line of inquiry towards improving upon our system. We will conduct such experiments in the future.

F-Score\System	1	2	3	4	5
Green	0.82	0.85	0.78	0.83	0.82
Amber	0.57	0.54	0.42	0.54	0.51
Red	0.39	0.44	0.52	0.40	0.42
Crisis	0.33	0.25	0.24	0.33	0.35
Macro-Averaged	**0.53**	**0.52**	**0.49**	**0.52**	**0.52**
Official Score	**0.43**	**0.41**	**0.39**	**0.42**	**0.43**

Table 2: F-scores on development data. (Official Score is Macro-Averaged F-Score over crisis, red, and amber.)

F-Score\System	1	2	3	4	5
Green	0.83	0.87	0.84	0.83	0.85
Amber	0.41	0.5	0.33	0.43	0.48
Red	0.47	0.44	0.4	0.48	0.44
Crisis	0.00	0.00	0.00	0.00	0.00
Macro-Averaged	**0.43**	**0.45**	**0.39**	**0.44**	**0.44**
Official Score	**0.29**	**0.31**	**0.24**	**0.30**	**0.31**

Table 3: F-scores on test data. (Official Score is Macro-Averaged F-Score over crisis, red, and amber.)

Our system #3, which used Euclidean distance based emotion-sensitive representation of documents, was submitted because of its outstanding red prediction performance on development data. Given the importance of red and crisis recall in this domain, a system that perfomed particularly well in such an area seems worth exploring. Unfortunately, this red recall rate did not carry over to the test data, so it seems likely that our model simply overfit to the red data.

An examination of Table 4 suggests that it may be difficult to find features that are significantly more effective for this task than bag of words features. In particular, all of the systems listed that outperformed bag of words overall (whether on Macro-Averaged F-Score or Macro-Averaged F-Score over the amber, red, and crisis classes) seem to have done so only minimally. Interestingly, many of the feature sets did outperform bag of words on F-Score for the red class in development data, but this result does not seem to replicate in the test data.

4 Conclusions and Future Directions

In this paper we have summarized our contribution to the CLPSych 2016 shared task on triage of mental health forum posts. Our approach used class-weighted multi-class SVM classifiers with a linear kernel, and we found binary bag of words features to

Features\F-Scores	Green	Amber	Red	Crisis	Macro-Averaged	Official Score
BOW	0.82	**0.57**	0.39	0.33	**0.53**	0.43
Topics	0.77	0.37	0.34	0.24	0.43	0.32
Context Sensitive	0.80	0.43	0.28	0.32	0.46	0.34
Emotion Sensitive (Euclidean)	0.78	0.42	**0.52**	0.24	0.49	0.39
Emotion Sensitive (Cosine)	0.67	0.19	0.28	0.07	0.31	0.18
BOW + Topics	0.83	0.54	0.40	0.33	0.52	0.42
BOW + Context Sensitive	**0.85**	0.54	0.44	0.25	0.52	0.41
BOW + Emotion Sensitive (Euclidean)	0.82	0.45	0.45	0.13	0.46	0.34
BOW + Emotion Sensitive (Cosine)	0.82	0.54	0.42	**0.35**	**0.53**	**0.44**
BOW + Topics + Context Sensitive	0.84	0.52	0.44	0.25	0.51	0.40
BOW + Topics + Emotion Sensitive (Euclidean)	0.82	0.45	0.45	0.125	0.46	0.34
BOW + Topics + Emotion Sensitive (Cosine)	0.82	0.51	0.42	**0.35**	0.52	0.43
All	0.82	0.44	0.45	0.13	0.46	0.34

Table 4: Multi-class F-scores of different feature combinations on development data. (Official Score is Macro-Averaged F-Score over crisis, red, and amber.)

be reasonably effective for this task. Though topic models and context- and emotion-sensitive vector representations did not perform well independently on this task, when used to supplement bag of words features they did lead to some improvement in test data prediction.

In future work, one direction for potential improvement is the exploration of more complex topic models. In particular, our work utilized "vanilla" Latent Dirichlet Allocation, but Resnik et al. (2015) found some success in applying supervised topic modelling techniques to this domain. Furthemore, it would be interesting to introduce domain expertise into the models, whether by interactive topic modelling (Hu et al., 2014) or by providing informed priors, and seeing how that affects performance.

Another interesting direction we hope to explore is tracking changes amongst a user's posts over time. While we only used the four class labels, available sublables included "followupOk" for some amber posts and "followupWorse" for some red posts. Tracking how a user's language has changed both since the start of their time on the forum and from the start of a given thread seems likely to be able to provide useful features for classification of such cases.

Finally, the labeled data available for this task was rather limited, and while we used the unlabeled data in the creation of the topic models, our system in general focused on the labeled data. Future work might explore application of semi-supervised models, integrating both the unlabeled ReachOut data and mental health posts from other forums.

References

David M Blei, Andrew Y Ng, and Michael I Jordan. 2003. Latent Dirichlet allocation. *Journal of Machine Learning Research*, 3:993–1022.

Geoffrey E Hinton and Ruslan R Salakhutdinov. 2006. Reducing the dimensionality of data with neural networks. *Science*, 313(5786):504–507.

Yuening Hu, Jordan Boyd-Graber, Brianna Satinoff, and Alison Smith. 2014. Interactive topic modeling. *Machine learning*, 95(3):423–469.

Thomas R Insel. 2008. Assessing the economic costs of serious mental illness. *American Journal of Psychiatry*, 165(6).

F. Pedregosa, G. Varoquaux, A. Gramfort, V. Michel, B. Thirion, O. Grisel, M. Blondel, P. Prettenhofer, R. Weiss, V. Dubourg, J. Vanderplas, A. Passos, D. Cournapeau, M. Brucher, M. Perrot, and E. Duchesnay. 2011. Scikit-learn: Machine learning in Python. *Journal of Machine Learning Research*, 12:2825–2830.

Philip Resnik, William Armstrong, Leonardo Claudino, and Thang Nguyen. 2015. The University of Maryland CLPsych 2015 shared task system. *NAACL HLT 2015*, page 54.

Using Linear Classifiers for the Automatic Triage of Posts in the 2016 CLPsych Shared Task

Juri Opitz
Computational Linguistics
Heidelberg University
69120 Heidelberg, Germany
opitz@cl.uni-heidelberg.de

Abstract

The 2016 CLPsych Shared Task was to automatically triage posts from a mental health forum into four categories: *green* (everything is fine), *amber* (a moderator needs to look at this post), *red* (a moderator urgently needs to look at this post) and *crisis* (the person might hurt himself or others). The final results for the task revealed that this problem was not an easy task. I chose to treat the problem as a text categorization task using a system composed of different Support Vector Machines (SVMs) in a one-vs-rest setting. This approach was straight-forward and achieved good performance in the final evaluation. The major difficulty was to find suitable features and feature combinations.

1 Approach

Treating the problem as a multi-class text categorization problem motivated the usage of linear SVMs. SVMs promise good regularization in high dimensional spaces (as this and most other text spaces are) and have demonstrated empirical success for many kinds of text categorization problems (Joachims, 1998), (Manevitz and Yousef, 2002).

To map the posts into vector space, suitable features had to be chosen. I experimented with three different types of features. First and foremost the traditional *bag-of-ngram features*: In information retrieval and document classification tasks, documents are often treated as bag-of-words or bag-of-ngrams. One distinct dimension represents each distinct n-gram. These features simply assumed a boolean value of 1 at index i in the feature vector, when the document in question contained the n-gram represented by i, and 0 otherwise. I created 1,2 and 3 grams based on the available data and discarded those which appeared in less than twelve documents. This resulted in a maximum number of 65287 features. The ngrams were drawn from the tokenized main message text and the title (if the title did not contain "Re:", indicating that the title-text might be from another user).

The second category of features were *user features*: These described i.a. the ratios of *green*, *amber*, *crisis* and *red* labels in a user's history and the label of his last post (if there was one). Motivation were assumptions like: given a user posted a *crisis* post, chances are higher that the next post of this user is also a *crisis* post.

Also manually created were *post features*: these features described the number of kudos and the time of the post (in a categorical way). Motivation: Was the post created very late in the night? This could indicate sleep problems, which again could indicate a *crisis* or *red* label.

For each label a different SVM was trained. The best feature combination for each of the four SVMs was searched on 250 development posts (these were cut off at the end of the 947 training posts). Of course, it was intractable to validate all different possible combinations of features. I chose to focus on the following options:

1. all features

2. 1-grams

3. 1,2-grams

Proceedings of the 3rd Workshop on Computational Linguistics and Clinical Psychology: From Linguistic Signal to Clinical Reality, pages 162–165,
San Diego, California, June 16, 2016. ©2016 Association for Computational Linguistics

4. 1,2,3-grams

5. 1,2 grams using 1k,5k..., 40k of the 2 grams

6. 1,2,3 grams using the best of 5. and 1k,5k,..., 15k of the 3 grams

7. The best of the above combinations with user and/or post features

Taking also the 20 different options for the SVM regularization parameter into account, more than 400 parameter combinations for each label were checked. The four SVMs representing the labels achieving the best label-wise F1-measure were chosen for the multi-class classification.

The decision for the final label was based on the soft outputs of the decision functions (dot-product of weights and feature values) of the four one-vs-rest classifiers. Here I chose to experiment with two options: 1., argmax and 2., train another classifier (used AdaBoost) on the output scores of the four SVMs as a "meta-classifier".

2   Results

Table 1 shows the F1-scores on the development and test set of the best combination of parameters found on the development set. For each single label (vs. rest) and for the final multi-class classification where the single binary classifiers were combined to make a final decision. The evaluation measure of the Shared Task was Macro F1, averaged over *amber*, *red* and *crisis*. The argmax decisions of the soft

label	feature option	F1 Dev	F1 Test
green	1,2 grams	0.88	0.89
amber	1,2 grams	0.60	0.62
red	$1,2_{1k},3_{1k}$ grams	0.48	0.48
crisis	$1,2_{1k},3_{1k}$ grams	0.37	0.0
all, argmax	-	0.44	**0.37**
all, AdaBoost	-	0.34	0.31

Table 1: Results of the best parameter options found on the development set. In the final multi class classification, F1 means Macro F1 averaged over all labels but *green*.

SVM-outputs outperformed the AdaBoost decisions by 10% on development and 6% on test. For *green* an F1 score of 0.89 was achieved. All labels but

"crisis" yielded better scores on test set. The significant drop in performance from the development data (44% Macro F1) to the test data (37% Macro F1) mainly originated in the could-not-be-worse performance for finding the *crisis* posts (37% F1 development, 0% test).

3   Analysis

3.1   Why the total fail at labelling *crisis*?

Achieving 0.0 F1 for the label *crisis* had a very negative impact on the final Macro F1 measure. A possible explanation of the bad performance for *crisis* is indicated by Figure 1. With respect to the ratio of *crisis*, both train- and development set are not representative for the held-out test set. Indeed, in the test set, there was only one *crisis* in 241 test samples. As the final evaluation measure was Macro F1,

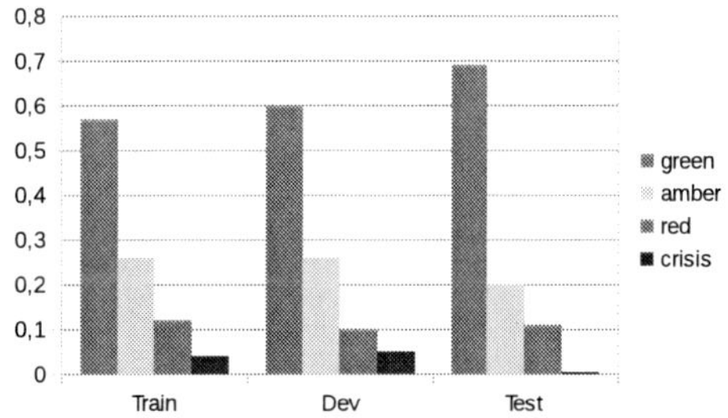

Figure 1: Label distirbutions in the different data sets used. From left to right: *green*, *amber*, *red* and *crisis*.

this was the major reason for the heavy drop in performance on the test data. Finding the only positive sample out of 241 negative ones without making to many guesses is very difficult. This again makes it very likely for recall (and hence F1) to be zero. With more guesses, the chances of finding this one sample may be still small while the precision (and hence F1) for *crisis* drops (and probably also the scores of the three other labels). With $F1 = 0$ for one out of three labels, the Macro F1 was already bounded by 0.67. The best of my systems (Macro F1 $= 0.37$) fired once on *crisis* and missed (the true *crisis* post was labelled *red* - maybe not the worst of an error). Another system I submitted fired 12 times on *crisis*, but missed it every time. In fact, none of the five systems I submitted was able to find this needle in a haystack.

Two things I find important to conclude from that:

1. Macro F1 was an evaluation measure bringing a "harsh" punishment for mislabelling one specific sample.

2. a not-so-good F1 Macro score does not necessarily imply a not-so-good system. As the F1 for one out of three labels was always zero, classifying the other two non-*green* labels worked better (*amber* 0.62 F1 and *red* 0.48 F1).

3.2 The manually designed features did not work well

In the first section I proposed two types of feature sets, which intuitively made sense for me.

These features were designed manually and originated from motivations like: A user who posted a *crisis* post before might be more likely to have another *crisis* in his next post. *Post features*, also i.a. described the time a post was submitted. However, as it turned out, these features led to over-fitting problems as indicated by figure 2. The figure describes functions of the SVM regularization parameter C with regard to 1. a feature vector containing only uni-grams, 2. post and user features appended and 3., only user features appended and 4., only post features append. It is clearly visible that the usage of the hand-crafted features led to problems on the unseen development data.

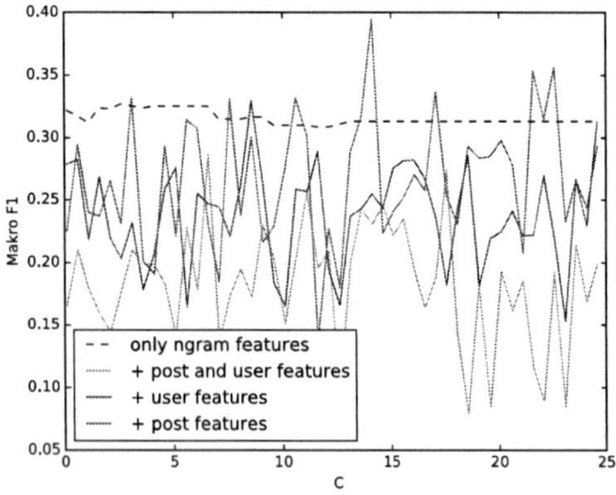

Figure 2: Performance of different feature combinations on the unseen development set. Severe over-fitting problems occurred when including the manually designed features.

3.3 Phrases with high weights assigned

The ranking of features by their respective squared weights can be interpreted as metric of feature relevance (Guyon et al., 2002). High weights (their squared value to take negative weights into account) influence the output of the decision function by tendency more than low weights.

Table 2 displays, for each possible label, the phrases with the highest weights (positive and negative). This analysis i.a. shows that emoticons were of importance for the discrimination of posts. For example,
:-) is negatively correlated with *crisis*, *red* and *amber* and positively correlated with *green*. 72% of 65026 posts contained emoticons. Further interpretation of the high weighted phrases is left to the reader.

4 Conclusion and Outlook

The approach I proposed was to train one SVM for each label and do the final vote between the four SVMs with an argmax of the soft-outputs of their respective decision functions. The system led to above-median performance in the final evaluation of the Shared Task. The approach is also straight forward, the major difficulty being the search for good features and feature combinations there are very many of these possible. The best performing features turned out to be bag-of-phrase features: uni-grams plus partially bi- and tri-grams. The SVMs appeared to cope well with high dimensions (as expected), but not so well with the manually designed features (as not expected). These features led to problems on unseen data. It is very likely that there exist features or sets of features which are able to further enhance the automatic triage of posts, making the SVM approach all in all a promising technique for this task.

As the results of all systems of all participants on the held-out test set show, the automatic triage of posts in a psychology forum is not an easy task. I think that deciding whether a post is to be labelled *red* (a moderator needs to look at the post as soon as possible and take action) or *crisis* (the author might hurt himself) is often not only difficult to decide for machines, but also for humans themselves (maybe even for psychological experts, especially without knowing the author in person). Thus, for further ex-

label	phrases
green (-)	don't, cant, just, I'm, negative, want, help, don't know, feeling, not, everything, do, scared, know, anymore, help me, guess, feel, don't want, has, nothing, : – (
green (+)	be lonely, you, : –) , your, : –D, awesome, proud, you are, love, 1, we, you can, good, for, hope, well, you're, if you, by, hey, morning, for you, how, 2, some, there
amber (-)	: –) , be lonely, your, you are, there, 1, day, I'm so, can, love, well, hope, anymore, will, : –D, 3, sorry, hey, out, how, if you, into, you have, awesome, coming, you can, friend
amber (+)	don't, me, help, think, but, other, not, thanks, about, I'm, all, yeah, just, help me, those, have, put, negative, services, thank, anxious, lot, there's, don't have, thank you, isn't, guess
red (-)	for, thanks, you, about, : –) , hope, too, good, proud, : –D, an, put, think, one, awesome, still, me but, thought, but don't, make, phone, week, other, sitting
red (+)	breathe, : – (, passed, empty, ..., family, worse, should, feeling so, hospital, anymore, things are, disappointment, incapable, shit, afraid, please, cant, practically, through this, identical, can not, failed
crisis (-)	you, my, your, I've, : –) , some, was, been, with, its, people, things, all, would, have, we, are, them, love, see, there, said, much, after, not, good, someone, thing
crisis (+)	can't, life, just, for me, just want, back, negative, home, want, I'm so, thought about, me, sorry for, anymore, worth, everything, feel like, die, harm, sorry, self, bad, unsafe, don't know, tips, useless

Table 2: Features with the highest positive (+) and negative (-) weights for each label. Emoticons: : –) = happy emoticon, : –D = very happy emoticon, : – (= sad emoticon.

amination and comparison of systems in this classification problem, I would suggest to also consider other evaluation measures, which take not only *error yes-no* into account, but also the severity of an error. With respect to a real world application, a *crisis* post labelled *red* should not be as severe of an error as handing out a *green* label: *red* and *crisis* (by definition) are very close neighbors, *crisis* and *green* are opposites.

References

Isabelle Guyon, Jason Weston, Stephen Barnhill, and Vladimir Vapnik. 2002. Gene selection for cancer classification using support vector machines. *Mach. Learn.*, 46(1-3):389–422, March.

Thorsten Joachims. 1998. Text categorization with suport vector machines: Learning with many relevant features. In *Proceedings of the 10th European Conference on Machine Learning*, ECML '98, pages 137–142, London, UK, UK. Springer-Verlag.

Larry M. Manevitz and Malik Yousef. 2002. One-class svms for document classification. *J. Mach. Learn. Res.*, 2:139–154, March.

The GW/UMD CLPsych 2016 Shared Task System

Ayah Zirikly
George Washington University
Washington, DC
ayaz@gwu.edu

Varun Kumar
University of Maryland
College Park, MD
varunk@cs.umd.edu

Philip Resnik
University of Maryland
College Park, MD
resnik@umd.edu

1 Introduction

Suicide is the third leading cause for death for young people, and in an average U.S. high school classroom, 30% have experienced a long period of feeling hopeless, 20% have been bullied, 16.7% have seriously considered suicide, and 6.7% of students have actually made a suicide attempt.[1] The 2016 ACL Workshop on Computational Linguistics and Clinical Psychology (CLPsych) included a shared task focusing on classification of posts to ReachOut, an online information and support service that provides help to teens and young adults (aged 15-24) who are struggling with mental health issues.[2] The primary goal of the shared task is to identify posts that require urgent attention and review from the ReachOut team (i.e. moderators).

2 System Overview

We use Stanford CoreNLP (Manning et al., 2014) for preprocessing (tokenization, lemmatization, POS tagging) and a supervised learning approach for classification. Section 2.1 describes the features we use, and Section 2.2 describes our classifiers.

2.1 Features

The features used in our model range from simple unigrams to more complex features such as syntactic, sentiment, psychological, and other data-driven features.

- Unigram features: We choose the n most important unigrams based on their TF-IDF values, restricting attention to unigrams appearing in between 2 and 60% of documents.

- Part-of-speech features: We use part-of-speech (POS) tag counts for adverbs, pronouns, and modal auxiliaries (e.g. can, cannot, couldn't, might).

- Sentiment features: For every post we generate three sentiment features, calculated as follows: i) split the post into sentences; ii) tag each sentence as one of {positive, negative, neutral} using Stanford CoreNLP; iii) as three document-level features, include the number of sentences that are tagged as *negative*, *positive*, and *neutral*.

- ReachOut meta-data features: From the meta-data of the posts, we use: number of views, time of day of the post, and the board on which the post appeared. The *time* feature is bucketed into eight categories, where each category represents a three hour window. (This feature is based on observations in the literature showing that depressed users tend to be more active on social media at night (Choudhury et al., 2013).) The *board* is represented as six binary features, one each for *Everyday_life_stuff*, *Feedback_Suggestion*, *Getting_Help*, *Intros*, *Something_Not_Right*, and *mancave*. For any post in the test set where the board is not among these, the six board features is set to zero.

- Emotion features: We use the count of emotion words occurring in the post, based on the NRC Word-Emotion Association Lexicon (Mohammad and Turney, 2013). The emotions included are anger, anticipation, disgust, fear, joy, sadness, surprise, and trust. To expand the number of matches, we do lookups in the NRC for words, tokens, and lemmas and use the maximum value.

---

[1] http://us.reachout.com/about-us/what-we-do/; see also Centers for Disease Control and Prevention 2015

[2] http://us.reachout.com

Proceedings of the 3rd Workshop on Computational Linguistics and Clinical Psychology: From Linguistic Signal to Clinical Reality, pages 166–170,
San Diego, California, June 16, 2016. ©2016 Association for Computational Linguistics

- Linguistic Inquiry and Word Count (LIWC): We include the category for each LIWC category (Tausczik and Pennebaker, 2010) using the post's lemmas.

- Positive/negative counts: In non-green posts, some users list "positives" and "negatives" associated with the issue or situation the user is facing. For example, a user might say *Negative: Everything is going wrong in my life, I feel so depressed and worthless. Positive: I need to appreciate small things and be grateful to what I have.* We include the total number of such positive or negative lists as a single feature whose value is the frequency of any of the following tokens: *(positive:, negative:, pos:, neg:).* In the above example the value of the feature would be 2.

- Mention features: As the *mention* feature, we use the count of explicit user mentions (identified using @) within the post.

- The *word_count* feature is the number of words in the post.

In work after the the shared task was completed, we also experimented with additional features that were not part of our official submission.[3]

- ReachOut author: This binary feature is enabled when the user is ReachOut-affiliated (e.g. moderator, staff). This feature is a cue that the post is *green* (no further follow-up is needed).

- Mental Disease Lexicon *mentalDisLex*: This feature is a count tokens in the post that match entries in a mental disease lexicon.[4]

- Word shape: We include two binary features that reflect the occurrence of words that either have character repetitions like "hmmm" or all capitalized letters like "DIE".

- Word embeddings: We use word2vec to generate word embeddings as described in (Mikolov et al., 2013).[5] The post's document-level embedding is calculated as the average of all the words' vectors.

---

[3]For the rest of the document, when we mention features, we mean the above features that were used in the official runs, unless otherwise stated.

[4]http://mental-health-matters.com/psychological-disorders/alphabetical-list-of-disorders

[5]http://word2vec.googlecode.com/svn/trunk/

2.2 Framework

We experimented with a diverse set of multi-class balanced supervised classifiers.

2.2.1 Lexically based classifier

In this setup we used both the SVM *(uniSVM)* and logistic regression *(uniLR)* classifiers. We use unigrams as binary features. We pick the top n unigrams based on their TF-IDF weighting scores and combine them with the other features.

2.2.2 Non-lexical classifier

In this setup *(nonLexLR)*, we incorporate all features (Section 2.1) except the unigram features and classify using the logistic regression classifier.

2.2.3 Two-stage classifier

This setup *(2stage)* is based on an ensemble supervised learning approach as depicted in Figure 1. The first stage is a support vector machine clasifier (Cortes and Vapnik, 1995) using lexical features with TF-IDF weighting. The second stage is a logistic regression classifier which uses the output probabilities of the SVM classifier, along with the features described in Section 2.1.

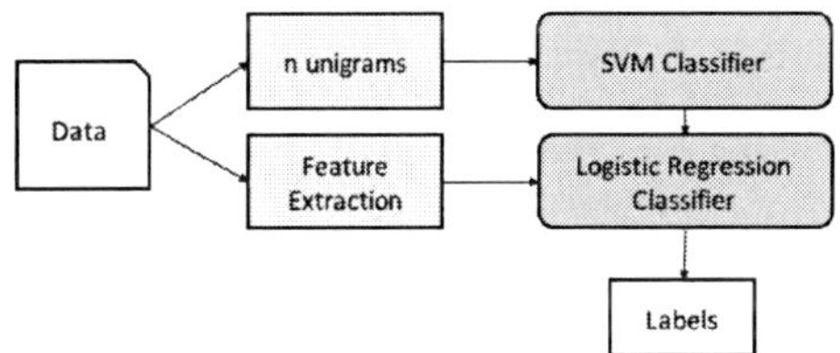

Figure 1: Two-stage classifier

Ensemble methods have proven to be more effective than individual classifiers when the training data is significantly small (as shown in Table 1) and not a good representative of the classes (Polikar, 2006).

2.2.4 Majority vote classifier:

In this setting *(maj1)*, we use the majority vote based on the *uniSVM*, *uniLR*, and *nonLexLR* classifiers.

3 Experiments

3.1 Dataset

The shared task dataset contains posts annotated with four classes (green, amber, red, and crisis), and the main goal is to correctly classify the posts

167

that belong to the last three classes. Table 1 shows the number of posts per class.

Subset	green	amber	red	crisis	total
Train	549	249	110	39	947
Test	166	47	27	1	241

Table 1: Dataset Train-Test Stats

3.2 Metrics

For evaluation, we used the script provided by the shared task organizers, which does not include the green labels.[6] The evaluation metrics are precision, recall, and F1-score for each of the three classes (amber, red, crisis), in addition to the macro F1 (official score).

3.3 Results & Discussion

During the system building phase, we experimented with the models in Section 2.2 using 5-fold cross validation (CV) on the training data, making use of all the features mentioned in Section 2.1 except word shape, author ranking, mental disease lexicon, and word embedding features. For the *uniLR, uniSVM*, and *2stage* classifiers, we empirically choose $n = 300$ as the number of most-important unigrams based on best results of the 5-fold CV.

Table 2 depicts the models' performance on the test data. Although they were not included in the official submissions, Table 4 also includes the extra features we explored.

Model	Test data
uniLR	0.32
uniSVM	0.34
nonLexLR	0.34
2stage	**0.36**
maj1	0.32

Table 2: Macro F1-Scores on Test Data

Two key challenges in this shared task turned out to be the highly imbalanced data and the extremely small number of *crisis* and *red* posts, with just 39 crisis posts in the training data and one (!) crisis post in the test set. We addressed the imbalanced dataset problem by using multi-class balanced classifiers, and using five-fold cross validation on training data (941 posts) helped to

avoid design choices based on a particularly lucky or unlucky training/test split (Khoshgoftaar et al., 2007). However, in order to tackle the second issue, we need a feature set that is capable of capturing red and crisis posts, which are the most important classes since they require immediate action from ReachOut's moderators and/or administrators.

From Table 4, we observe that the mental disease lexicon feature set was the one capable of capturing the single instance of *crisis* in the test data; additionally, it improved the recall of *red* and precision of *amber*. This results in our best system performance, an unofficial post-shared-task macro-F1 score of 0.45, which improves on the best shared-task official score of 0.42. The LIWC features also provide a major boost in performance (on both CV and test data) which aligns with the results in Table 2; there a feature set that does not include any lexical features (0.34) performs equally to a single classifier using a combination of lexical and non-lexical features.

4 Conclusion & Future Work

We have presented a collaborative effort between George Washington University (GW) and University of Maryland (UMD) to tackle the CLPsych 2016 ReachOut shared task. Using a 2-stage ensemble classification approach, our best official submission yielded 0.36% macro-F1, which is 6% short of the best system. However, further feature experimentation after the conclusion of the shared task yielded a macro F1 score of 0.45%. In future work, we plan to experiment with an extended ReachOut meta-data feature set and to expand LIWC features using word embeddings.

---

[6] https://github.com/clpsych-2016-shared-task/ro-evaluation

Features	F1 CV	macro-F1	Accuracy	crisis			red			amber		
				Precision	Recall	F1	Precision	Recall	F1	Precision	Recall	F1
U=unigrams	0.12	0.33	0.75	0	0	0	0.5	0.41	0.45	0.48	0.64	0.55
U+POS	0.11	0.29	0.73	0	0	0	0.42	0.3	0.35	0.46	0.62	0.53
X=U+sentiment	0.12	0.33	0.75	0	0	0	0.5	0.41	0.45	0.48	0.62	0.54
+LIWC	0.36	0.36	0.75	0	0	0	0.59	0.48	0.53	0.49	0.62	0.55
+emotion	0.33	0.35	0.74	0	0	0	0.57	0.44	0.5	0.48	0.62	0.54
+meta_data	0.35	0.36	0.77	0	0	0	0.59	0.48	0.53	0.51	0.60	0.55
+positive/negative counts	0.34	0.36	0.76	0	0	0	0.57	0.48	0.52	0.51	0.62	0.56
Y=..+mention	0.36	*0.36*	0.77	0	0	0	0.56	0.52	0.54	0.51	0.60	0.55
Z=..+word_count	0.356	0.36	0.76	0	0	0	0.54	0.48	0.51	0.52	0.62	0.56
Y+wordShape	0.356	0.36	0.77	0	0	0	0.59	0.48	0.53	0.5	0.57	0.53
Y+authorRanking	0.36	0.36	0.78	0	0	0	0.57	0.48	0.52	0.52	0.60	0.55
Y+mentalDisLex	0.364	0.44	0.78	0.12	1	0.22	0.57	0.48	0.52	0.54	0.6	0.57
Y+word2vec	0.356	0.36	0.78	0	0	0	0.59	0.48	0.53	0.52	0.62	0.56
Z'=Y+mentalDisLex+authorRanking	**0.37**	**0.45**	0.78	0.12	1	0.22	0.58	0.52	0.55	0.56	0.60	0.58
Z'+wordShape+word2vec	**0.37**	**0.43**	0.78	0.11	1	0.20	0.57	0.48	0.52	0.54	0.6	0.57
All	0.35	0.35	0.77	0	0	0	0.52	0.48	0.50	0.51	0.57	0.54

Table 3: Features' impacts on system performance, using 5-fold cross-validation and evaluation on test data

References

Munmun De Choudhury, Scott Counts, Eric Horvitz, and Michael Gamon. 2013. Predicting depression via social media. AAAI, July.

Corinna Cortes and Vladimir Vapnik. 1995. Support-vector networks. *Mach. Learn.*, 20(3):273–297, September.

T. M. Khoshgoftaar, M. Golawala, and J. V. Hulse. 2007. An empirical study of learning from imbalanced data using random forest. In *Tools with Artificial Intelligence, 2007. ICTAI 2007. 19th IEEE International Conference on*, volume 2, pages 310–317, Oct.

Christopher D. Manning, Mihai Surdeanu, John Bauer, Jenny Finkel, Steven J. Bethard, and David McClosky. 2014. The Stanford CoreNLP natural language processing toolkit. In *Association for Computational Linguistics (ACL) System Demonstrations*, pages 55–60.

Tomas Mikolov, Ilya Sutskever, Kai Chen, Greg S Corrado, and Jeff Dean. 2013. Distributed representations of words and phrases and their compositionality. In *Advances in neural information processing systems*, pages 3111–3119.

Saif M. Mohammad and Peter D. Turney. 2013. Crowdsourcing a word-emotion association lexicon. 29(3):436–465.

Robi Polikar. 2006. Ensemble based systems in decision making. *Circuits and systems magazine, IEEE*, 6(3):21–45.

Yla R. Tausczik and James W. Pennebaker. 2010. The psychological meaning of words: LIWC and computerized text analysis methods.

A Semi-supervised Approach for the CLPsych 2016 Shared Task

Nicolas Rey-Villamizar and **Prasha Shrestha** and **Thamar Solorio**
University of Houston
nrey@uh.edu, pshrestha3@uh.edu, solorio@cs.uh.edu

Farig Sadeque and **Steven Bethard**
University of Alabama at Birmingham
farigys@uab.edu, bethard@uab.edu

Ted Pedersen
University of Minnesota, Duluth
tpederse@d.umn.edu

Abstract

The 2016 CLPsych Shared Task is centered on the automatic triage of posts from a mental health forum, au.reachout.com. In this paper, we describe our method for this shared task. We used four different groups of features. These features are designed to capture stylistic and word patterns, together with psychological insights based on the Linguistic Inquiry and Word Count (LIWC) word list. We used a multinomial naive Bayes classifier as our base system. We were able to boost the accuracy of our approach by extending the number of training samples using a semi-supervised approach, labeling some of the unlabeled data and extending the number training samples.

1 Introduction

The 2016 ACL Workshop on Computational Linguistics and Clinical Psychology (CLPsych) included a shared task focusing on classification of user posts in the mental health forum, au.reachout.com. Our system is based on two main ideas: the use of word lists that group words into psychologically meaningful categories, and a semi-supervised approach in order to increase the size of the training data. For the word list we used, the Linguistic Inquiry and Word Count (LIWC) (Pennebaker et al., 2007). LIWC is a psychometrically validated lexicon mapping words to psychological concepts and has been used extensively to examine language in order to understand mental health. For using some of the unlabeled data to train our system we leveraged the idea of self-training. This method consists of expanding the number of label samples from the unlabeled data by using the most confident samples, based on a pretrained system on the label data. We were able to combine these two ideas and develop a system that performs significantly better than the baselines.

2 Task Description

The 2016 CLPsych Shared Task is based on the automatic classification of user posts from an online mental health forum *ReachOut*[1] into four different categories according to how urgently the post needs a moderator's attention.

For the shared task, a corpus of posts tagged with four different categories *crisis/red/amber/green* has been provided. Table 1 describes each of the different categories. A dataset of unlabeled data was also provided. Table 2 describes the number of samples of both the labeled and unlabeled data as well as the test data.

The evaluation metric of the task is a macro-averaged F-score over *crisis*, *red* and *amber* labels. This was motivated by a system needing to get the critical cases correct.

3 System description

In our system, we used a Multinomial naive Bayes classifier together with features that aim to capture the user's cognitive processes and writing style. We used a cross-validation approach in combination with a Bayesian optimization for the parameter selection using the provided training set.

---

[1]http://www.au.reachout.com

171

Proceedings of the 3rd Workshop on Computational Linguistics and Clinical Psychology: From Linguistic Signal to Clinical Reality, pages 171–175,
San Diego, California, June 16, 2016. ©2016 Association for Computational Linguistics

Post's label	Description
crisis	The author (or someone they know) might hurt themselves or others (these are red instances that are of immediate importance).
red	A moderator needs to look at this ASAP and take action.
amber	A moderator needs to look at this and assess if there is enough responses and support from other or if they should reply.
green	A moderator does not need to prioritize addressing this post.

Table 1: Categories of the post

Data	Description
Train set	39 *crisis*, 110 *red*, 249 *amber*, 549 *green* posts
Test set	1 *crisis*, 27 *red*, 47 *amber*, 166 *green* posts
Unlabeled set	63797 posts

Table 2: Data distribution

3.1 Classifier

We explored different classifiers in our experimentation. Based on a cross-validation study on the training set we choose to use Multinomial naive Bayes for our final submission. We used the implementation of the *scikit-learn*[2] module (Pedregosa et al., 2011). To account for the words not present in the training vocabulary we explore the use of different smoothing parameters. Using a smoothing parameter of 1 corresponds to the classic Laplace smoothing, and values below 1 correspond to Lidstone smoothing.

3.2 Features

We used the following features in our system:

- Unigrams and bigrams of words

- Prefixes and suffixes of lengths 2, 3, 4 and 5

- Number of kudos in the post

- For each category of the LIWC word lists, we counted how many occurrences of each word in the list the post has, and we created a vector

---

[2]scikit-learn.org/

representation for each post. The LIWC 2007 word list has 64 different word categories.

The unigram and bigram features are intended to capture writing patterns of words that are associated with each label. For example, unigrams and bigrams such as *harm*, *overwhelmed*, *hurts*, and *can't handle* are usually associated with negative feelings that we want our system to be able to capture as *red* and *crisis* labels. The same happens with positive words that are more typically associated with the *green* label.

The number of kudos of the post was used to better distinguish positive posts from the others. In general, posts labeled as *green* have more kudos than the rest. Prefixes and suffixes are added since they have shown to perform well in many text classification tasks.

3.3 Parameter Optimization

We used the Bayesian optimization framework provided by SigOpt[3]. This framework is an alternative to the classic grid search approach, where parameters are explored in an exhaustive way. Table 3 describes the ranges of values explored for the classifier. We also tested the same set of parameters with a different combination of features. We found that using trigrams decreased the performance as well as using more than five character prefixes or suffixes as a feature.

Parameter	Range of values
Smooth term(α)	(1, 0.8, 0.4, 0.2, 0.1)
Class weight	exhaustive search of 10% increase for each class

Table 3: Parameter exploration for the classifier

We also explored feature selection algorithms. However in the 8-fold cross validations over the training set that we performed none of them gave us better performance than when all the features were used.

4 Self-training

Self-training is a method to expand the number of labeled samples given the high cost of labeling samples in the text processing domain (Nigam et al., 1998). We optimized our system in order to achieve the maximum possible f1-macro-average that is used as the

---

[3]https://sigopt.com/

official score using an 8-fold cross validation on the training dataset. We ranked each system as the mean over all the f1-macro-average of the three classes of the 8 runs. We then ran our algorithm in the unlabeled data and selected the most confident samples for each class. The confidence was measured based on the posterior probability of the Multinomial naive Bayes classifier. In order to keep the class balanced in the same way as the training data, we selected only 100 samples in this way 4 *crisis*, 11 *red*, 26 *amber*, and 59 *green*. In our experimentation with the 8-fold cross-validation of the training set, including the samples found by self-training improved the f1-macro average of our system by 0.12. It also helped to extend the vocabulary of some of the words not present in the training samples.

5   Results

In this section, we present the results of our system. We used two baseline systems. The first baseline consists of random assignment of labels with any of the three classes *crisis/red/amber*. The second is a majority class, always predicting *amber*. The first baseline achieves a macro average f1-score of 0.11, and the second system achieves a macro average f1-score of 0.10.

5.1   Official results

Our system results are summarized in Table 5 and Table 4, and the overall official statistics of all the teams submissions are summarized in Table 6. From the precision and recall results of Table 4 we can conclude that our system was balanced in terms of achieving a similar precision and recall for each one of the classes. The system incorrectly assigned three posts a *crisis* label and was not able to predict the only *crisis* post present in the test data. This post in particular contained vocabulary not seen in the training set, which made it difficult for our system to detect it correctly, instead our system assigned it a *red* label.

Our system performed a little above the median of all the team best scores with a 0.34 official score. Our system would require an increase 0.08 in the f1-average-macro to score as the best participant. In the non-*green* vs. *green* macro f-score and the non-*green* vs. *green* accuracy we performed above the median

label	precision	recall	f1-score
crisis	0.00 (0/3)	0.00 (0/1)	0.00
red	0.46 (11/24)	0.41 (11/27)	0.43
amber	0.53 (30/57)	0.64 (30/47)	0.58

Table 4: Precision, recall, and f1-score of our system for the three classes used for the official score.

Measurement	Our Score
official score (f1-macro)	**0.34**
accuracy	0.77
non-*green* vs. *green* macro f-score	0.79
non-*green* vs. *green* accuracy	0.86
random *crisis/red/amber* (f1-macro)	0.11
all *amber* (f1-macro)	0.10

Table 5: Official results of our system together with baseline 1 and 2

Measurement	min.	max.	median of team bests
official score (f1-macro)	**0.13**	**0.42**	**0.335**
accuracy	0.42	0.85	0.775
non-*green* vs. *green* macro f-score	0.58	0.87	0.77
non-*green* vs. *green* accuracy	0.60	0.91	0.85

Table 6: Official statistics of the overall results

of the team bests. It is important to mention that the selected metric is very sensitive to the *crisis* label. If the *crisis* post was labeled correctly, the official score would have increased to around 0.50.

5.2   Analysis and discussion

The most difficult part of the shared task was the highly skewed distribution of the training samples. The smallest class, *crisis*, has 39 samples and the largest class, *green*, has more than 500 samples. We assumed the distribution of each class to be representative of the distribution of the whole population. If more information can be known a priori about the class distribution, our system could be adjusted to model such a distribution. During the cross-validation study of the training samples, we found that distinguishing between the *red* and the *crisis* class was the most challenging part of the problem.

We found that sometimes even for a human it is difficult to distinguish between one or the other, given the informal language used in the online posts.

In order to understand the types of posts present in the unlabeled data, we ran our self-training algorithm multiple times to understand how it will be biased towards the classes and to get familiar with data. We found that in the forum there were some particular threads where users tend to post very negative posts. We found that many of the posts in this thread were either *crisis* or *red*. We performed a study to replace the given training sample with some of these posts and study the mean performance in an 8-fold cross validation. We found that the performance was lower. In particular, those posts were structured in a specific way, people will post something very positive, followed by something very negative. This structure of the post was very challenging for our system. Either the posts were assigned to *green* or *crisis* label depending on the data present in each fold of the cross-validation iteration.

From the gold data, we could see that most of the errors of our system were due to new vocabulary not present in the training set. We tried to account for this with the use of a smoothing parameter in the classifier but more work is needed in this respect. One way could be to train a word embedding using the unlabeled data in such a way that semantic similarities of words not present in the training samples can be modeled in the test set.

6   Related work

In the previous versions of the workshop some systems have been proposed to solve similar challenging problems using some or similar features to the ones we used in our system. In (Mitchell et al., 2015) a system was developed for quantifying the language of schizophrenia in social media based on the LIWC lexicon. This study also showed that character n-grams over specific tweets in the user's history can be used to separate schizophrenia sufferers from a control group. In (Pedersen, 2015) a system based on decision lists was developed to identify Twitter users who suffer from Depression or Post Traumatic Stress Disorder (PTSD). The features in this system are based on n-grams of up to 6 words. In this system, the usage of larger n-grams performed better than bigrams. In our experiments, we only tried with n-grams up to length 3 and found that the best performing system in the cross-validation of the training data was obtained using bigrams.

7   Conclusion

In this paper, we have briefly described our submission to the CLPsych 2016 shared task. We found that the best result was achieved when the number of label samples was expanded by using a self-training approach. We also saw that the performance of the system degraded when some challenging posts with both very positive and negative information were included. We also used a method for parameter tuning that accelerated our experimentation significantly as compared with the exhaustive grid search algorithm and we expect this to be useful for other researchers in the field.

In future work, we plan to study the use the unlabeled data to extend the vocabulary and in this way help us model words not present in the training sample. We also plan to do a more exhaustive experimentation on different algorithms to label the unlabeled data to increase the amount of training data used to train our system. Finally, we expect to study in more detail how the pattern of posts over a period of time can be used to predict the likelihood of a user to post a *crisis* or *red* kind of post.

Acknowledgments

We thank the organizers of this shared task for their effort towards building a community able to solve this challenging problem.

References

Margaret Mitchell, Kristy Hollingshead, and Glen Coppersmith. 2015. Quantifying the Language of Schizophrenia in Social Media. In *Proceedings of the 2nd Workshop on Computational Linguistics and Clinical Psychology: From Linguistic Signal to Clinical Reality*, pages 11–20. North American Chapter of the Association for Computational Linguistics.

Kamal Nigam, Andrew McCallum, Sebastian Thrun, and Tom Mitchell. 1998. Learning to classify text from labeled and unlabeled documents. In *Proceedings of the Fifteenth National Conference on Artificial Intelligence*, page 792799.

Ted Pedersen. 2015. Screening Twitter Users for Depression and PTSD with Lexical Decision Lists. In *Proceedings of the Workshop on Computational Linguistics and Clinical Psychology: From Linguistic Signal to Clinical Reality*, pages 46–53. North American Chapter of the Association for Computational Linguistics.

Fabian Pedregosa, Olivier Grisel, Ron Weiss, Alexandre Passos, and Matthieu Brucher. 2011. Scikit-learn : Machine Learning in Python. *The Journal of Machine Learning Research*, 12:2825–2830.

James W Pennebaker, Cindy K Chung, Molly Ireland, Amy Gonzales, and Roger J Booth. 2007. *The Development and Psychometric Properties of LIWC2007 The University of Texas at Austin*.

Combining Multiple Classifiers Using Global Ranking for ReachOut.com Post Triage

Chen-Kai Wang[1], Hong-Jie Dai[1*], Chih-Wei Chen[2], Jitendra Jonnagaddala[3] and Nai-Wen Chang[4]

[1]Department of Computer Science and Information Engineering, National Taitung University, Taitung, Taiwan
[2]Graduate Institute of Biomedical Informatics, College of Medical Science and Technology, Taipei Medical University, Taiwan
[3]School of Public Health and Community Medicine, University of New South Wales, Sydney, Australia
[4]Graduate Institute of Biomedical Electronics and Bioinformatics, National Taiwan University, Taipei, Taiwan

Abstract

In this paper, we present our methods for the 2016 CLPPsych shared task. We extracted and selected eight features from the corpus consisting of posts from ReachOut.com including the information of the post's source board, numbers of kudos and views, post time, ranks of the authors, unigram of the body and subject, frequency of the used emotion icons, and the topic model features. Two support vector machine models were trained with the extracted features. A baseline system was also developed, which uses the calculated log likelihood ratio (LLR) for each token to rank a post. Finally, the prediction results of the above three systems were integrated by using a global ranking algorithm with the weighted Borda-fuse (WBF) model and the linear combination model. The best F-score achieved by our systems is 0.3 which is based on the global ranking method with WBF.

1 Introduction

The Internet and the WWW (World Wide Web) provide ubiquitous access to the information all around the world, drastically remodeling how humans acquaint facts, comprehend knowledge and communicate with others. For example, at online health communities, patients and their close persons learn diseases and gain insights, seek and offer helps and supports, and become familiar with others with similar conditions (Neal et al., 2006). Physicians and other medical professionals also involves online health communities through content sites, web forums, social media, or other means, providing advices and services (Guseh et al., 2009).

Online board moderators save psychiatric patients from emotional distresses and suicidal attempts (Barak 2007). With proper modulation, even previous self-harm patients become altruistic board members and helpers (Smithson et al., 2011). However, some unmodulated online forums may contain improper posts and messages, influencing and guiding patients' judgements and behaviors in deviant ways. Some self-harm victims report learned behaviors from online forums (Dunlop et al., 2011).

As the messages at online forums are numerous, manual evaluations and responses by broad modulators become tedious and helps may be delayed. With the advances in natural language processing

---

* Corresponding author.

Proceedings of the 3rd Workshop on Computational Linguistics and Clinical Psychology: From Linguistic Signal to Clinical Reality, pages 176–179,
San Diego, California, June 16, 2016. ©2016 Association for Computational Linguistics

(NLP), automatic text categorization become possible and might be integrated into the code base of online forums to assist modulators. The third annual computational linguistics and clinical psychology (CLPsych) workshop, held by Association for Computational Linguistics, focus on language technology applications in mental and neurological health. As a participant of the 2016 CLPPsych shared task, we develop a NLP system to automatically classify posts from ReachOut.com mental health forum into one of the red/amber/green/crisis semaphore that indicates how urgently a post needs moderator attention.

2 Methods

The input of our system is the ReachOut.com forum posts represented in the XML format. The following features are extracted from the structural content and selected by the information gain algorithm using tenfold cross validation (CV) on the training set.

1. Source board: The link of the board contains the post, such as "/boards/id/Something_Not_Right", and "/boards/id/Tough-Times_Hosted_chats" is extracted as a nominal feature.

2. Kudos: The number of kudos (equivalent of up-vote) given to a post is extracted as a numeric feature.

3. Post and the last edit time: The creation and the most recent edit timestamp for the post. In this work, the value was equally discretized into 24 distinct ranges and encoded as a nominal feature to indicate a certain hour of a day.

4. Views: The number of times the post has been viewed is extracted as a numeric feature.

5. Rank of the author: The rank, such as "Mod Squad", and "Frequent scribe", of the author of the post in the forum was extracted and encoded as a nominal feature.

6. Subject and body: The text of the post's subject and the body of the post were extracted.

Because the content of the body includes escaped HTML tags, Apache Tika[1] was used to extract all of the plain texts from these HTML tags. Twokenizer (Owoputi et al., 2013) was then used to tokenize the extracted texts. Finally, the normalization process proposed by Lin et al. (2015) was used to normalize all tokens. The unigrams of the normalized texts from both the subject and body were extracted as features.

7. Emotion icon frequency: Based on all of the extract body contents, twelve emotion icon types used in the forum were observed, which include "Happy", "VeryHappy", "Tongue", "Embarassed", "Frustrated", "Wink", "Surprised", "Heart" "LOL", "Indifferent" and "Mad". The frequencies of the occurrences of the above icons were determined by parsing the body content for each post.

8. Topic model: The features were produced in two steps. The first step was to train a topic model using the training set and the second step was to use the trained model to generate features. The type of topic modelling features extracted in this study include (1) the topic distribution weights per instance and (2) the binary features to represent the presence of a keyword term (obtained from the topics generated) in a given instance. Above features were created by using Stanford topic modeling toolbox[2].

The extracted features trained with the support vector machine (SVM) (Cortes et al., 1995). Two SVM models were created. One used features one to seven and the other used all eight features. In addition to the supervised learning method, a baseline system based on the log likelihood ratio (LLR) was developed. In this system, we ranked the tokens observed in the training dataset based on their values calculated by using LLR and selected the tokens with positive values to compile a keyword list for each triage label. The compiled lists were then used to rank a given post. The triage label with the highest LLR value is selected as the output for the post.

---

[1] https://tika.apache.org
[2] http://nlp.stanford.edu/software/tmt/tmt-0.4/

Run	Official F-score	Accuracy
1	0.29	0.76
2	0.26	0.63
3	0.22	0.66
4	0.3	0.73
5	0.28	0.69

Table 1: Official F-score and accuracy of the submitted runs.

Run	Non-green vs. green macro F-score	Non-green vs. green accuracy
1	0.8	0.87
2	0.66	0.74
3	0.62	0.76
4	0.76	0.83
5	0.69	0.79

Table 2: Non-green vs. green F-score and accuracy of the submitted runs.

Finally, we merge all results of above three systems by using a global ranking method based on two data fusion algorithms (Dai et al., 2010). First of all, the outputs of all three systems were collected and their performance on the tenfold CV training set were determined. The simple weighting scheme based on the weighted Borda-fuse (WBF) model was employed, which multiply the points assigned to a semaphore determined by a system by the F-score of that system. The second fusion algorithm is the linear combination (LC) model which multiplies the predictions probability of a semaphore determined a system by the F-score of that system.

3   Results

We submitted five runs. Both the first and the second runs are based on SVM. As mentioned in the Methods section, the first run includes features one to seven, while the second run further adds the topic model feature. The third run is the baseline system based on LLR. The fourth and fifth runs are created by using the global ranking method with WBF and LC, respectively. Table 1 and 2 shows the results of the submitted runs.

As shown in Table 1, the best run of our system achieves an F-score of 0.3, which is based on the global ranking with WBF. The second best run is the SVM model w/o topic model features. However, the difference between the two runs may not be significant.

4   Discussion

Here we only focus on the comparison between the run 1 and 2. A manual inspection of the keyword terms within the topics generated from the training set shows that the topics didn't quite capture the themes correctly, as the words within the topic don't belong to a particular theme. For example, if we see the top keyword terms within the topics for 4-topic model, negative sentiment is not captured effectively though the dataset had several negative sentiment themed topics. In addition, words which stand for positive and negative sentiments are grouped under the same topic. Also, the analysis of the document topic distribution shows that in almost all the instances, one particular topic is having the most weight, making it hard for our classifier to discriminate themes and sentiments.

5   Conclusion

This work selected eight features and studied their impact for the triage task of ReachOut.com posts. The global ranking algorithm is then used to combine the generated results from three systems. In the future work, we consider to apply ensemble classifiers and compare the results with the ranking-based method.

References

Azy Barak. 2007. *Emotional support and suicide prevention through the Internet: A field project report*, Computers in Human Behavior 23(2): 971-984.

Corinna Cortes and Vladimir Vapnik. 1995. *Support-vector networks*, Machine Learning 20(3): 273-297.

Hong-Jie Dai, Po-Ting Lai, Richard Tzong-Han Tsai and Wen Lian Hsu. 2010. *Global Ranking via Data Fusion*, Proceedings of the 23rd International Conference on Computational Linguistics. Beijing, China, 223-231.

Sally M. Dunlop, Eian More and Daniel Romer Dunlop. 2011. *Where do youth learn about suicides on the Internet, and what influence does this have on suicidal ideation?*, Journal of Child Psychology and Psychiatry 52(10): 1073-1080.

James S. Guseh, Rebecca W. Brendel and D. H. Brendel 2009. *Medical professionalism in the age of online social networking*, Journal of Medical Ethics 35(9): 584-586.

Wei-San Lin, Hong-Jie Dai, Jitendra Jonnagaddala, Nai-Wun Chang, Toni Rose Jue, Usman Iqbal, Joni Yu-Hsuan Shao, I-Jen Chiang and Yu-Chuan Li Lin. 2015. *Utilizing Different Word Representation Methods for*

Twitter Data in Adverse Drug Reactions Extraction, Proceedings of the 2015 Conference on Technologies and Applications of Artificial Intelligence (TAAI). Tainan, IEEE: 260-265.

Lisa Neal, Gitte Lindgaard, Kate Oakley, Derek Hansen, Sandra Kogan, Jan Marco Leimeister, and Ted Selker. 2006. *Online health communities*, CHI '06 Extended Abstracts on Human Factors in Computing Systems. ACM: 444-447.

Olutobi Owoputi, Brendan O'Connor, Chris Dyer, Kevin Gimpel, Nathan Schneider, and Noah A. Smith. 2013. *Improved part-of-speech tagging for online conversational text with word clusters*, Proceedings of the Conference of the North American Chapter of the Association for Computational Linguistics, Association for Computational Linguistics.

Janet Smithson, Siobhan Sharkey, Hewis Elaine, Ray B Jones, Tobit Emmens, Tamsin Ford and Christabel Owens. 2011. *Membership and Boundary Maintenance on an Online Self-Harm Forum*, Qualitative Health Research.

Classification of mental health forum posts

Glen Pink [†]   **Will Radford** [‡]   **Ben Hachey** [†]
[†]ə-lab, School of Information Technologies   [‡]Hugo Australia
University of Sydney   58-62 Kippax Street
NSW 2006, Australia   NSW 2010, Australia

{glen.pink,ben.hachey}@sydney.edu.au
wradford@hugo.ai

Abstract

We detail our approach to the CLPsych 2016 triage of mental health forum posts shared task. We experiment with a number of features in a logistic regression classification approach. Our baseline approach with lexical features from a post and previous posts in the reply chain gives our best performance of 0.33, which is roughly the median for the task.

1 Introduction

The CLPsych 2016 shared task requires the triage of forum posts from the ReachOut.com forums, a support forum for youth mental health issues. The triage task centres on directing forum moderators to posts which required the most immediate attention (Calvo et al., 2016). For this task, a set of posts from the forum are each annotated with one of the labels *crisis*, *red*, *amber* or *green*, which indicate decreasing degrees of urgency of moderator addition. All unlabelled posts are made available for systems.

This task follows other studies of social media discourse as it relates to clinical psychology (Thompson et al., 2014; Schwartz et al., 2014; Coppersmith et al., 2015; Schrading et al., 2015). Analysis of ReachOut.com posts is interesting as posts are made by young individuals who have originally come to the forum seeking some kind of help, but over time may participate in several different capacities. Typically most users will initially need support, but this need may substantially increase or decrease over time; users may also support each other or use the forums for activity unrelated to mental health.

Our approach to this task was primarily focussed on implementing a straightforward baseline and experimenting with a few ideas derived from experience looking at the data in detail. While the data itself is definitely sequenced, we choose not to model this as a sequence problem, primarily because we expect the meaningful sequences to be fairly short: typically users either create new posts that are generally relevant to the original post in a thread, or reply to a specific post.

We further motivate this local post comparison by considering the annotation flowchart distributed with the data. Many labelling decisions are affected by whether the user's state is considered to be the same, or if their condition has gotten worse. Key to this task is capturing change in author language, and identifying how this reflects a change in their state-of-mind and change of condition.

We implement a feature set based on basic post features and author history and thread context, using the sequence of replies that lead to a post as the context for that post. We experiment with a number of additional features, but our baseline approach provides our best result of 0.33, which puts our performance at the median overall.

2 Features

We make use of post lexical features, author history and thread history for classification.

2.1 Preprocessing

Prior to extracting features, we perform some basic preprocessing on post text. We unescape HTML entities, remove images and replace emoticons with the

Proceedings of the 3rd Workshop on Computational Linguistics and Clinical Psychology: From Linguistic Signal to Clinical Reality, pages 180–182,
San Diego, California, June 16, 2016. ©2016 Association for Computational Linguistics

name of the emoticon to simplify processing. We remove blockquotes entirely, as we want extracted features to be from the content of the current post. We tokenise using the NLTK TweetTokenizer, as we expect the web forum text to be fairly casual and similiar to the Twitter domain for the purposes of tokenisation.

2.2 Lexical features

We extract unigrams and bigrams as post features, and continue to use this feature space for the below contexts.

2.3 Reply chain features

Instead of using the sequence of posts in a thread as context, we make use of the chain of replies to a post as the context for that post. We make use of two posts in that context: the most recent post before the current post that has the same author as the current post, and the most recent post to the current post. We retrieve unigrams and bigrams for these posts. We then extract three different types of features: the intersection of unigrams and bigrams with the current post; those that occur in the current post but not the previous post; and those that occur in the previous post but not the current. Note that there are separate feature spaces for author posts and non-author posts.

2.4 Unused features

We experimented with a number of features which did not improve results. These include use of n-gramfeatures from the first post in thread of the post; use of lemmas instead of words; cosine similarity between post bag-of-words; and thread type. We manually identify these thread types for threads which have a substantially different structure to others, such as the Turning Negatives Into Positives and TwittRO. We identify 1 post as `game`, 2 as `media` (e.g. image threads), 5 as `semi-structured` and 5 as `short` (e.g. TwittRO).

3 Data and training

The released training corpus contains 65,024 posts, 947 of which are annotated with triage labels. For development, we split this into a train set of 797 posts and a development set of 250 posts. We use a scikit-learn logistic regression classifier, using a grid search over a regularization hyperparameters

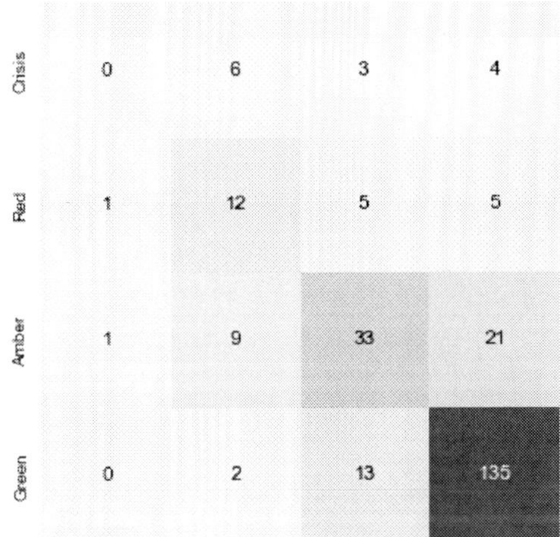

Figure 1: Confusion matrix on the development data.

Label	Precision	Recall	F-score
macro-avg	0.42	0.41	0.42
crisis	0.00 (0/0)	0.00 (0/13)	0.00
red	0.58 (14/24)	0.61 (14/23)	0.60
amber	0.68 (40/59)	0.62 (40/64)	0.65

Table 1: Final scores for run 1 settings on development data.

over 10-fold cross validation over the train set. Results on development data in Table 1. Figure 1 shows the confusion matrix, including green classifications. We note that a large number of confusions happen between amber and green, largely due to their larger representation in the data. For the full task we use the full 947 posts for training. The test set adds an additional 731 posts.

We experimented with using a cascaded classification approach, classifying crisis v. non-crisis, red v. non-red and amber v. non-amber in sequence, however this approach did not perform well. We also experimented with treating the task as a regression task, mapping *crisis* to a value of 1.0, *red* to 0.66, *amber* to 0.33, and *green* to 0.0. The idea is that we expect there to be a gradient to post severity rather than a distinct underlying set of 4 labels, and this gradient may be better modelled via a regression approach. Our implementation has lower results than our approach using discrete labels, but we consider this to be a possible direction for future approaches to this task.

run	score	accuracy	ngvg	ngvg accuracy
1	0.33	0.78	0.73	0.85
2	0.32	0.76	0.72	0.83

Table 2: Official results. *ngvg is non-green vs green.*

Label	Precision	Recall	F-score
crisis	0.00 (0/0)	0.00 (0/1)	0.00
red	0.61 (11/18)	0.41 (11/27)	0.49
amber	0.50 (23/46)	0.49 (23/47)	0.49

Table 3: Run 1 per-label scores.

4 Results

We submit two runs, for both L2 (run 1, with regularisation parameter $C = 1$) and L1 (run 2, with regularisation parameter $C = 100$) regularisation. Our official results are in Table 2, with per-label breakdowns of each run in Tables 3 and 4.

While other labellings fall outside the official metric for the shared task, we are interested in the performance of a system trained on only *non-green* vs *green* as opposed to all 4 triage labels. We run this configuration with the same settings as run 1. This configuration has an F-score of 0.80 on our development data, and a score of 0.82, which above our multiple label F-score of 0.73. This may be a useful setup for a two-stage classification or an actual implementation for ReachOut.com moderators.

5 Discussion

Run 1 performs at the median, and may be an informative baseline. Interestingly, many of the features that we explored decreased or did not significantly improve performance. This is possibly due to feature sparsity: the amount of training data is relatively small, and most of these features likely are not informative. We note that L2 regularisation gives our best performance, the data set is small, and L2 keeping more features from the training data helps compensate for feature sparsity better than L1 regularisation.

Notably, both of our runs returned very few crisis

label	Precision	Recall	F-score
crisis	0.00 (0/0)	0.00 (0/1)	0.00
red	0.52 (11/21)	0.41 (11/27)	0.46
amber	0.50 (23/46)	0.49 (23/47)	0.49

Table 4: Run 2 per-label scores.

labellings: both returned 1 labelling which was incorrect. This is somewhat surprising, particularly as a label F-score of 0% is particularly penalised with a macro-averaged metric, however given the lack of instances for training this is not unreasonable.

6 Conclusion

We participated in the CLPsych 2016 shared task, providing a baseline approach using a small feature set that gave a near-median performance of 0.33. We look forward to continuing to work on this task.

References

Rafael A Calvo, M Sazzad Hussain, Kjartan Nordbo, Ian Hickie, David Milne, and P Danckwerts. 2016. Augmenting Online Mental Health Support Services. *Integrating Technology in Positive Psychology Practice*, page 82.

Glen Coppersmith, Mark Dredze, Craig Harman, Kristy Hollingshead, and Margaret Mitchell. 2015. CLPsych 2015 Shared Task: Depression and PTSD on Twitter. In *Proceedings of the 2nd Workshop on Computational Linguistics and Clinical Psychology: From Linguistic Signal to Clinical Reality*, pages 31–39, Denver, Colorado, June 5. Association for Computational Linguistics.

Nicolas Schrading, Cecilia Ovesdotter Alm, Ray Ptucha, and Christopher Homan. 2015. An Analysis of Domestic Abuse Discourse on Reddit. In *Proceedings of the 2015 Conference on Empirical Methods in Natural Language Processing*, pages 2577–2583, Lisbon, Portugal, September. Association for Computational Linguistics.

H. Andrew Schwartz, Johannes Eichstaedt, Margaret L. Kern, Gregory Park, Maarten Sap, David Stillwell, Michal Kosinski, and Lyle Ungar. 2014. Towards Assessing Changes in Degree of Depression through Facebook. In *Proceedings of the Workshop on Computational Linguistics and Clinical Psychology: From Linguistic Signal to Clinical Reality*, pages 118–125, Baltimore, Maryland, USA, June. Association for Computational Linguistics.

Paul Thompson, Craig Bryan, and Chris Poulin. 2014. Predicting military and veteran suicide risk: Cultural aspects. In *Proceedings of the Workshop on Computational Linguistics and Clinical Psychology: From Linguistic Signal to Clinical Reality*, pages 1–6, Baltimore, Maryland, USA, June. Association for Computational Linguistics.

Automatic Triage of Mental Health Online Forum Posts
CLPsych 2016 System Description

Hayda Almeida
Concordia University
Montreal, QC, Canada

Marc Queudot
Université du Québec à Montréal
Montreal, QC, Canada

Marie-Jean Meurs
Université du Québec à Montréal
Montreal, QC, Canada
meurs.marie-jean@uqam.ca

Abstract

This paper presents a system capable of performing automatic triage of forum posts from ReachOut.com, a mental health online forum. The system assigns to each post a tag that indicates how urgently moderator attention is needed. The evaluation is based on experiments conducted on the CLPsych 2016 task, and the system is released as an open-source software.

1 Introduction

This paper describes a system that was presented at the CLPsych Shared Task 2016[1]. The goal of the task is to perform automatic triage of user posts gathered from the ReachOut.com mental health online forum[2]. Posts must be classified into four categories (green, amber, red, and crisis), which indicate how urgently any intervention from forum moderators is required. The automatic triage of ReachOut forum posts is a challenging task. First, the targeted documents - from the amber, red, and crisis classes - are highly underrepresented in the data to be analyzed. Second, forum post content can be highly noisy, since posts commonly present symbols, emoticons, pictures, and mispelled words.

The objective of an automatic triage of ReachOut posts is to allow forum moderators to quickly identify posts that require urgent intervention. Posts labeled as red or crisis could indicate an imminent dangerous or harmful condition, for example, an author that suggests a possibility of self-harm.

To handle the task of ReachOut post automatic triage, we propose a system relying on the combination of two text classification techniques, namely supervised learning and rule-based classification. Our experiments are performed utilizing three classification algorithms, and classification rules designed based on discriminative vocabularies selected from documents of the minority classes. In addition, we studied the use of different feature types and subsets.

This paper is organized as follows: Section 2 describes some related works while Section 3 provides details about our approach, and the system architecture. Experiments and results are reported in Section 4, and we conclude in Section 5.

2 Related Work

The automatic triage of documents can be used to support a variety of data handling processes. It supports professionals and researchers working in the medical (Tuarob et al., 2014; Almeida et al., 2015) or biological fields (Almeida et al., 2014). Data gathered from forum posts have been used in several related classification tasks. In (Huh et al., 2013), the triage supports patients handling several health conditions, while it was used to identify mental health issues in (Saleem et al., 2012), and to recognize user sentiments in (Thelwall et al., 2012).

Designing efficient automatic approaches for textual data triage can be challenging, especially when documents of interest represent a very small part of the entire dataset. Machine learning approaches are impacted by the class distribution, and many classifiers do not perform well in unbalanced contexts. Support Vector Machines (SVM) (Vapnik,

---

[1] http://clpsych.org/shared-task-2016/
[2] http://au.reachout.com/

183

Proceedings of the 3rd Workshop on Computational Linguistics and Clinical Psychology: From Linguistic Signal to Clinical Reality, pages 183–187,
San Diego, California, June 16, 2016. ©2016 Association for Computational Linguistics

1995) were previously utilized in forum post triage handling mental health subjects (Saleem et al., 2012). Models using Sequential Minimal Optimization (SMO) (Platt, 1998) for optimizing SVM, were applied to perform sentiment analysis in forum data, outperforming other methods when used on large datasets (Thelwall et al., 2012). Logistic Model Trees (LMT) (Landwehr et al., 2005) were shown to outperform other classification algorithms in tasks that handle (highly) imbalanced data (Charton et al., 2013; Almeida et al., 2014). Previous studies have combined rule-based and supervised classification approaches to handle forum posts (Saleem et al., 2012), patients medical records (Xu et al., 2012), or sentiment in social media (Chikersal et al.,). In these works, combined strategies usually obtained better performance compared to supervised only or rule-based only approaches.

The use of lexical features, such as n-grams, Part-Of-Speech (POS) tags, and lemmas, as well as sentiment dictionaries, were shown to perform well in tasks handling forum posts (Biyani et al., 2014), and mining sentiments or opinion (Thelwall et al., 2012). Feature selection methods have been studied to choose relevant attribute subsets (Liu et al., 2010; Basu and Murthy, 2012). Among these methods, Correlation-based Feature Selection (CFS) selects a subset of attributes that are *highly correlated with the class, yet uncorrelated with each other* (Hall, 1999). Methods to determine relevant vocabulary for specific class labels were previously studied (Melville et al., 2009; Charton et al., 2013). Melville et al. (2009) built a discriminative vocabulary to represent sentiment polarity, while Charton et al. (2013) used one to represent minority classes. In both cases, the use of discriminative vocabularies in the classification models improved performance.

3 Methodology

To tackle the task of automatic triage of forum posts, the proposed system combines rule-based and machine learning based classification. Our approach makes use of several feature types, such as n-grams, POS tags, and a sentiment dictionary generated from two sentiment libraries. Various features subsets were filtered using the CFS feature selection method. In the following sections we explain with more details the system pipeline, and the methods

| | Training | | Test | |
Class	# posts	ratio (%)	# posts	ratio (%)
Green	549	57.49	166	68.88
Amber	249	26.30	47	19.50
Red	110	11.61	27	11.20
Crisis	39	4.18	1	0.42
Total	947	100	241	100

Table 1: Statistics on the CLPsych Shared Task 2016 dataset

utilized in each step.

3.1 CLPsych Dataset

The CLPsych corpus consists of 65024 publicly available posts gathered from the ReachOut forum, which have been posted between July 2012 and May 2015. Among these posts, 1188 posts were manually annotated with class labels, then split into a training and a test set. The training set is composed of 947 posts while the test set contains 241 posts. The class distribution on the training and the test data is shown in Table 1.

3.2 Feature Extraction and Selection

Prior to performing feature extraction, the forum posts were pre-processed by normalization procedures, which included normalizing HTML characters, symbols, punctuation, smiley pictures, and smiley symbols. Each smiley was replaced by a corresponding word extracted either from the picture URL, or from a concise mapping containing the smiley textual meaning (e.g., `:)` or `=]` or `:D` are all replaced by `happy`). The features used in our experiments were of type bigrams, POS tags, and sentiments. Extraction of POS tags was performed using the POSTaggerAnnotator from the Stanford CoreNLP suite (Manning et al., 2014). POS features are composed of forum post words annotated with discriminative POS tags, which were adjective (JJ*), nouns (NN*), predeterminer (PDT), particle (RP), and verbs (VB*). The selection of discriminative POS tags was based on experimental results. Sentiment features are dataset lemmas found within a sentiment dictionary. The dataset lemmas were extracted using the Stanford CoreNLP suite. We built a sentiment dictionary based on a list of feeling words used in mental status exams (see `http://psychpage.com/learning/library/assess/feelings.html`), and a conceptual feature

Feature type	# features	# CFS features
Bigrams	35,442	73
POS	5,828	43
Sentiments	2,387	45

Table 2: Number of unique features in CLPsych dataset

map from SenticNet (Cambria et al., 2014). Stop-words were not removed from the data, since they seem to carry relevant discriminative power for the task, as previously demonstrated by (Saif et al., 2014). All feature lists were separately filtered by the CFS method. Feature distributions by type before and after CFS filtering are reported in Table 2.

3.3 Classification Algorithms

We performed experiments utilizing three classification algorithms: Bayesian Network (BN) (Pearl, 1988), SMO, and LMT. A BN is a probabilistic directed acyclic graph, in which nodes are random variables with arcs representing their conditional dependencies. BN was used as a baseline classifier. SMO-SVM were previously applied in similar tasks as described in Section 2. SMO (Platt, 1998) is an optimization algorithm for training SVMs. SMO is an iterative algorithm that solves the quadratic programming problem of SVM training by breaking it into smaller sub-problems easier to solve. As described in Section 2, LMT previously demonstrated good performance in classification tasks on imbalanced datasets. LMT is an algorithm that produces decision trees with linear logistic models at the leaves.

3.4 Discriminative Vocabulary Rules

For the red and the crisis classes, a discriminative vocabulary was utilized to develop classification rules. The discriminative vocabulary was extracted from red and crisis labeled documents. The extraction of the discriminative vocabulary was implemented with the approach described in (Charton et al., 2013). The relative frequency of each word is computed for each class. Then, the average difference of word frequencies between the red/crisis classes and the green and amber classes is computed. Each word for which the average difference is above an experimentally set threshold is added to the discriminative vocabulary of a given class. After defining the discriminative vocabularies for the red

model	LMT & rules (5 words)		
class	Precision	Recall	F-measure
crisis	0.22 (15/69)	0.38 (15/39)	0.28
red	0.24 (36/150)	0.33 (36/110)	0.28
amber	0.26 (51/196)	0.20 (51/249)	0.23
accuracy	0.45		
macro-averaged F-score	0.26		
model	SMO & rules (5 words)		
class	Precision	Recall	F-measure
crisis	0.25 (14/56)	0.36 (14/39)	0.29
red	0.24 (33/136)	0.30 (33/110)	0.27
amber	0.25 (51/169)	0.17 (42/249)	0.20
accuracy	0.47		
macro-averaged F-score	0.25		
model	BN		
class	Precision	Recall	F-measure
crisis	0.08 (2/26)	0.05 (2/39)	0.06
red	0.09 (9/98)	0.08 (9/110)	0.09
amber	0.27 (55/205)	0.22 (55/249)	0.24
accuracy	0.44		
macro-averaged F-score	0.13		

Table 3: Results obtained on training set

and the crisis classes, we utilized up to the five best ranked vocabulary terms to build classification rules based on the appearance of these words in a forum post. The rules were applied on top of the predictions made by the supervised classifiers.

4 Experiments and Results

We performed a set of experiments to evaluate the usage of different classifiers, feature sets (combining different feature types), as well as the use of CFS, and finally the integration of classification rules to the supervised approach. The system pipeline is implemented as follows:

1. Dataset pre-processing and normalization

2. POS and lemma annotation

3. Feature extraction (POS tags, bigrams, sentiments)

4. CFS filtering of feature sets

5. Generation of documents versus features matrix using selected feature subsets

6. Output of predictions by machine learning based classifiers

7. Re-evaluation of predictions using classification rules

Run 1	model	LMT & rules (5 words)	
class	Precision	Recall	F-measure
crisis	0.00 (0/10)	0.00 (0/1)	0.00
red	0.33 (8/24)	0.30 (8/27)	0.31
amber	0.49 (20/41)	0.43 (20/47)	0.45
accuracy	0.72		
macro-averaged F-score	0.26		

Run 2	model	LMT & rules (3 words)	
class	Precision	Recall	F-measure
crisis	0.00 (0/9)	0.00 (0/1)	0.00
red	0.36 (9/25)	0.33 (9/27)	0.35
amber	0.49 (20/41)	0.43 (20/47)	0.45
accuracy	0.72		
macro-averaged F-score	0.27		

Run 3	model	SMO & rules (5 words)	
class	Precision	Recall	F-measure
crisis	0.00 (0/8)	0.00 (0/1)	0.00
red	0.43 (10/13)	0.37 (10/27)	0.40
amber	0.59 (19/32)	0.40 (19/47)	0.48
accuracy	0.74		
macro-averaged F-score	0.29		

Run 4	model	LMT only	
class	Precision	Recall	F-measure
crisis	0.00 (0/6)	0.00 (0/1)	0.00
red	0.46 (6/13)	0.22 (6/27)	0.30
amber	0.45 (21/47)	0.45 (21/47)	0.45
accuracy	0.75		
macro-averaged F-score	0.25		

Table 4: Results obtained on test set

Our results run	official macro F-m	accuracy	non-green v. green macro F-m	non-green v. green accuracy
run 1	0.26	0.72	0.72	0.83
run 2	0.27	0.72	0.72	0.83
run 3	0.29	0.74	0.68	0.82
run 4	0.25	0.75	0.75	0.85

Table 5: Official results for our system

Overall summary	max	min	median (all runs)	median (team bests)
official score	0.42	0.13	0.32	0.335
accuracy	0.85	0.42	0.77	0.775
non-green v. green macro F-m	0.87	0.58	0.765	0.77
non-green v. green accuracy	0.91	0.60	0.85	0.85

Table 6: Overall summary results for all teams

On the CLPsych training data, the best results were obtained by LMT and SMO algorithms trained on bigrams, sentiment features, and specific POS features. Rule-based classification was applied on the predictions, using a subset of 5 discriminative words from the vocabularies of each red and crisis classes. Table 3 presents the results obtained on the training data while Table 4 shows the results obtained on the test data. We submitted 4 runs using the models that performed best on the training data, namely LMT with and without rules (using 5 or 3 words), and a SMO with rules (5 words). None of our approaches found the unique crisis post present in the test. Posts from the crisis class are indeed the most difficult to find since they are rare, but we also explain this by the difference between crisis ratio in the training set (4.18%) and the test set (0.42%). The system performed consistently on the other classes. Our official results are presented in Table 5, and official results for the 16 teams that participated in the task are provided in Table 6.

5 Conclusion

We presented a system capable of performing automatic triage of forum posts from a mental health online forum. The system assigns to each post a tag that indicates how urgently moderator attention is needed. The evaluation is based on experiments conducted on the CLPsych 2016 task, and the system is available as an open-source software in the following repository: https://github.com/BigMiners/CLPsych2016_Shared_Task

Acknowledgments

The presented system was developed as a Master's student's project. We would like to thank Adrien Appelgren, Antoine Briand, and Sara Zacharie for their contribution.

References

Hayda Almeida, Marie-Jean Meurs, Leila Kosseim, Greg Butler, and Adrian Tsang. 2014. Machine Learning for Biomedical Literature Triage. *PLOS ONE*, 9(12), 12.

Hayda Almeida, Marie-Jean Meurs, Leila Kosseim, and Adrian Tsang. 2015. Supporting HIV Literature Screening with Data Sampling and Supervised Learning. In *Proceedings of IEEE International Conference on Bioinformatics and Biomedicine (BIBM), 2015*, pages 491–496, Washington, USA, November, 2015. IEEE.

Tanmay Basu and C.A. Murthy. 2012. Effective Text Classification by a Supervised Feature Selection Approach. In *Proceedings of the IEEE 12th International Conference on Data Mining Workshops (ICDMW)*, pages 918–925, Brussels, Belgium, December 2012. IEEE.

Prakhar Biyani, Sumit Bhatia, Cornelia Caragea, and Prasenjit Mitra. 2014. Using Non-lexical Features for Identifying Factual and Opinionative Threads in Online Forums. *Knowledge-Based Systems*, 69:170–178.

Erik Cambria, Daniel Olsher, and Dheeraj Rajagopal. 2014. SenticNet 3: a Common and Commonsense Knowledge Base for Cognition-driven Sentiment Analysis. In *28th AAAI conference on artificial intelligence*, Quebec City, Canada, July 2014.

Eric Charton, Marie-Jean Meurs, Ludovic Jean-Louis, and Michel Gagnon. 2013. Using Collaborative Tagging for Text Classification. *Informatics 2014*, pages 32–51.

Prerna Chikersal, Soujanya Poria, and Erik Cambria. SeNTU: Sentiment Analysis of Tweets by Combining a Rule-based Classifier with Supervised Learning. In *Proceedings of the International Workshop on Semantic Evaluation, SemEval*, pages 647–651, Denver, Colorado, June 2015.

Mark Hall. 1999. *Correlation-based Feature Selection for Machine Learning*. Ph.D. thesis, The University of Waikato.

Jina Huh, Meliha Yetisgen-Yildiz, and Wanda Pratt. 2013. Text Classification for Assisting Moderators in Online Health Communities. *Journal of Biomedical Informatics*, 46(6):998–1005.

Niels Landwehr, Mark Hall, and Eibe Frank. 2005. Logistic Model Trees. *Machine Learning*, 59(1-2):161–205.

Huan Liu, Hiroshi Motoda, Rudy Setiono, and Zheng Zhao. 2010. Feature Selection: An Ever Evolving Frontier in Data Mining. In *Proceedings of the 4th Workshop on Feature Selection in Data Mining*, pages 4–13, Hyderabad, India, June 2010.

Christopher D. Manning, Mihai Surdeanu, John Bauer, Jenny Finkel, Steven J. Bethard, and David McClosky. 2014. The Stanford CoreNLP Natural Language Processing Toolkit. In *Association for Computational Linguistics (ACL) System Demonstrations*, pages 55–60.

Prem Melville, Wojciech Gryc, and Richard D. Lawrence. 2009. Sentiment Analysis of Blogs by Combining Lexical Knowledge with Text Classification. In *Proceedings of the 15th ACM SIGKDD International Conference on Knowledge Discovery and Data Mining*, KDD '09, pages 1275–1284, New York, NY, USA. ACM.

Judea Pearl. 1988. *Probabilistic Reasoning in Intelligent Systems: Networks of Plausible Inference*. Morgan Kaufmann.

John Platt. 1998. Sequential Minimal Optimization: a Fast Algorithm for Training Support Vector Machines. *Microsoft Research Technical Report MSR-TR-98-14*, April 1998.

Hassan Saif, Miriam Fernández, Yulan He, and Harith Alani. 2014. On Stopwords, Filtering and Data Sparsity for Sentiment Analysis of Twitter. In *Proceedings of 9th of the Language Resources and Evaluation Conference (LREC)*, pages 810–817, Reykjavik, Iceland, May 2014.

Shirin Saleem, Rohit Prasad, Shiv Naga Prasad Vitaladevuni, Maciej Pacula, Michael Crystal, Brian Marx, Denise Sloan, Jennifer Vasterling, and Theodore Speroff. 2012. Automatic Detection of Psychological Distress Indicators and Severity Assessment from Online Forum Posts. In *COLING*, pages 2375–2388.

Mike Thelwall, Kevan Buckley, and Georgios Paltoglou. 2012. Sentiment Strength Detection for the Social Web. *Journal of the American Society for Information Science and Technology*, 63(1):163–173.

Suppawong Tuarob, Conrad S Tucker, Marcel Salathe, and Nilam Ram. 2014. An Ensemble Heterogeneous Classification Methodology for Discovering Health-related Knowledge in Social Media Messages. *Journal of Biomedical Informatics*, 49:255–268.

Vladimir Vapnik. 1995. *The Nature of Statistical Learning Theory*. Springer.

Yan Xu, Kai Hong, Junichi Tsujii, I Eric, and Chao Chang. 2012. Feature Engineering Combined with Machine Learning and Rule-based Methods for Structured Information Extraction from Narrative Clinical Discharge Summaries. *Journal of the American Medical Informatics Association*, 19(5):824–832.

Automatic Triage of Mental Health Forum Posts

Benjamin Shickel and **Parisa Rashidi**
University of Florida
Gainesville, FL
{shickelb, parisa.rashidi}@ufl.edu

Abstract

As part of the 2016 Computational Linguistics and Clinical Psychology (CLPsych) shared task, participants were asked to construct systems to automatically classify mental health forum posts into four categories, representing how urgently posts require moderator attention. This paper details the system implementation from the University of Florida, in which we compare several distinct models and show that best performance is achieved with domain-specific preprocessing, n-gram feature extraction, and cross-validated linear models.

1 Introduction

As more and more social interaction takes place online, the wealth of data provided by these online platforms is proving to be a useful source of information for identifying early warning signs for poor mental health. The goal of 2016 CLPsych shared task was to predict the degree of moderator attention required for posts on the ReachOut forum, an online youth mental health service that provides support to young people aged 14-25.[1]

Along with the analysis of forum-specific meta-information, this task includes aspects of sentiment analysis, the field of study that analyzes people's opinions, sentiments, attitudes, and emotions from written language (Liu, 2012), where several studies have explored the categorization and prediction of user sentiment in social media platforms such as Twitter (Agarwal et al., 2011; Kouloumpis et

[1] https://au.reachout.com/

al., 2011; Spencer and Uchyigit, 2012; Zhang et al., 2011). Other studies have also applied sentiment analysis techniques to MOOC discussion forums (Wen et al., 2014) and suicide notes (Pestian et al., 2012), both highly relevant to this shared task.

Our straightforward approach draws from successful text classification and sentiment analysis methods, including the use of a sentiment lexicon (Liu, 2010) and Word2Vec distributed word embeddings (Mikolov et al., 2013), along with more traditional methods such as normalized n-gram counts. We utilize these linguistic features, as well as several hand-crafted features derived from the meta-information of posts and their authors, to construct logistic regression classifiers for predicting the status label of ReachOut forum posts.

2 Dataset

As part of the shared task, participants were provided a collection of ReachOut forum posts from July 2012 to June 2015. In addition to the textual post content, posts also contained meta-information such as author ID, author rank/affiliation, post time, thread ID, etc. A training set of 947 such posts was provided, each with a corresponding moderator attention label (*green*, *amber*, *red*, or *crisis*). An additional 65,024 unlabeled posts was also provided. The test set consisted of 241 unlabeled forum posts.

3 System

In this section, we describe the implementation details for our classification system. In short, our relatively straightforward approach involves selecting and extracting heterogenrous sets of features for

Proceedings of the 3rd Workshop on Computational Linguistics and Clinical Psychology: From Linguistic Signal to Clinical Reality, pages 188–192,
San Diego, California, June 16, 2016. ©2016 Association for Computational Linguistics

Name	Type	Description
View Count	Numeric	The number of times the post was viewed.
Kudos Count	Numeric	The number of kudos given to the post.
Reply Count	Numeric	The number of posts which were made in reply to the current post.
# Replying Authors	Numeric	The number of unique authors replying to the current post.
Board Name	Categorical	Which of the 25 subforums (boards) the post was made in.
Reply Status	Binary	Whether the current post is a reply or a new post.
Thread Size	Numeric	The number of total posts involved in the current post's thread.
Sibling Count	Numeric	The number of *other* posts replying to the same post that the current post is replying to.
Total Post Count	Numeric	The total number of posts made by the current author.
Total View Count	Numeric	The total number of views for posts made by the current author.
Total Kudos Count	Numeric	The total number of kudos given to posts created by the current author.
Mean View Count	Numeric	The average number of views for posts created by the current author.
Mean Kudos Count	Numeric	The mean number of kudos given to posts created by the current author.
Rank	Categorical	The forum "ranking" of the current author.
Affiliation	Binary	Whether the current author is a member of the ReachOut forum staff.
Board Fraction	Numeric	The fraction of the current author's total posts that were made in the current post's subforum.

Table 1: List of attributes extracted for each post. The upper half of the table contains attributes unique to the post itself, while the lower half contains attributes derived from the post's author.

each post, which are then used to train separate logistic regression classifiers for predicting the moderator attention label. We report results for each model individually, and experiment with various classifier ensembles. Results were obtained following a randomized hyperparameter search and 10-fold cross-validation process.

For clarity, we subdivide our features into two categories: post attributes and text-based features. We only extracted features for the 947 posts in the labeled training set; however, several of our features were historical in nature, utilizing information from the entirety of the unlabeled dataset of 65,024 posts.

3.1 Attribute Features

As a starting point for classifying posts as *green*, *amber*, *red*, or *crisis*, we began by examining several attributes of each post and its corresponding author.

Many of our attribute features were immediately available from the raw dataset, and required no further processing. A small sample of these statistics include the post's view count, kudos count, author rank, and in which subforum the post is located.

We also incorporated historical attributes that were derived from the entirety of the unlabeled dataset. These include items such as thread size, mean author kudos/views, number of unique reply

authors, etc. Our full list of post attributes is shown in Table 1.

3.2 Text Features

Each post in the dataset was associated with two sources of free text - the subject line and the body content. Since the post content itself is what moderators themselves look to when deciding whether action should be taken, we speculated that these features were of the greatest importance. We applied several text-based feature extraction techniques, and began with an in-depth preprocessing phase.

3.2.1 Preprocessing

Since the textual information of each post was formatted as raw HTML, our first preprocessing step involved converting the post content to plain text. During this process, we replaced all user mentions (i.e., @user) with a special string token. We also built a map of all embedded images, of which the majority were forum-specific emoticons, and replaced occurrences in the text with special tokens denoting which image was used. We performed a similar technique for links, replacing each one with a special link identifier token. Finally, in an effort to reduce noise in the text, we removed all text contained within <BLOCKQUOTE> tags, which typically contained text that a post is replying to. After these conversions, we stripped all remaining HTML tags from each post, resulting in plain-text subject and body content.

While examining the corpus, we also noticed the frequent presence of text-based emoticons, such as ':)' and '=('. We employed the use of an emoticon sentiment lexicon[2], which maps text-based emoticons to either a positive or negative sentiment, to convert each textual emoticon to one of two special tokens denoting the corresponding emoticon's polarity. We manually annotated 12 additional emoticons that were not present in the pre-existing lexicon.

Since we found the subject and body text to be highly related, we concatenated these texts into a single string per post. In an effort to further reduce noise in the text, we examined the subject line of each post, and if it was of the form "Re: ..." and contained the same subject text of the post it was replying to, we discarded the subject line.

Finally, we finished our preprocessing phase with several traditional techniques, including converting all text to lowercase and removing all punctuation. We also converted non-unicode symbols to their best approximation. Due to experimental feedback, we did not remove traditional stop words, as doing so decreased classifier performance for this domain.

3.2.2 N-Gram Features

The majority of our text features are derived from traditional n-gram extraction methods. Given the large amount of unlabeled posts in the dataset, we trained our text vectorizers on the entire corpus (minus the test set posts). After constructing a vocabulary of n-grams occurring in the corpus, we counted the number of each n-gram occurring in each post's text, and normalized them by term-frequency inverse-document frequency (tf-idf). Following initial feedback, our n-gram methods employed normalized unigram counts.

3.2.3 Sentiment Lexicon Features

Because a primary goal of the shared task was to gauge the mental state of posting authors, we borrowed a basic technique from sentiment analysis and utilized a pre-existing sentiment lexicon[3], which contains a list of words annotated as *positive* or *negative*. We count the number of occurrences of both *positive* and *negative* words in the text of each post.

3.2.4 Embedding Features

Since the amount of unlabeled text was so large relative to the labeled posts, we sought to learn a basic language model from past forum discussions. Our word embedding features are based on the recent success of Word2Vec[4] (Mikolov et al., 2013), a method for representing indidivual words as distributed vectors. Our specific implementation utilized Doc2Vec[5] (Le and Mikolov, 2014), a related method for computing distributed representations of entire documents. Our model used an embedding vector size of 400 and a window size of 4. After training the Doc2Vec model on the entire corpus of post text (minus test posts), we computed a 400-dimensional vector for the text of each training post.

3.2.5 Topic Modeling Features

As a final measure to incorporate the abundance of unlabeled text in the dataset, we trained a custom Latent Dirichlet Allocation (LDA) (Blei et al., 2003) model with 20 topics on the entire corpus of post text (minus test posts). LDA is a popular topic modeling technique which groups words into distinct topics, assigning both word-topic and topic-document probabilities. Once trained, we used our LDA model to predict a topic distribution (i.e, a 20-dimensional vector) for the text of each post.

4 Results

After extracting features for each of the 947 posts in the training set, we trained a separate logistic regression classifier on each source of text features, plus one trained on all of the attribute-based features. Because we hypothesized that the content of the replies to a particular post could be indicative of the nature of the post itself, for each set of text features we trained an additional model on the concatenated text of all direct reply posts only, ignoring the text of the post itself.

For each model, we performed a randomized hyperparameter search in conjunction with a 10-fold cross-validation step based on macro-averaged F1

---

[2]http://people.few.eur.nl/hogenboom/files/
EmoticonSentimentLexicon.zip

[3]https://www.cs.uic.edu/ liub/FBS/sentiment-analysis.html

[4]https://code.google.com/archive/p/word2vec

[5]https://radimrehurek.com/gensim/models/doc2vec.html

Feature Set	Accuracy	F1	Green vs. Non-Green Accuracy	Green vs. Non-Green F1
Post Attributes	0.76	0.72	0.78	0.66
Sentiment Lexicon	0.71	0.64	0.76	0.64
N-Grams (Post)	**0.83**	**0.82**	**0.90**	**0.88**
N-Grams (Replies)	0.73	0.68	0.80	0.72
Doc2Vec (Post)	0.74	0.70	0.80	0.72
Doc2Vec (Replies)	0.72	0.65	0.76	0.62
LDA (Post)	0.73	0.67	0.78	0.70
LDA (Replies)	0.71	0.63	0.78	0.66

Table 2: Classification results on the test set using a single logistic regression model trained on each set of features. (Post) denotes features extracted from each post itself, while (Replies) indicates that features were extracted from only replies to the post.

Label	Precision	Recall	F1
Green	0.91	0.95	0.93
Amber	0.59	0.72	0.65
Red	0.90	0.33	0.49
Crisis	0.00	0.00	0.00
Average	**0.84**	**0.83**	**0.82**

Table 3: Detailed classification results for our final model. No *crisis* labels were predicted, resulting in metrics of 0.0; however, the test set only included a single *crisis* post. Average reported metrics consider the support of each label.

Green	Amber	Red	Crisis
<E0>	(@user)	worse	cant
awesome	phone	feeling	anymore
<E1>	anxious	<E2>	life
hope	talk	empty	dont
love	not	sick	screwed
proud	school	hate	negative
amazing	think	family	f**k
fun	going	hospital	unsafe
favourite	help	scared	intense
first	feeling	s**t	die

Table 4: Top 10 features per label via the largest per-class feature coefficients of our final model. From an informal inspection, there appears to be a clear trend in the polarity of the word lists from *green* posts to *crisis* posts. **Notation:** <E0> = emoticon with alt text 'Smiley Happy', <E1> = emoticon with alt text 'Smiley Very Happy', <E2> = emoticon with alt text 'Smiley Sad', (@user) = special token for any user mention.

score. Results for each feature set are shown in Table 2, where it is clear that the model trained on n-grams of the post text (subject + body) performs the best across all metrics. We show a more detailed breakdown of this model's performance in Table 3, which includes per-label metrics.

4.1 Discussion

Given the relatively small amount of labeled data, it comes as no surprise that the traditional n-gram approach performs better than the more complex text-based methods. Because our vectorizers and vocabulary were trained on the full corpus of unlabeled and training posts before fine-tuning predictions on the test posts, this model is able to capture trends in word usage across all four labels.

We sought to combine the models shown in Table 2 with various ensemble methods, but found that no combination of classifiers trained on heterogeneous feature sets produced better results than the straightforward n-gram technique. Thus, the simplest text-based method proved also to have the best performance, a benefit for deploying such a system.

To gain better insight into our best-performing model, we show the top 10 features per label in Table 4, obtained by inspecting the model coefficients of the fully-trained logistic regression classifier. Here (aside from the *Amber* label, which is a bit more ambiguous, as expected), there is a clear distinction and trend in the type of language used between posts of different labels.

5 Conclusion

In this paper, we detailed our system implementation for the CLPsych 2016 shared task. We compared several types of models and feature sets, and showed the benefit of combining rigorous preprocessing with straightforward n-gram feature extraction and a simple linear classifier. Additionally, using the entire corpus of forum text, we identified several discriminative features that can serve as a launching point for future studies.

References

Apoorv Agarwal, Boyi Xie, Ilia Vovsha, Owen Rambow, and Rebecca Passonneau. 2011. Sentiment analysis of Twitter data. In *Proceedings of the Workshop on Languages in Social Media*, pages 30–38.

David M. Blei, Andrew Y. Ng, and Michael I. Jordan. 2003. Latent dirichlet allocation. *The Journal of Machine Learning Research*, 3:993–1022.

Efthymios Kouloumpis, Theresa Wilson, and Johanna Moore. 2011. Twitter sentiment analysis: The good the bad and the omg! In *Proceedings of the Fifth International AAAI Conference on Weblogs and Social Media (ICWSM 11)*, pages 538–541.

Qv Le and Tomas Mikolov. 2014. Distributed representations of sentences and documents. In *Proceedings of the 31st International Conference on Machine Learning*, volume 32, pages 1188–1196.

Bing Liu. 2010. *Sentiment Analysis and Subjectivity*. 2 edition.

Bing Liu. 2012. Sentiment analysis and opinion mining. *Synthesis Lectures on Human Language Technologies*, 5(1):1–167.

Tomas Mikolov, Kai Chen, Greg Corrado, and Jeffrey Dean. 2013. Efficient estimation of word representations in vector space. In *Proceedings of International Conference on Learning Representations (ICLR)*, pages 1–12.

John Pestian, John Pestian, Pawel Matykiewicz, Brett South, Ozlem Uzuner, and John Hurdle. 2012. Sentiment analysis of suicide notes: A shared task. *Biomedical Informatics Insights*, 5(1):3–16.

James Spencer and Gulden Uchyigit. 2012. Sentimentor: Sentiment analysis of Twitter data. In *Proceedings of European Conference on Machine Learning and Principles and Practice of Knowledge Discovery in Databases*, pages 56–66.

Miaomiao Wen, Diyi Yang, and Cp Rosé. 2014. Sentiment analysis in MOOC discussion forums: What does it tell us? In *Proceedings of Educational Data Mining*, pages 1–8.

Lei Zhang, Riddhiman Ghosh, Mohamed Dekhil, Meichun Hsu, and Bing Liu. 2011. Combining lexicon-based and learning-based methods for Twitter sentiment analysis. Technical report.

Text-based experiments for predicting mental health emergencies in online web forum posts *

Hector Franco-Penya
hector.franco@dit.ie
Dublin Institute of Technology

Liliana Mamani Sanchez
mamanisl@tcd.ie
Trinity College Dublin

Abstract

This article explores how to build a system for detecting users in a need of attention on *ReachOut.com* forums. The proposed method uses Tree Kernels over binary Support Vector Machines classification and linear regression, comparing these two machine learning techniques. Predictions from one of these systems were submitted to the CLPsych 2016 Shared Task. Nonetheless, results indicate that it is possible to build an accurate system using only text features without the use of other meta data.

1 Introduction

Online communities such as web forums have become places where people participate according to common interests with other members of such communities. Language and interaction analysis may be done in these forums as to test hypothesis related to participation. Particularly, in web forums where the main topic of conversation is about issues related to their mental health, analysis may help address some situations where the well being of participants is compromised.

One of the duties of web forums moderators is to detect abnormal behaviour and take action over it. In the case of mental health web forums, the moderator should detect conversations that reveal a seemingly dangerous situation for the participants. For instance, conversations that might reveal that one of the participants wants to commit self-harm. The

---

CLPsych Shared Task 2016 has the goal of evaluating systems that address the identification of web forum posts that reveal this kind of risk situations.

In order to assist moderators, this shared task consists on creating a system to automatically label posts, so moderators can identify where to focus their attention with more ease.

This report is structured as follows: Section 2 briefly describes the task and dataset, Section 3 presents all the details about the systems we built, Section 4 summarizes the results, Section 5 presents the discussion of these results, and finally we conclude with Section 6.

2 Task and dataset

The system has to classify each post into four categories that indicate how urgently a post needs the moderator's attention: green, amber, red or crisis. According to the annotation procedure carried on by the task organizers, those labels may be subdivided into twelve fine-grained categories shown in Table 1. This table also shows how many examples are present on the training dataset for each fine-grained category. For our experiments we only used the dataset of posts that have a label.

3 Systems description

Our systems are based on two machine learning techniques: 1) linear regression, and 2) three-step binary classification. For each technique, two types of features were extracted: grams (unigrams and bigrams), and grammatical tree structures. The system we submitted to the official CLPsych shared task is a

* Both authors contributed equally to the contents and experiments described in this paper.

Proceedings of the 3rd Workshop on Computational Linguistics and Clinical Psychology: From Linguistic Signal to Clinical Reality, pages 193–197,
San Diego, California, June 16, 2016. ©2016 Association for Computational Linguistics

Label	Fine-grained	Samples
green	allClear	366
	supporting	166
	followupBye	16
amber	followupOk	165
	currentMildDistress	40
	underserved	34
	pastDistress	10
red	currentAcuteDistress	87
	followupWorse	20
	angryWithReachout	2
	angryWithForumMember	1
	crisis	39

Table 1: Fine-grained distribution of labels in the training dataset.

gram-based linear regression system. From now on wards, we will refer to this as *baseline* system.

3.1 Pre-processing of web forum posts

In order to prepare the data for training a classifier system, text normalization was performed over two kinds of elements in posts: a) quoted text, and b) emoticons.

The inclusion of quoted text in post is frequent as it serves the purpose of clarifying which statements the post's writer is replying to. Since we are aiming to develop a text-based classification of posts into distinct categories, it is important to identify what is original post content and what is not. We consider quoted text cannot be deemed as original content, and can lead to missclassification. Therefore, we replaced quotations with a wilcard term.

Emoticons are signals of emotion expressed by using pictorial elements, or made up mostly of punctuation characters. We consider emoticons are essential on determining the writer's mood and are language independent to some extent. In the dataset provided, there is a large variation of emoticons instances that may convey similar mood, e.g. happy-smiley and very-happy-smiley. We reduced the possible set of emoticon labels and replaced them by wildcards. This approach is similar to the one followed in (Vogel and Mamani Sanchez, 2012) as they work with a dataset of pictorial emoticons extracted from the same web forum platform.

Other types of standardization were applied such as replacing HTTP links by wildcards.

3.2 Feature extraction

We describe here the linguistic and non-linguistic features that were extracted. Linguistic features were extracted after normalization.

N-grams Our baseline system uses unigrams and bigrams to create binary features to indicate if those grams occur in a post or not.

Tree kernels We used the Stanford parser (Klein and Manning, 2003b; Klein and Manning, 2003a) to generate constituent trees for all sentences from a single post. This generates a collection of trees, which where co-joined to have a tree representing the entire post. This structure was used thereafter in a tool that extract subtrees from such a tree and uses them as features to train a Support Vector Machine. For this purpose, we used the SVM-light implementation by (Joachims, 1999) and SubSet Tree kernel (SST) computation tool (Moschitti, 2006).

To our knowledge, SVMs over grammar trees for entire documents have not been explored before. Tree kernels are usually used to classify single sentences but not large pieces of text that could contain multiple paragraphs. This is due to the quadratic complexity of computing this kind of kernels.

Additional meta features In addition to text-based or linguistic features, we consider some additional features extracted from a post metadata. This metadata comprises the board name, a flag indicating if a posts is the first one in the thread or not, the rank (user category) of the post's author, and the base 10 logarithm plus one of number of views and the number of kudos. Names for our systems that used these additional features are suffixed with "full", while those that only use text features are suffixed with "textOnly". This naming convention is used in results in Table 3.

Table 2 shows the 20 user ranks labels and the number of users per rank. This table shows an unbalanced distribution of user across ranks: the first four categories ("Rookie scribe", "Casual scribe", "Rookie" and "Visitor") make 80% of the total of users, this produces a perplexity value of 7.3 (far from the value of 20 that could be reached if users were uniformly distributed across user categories).

rank	members
Rookie scribe	420
Casual scribe	402
Rookie	351
Visitor	151
Frequent scribe	90
Super frequent scribe	64
Youth Ambassador	39
Special Guest Contributor	24
Star contributor	20
Frequent Visitor	12
Staff	12
Contributor	11
Post Mod	11
Mod Squad	8
Community Manager	6
Mod	5
Uber contributor	5
Reachout.com Crew	4
Mod In Training	3
Super star contributor	2

Table 2: Author ranking

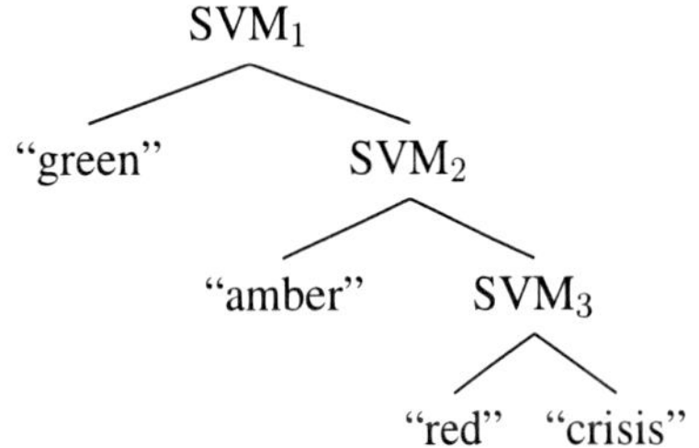

Figure 1: SVM classification

System	non-green		all-labels	
	acc	F1	acc	ma-F1
baseline	60%	.58	42 %	.13
reg_tree_full	**89%**	**.85**	73%	.28
reg_tree_textOnly	**89%**	**.85**	**78%**	**.38**
3s_tree_full	85%	.76	**78%**	.32
3s_tree_textOnly	77%	.67	69%	.29

Table 3: Results in terms of accuracy and F1 measures for green vs non-green classification, and for green vs all the other labels classification.

3.3 Architecture design

3.3.1 Linear regression systems

For the linear regression models, labels for the training set posts were mapped to an ordinal scale according to how urgently a post needs attention: "green" was mapped to 0, "amber" to 1, "red" to 2 and "crisis" to 3.

Then SVM-light software was used to create the model. In the evaluation stage, the predicted values for the test set were used to rank the posts according to their need of attention, for which the higher values where labelled as "crisis", then "red", "amber" and "green" following the same distribution as in the training set: "crisis" 4.1%, "red" 11.7%, "amber" 26.3% and "green" 57.9%. Linear regression systems are prefixed with "reg".

3.3.2 Three step binary classification systems

The three-step binary classification systems are developed as decision trees of three nodes. Decisions in each node are calculated according to classification performed by a Support Vector Machine (SVM). The first SVM decides if the post has "green" or "non-green" as a label. If the example is labelled as "non-green", the second SVM decides if the posts is labelled "amber" or "non-amber". If the example is labelled as "non-amber", the third SVM decides if the label is "red" or "crisis". Figure 1 illustrates this procedure.

The training set for each SVM only contains relevant examples for the specific step. This means that the first SVM is trained with all examples that have a "green" label as negative samples, and the remaining examples are deemed positive examples. The examples labelled as "green" are not used to train the second and third SVMs. Three-step binary classification systems are prefixed with "3s".

4 Results

Table 3 reports results for the systems accuracy and macro F1 measures. The first two columns report the results of predicting posts that need attention, where all the labels but "green" were unified into a single category "non-green". The last two columns report results for all labels. The macro-F1 measure is low mainly because all systems failed to identify the single "crisis" post. This lead to a F1 value of zero for prediction of "crisis", this drags down the macro accuracy value since all labels have the same weight.

It is puzzling, that the system that which produces best results is the tree kernel based linear regression based uniquely on the text of the posts, as our in-

	positives	negatives	n/p ratio
SVM$_1$	42.1%	57.9%	1.375
SVM$_2$	37.5%	62.5%	1.666
SVM$_3$	25.9%	74.1%	2.861

Table 4: Positives and negatives per SVM step

tuition suggests this should have been outperformed by the variation that includes metadata, which is the case when comparing the two tree kernel systems based on three binary classification steps. Also, the regression models seem to outperform the other systems in the detection of non-green labels. The success of the linear regression systems could be related to the fact that the regression models do have a quota of predictions for each type of labels.

Due to time limitations only the baseline system was submitted on time for the public evaluation.

5 Discussion and future work

The tree model shown in Section 3.3.2 was designed as a three-step decision tree based on machine learning classifiers. These steps decide first the label in growing order, this way each machine learning step has a fairly balanced training set, which gets more unbalanced as the labels involved in the decision have higher priority than in the first step. Figure 4 illustrate this observation. Any other combination of steps would lead to more unbalanced training sets; it would be necessary to use balancing techniques.

Another possible design would involve the use of the eleven binary classification steps as described in the annotation procedure document provided by the organizers. Therefore, the classifier systems should be designed to mimic this annotation procedure. As a final step, the eleven fine-grained labels should be converted back the original four-label range used in the competition. This system would had been substantially more complex, the first step would have had to classify a sample as a "crisis" or "non-crisis". In such case, the first machine learning classifier would had dealt with a very unbalanced training set as only 4.1% of samples are labelled as "crisis".

Some sparse fine-grained labels would had been very difficult to predict such as "angryWithForum-Member" (1 example in the training set), or "angry-WithReachout" (2 examples in the training set).

The prediction of the labels: "followupBye", "fol-lowupOk", and "followupWorse" could benefit from analysing and labelling previous posts in a thread as they only exist as following posts labelled as "red" or "crisis", and features extracted from these posts may not help the prediction of other labels.

These observations suggest a major change on the design of the system in which all posts of a thread should be labelled and re-labelled based on the previous posts in the thread and according to author roles. We consider this fine-grained model as future work. The linear regression model proposed in Section 3.2 only requires one step of machine learning classification. However, it requires to map ordinal data into numerical to create the training set and numerical into ordinal to interpret the predictions. For the proposed system, labels are mapped into consecutive numbers, this assumes that the difference between consecutive labels are the same. Which may not be the case, perhaps "crisis" posts should be mapped to a much larger value than "red" posts. Perhaps the mapping function should be related to the percentile in which the (mapped) values appear, or some other feature. The problem of mapping ordinal data into numerical is another open research topic outside the scope of this experiment. Tuning of the mapping procedure is left for future work.

6 Conclusions

We have described the basic setup for systems that address the CLPsych 2016 Shared Task. Our systems do not reach top positions in the ranking for this competition, however they provide some opportunities to explore ideas on how to deal with this kind of classification task. The main principle followed on designing these systems was to make them as portable as possible and independent of exogenous features to the post's contents. There is several aspects to improve if the goal is to build system for post classification that are uniquely based on text. Besides our goals summarized in the section for future work, one issue to explore further is to determine how noisy text affects classification.

Overall, we also have to explore the corresponding caveats of relying only on text for building classifier systems.

References

Thorsten Joachims. 1999. Making large scale svm learning practical. Technical report, Universität Dortmund.

Dan Klein and Christopher D. Manning. 2003a. Accurate Unlexicalized Parsing. *Proceedings of the 41st Annual Meeting on Association for Computational Linguistics - ACL '03*, 1:423–430.

Dan Klein and Christopher D Manning. 2003b. Fast Exact Inference with a Factored Model for Natural Language Parsing. *Advances in Neural Information Processing Systems*, 15:3–10.

Alessandro Moschitti. 2006. Making tree kernels practical for natural language learning. In *EACL*, volume 113, page 24.

Carl Vogel and Liliana Mamani Sanchez. 2012. Epistemic signals and emoticons affect kudos. In *Cognitive Infocommunications (CogInfoCom), 2012 IEEE 3rd International Conference on*, pages 517 –522, Dec.

Association for Computational Linguistics
209 N. Eighth Street
Stroudsburg, Pennsylvania 18360

ISBN 978-1-5108-2527-7